TRACING THE AUTOBIOGRAPHICAL

Life Writing Series

In the **Life Writing Series**, Wilfrid Laurier University Press publishes life writing and new life-writing criticism in order to promote autobiographical accounts, diaries, letters, and testimonials written and/or told by women and men whose political, literary, or philosophical purposes are central to their lives. **Life Writing** features the accounts of ordinary people, written in English, or translated into English from French or the languages of the First Nations or from any of the languages of immigration to Canada. **Life Writing** will also publish original theoretical investigations about life writing, as long as they are not limited to one author or text.

Priority is given to manuscripts that provide access to those voices that have not traditionally had access to the publication process.

Manuscripts of social, cultural, and historical interest that are considered for the series, but are not published, are maintained in the **Life Writing Archive** of Wilfrid Laurier University Library.

Series Editor
Marlene Kadar
Humanities Division, York University

Manuscripts to be sent to
Brian Henderson, Director
Wilfrid Laurier University Press
75 University Avenue West
Waterloo, Ontario, Canada N2L 3C5

TRACING THE AUTOBIOGRAPHICAL

edited by Marlene Kadar, Linda Warley,
Jeanne Perreault, and Susanna Egan

Wilfrid Laurier University Press
WLU

We acknowledge the financial support of the Government of Canada through the Book Publishing Industry Development Program for our publishing activities. We acknowledge the Government of Ontario through the Ontario Media Development Corporation's Ontario Book Initiative.

Library and Archives Canada Cataloguing in Publication Data

Tracing the autobiographical / edited by Marlene Kadar ... [et al.].

(Life writing series)

Includes bibliographical references.
ISBN 0-88920-476-4

1. Autobiography.   I. Kadar, Marlene, 1950–   II. Series.

PN56.A89T72 2005   920   C2005-902659-6

© 2005 Wilfrid Laurier University Press
Waterloo, Ontario, Canada
www.wlu.press.wlu.ca

Cover design by Leslie Macredie. Photograph courtesy the J. Paul Getty Museum, Los Angeles. Eugène Atget (photographer), "Petit Bacchus, rue St. Louis en l'Isle (The Little Bacchus Café, rue St. Louis en l'Ile)" (detail), 1901–1902. Albumen silver, 22.1 x 17.8 cm. Text design by Catharine Bonas-Taylor.

Every reasonable effort has been made to acquire permission for copyright material used in this text, and to acknowledge all such indebtedness accurately. Any errors and omissions called to the publisher's attention will be corrected in future printings.

∞

Printed in Canada

Dedicated to the memory of Gabriele Helms, 1966–2004,
scholar, colleague, and friend

CONTENTS

JEANNE PERREAULT AND MARLENE KADAR

....

INTRODUCTION
TRACING THE AUTOBIOGRAPHICAL: UNLIKELY DOCUMENTS, UNEXPECTED PLACES

Tracing the Autobiographical brings to the forefront of critical thought innovations in our current understanding of the genre of autobiography. The power of this collection rests in the variety of reading practices of the authors, whose questions about identity, community, and history extend beyond the reach of autobiography as most of us know it. We chose the title Tracing the Autobiographical because we seek the traces of autobiographical self-representation in fragments of document and image, or we outline their possibilities by considering the implications of images, documents, and practices that may be read as autobiographical. It is not our wish to stress the limits of autobiography, but rather the scope of the autobiographical. Nor is it our objective to focus on the exclusions of autobiography as many have done so well before us. Instead, we underline the inimitable potential for autobiography and its renovations to address the life of the individual, the lives of groups of individuals, or some self-representational aspect of the individual or her group. No matter what we do to autobiography, it continues to flourish in one form or another. The authors thus share a crucial starting point: that the varieties of representation of the autobiographical are multiplying, and in spite of troubled contexts or specious features, need to be examined as seriously as their predecessors.

The authors work with the literatures of several nations to suggest connections between broad agendas, such as national ones, and the personal, the private, the individual. Feminism has been for each of us an informing perspective, one that makes itself known in both the questions we ask and how we ask them. We do not, however, claim this as a feminist project per se, as that would indicate a degree of specific political accord we have not sought. Instead, traces of the autobiographical relentlessly inform, or allow us to revisit and critique, disciplinary and historical questions with complexity and passion, including feminist questions of identity and agency.

Referencing the autobiographical is, for us, referencing new ways of knowing. Many of the authors return to the question of text or traces of text, demonstrating that the language of autobiography, as well as the textualized identities of individual persons, can be traced in multiple media and sometimes in unlikely documents—a deportation list, an art exhibit, reality TV, Internet websites and chat rooms, memos and propaganda documents, memories—as well as familiar literary genres, such as the play, the long poem, the short story. *Tracing the Autobiographical* assumes an identity between the unlikely documents and the more familiar literary genres; at the very least, we propose, there are generic similarities that override a focus on the differences. What do all of these "unlikely documents" have in common? Depending on the privileges and constraints offered by the context, they bespeak either an extended or a limited story about a person's life.

The forces at the heart of this collection are the inexhaustible variety of human identity and experience, and the irrepressible impulse to explore, express, and understand it. All the essays that appear here are driven by the curiosity that breathes life into any intellectual effort; what shapes this volume is each author's attention to the complexity of the voice that shapes or performs selfhood. Those voices may appear in multiple forms, some textual, some three-dimensional, some with no dimension at all as virtual cyberpresences. Some are haunting echoes of loss, apparent only in traces; others are forceful claims demanding attention. Readers of life writings are easily familiar with some of these modes; other modes are just now coming into being or are surfacing under the expanding reading practices of auto/biographical[1] scholarship.

These reading practices involve using the interpretative skills and strategies scholars have developed in thirty years of close academic attention to texts that can be defined as "autobiography." From early writings like St. Augustine's and Margery Kempe's, designed to edify readers by showing them how God might be found, to the travel journals of adventurers in every generation, to the individual representative of a suppressed people, to the "healing" narratives of abuse survivors, life writing has taken many forms for many purposes. Even some of the earliest scholars recognized that refining genre definitions would present not a limitation but an opportunity to shape a discourse and a naming appropriate to these diverse expressions. Since the early 1980s, autobiography theory in English has integrated feminist theories of the self and the body with various branches of poststructuralist and postcolonial theories of identity and agency, language and self-representation. All the essays here draw from this admixture.

We have structured this collection to highlight these generative impulses. Contemporary anxieties of identity, technology, and self-representation inform the first three pieces. Helen Buss, Linda Warley, and Gabriele Helms all explore digital or electronic media, raising questions about the effects of self and community when the nature of mediation between subject and audience is fluctuating. "Reading" practices are reconsidered and expectations revised as divergent forms of self-expression come into being. Sherrill Grace's essay on the stage as an autobiographical medium can be read as a kind of bridge between these three essays and those that follow, in that Grace also deals with medium, genre, and audience. Kathy Mezei and Susanna Egan look to home as a concept central to ideas of selfhood and to expressions thereof. The politics of location and the politics of subjectivity also inform the essays of Cheryl Suzack, Jeanne Perreault, and Bina Freiwald. And the ambiguities of place, trace, and memory complete the volume in Adrienne Kertzer's and Marlene Kadar's journeys into loss. These essays reflect on similar questions and grapple with concepts of self, place, identity, and memory in ways that cross-pollinate recent thought.

This is not the place to rehearse the variety of alternatives scholars have devised to make their discussions meet the texts they are reading. Our own choices you will find in the individual articles. We have, however, as a group found "auto/biography" to be a flexible term, one that implicates self and other(s) in a context in which a dialectic of relationality is both acknowledged and problematized. This kind of autobiographical practice, as we see in the poetics of exile in Daphne Marlatt, the cautionary work of Katie relating her dot-com experience, the political urgings of Muriel Rukeyser, or the generational accounts of Israeli women building a nation, requires the reader to listen for the memory and the ethics of the text. When the scholar of autobiography reads life stories in the performance of plays, the arrangement of domestic spaces, or the legislative acts of a government, cultural context is the essential lens though which she looks. In these cases, location takes on highly mobile meanings. When a play is read auto/biographically, the multiple interpretations of directors, actors, stage settings, and so on act upon the playwright's words and the audience's reception of them. Similarly the performance of "reality" on television shows or representations of "identity" on websites must be taken into account as they offer another location of auto/biographical significance.

When the setting is a house, a home, "location" extends its metaphorical authority and enters the material world. And when location is the intersection of individuals and the laws that control their lives or the violence that shatters lives, their auto/biographical texts open new ways to comprehend interpellation and agency. Agency itself may be the most elusive of concepts when only documents and laments remain of the life experience of many. Indeed, under extreme circumstances, a critic might argue that no "agent" can be found in the traces of a life.

Naming the genre of our own study is of less importance to us than the responsibility we have undertaken in the practice of reading for auto/biographical insight. The questions we ask in this reading process are as varied as the texts we engage: what do self, subject, agent, person, and identity mean, and how does that meaning get made? What have aspects of identity to do with each other? What has specific context to offer in our desire to understand how the world (society, culture, history) has made the person? What is the relation between the text(s) of selfhood, the writer, and the reader? What kinds of materials can be considered articulations of self or of life? Any reader might be entertained by imagining the critic as auto-critical, using the process of reading publicly as a screen for her own autobiographical assertions. The conscious presence of the critic in the criticism engages some analysts in the recursive spirals of writers and readers. Some of the ways writers in this collection seek and create knowledge rely on intensive readings of specific texts—websites, poems, television programs, memoranda; others look to fragments of history, hoping to recognize or create meaning against all efforts to negate it; some even look to the "rag-and-bone shop of the heart" (Yeats 935) for insight. Hence, unlikely documents in unexpected places.

With the rise of feminist, literary, and postcolonial theories, auto/biography theorists and critics have elaborated the potential of location as a category. Rosi Braidotti, like many others, notes that "axes of differentiation such as class, race, ethnicity, gender, age, and others intersect and interact with each other in the constitution of subjectivity" (4). These "axes of differentiation" both extend and limit readers. Attending to each element of identity is impossible, analyzing the intersections as complex as reiterating a human life. Like the author, the critic must select some elements for particular attention or risk being overwhelmed and falling into the catatonia of too-muchness; at the same time, the recognition of historical or cultural patterns made visible through gender or race or class practices invites readers and critics to grasp the ground as well as the figure upon it. Understanding the context or location of the life being written or enacted informs the critic of the particular significance of a gesture or an absence of reaction to local circumstances. Here, we are speaking of the writing-as-resistance mode of expression, crucial to a complex of literary and political practices in which the explicit presence of the subjected person (in voice, image, text) exposes and challenges oppression, trauma, and cultural norms. When the speaking presence is narrating the story of a community, as in *testimonio* (Beverley), the "I" blurs with the "we," and the axes of differentiation move less among differences or similarities within a collective and more in the commonality of the "we" in struggle against the "them." Leigh Gilmore observes that texts resisting the genre category of autobiography "have resisted being coopted into the service of...saving autobiography for the politics of individualism" ("The Mark" 9). Form, however, may not be the deciding characteristic of materials that manifest "the politics of individualism." While Gilmore argues that the stability of the form, and of history and subjectivity, establishes the conditions upon which traditional autobiography—and the politics of individualism— flourish (5), other autobiography scholars are noting that the assumptions of postmodernity regarding form are not always correct. The most experimental or unconventional manner of expression can convey a celebration of individualism while a formally unadventurous life narrative may effectively defy that world view. The values of autobiography scholars surely are as diverse as the values inherent in the texts they analyze. In this collection, no effort has been made either to restrict perspective or to cover the field. This means that some very important questions are not addressed here: no text in which lesbianism, gayness, heterosexuality, or queerness as a central concern is discussed here, although several writers (including Daphne Marlatt and Muriel Rukeyser) have made sexuality a vital force in their life writings. Other important topics in autobiography literature are also absent: disability, health, aging; spirituality; mental illness; and physical work. These issues make up crucial dimensions of life writing, and important scholarship on these topics is being undertaken. The present collection, of course, attends to concerns that are equally important: ethics, exile, tyranny, and hope (or an impatience for it).

Making meaning and creating knowledge are tasks usually undertaken by author/subject and reader (used here metaphorically) jointly in scholarly projects. Some of the questions readers bring to this narrative form parallel a central issue of reading the individually authored and centred text: what is the place of memory and how is it engaged? The painstaking investigations into Holocaust post-memory, the Roma Great Devouring, and Aboriginal survival narratives live at the blurred edges of these questions of "I" and "we" and "they." Texts, in these cases, may exist only as traces, echoes, or chilling formal documents. The only way through to these lives is via "difficult knowledges," a process of intellectual, emotional, and ethical engagement that exerts enormous demands on the reader.[2] Memory is, Susan Engel asserts, profoundly contextual: "Memory never stands alone" (52). From the turn toward the inner life, the site of consciousness and the terrain from which memory is drawn, Engel directs us to the collaborative and contextual in the making of memory and, as importantly, the meaning of memories (123). Meaning is intersubjective, shared, though erratically realized. Only when the audience (the reader, the watcher, the witness) is part of the event can it matter, for only then does it fulfill its mandate: to communicate. Avishai Margalit undertakes a philosophical analysis of the meaning of memory. He is not concerned with auto/biography, but with memory as an ethical and moral question. Margalit draws our attention because he is acutely sensitive to the powerful force of the "we" composing its collective memory. When that "we" is dominant rather than resistant, memory enters the narrative of history, and engaging an "ethics of memory" is essential. Margalit maintains that "the obligation to remember…comes from the effort of radical evil forces to undermine morality itself by, among other means, rewriting the past and controlling collective memory" (83). Auto/biography is essentially, though not exclusively, a work of memory. It is important because it offers exactly what Margalit calls for: "the obligation to remember." Every articulation of a life invites the reader to participate in the memories of the writer (or artist) and enjoins us to understand the context in which the memories were both formed and then expressed. We do not mean to argue that auto/biography is a pure record of truth or even fact; rather, it is a rendering, often in a single voice, of experience framed by time and place, and as such, it will rarely speak in the official ventriloquist's collective parody of truth that Margalit warns against. However, when an author's voice takes on the imprint of conventional perspectives, autobiography readers may be in a position to recognize that formula—whether the convention is that adopted by a dominant discourse or by counternarrative practices. By examining the language offered (in words or otherwise), we can tease out some of the great questions of our time: Can autobiographical practices help us evade or at least recognize the overwhelming colonizing forces of global economies and media? Will the possibility of connection among readers, writers, and theorists of life documents dissipate the ill effects of exile? Will the powers of analysis and the recreation of life narratives we enact here counteract forces that seem ranged against life itself?

All the writers of this collection are Canadians; all are women; all self-identify as feminists (without requiring definition of that capacious term); and all are academics. While these facts may not cohere to produce a uniform vision of Canada or of anything else closely scrutinized, and while it is obvious that our interests and approaches vary, we share the view that it is our responsibility to listen for echoes and murmurs, as well as for clear authoritative declarations; to watch for the appearance of auto/biography in unexpected places; to trace patterns from the materials left behind; and to undertake the struggle with words and meanings that will extend our sensitivity to the world we are making and the peoples with whom we share it.

....

Note: Some of the essays in this collection were initially presented at a conference on Auto/biography: Contemporary Issues held at the University of Calgary in December 2001, organized by Jeanne Perreault, Helen Buss, and the Feminism and Cultural Texts Research Group. Marlene Kadar would like to thank Shannon Gerard and Leslie Ambedian, Nancy Gobatto and Rai Reece for excellent research assistance with the original papers.

NOTES

1　The word is used with the virgule to indicate the intimate yet blurred relationship between the genres of autobiography and biography.
2　The phrase comes from Deborah Britzman's book *Lost Subjects, Contested Objects* (1998).

HELEN M. BUSS

KATIE.COM: MY STORY

MEMOIR WRITING, THE INTERNET, AND EMBODIED DISCURSIVE AGENCY

The birth of a new medium of communication is both exhilarating and frightening. — Janet H. Murray, *Hamlet on the Holodeck* (1)

At the turn of our new millennium, a teenager published a memoir about her experience of sexual abuse arising from a contact made through the Internet. This new abuse of the Internet alerted parents and law enforcement to a powerful access to potential victims that technology has given sexual predators. But also, because Katherine Tarbox wrote a memoir of her encounter, *Katie.com*, her experience can be used to demonstrate the ways in which agency develops as a result of discursive acts. Through a fortuitous coming together of two media dependent on written language, the internet and the book, both discursively constructing the experience of her life during and after her ordeal, Katie constructs a changed sense of self. In demonstrating this process of self-making, I wish to illustrate the embodied nature of a sense of self and to question the ways in which Internet activities seem to promise a disembodied sense of self.

Agency, in this context, is the ability of individuals to negotiate societal systems to make meanings for themselves that allow them to act, in however circumscribed a manner, in the world. Autobiographical practices "effectively reveal agency or the desire for agency because they show how meanings are created for people, how people create meanings for themselves, and how people engage in the world around them" (T. Smith 28) as a result of this meaning-making activity. Like Thomas Smith, I must add the caveat that a concept of agency does not imply a return to "individualist ideology," but rather a learned ability of individuals to piece together a meaningful subjectivity from the "hegemonic and non-hegemonic discourses around them" (28). I am especially interested in not

9

only the way autobiographical practices "reveal agency," but also how they help to construct agency. Because Katherine Tarbox begins by "chatting" with the written word on an Internet site and ends by processing the life-changing experiences that happened as a result of that "chat" though the written words of a memoir, I am able to observe the movement from an agency that is largely made up of meanings created for her by others, to her nascent ability to make meaning for herself from the discursive influences in her life, meaning that becomes embodied through discursive activity.

By "embodied" I refer to the result of the meaning-making process by which what is perceived becomes incorporated into an individual's physical, psychic, and emotional life so that a maturation process happens whereby that individual gains a more conscious agency. I connect that maturation process with the activities of written discourse, especially those of the memoir form. In making this argument, I implicitly take stands on complex theoretical issues involving concepts of materialism and discourse that cannot be fully explicated in this essay. In terms of materialism and what I call embodiment, I am not attempting to construct a dichotomy in which there is a "real" material body and a separate "body" that is constituted by cultural influences. As in Elizabeth Grosz's effort to describe a "corporeal feminism," I accept that bodies are "quite literally" the representations and cultural inscriptions that constitute them (x), but I also insist on the implication of that insight, that such inscriptions cannot take place without bodies, outside of embodiment, just as speaking, listening, reading, and writing, the discursive activities of meaning-making, cannot take place without a body to process these discursive activities. As Jack Selzer observes in *Rhetorical Bodies*, "the body, flesh, blood and bones, and how all the material trappings of the physical are fashioned by literate practices" along with "the speeches and texts that are the traditional staple of rhetoric, as well as the ads and virtual spaces and languages associated with the new media" need to be considered as interrelated, complementary phenomena (10). I emphasize the fact that cultural inscription, "quite literally," cannot take place without bodies. The existence of individual bodies, ones that suffer, take pleasure, learn, live, and die, always implies physical, civil, and legal realities that much theorization of subjectivity ignores. Thus, for the purposes of my argument, I need to reiterate "embodiment" as a condition of all discursive activity.

As with the dawning of any new discursive technology, the arrival of the Internet as a tool of language has been accompanied by considerable positivist as well as negative analysis. Donna Haraway describes the cyborgian identity that awaits us in our future "informatics" world as "a source of power" through which "fresh sources of analysis and political action" can produce a "subtle understanding of emerging pleasures, experiences, and power with serious potential for changing the 'rules of the game'" (215). Sidonie Smith agrees with Haraway that we are offered a new "integrated circuit" of linguistic possibilities and therefore self-making possibilities in the cyberspace cultures of the Internet, but points out that women may also be subject to effects that are "constraining and colonizing in new ways and render former oppressions nostalgically preferable" (180). I agree with Smith's caution and advocate against viewing Internet culture in entirely positive terms. Eleanor Wynn and James E. Katz strike a similar warning against assuming that "technology liberates the individual from the body and allows the separate existence of multiple aspects of self that otherwise would not be expressed and that can remain discrete rather than having to be resolved or integrated as in ordinary social participation" (297). Such a view, while seeming to be fashionably postmodern, ironically depends on viewing the self more in terms of individualist ideology, as a discrete, powerfully sovereign (rather than agential) unity that can freely multiply its selves without negative psychic and bodily consequences. If, instead, one views the sense we have of self (or selves)—that conviction we have that our thoughts and acts are coming from inside our own bodies—as a set of relational reactions to many social, psychological, and embodied situations, a self that is only occasionally agential, lodged in a body that is vulnerable to the effects of this external/internal self-making process, then unqualified optimism about the cyborgian identity becomes less easy. With a more relational, embodied, and contingent view of self-making, we discover "evidence that the 'virtualness' and alleged anonymity of the Internet are illusionary and therefore could not over time support a plausibly disembodied depoliticized, fragmented self" (Wynn and Katz 297).

This caution concerning the "illusionary" nature of disembodiment is especially well illustrated in the lives of some of the most active users of the Internet: teenagers. Both they and their parents, until very recently, have accepted the relative harmlessness of their self-representations on the Internet. For young people the idea that one could transcend the awkward, adolescent body has been a boon. Parents' ignorance of the medium often led them to believe their children's conviction regarding its harmlessness and to rest assured that children whose bodies remain safely in the confines of their homes are also safe from harm. Indeed, the young girl in my cautionary tale had to educate both parents and the FBI in how chat-rooms work before these authority figures could understand the way in which a friendship begun in disembodiment could lead to the abuse of her very vulnerable body.

Katherine Tarbox, the "author" of *Katie.com: My Story*, was thirteen years old in 1995 when she began exchanging email chat with a man who called himself "Mark" and who claimed to be twenty-three years old. Theoretically, as Waskul and Douglass define it, in "on-line chat-interaction, a 'cyberself' emerges, rooted in a unique form of communication that is disembodied, dislocated, anonymous, multiple-simultaneous, and faceless." What happens in such a virtual space is "a kind of communication 'self-game' where participants enact a multiplicity of selves" (375). Only once in their theorization of the positive aspects of "The Emergence of Self in On-Line Chat" do Waskul and Douglass speculate on what we do not know about this process of cyberself. When they briefly comment that "the [chat] relationship seems so natural that we have yet to realize the implications of dislocating social situations from physical places" (392), they imply important questions that need to be asked of their own positivist theorization, and about the interrelationships between self, location, and virtuality. Indeed, Sherry Turkle, in *Life on the Screen* (1995), has posed many of the relevant questions about self-formation on the Internet:

> The internet has become a significant social laboratory for experimenting with the constructions and reconstructions of self that characterize postmodern life. In its virtual reality, we self-fashion and self-create. What kinds of personae do we make? What relation do these have to what we traditionally thought of as the "whole" person? Are they experienced as an expanded self or as separate from the self? Do our real-life selves learn lessons from our virtual personae? How do they communicate with one another? Why are we doing this? Is this a shallow game, a giant waste of time? Is it an expression of an identity crisis of the sort we traditionally associate with adolescence? Or are we watching the slow emergence of a new, more multiple style of thinking about the mind? (180)

In following the case of Katherine Tarbox, particular questions come to my mind that insist on our not ignoring the connections between virtual life and real life (RL to cyberspace fans). How can a sense of self capable of any agency in the acts of living on a day-to-day basis in the social constructions of family, study, work, and play be formed without attention to the embodied processes of living? Indeed, given our formation as persons immersed from prenatal development in a very tactile physicality, does it not seem reasonable that we will (and should) seek to involve the body in our cyberselves, that in fact the urge to embody the new seemingly disembodied constructions may be a logical part of the process?

Certainly Katherine Tarbox's memoir illustrates the inevitability of bodies as the locus of all our selves. After six months of contact by both Internet and phone with the man who will become her abuser, whom she knows as "Mark," and after Katie, the narrator of the memoir,[1] has qualms about the wisdom of flying out to California to meet him (at his expense), her correspondent insists on coming to meet Katie while she is in Texas at a school swim meet. Katie's desire to be with "Mark" in person seems almost as compelling as his desire, causing her to ignore the conventional warnings of her culture, expressed by her roommate at the swim meet. The facts of the case (as later established in court) are that they met briefly in his hotel room where Frank Kufrovich (Mark's real name), an experienced child molester in his forties, molested Katherine. If rape was his goal, it was interrupted by her mother, who had been informed of her whereabouts by Katherine's roommate. After a week of insisting nothing happened, Katherine finally confessed the molestation to her mother and at the mother's instigation charges were eventually brought against Kufrovich. Because he crossed state lines for the purposes of sexual activity with a minor, the case became a federal one, involving the FBI and the first full-scale, nationally prominent prosecution in the US of a sexual crime that was initiated through the Internet. In 1998 Kufrovich, through a plea-bargaining process, was sentenced to eighteen months in jail, a time shorter than the "two years" of her life that Katherine claimed, in her court statement contained in the memoir, that he had "stolen" from her "childhood" (182–83).

"Katie" and "Mark" as an underage subject and an aberrant subject respectively, are extreme illustrations of how the body cannot be left out of our thinking on cyberself. Yet, as subjects, they are not different in kind from other subjectivities, but only in degree, in terms of how bodies cannot be separated from our cyberselves. Eventually, all the liberating (read disembodying) possibilities of postmodernity's positivism concerning the cyberself must meet on the ground of the human body, which processes and constructs our sense of self. This is not to say that I advocate a deterministic solution by which we would severely limit Internet access through fear of its ability to coerce our bodies. Such a solution would be similar to the route taken by my puritan ancestors in banning novels as the work of the devil seeking to lead young girls astray. We know the result of that effort. Rather, I would have us (and by us I mean everyone from academics through lawmakers to parents, all adults who have some conscious agency in deciding the cultural place of the Internet) understand the medium as a new and powerful way to use language to make and change selves; and therefore I advocate the inculcation of linguistic sophistication in those that use it. I would also hope for us to understand and shape this new linguistic tool through ethically informed approaches. The first understanding would lead to better education in the use of the Internet (think of the amount of time we spend educating children in the reading of fiction); the second would lead to a recognition that we all live in bodies, bodies that are vulnerable and bodies that must be ultimately responsible for their actions.

In thinking of the discursive potential of the Internet for both helpful and harmful results, I find it interesting that while Katherine's victimization was the product of Internet and telephone conversations, the vehicle she uses to rescue her reputation and to gain a more effective agency in her culture than that offered by her previous cultural inscriptions, is the personal memoir, a discursive form that reaches back to one of the oldest print genres.[2] I would like to examine the way this memoir takes up various cultural scripts open to a young girl, scripts that I see as preceding any possible agency in self-making. In fact, reading this memoir allows me to see how the ability to make new versions of the self is limited to gaining agency. This agency is hard won. Reiterative experiences of various scripts lead to the embodiment of some portions of those scripts, which in turn can produce a discursive competence that leads to increased agency. Yet Judith Butler proposes that this is not an easy or always positive experience, since these scripts, particularly those that construct gender, are multiple and often conflicting, and their insistent demand on us "produces necessary failures" (*Gender Trouble* 145), and in those failures lie the possibility of a difficult and fraught agency. The controlling scripts that inform the life of Katie—love object, athlete, teenage consumer, good/bad daughter, victim, scapegoat, and survivor (to name a few)—predate her life in cyberspace and involve powerful discursive appeals that control the direction of that experience.

LOVE OBJECT

Katie is seduced into her predicament by two of the most powerful "discourses of desire" (Kauffman), secret letters (emailed in this case) and secret telephone calls. Both venues (letters in former times, telephones in modern times) are traditional linguistic vehicles for intensifying the body-absent yearning that makes romantic attachment bloom with the desire for embodiment. While the emails that Katie and Mark exchange are more like conversation, they still maintain the aura of the letter's appeal to empowerment through the love object's absence. As Linda S. Kauffman observes of love letters, they are the way a girl escapes a restricted life and finds a mode of "nurturing illusions: of his presence…[of] her own identity as his beloved, of their mutual passion" (17-18). Or, as Katie observes, "Something about the secrecy was seductive. There was a certain kind of power, control, even romance in knowing that together we were building our own relationship that no one else could influence, control or see" (78). We enter discourse as we enter the river of life. The currents and eddies, the calm waters and whirlpools are already there. Gaining discursive agency requires first learning to navigate the river, taking on the mapped scripts already established, before we map our new versions of them. Katie is a fast learner, and she often sounds more mature than her correspondent, but the discourse of romance is strong and eventually his insistence that they meet wins out over her reservations. What begins as a "liberation" from the awkwardness, the loneliness of being thirteen, becomes, because of the desire implicit in the discourses of romance, an embodiment of cyberself that is the opposite of freedom.

ATHLETE

Katie has reason to want power and control. Her identity as a person is, to a large extent, dependent on her participation in a nationally ranked swimming team in which she has won a top rank until turning thirteen and entering puberty, at which time younger girls are beginning to receive more attention from coaches. The lives of young girls in amateur sports in which they are expected to "peak" very young (e.g., swimming and gymnastics) are more disciplined, that is, more physically demanding (and at times abusive in the training methods), more isolating, and more emotionally and psychological controlled by others than in most youth activities in this culture. Indeed, I think that the training of very young girls in elite amateur sports would have provided Foucault with a subtler model of oppression than either prisons or insane asylums. Her training as an athlete contributes to Katie's decision to finally accept the meeting her abuser requires. She is so disciplined by severe coaches, including one who actually throws chairs at slow swimmers, that she is very accustomed to giving over her body to insistent adults; she has been readied by her embodied cultural scripts as an athlete to give in to her Internet lover.

Perhaps more controlling than tough coaching is the way her sport separates her from peer support. Since everyone on the team is a potential competitor, opportunities for learning positive deviations from the scripts through peer bonding are limited. As Katie observes in the hindsight of memoir, what such disciplines do is keep the girl in a childlike dependence and in isolation from her peer group: "I was missing key opportunities to compare myself with people my age, to talk about what was ahead of us in high school, and to try to figure out if I was normal" (45). Swimming makes it impossible for her to maintain friendships and makes her more vulnerable to exploitation on the Internet: "As time passed, Mark replaced Karen [her best friend] as my main confidant. It wasn't something I planned. But I just never seemed to have time to be with her. I had swim meets on Saturdays, and that obliged me to have a good night's sleep the evening before. So it never seemed practical to go out on the weekends. I began declining invitations more and more" (59). Her Internet pal, Mark on the other hand, is available at all times, his letters waiting for her in any free minutes Katie can spare from her busy schedule.

TEENAGE CONSUMER

One of the ways in which our culture keeps its young girls onside in our colonization and oppression of them is to substitute consumer choices for maturity choices; a script of consumerism, especially effective because of its emphasis on the girl's body as its grounds of interpellation, replaces growth that might lead to more useful maturation activities. Katie lives in the upscale suburb of New Canaan, Connecticut, where she is permitted and encouraged to assemble an array of expensive clothing that allows her to go four full months of school days without wearing the same outfit twice. Her many beauty products, her teen magazines that dwell on an array of clothing, makeup, and body enhancement, and the sense of identity she gets from grooming her correctly blond, straight hair, give her a limited agency firmly tied to the external decoration of her body. Indeed, so much time is taken up in preparing the body for public presentation that little time is available for learning about that very body, its desires, its needs, and its vulnerabilities. At the same time, as she enters puberty and the fat measurements at swim practices indicate that she has too much (she is size ten but short), she increasingly wants to hide her body, even from herself. Thus, despite her adherence to one script, girl consumerism, she has failed to obey the script of the girl athlete. She also finds that her male peer group, middle-school boys, "picked everything apart. Your hair, your eyes, your smile, your breasts, your waist, your butt, your legs" (24). Her body shame is reinforced not only by the outside world, but also by those closest to home. As Katie observes, "I couldn't stand to leave zits on my face. I never had a lot of them, though the occasional few did come along and needed proper attention. If I didn't take care of them, my mom was sure to say something, which was a lot more painful than any squeezing could be" (5).

The only discourses of the body available to Katie are negative ones, and her community's ideals of intimacy and friendship seem to be based on status. She yearns for the transcendence of the body that some theorists of the Internet believe is possible. She desires a friendship not based on body or status, but on commonality of interest. In entering chat rooms, Katie seeks "someone who would share my interests—music, reading, movies—someone who was intelligent and kind and funny. Someone I could learn from" (24). Like those who see the Internet as a mode of transcendence, Katie seeks to leave the body out, to escape an embodiment that is informed by unsatisfactory scripts that she has failed to perform to perfection.

GOOD/BAD DAUGHTER

Katie's only involved parent is her mother, but Andrea's involvement is compromised by her own addiction to the beauty scripts of our culture. Katie has a biological father who has not seen her since she was a baby, and a live-in stepdad who is little involved in her life (until after the abuse incident when he becomes a vocal advocate of psychiatric therapy and a fascinated voyeur of the trial process). Katie and her mother have a typical post second-wave feminism mother/daughter relationship, an unexamined hodge-podge of scripts in which they feel emotions of both love for each other because of family values, and hatred of each other because they live in a culture in which being female is devalued. These unexamined emotions are projected onto each other and represent cultural scripts that exemplify our ideology's failure to take up the mother/daughter plot in any meaningful way (see Hirsch, *The Mother/Daughter Plot*). There is no satisfactory mother/daughter discourse available to Katie, except the stereotypes of mass media, which demand the impossible: mothers who are both independently self-supporting in the way second-wave feminism advocates, and totally fulfilled by constant service to husband and children as prescribed by traditional feminine scripts. This whole text is riddled with the ambiguities and contradictions of the scripts that cause the failure of mother/daughter relationships.

Katie admires her mother's work ethic and achievements, but also sees herself as victimized by them in terms of maternal neglect. Her mother, burdened with too many responsibilities and expectations, sees keeping her daughter busy as the way through adolescence. Andrea, a workaholic "glass-ceiling breaker," mostly enters her daughter's life in the roles of co-shopper and enforcer of swimming disciplines. However, during the memoir process, Katherine eventually learns through writing to recognize and embody another Andrea: the mother who, by acting quickly when told that Katie is meeting her Internet pal, by commanding the reluctant team coaches and hotel security staff, interrupts what might well have become a rape. After the molestation, Andrea is the only person who embraces her and cries with Katie. It is in the course of memoir writing that the daughter seems to become aware of some part of the significance of this fact. Katie observes: "I knew she loved me, and I just wanted to make everything right again" (101).

VICTIM/SCAPEGOAT

The positive agency to be gained from realizing that your mother is not only neglectful, but may also love you, is dampened by another cultural script. It is a typical inculcated female cultural script, as old as the women's romance genre, as old as misogyny, which makes young girls who have become victims feel that it is they who must "make everything right." This blaming-the-victim script, one that places impossible responsibilities on young females, given their actual power, infects everyone in Katie's cultural milieu. From her first required public apology to her swim team the day after the event (an apology for soiling their reputations and distracting them from swimming), to the angry moments when mother, sisters, and friends blame her for the negative impacts on their lives that the event of the molestation has caused, Katie, as victim, is also a scapegoat. Her stepfather asks her, when driving her home after her molester's sentencing hearing: "feeling guilty about screwing up a man's life?" (163).

Not only the stepfather and the family, and intermittently the mother, but the whole prosperous, well-educated, white-populated town of New Canaan, Connecticut, demonize Katie so that they need not examine their own cultural assumptions and responsibilities. This is not Salem, Massachusetts, of the seventeenth century, nor medieval Europe during the witch hunts, nor Mary Magdalene's Jerusalem; this could be any prosperous North American suburb. However, the similarity of persecutions of women over time indicate that the Internet has introduced no "new ways" of "constraining and colonizing" women, but has merely refined some very old oppressions and colonizations. I am not arguing here for an essentialist understanding of female victimhood, but rather arguing against the contemporary positivism of Western culture that likes to see the historical conditions of women's victimization as radically changed by humanist and/or feminist progress. The seduction scenario used to accomplish the molestation is as old as patriarchy and is merely enhanced by the Internet, which allows the predator more access more quickly to more teenagers. The community's scapegoating reaction is also unchanged from other patriarchal regimes. This is not to propose an essential and unchangeable female condition, but to insist that we recognize the similarities between cultural scripts over time in order to gain more conscious agency. In this way we may see the Internet as a new "source of power" for women but also advocate modes of survival available to women using the Internet. It is in this sixth cultural script, as a "survivor," that I find Katherine's case most instructive.

SURVIVOR

Memoir has become, in our present times, the literature of survivors, including the survivors of sexual and physical abuse. As someone who writes about memoir and who has written a memoir, I know that the disclosure of anything sexual in nature by a woman is always viewed as confessional. Any confessional act by a woman tends to make the writer vulnerable to the appropriation of the pornographic, victimizing, and blaming gaze that Irene Gammel and the essayists in the book *Confessional Politics* describe. In that book, only the sophisticated productions of postmodern poets writing for an elite audience would seem to be immune from such appropriation. On the other hand, although she recognizes that "to give testimony is an uncertain enterprise, especially for women," Janet Mason Ellerby in her book *Intimate Reading* finds the risk necessary; if undertaken with honesty, giving testimony can "guide us toward transformation, stability and empowerment" (xx). I contend, in *Repossessing the World*, that the difference between writing a memoir that further victimizes the writer and writing one that can lend her more agency in her own survival lies in the way the memoirist takes up the challenges of authorship. I do not contend that agency must be achieved through literary authorship, nor that authorship is always productive of agency, but I do propose that the discursive acts involved in writing a memoir can lead to a greater conscious agency in the lived life—indeed, that discursive acts can be embodied into lived lives. The specific literary acts of the memoirist that I find to be conducive to gaining greater conscious agency lie in the way she shapes the three narrative stances of the voice of memoir: the participant, the witness, and the reflective/reflexive consciousness. These narrative positions need to be cultivated in those using the Internet, especially the third, the function that internalizes and makes use of—in an embodiment that has mental, emotional, and physical effects—the new opportunities that the Internet provides for extending and shaping the self.

Katie.com has a surprising selectivity and balance in terms of the narrator's functions. Surprising in that the author was thirteen at the time of the events, and sixteen and seventeen at the time of writing. I have to assume that she had a really good editor who had the sense to leave in Katie's teenage voice while helping her craft the anecdotes, the reflections, the observations on her own growth and maturity. In quoting from the emails exchanged between Katie and her correspondent "Mark" and in recreating their telephone calls, there is never a sense that Katie is entirely the gullible, passive victim, or "Mark" the stereotypical villain. They discuss the benefits of watching the *Simpsons*, the problems of being a serious swimmer, the need for someone in your life who listens and doesn't judge. Katie is often more mature in her opinions than "Mark." And "Mark," before his ulterior motives are revealed, does seem to offer the kind of approval and support that Katie seeks from parents and community. The quoting of actual emails creates in the reader a sense of intimate narrative participation that never allows us to relax into the idea that we, or our children, would be too smart to get ourselves into such a situation. The unique power of letters to involve the reader as if she were one of the correspondents holds true for email exchanges as well as for older paper forms. Also, because memoir is the product of a "recollection in tranquility" (*Repossessing* 14–15), in reflecting on the correspondence, Katie is observant of her own loneliness, her isolation, and her values as beliefs produced by her upbringing. She gains a reflexivity that comes from working through experience over time and over the various drafts that writing a book-length work require. The embodiment I see as essential to agency is not a mysterious quality, but rather this process of realization over time, of incorporation of the experience through reflection and reflexive speaking and writing, respeaking, rereading, and rewriting, into the action and habits of daily life lived in a body.

Katherine Tarbox's memoir is a product of considerable psychotherapy in which writing every day was a principle feature. She has, in part through writing a therapy diary, developed some reflexivity, which allows her to assess her place in culture with a measure of maturity. The author of *Katie.com* has had considerable support in shaping that maturity. Chastened by their own share of the blaming and isolation that their daughter is subjected to, her parents eventually come to encourage Katherine in her healing gestures, all of which involve discursive acts: her research on sexual abuse for a school essay, her detailed court statement as the victim of a crime, her speech to a student assembly at her private school (to which her parents send their daughter after the ostracism at her home school becomes unbearable). Katherine finally decides not to live the double life caused by hiding her past, and that leads to her writing of this memoir (with the help of an internship won at the prestigious Bread Loaf workshops) and the joint Internet home page her parents have established with her. That home page is the accomplishment of an increased agency in using the Internet rather than being used by it. Katherine Tarbox has won this agency through her own work of healing, a healing that manifests itself as discursive competence. This new agency becomes an interactive tool for encouraging awareness among other teens as the site fills up with the comments of readers of the memoir, a constant feedback of others' stories and reactions to the memoir. The memoir itself ends with a list of advice for parents wanting to help their children use the Internet productively: a practical outreach gesture.

It is important to note, however, that despite this "happy" ending Katherine's agency is not only a product of her growing discursive sophistication. It is also the product of her privileged class position. Katie has access to therapy (she even has the luxury of turning down therapists until she finds the right one), to writing opportunities, and to less oppressive cultural scripts offered by the influential alternative community she is able to enter through her new school and her therapist; she does not directly recognize that this access is a result of her class position and her parents' assertive use of their financial and other resources. However, Katie does acknowledge that she learned through the trial that the man who molested her has done much worse to other teens, teens who did not have her privilege and protection; she also acknowledges the activist participation of a mother who eventually mobilizes her own cultural agency to fight the community's attempt to victimize her daughter. From the beginning of the memoir, Katie is aware of the disadvantages of her class position as upper-class, white, female overachiever; at the end she is aware of only some of her advantages in that class position.

In her acknowledgments, it becomes obvious that this book, like her process of agential self-formation, is a communal effort on the part of professionals that have aided her survival: her therapist, editor, lawyer, and others receive Katherine's heartfelt thanks. She feels an increased sense of female community as part of her profits from the memoir have been donated to RAINN (the acronym for Rape, Abuse and Incest National Network). She is writing a second book about the trials of the college application process for young students (a process that may well occasion her traumatic recall of feelings of isolation and helplessness). She asks other young people entering college to email her their stories, thus seeking an interactive mode for her second book through the vehicle of the Internet.

Her new agential ability to critically negotiate discourse in general is indicated by an incident close to the end of the memoir, in which young Katie waits for her first visit with the counsellor with whom she will begin her healing. In the waiting room, she watches *The Jerry Springer Show* on television. The topic of the show is "Teens and Their Lovers," and Katie enacts this moment as a reflective/reflexive narrator: "I began to think the entire world was a sex-crazed mess. I know Jerry Springer is entertainment, but what are you supposed to think when grown-ups make a twelve-year-old the object of their desire and then go on TV to talk about it like it's normal. When my mother was a kid, she came home to reruns of *Father Knows Best*. I get transsexuals, hookers, and pedophiles. Sometimes it makes me laugh. This time it made me feel dirty" (175). Although ironically unaware of her own biases (including her implication that *Father Knows Best* is ideologically harmless), Katie has arrived at a degree of narrative reflexivity that will aid her survival. It is interesting to note that in her statement that such negative scripts "make me feel dirty" she indirectly recognizes the way the body is the ground on which a sense of self is established. Recognition of the invasive nature of negative scripts and the vulnerability of the body to their effects, even when the body is not actually in physical contact with the abusive agents of the scripts, is an important step in developing her agency.

I find that, in her increasing ability to manipulate and change her cultural scripts through a sophistication in the use of the form of the memoir and ultimately in translating that sophistication to her uses of the Internet, Katherine Tarbox gains, not the freedom of multiple selves, but the agency of a embodied selfhood able to protect, serve, and enhance the self-making potential of the body of which her human subjectivity is a part and in which her human subjectivity grows and changes over time. Even though she has experienced some old oppressions made new by new media, she may also have some opportunity, ironically through the old-fashioned agency of book making, to experience what Haraway calls the "emerging pleasures, experiences, and power" of the new "informatics" world we live in (215). Through the agency gained in memoir writing, Katherine is able to return to the Internet to seek community with other youths who have suffered similar exploitation. Through such a community, she may indeed become a part of the cohort that may fulfill some of Harraway's optimism by changing the "rules of the game."

NOTES

1 I use "Katie" to refer to the narrator and "Katherine" to refer to the author of the memoir.

2 See "Introduction" (chapter 2) of my *Repossessing the World*.

LINDA WARLEY

READING THE AUTOBIOGRAPHICAL
IN PERSONAL HOME PAGES

In their recent book *Reading Autobiography*, Sidonie Smith and Julia Watson list as an appendix "Fifty-Two Genres of Life Narrative."[1] A personal home page published on the Internet is not one of the fifty-two listed. Smith and Watson acknowledge that "cyber narratives" are an increasingly important form of self-representation; however, they note, "As yet no single generic term has emerged as a critical concept to describe how the practices of a digitized imaginary in cyberspace life writing will differ from the analogue writings of lines on a page" (150). I do not propose here a "single generic term" as a "critical concept" that would account for all forms of life writing published on the Internet (it would be hard to imagine such an overarching term). What I do engage is the question of how such texts differ—or not—from print-based life writing and what those differences mean for critics of autobiography. The sheer number and diversity of Internet-based texts precludes broad generalizations about how new media might shape new human identities.[2] However, close analysis of the design, as well as the content, of specific texts such as home pages can highlight the ways in which digital media impact individuals' self-representations. Such analyses might also help us begin to answer the question of whether authors who create and publish life stories online draw on and reinforce existing models of identity or whether new media invite play with and even subversion of identities.

To be sure, personal home pages are not much like the lengthy, detailed, retrospective prose narratives that we generally think of as autobiography. Indeed, as many critics have noted, "autobiography" does not apply precisely to many forms of self-representation, perhaps especially at this historical and cultural moment. Smith and Watson make this point in their recent work and use the term "life narrative" rather than "autobiography," although they continue to find the adjectival form "autobiographical" use-

25

ful (see "Introduction" to *Interfaces*, and *Reading*). In the Canadian context, "life writing" has had much more currency than "autobiography." As Marlene Kadar explains, it is "an umbrella term for a kind of personal or self writing" that accounts for diverse forms and genres, including experimental ones, and invites readers to see "generic forms and changes as historically influenced, and also as unstable, unfixed categories still affected by historical and social context and by changing reading patterns" ("Life Writing" 660-61). The term "life writing" widens the field and makes it more inclusive; it also marks a deliberate intervention into the literary tradition of the lives of "great men" and the criticism that refuses to consider anything outside of that literary tradition worthy of study.

DIGITAL LIFE WRITING AND THE HOME PAGE AS GENRE

Internet-based texts are not just digitized forms of other prose genres. For one thing, they are not solely or even primarily written, and even the written elements need to be understood differently. Mark Poster distinguishes between analogue and digital writing: both draw attention to the materiality of language and both refer to the degree of resemblance between original and copy. In analogue writing, the copy is more closely analogous to the original: the letters of the alphabet stand in for the word. In digital writing, however, the copy is very different from the original since the code, regardless of the original word, image, sound, etc., is a series of zeros and ones. Digital writing is also distinctive because of how it is reproduced, transmitted, and stored.[3] The networked computer environment in which texts such as personal home pages exist, and through which they are read and interpreted, impacts both their design and their reception. Here I use the term "digital life writing." While "writing" still tends to privilege text over the visual or auditory elements that might also be included, the participle form "writing" does capture the sense of process, movement, and flux that tends to characterize digital texts such as home pages. I also think that it is possible to think of, for example, creating and importing other kinds of text objects (such as visual images) and shaping the hypertext structure as a new way of conceptualizing the activity of writing.

With significant numbers of people in the West now having access to literacy and to personal computers, different kinds of digital life writing are proliferating, as are the number and variety of resources upon which people draw in shaping their textualized identities. Among other strategies, people use their computers and the Internet to access genealogical information, to communicate with others to whom they might be related, to gain information about places, historical events, and figures that shape their lives, and, of course, to create their self-representations in word, image, sound, and movement. (Tactile and olfactory resources are not yet available, but might well be in the future.) The self that is represented on a personal home page is not a private self but a very public one—more public than a self represented in a printed book because of the (potential) global reach of the audience. Presumably, authors of personal home pages think that others might find their self-presentations interesting, useful, meaningful, or significant. In terms of motive, then, it seems to me that there are very few differences between those who publish digital life writing on the Internet and those who create other kinds of autobiographical texts. What is different is the sheer number of authors and texts out there. Indeed, anyone with access to the Internet can publish personal information about himself or herself; and life writing has come increasingly within the purview of so-called "ordinary" people.[4] Online publishing is fast and cheap. You don't have to rely on a publisher finding your story worthy of publication, nor do you necessarily have to pay for paper publication (as with vanity presses) or worry about making money from your book. Everyone's life story is potentially interesting, and online publishing encourages more people to make texts out of theirs precisely because the publishing and marketing institutions are no longer serving as exclusive gatekeepers. As Philippe Lejeune notes, "If a publisher turns down a novel, you curse him, but tell yourself that you are going to write a better one. If he turns down your autobiography, it is not only your text, but your self that he is turning down and you will certainly not write a second autobiography" ("Reading").

Each home page published on the Internet shapes a portrait of its author. This is true regardless of how much personal information is included. John Killoran finds that "personal home pages have not been all that autobiographical" (67), yet he also recognizes that home page authors draw on "past genres as heuristic cues, as starting points, as frameworks, but also struggl[e] to deploy them creatively—stretching them, combining them, answering back to them, all in an attempt to find a public voice and to fashion a public profile for themselves" (80). Certainly, many home page authors include elements familiar to readers of other kinds of autobiographical texts: descriptions of home and birth places, stories about significant relationships, and discussions of work, personal achievements, interests, obsessions, passions. Home pages also frequently include photographs, maps, identity documents, genealogical charts, short videos (like home movies), or other kinds of visual objects that can enhance the representation of self and can lend authenticity to it. Further, personal home pages conform to (at least in the most general ways) Philippe Lejeune's pact, the tacit understanding between author and reader that the narrator and the author are the same person (see "The Autobiographical Pact"). While the authorial signature in the case of a home page might be an invented name, most of the time authors of personal home pages do use their real names and claim to be the persons there represented. We do not have to believe them, of course (nor do we have to believe authors of book-form autobiographies, as the many disclosures of imposture teach us), but that is their claim. If we understand genres in terms of what they do rhetorically and how they are used, not by way of some list of common features that they share, then home pages are undeniably another genre of life writing.[5] Home page authors use machines and materials, including computer hardware and software, to construct representations of their identities just as other autobiographers have used pen and paper. Readers of personal home pages use them to gain information about authors and to enter into imaginative, virtual, or sometimes also real relationships with them.

HOW TO READ DIGITAL LIFE WRITING

What tools do we need to interpret digital life writing genres appropriately and fully? Critics can no longer rely solely on literary methods and literary theories, as has been the general practice of many autobiography critics thus far. Marie-Laure Ryan's general point about the shift from print to digital texts has relevance here: "For the literary scholar, the importance of the electronic moment is twofold: it problematizes familiar notions, and it challenges the limits of language. The emergence of a new form of writing has refined the concept of medium: we are now better aware that the medium...is affected by its material support" (10). The material support of computer hardware, phone or cable hookups, networked computer systems, and software programs structures digital life writing. The design features of such texts also require a more multi-faceted critical vocabulary than literary critics, including autobiography critics, have so far been called upon to develop.

This is not to say that critics of autobiography have not been cognizant of how media shapes life writing. On the contrary, the authors in this collection demonstrate that life writing can be found in a wide range of media from song to art exhibit to memorandum. In fact, much recent work in the field of autobiography studies (such as the collections *Getting a Life* and *Interfaces*, both edited by Smith and Watson) focuses on non-traditional autobiographical texts. In this most self-absorbed of cultures (Western, democratic, capitalist) and historical moments (early twenty-first century), almost anything—gesture, utterance, artifact—can be interpreted as life writing. Critics in the field are well positioned to analyze and theorize about this expanded corpus of materials, for they are adept at exploring the interconnections between medium, text, audience, and human subjectivity.

Yet there is still much to discover when it comes to digital life writing. While personal home pages have been the object of study for some time, especially by critics working in the social sciences (see Döring), the theories and methods developed in autobiography research have not had much impact on those studies. Similarly, critics in autobiography studies are only now beginning to turn their attention to computer-mediated texts. Philippe Lejeune led the way with his book "*Cher écran*," which is an ethnographic study of the experience of writing diaries on computers. More recently, a special issue of *Biography* titled *Online Lives* brings welcome attention to digital life writing such as blogs (as weblogs have come to be called)[6] and home pages. As the editor of that special issue notes, "life writing research, already profoundly interdisciplinary, opens onto even more fields of inquiry when it ventures into the domain of computer-mediated communication (Zuern, "Online Lives" viii). Before the digital revolution, it made sense for critics of autobiography to use the tools of literary analysis and theory in their scholarship because conventional autobiographers often draw on literary genres (such as the novel) and create narratives that follow literary conventions such as the quest narrative or the romance. Authors of digital texts, however, have other resources upon which they might draw. Two features that differentiate these texts are particularly significant: (1) they are interactive, and (2) they are multimodal. Interactivity means that authors are self-conscious about the addressee of their texts and readers are more directly involved both with the text and with the author than is generally the case with analogue texts. Multimodality suggests that the meanings of the text are achieved through numerous semiotic codes, of which written language is only one.

DIGITAL SELVES UNDER CONSTRUCTION

Gunther Kress and Theo Van Leeuwen comment that in Western cultures there has been a distinct preference until very recently for monomodality, exhibited both by those who create artifacts (a musical composition, a painting, a book) and those who interpret them (the musicologist, the art historian, the literary critic). Arguing that the situation is now reversing, with multimodality becoming increasingly the norm in all manner of composition from government documents to multimedia concerts, Kress and

Van Leeuwen develop a theoretical model for analyzing such artifacts. In their view, four "strata" are always working in relation to one another in any semiotically charged creation: discourse (socially constructed knowledges); design (the "conceptual side of expression"); production (the "organization of the expression"); and distribution (the mechanisms of dissemination) (*Multimodal* 5-6). As they note, one skilled person working in a digital environment can now control each of these strata. Authors of personal home pages create just such multimodal documents, and each design choice is just as capable of carrying meaning as the various contents. In fact, the design of personal home pages says a lot about how people understand themselves, as well as their audiences and the genres in which they work—a point on which I will elaborate below.

What kinds of selves appear in home pages? In her popular book *Life on the Screen: Identity in the Age of the Internet*, Sherry Turkle suggests that "The Internet has become a significant social laboratory for experimenting with the constructions and reconstructions of self that characterize postmodern life. In its virtual reality we self-fashion and self-create" (180). While she goes on to ask a number of important questions about what kinds of selves one can create on the Internet and what we can learn from those online personae, she is uncritical of and optimistic about the liberatory potential of online self-fashioning, and she accepts users' statements about their experience of "multiple selves" more or less at face value. Turkle finds that "Home pages on the Web are one recent and dramatic illustration of new notions of identity as multiple yet coherent" (259). But without detailed analyses of particular home pages, such comments must remain on the level of speculation. There is no particular evidence that personal home pages bring into being "new notions of identity" (258). In fact, in my reading of hundreds of them, I find most to be achingly traditional, especially in terms of content. Although the medium invites creative expression, the autobiographical form can reinforce traditional and often highly conservative ways of presenting the self. If a personal home page is "about me," what I have readily at hand are those discourses of the self that are most familiar—birthplace, family, work, home, interests, and so on. As Killoran implies, home page authors respond to "heuristic cues" of genre that are not just available to them but may also be hegemonic.

Perhaps ironically, given the global scope of the digital environment and the way in which it collapses time and space, home page authors are strikingly eager to locate themselves in specific times and places. While home pages are ephemeral, in that they can disappear or links to them or within them can be broken, the language home page authors use is quite conventional. Indeed, the discourse reveals a rather conservative desire to ground and domesticate the self—to be at home. Many have noted the prevalence of real estate, architectural, and domestic metaphors in cybertheory and practice (see Star, Zalis). Making and publishing a home page is called "homesteading"—which evokes rather troubling associations with other histories of colonization. A visitor to the home page is frequently greeted (at the door?) by the home page author and invited to "come in" and spend some time in his or her "little corner of cyberspace"—a cliché that now verges on banality. Home pages, like houses, are built, maintained, sometimes "under construction," and occasionally renovated. Home pages, like rooms, are decorated with background "wallpaper" against which text objects are arranged as one would arrange pictures on a wall. The metaphors are familiar. Just at the moment when identity is theorized as fragmented, flexible, contingent, and mobile, the language of digital life writing is all about grounding the self in time and space. Ironically, then, personal home pages often seem to enact shiny, vibrant, noisy *presence*. One can almost imagine the person just on the other side of the screen. Readers of autobiography have long recognized the seduction of the text in that we can identify with life writers and imagine ourselves in their places, but few of us would actually seek out and communicate with an author. Quite the opposite is the case with most digital life writing; readers are explicitly invited to "contact me." And many do.

That sense of presence is reinforced by the focus on the present self—the "I" that is "me now." Returning to Kress and Van Leeuwen's "strata," the digital environment brings the elements of design, production, and distribution of digital life writing into closer view. Unlike analogue texts, which, once published, are more or less fixed (and, thus, fix a certain image of the life writer), personal home pages feel very much alive and mobile, as does the self there represented. Makers of home pages edit, update, add, delete, change, and reshape the presentation of the self online. These texts are not at all stable, which perhaps demonstrates the theoretical point that human subjectivity is a constant process of fashioning and refashioning the self. The interactive aspects of digital texts also make a significant difference. Home pages speak out loud; they speak to a "you"; they invite response. A link to the author's email address offers an invitation to communicate directly with him or her. Right now. Readers are invited to sign guest books or to read the comments of other readers. Counters at the bottom of the first page keep track of the number of visitors. When we browse someone's home page we leave a trace—an "electronic footprint"—whether we are aware of it or not. Readers are *in* the text in ways unimaginable in the world of print, and neither the reader nor the author is as distant from each other as is the case with print texts. Home pages are communicative spaces that have the potential to link people together.

The interactivity of personal home pages provides perhaps our best example of the "self-in-relation" posited by some theorists of autobiography. A relational identity has been theorized by feminist scholars as one response to the sovereign self that supposedly defined Western bourgeois and patriarchal subjectivity.[7] Following from their work, Paul John Eakin has recently argued that "*all* identity is relational, and that the definition of autobiography, and its history as well, must be stretched to reflect the kinds of self-writing in which relational identity is characteristically displayed" (43-44). Whether Eakin's broad statement marks a return to the problematic universalism that has underscored Western thought for centuries is unclear; however, it is clear that autobiography theory must stretch if it is to address digital life writing. In such texts, as in other "everyday occasions" noted by Sidonie Smith and Julia Watson, "autobiographical narrators move out of isolation and loneliness into a social context in which their stories resonate with the stories of others in a group" (*Getting* 15). Authors of home pages are linked by a network infrastructure that makes different configurations of community possible. Furthermore, individual authors situate themselves in relation to others with whom they share something in common, by inserting hyperlinks to other websites, by joining web rings, and by engaging in email discussions with their readers. As Wynn and Katz note, interlinked personal home pages actually augment the social embeddedness of the individual (310). Indeed, they display the "tacit social contexts" in which authors participate (321).

Even further, the medium invites creative collaboration. Authors of personal home pages do not necessarily invest as much as do traditional authors (and the publishing industry that supports them) in the concept of individual and original authorship. Home page authors routinely cut and paste elements of someone else's page—a background pattern, for instance—into their own, or send virtual text objects to other home page authors. While some of this cutting and pasting is unacknowledged pilfering, practices of sharing and collaboration are more easily accomplished in the world of home page publication than in the world of print publication. Mark Poster comments that authorship in the digital environment requires a rethinking of issues of copyright (87-90). Certainly the ethical questions that arise when authors use other people's materials invite a more fulsome discussion than I can engage in here.

Interactivity is one significant difference between analogue and digital life writing; another is that digital life writing is almost always multimodal. While conventional autobiographers frequently include reproduced photographs and sometimes other kinds of documents (such as maps) in their texts, they still tend to valorize written language, as do their interpreters.[8] Home pages, on the other hand, seem to *require* more than writing. Authors of digital texts are much more aware than traditional authors need to be of aspects of multimodal design. They are not entirely free to design their pages in whatever way they want, because the software designers have already made certain choices available and not others. Moreover, as with available discursive resources about identity, design elements are ideologically loaded. For example, sites that sponsor home pages (for a fee) sometimes offer design advice—such as colour theory—or offer the home page maker a number of templates into which authors can simply plug their specific content. Such instruction can shape and homogenize texts in terms of existing ideologies (for instance, what is an appropriate subject for a home page or what is a "warm" or a "cool" colour). Nevertheless, home page authors are faced with a number of design choices that shape the text produced and, ultimately, communicate to the reader of the home page additional information about the author. These decisions vary depending on the desires, creativity, and skill of the author. They may include (among many other possibilities) choices about colour, "wallpaper" patterns, sound (music, voice, other sound effects), animation (video, moving objects), graphics (landscapes, photographs, maps, charts, and many other kinds of visual documents), and so on.

Readers access each element according to the structure of the home page. Digital texts are hypertextual: they present information not in linear form but in a web- or tree-like structure in which information is layered and layered again. Readers of a home page, like readers of other hypertexts, can move in different directions, and the order in which information is received is variable. The reader is not entirely free to move at random, as the author has made decisions about what she or he wants to be where. These choices about structure and arrangement reveal more than arbitrary decisions or personal preferences. What is on the front page? If there are topics listed in a menu, what appears at the top? How are objects arranged spatially on the page? Learning to interpret the significance of such design choices and connecting those insights to modes of self-representation is a new challenge for autobiography critics.

BUT IS IT ME? DESIGN CHOICES AND
WHAT THEY (MIGHT) MEAN

The semiotic potential and ideological implications of digital design choices became increasingly clear to me when I decided to create my own home page. Lacking the skill, the time, and the interest to do it myself, I hired a web designer to make a home page for me. But this turned out not to be a quick job that I could simply delegate. In fact, the designer and I had numerous discussions (on email and face to face) about what I wanted on that page and how it should look. These discussions became a complex process of sorting through my likes, dislikes, desires, and fears. In these discussions, my intellect, my emotions, my politics, and my aesthetic sense were all engaged. My idea of the home page was that it would serve a purely professional function. To my mind, what I look like is therefore not relevant; however, the designer convinced me that including a photograph was important. Taking some photographs also initiated a whole set of questions. What should the setting be? (Predictably the photographs were taken in my office and the one subsequently chosen shows me in front of my bookshelves.) Black and white or colour? Just a head shot or more of the body? Glasses on or off? What colour should I wear? How casual should my dress be? And so on. Then came the painful process of sorting through the photos. I tried to decide which one I could bear to be my very public and always accessible "face." The designer tried to get me to choose one that was "inviting" and "friendly." Apparently professors need to present images that students find inviting and friendly; otherwise we are judged to be too serious, even intimidating. I wonder if this is especially so for female professors.

Assembling the contents of the home page was easy enough, since all of that professional material—course syllabi, CV, and so on—existed in other forms. However, putting the contents together on a home page required other decisions, not least of which was how they were to be ordered and arranged—i.e., prioritized. And then there were the aesthetic questions: which colours and patterns do I like and do I think appropriate for the background, for the text, for the links? The larger question was how much additional information about my interests and life experiences did I want published on my home page. For me the answer was none. The home page is my professional self, not my personal self. However, some visitors have complained that the page is cold and boring (i.e., not "friendly"). Some have even suggested what they want to see there—lists of favourite books being a frequent request. I admit that I am considering "warming up" the site a bit by adding more material (photos of my garden? accounts of my travels to favourite places?). Why have I avoided adding that personal material? Privacy is important to me (and not just because I am a woman), and self-display makes me uncomfortable. My reticence about making myself too public speaks to a long personal history of self-effacement and insecurity. But I am also aware of wanting to maintain a separation between my professional life and my personal life. The genre of the home page, however, seems to demand display of the personal.

BUT IS IT HIM? A CASE STUDY

Smith and Watson remind us that all autobiographers draw on existing models of identity that are available in the culture (*Reading* 34). In my own case, the persona of the professor located in a Canadian university English department, and used to having to account for myself in terms of scholarly acts and achievements (teaching, publishing, etc.) shaped my sense of what is and what is not appropriate in terms of making a professional home page. However, not all home page authors are so reticent about themselves. Indeed, many home pages combine personal and professional information in ways that bring the two (or more) selves together. At this point I turn my attention to a home page that does just this. Originally found via the Yahoo! directory of personal home pages, Dr. Nick Bontis's home page offers a wealth of interpretive possibilities. I am interested in this particular page for several reasons. Partly I can identify with Dr. Bontis. Like me he is a youngish Canadian academic working at a university in southern Ontario. But in many ways he is not at all like me, and his detailed, multi-layered, and highly multimodal home page speaks to differences in gender, context, and sense of self.

Dr. Nick Bontis's home page is a remarkable example of a page created by a skilled author who can fully exploit the resources made available by computer technologies. A brief description is in order. Clicking on the web address shows us a royal blue screen, with a graphic of a brain at the centre and a statement telling us what technical resources we need to load the page. Clicking on the graphic brain takes us to the first and main page, an action that also activates a voice clip, which says "Welcome to Bontis.com," and continuous electronic-sounding background music. The same blue background colour remains, now augmented by the graphic of the brain pulsating and rotating, several white or lighter blue "spotlights" (giving the impression of a theatre marquee), small snapshot photos of the author and family members (including the dog), as well as menu buttons at the top and bottom of the screen (see fig. 1).

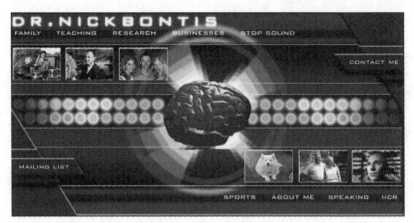

Figure 1. Bontis.com, copyright Nick Bontis

Clicking on menu items takes us to new pages, which include both written narrative and links to still more pages. These links lead us to, for example, several close-up photographs of family members, a family genealogical chart, detailed presentations of the author's work and achievements (including photos of him receiving awards), an academic CV, lists of courses, videos of his lectures and talks, a virtual tour of his office, and a video (made by others) of the author at work (which includes testimonials by students and colleagues). Included too are many links to other web pages, from universities at which the author has worked or studied and professional organizations to which he belongs, to the soccer association of which he is a member. Readers of the home page gain detailed information about the author, not just by reading his "bio" or by scanning the academic CV, but also from the various multimodal elements and their arrangement.

This personal home page is very much about "selling" the author in a professional academic context. The home page presents a portrait of a highly educated, middle-class, young man who is confident, savvy, energetic, and successful. It presents a person who, probably because of his training in business, fully understands the advantages of marketing the self. Much of the content is aimed at presenting the person at work, in his capacity as professor and as expert in the field of "knowledge management and business policy and strategy." Legitimization is a key theme. Even the field in which Dr. Bontis locates his research and teaching is legitimized on the home page. Apart from written explanations of the subject and excerpts from the author's lectures and interviews, colours and certain graphic elements communicate similar meanings and reinforce the presentation of the man and his job. The blue of the wallpaper, for example, is a cool colour, understated, "classy," which befits a professional man (the colour of a businessman's attire, for example). But this particular shade of blue, "royal blue," also signifies intellectual weight and social importance—it is the same colour blue as the trim on my own academic robe. Intellectual weight is also added by the graphic of the brain, which except for the colour is very realistic-looking (high modality, in communications theory terms). An obvious symbol of the human mind, it evokes the sciences and thus indirectly links the fields of business and knowledge management to the "hard" sciences. The connection to the sciences is also reinforced by sound—the electronic, almost robotic-sounding voice that welcomes the visitor and the "spacey" music track. The graphic presents the computer itself as a thinking machine. Rather than being asked to wait while information is "loaded," the reader is asked to wait while the site is "learning." This focus on learning highlights the author's own brainpower, as well as his position within an academic institution. It also invites the reader to identify as an equally "brainy" person. Certainly, the number of plug-ins and software downloads required to view all of the elements of the home page assumes a reader with updated computer resources and a high-speed Internet hookup, which, in turn, assumes a certain level of education, income, and class status.

Presumably this home page, like mine, serves a primarily professional function. But the number and variety of texts, videos, and graphic images included are noteworthy. To understand them only in terms of boastful arrogance is one predictable reaction, but it is not, it seems to me, enough. For one thing, we need to contextualize this self-representation in terms of the long history of male identity formation. The model of identity upon which Dr. Bontis draws is familiar: it is based on action, work, and personal achievement. The institutional context of the university reinforces this masculine model of the professor. All academics are required to sell themselves in these terms: our CVs, annual performance reports, applications for grants, sabbatical leaves, and tenure all require such shameless self-promotion. Modesty does not serve us well in this context. One could say that Dr. Bontis's home page is the digital equivalent of the academic cap and gown, the framed degree certificates and award plaques on the office wall. In addition, Dr. Bontis works partly in the corporate world, another arena where conventional masculine identity is assessed in terms of action, power, and individual accomplishment. He is both the professor and the corporate man, and the institutional contexts in which he spends much of his life shape the way in which he thinks and speaks of himself.

Significantly, this author uses the third person when writing about himself and refers to himself in three different ways: in the "Teaching" section he is "Professor Bontis"; in the "Research" and "Businesses" sections he is "Dr. Bontis"; and in the "Family" and "Sports" sections he is "Nick." Third-person narrative voice reinforces the fact that the textualized self is an artifact: not the private man but the public one; not the subjective being but the persona. Further, it keeps the focus on his actions and it keeps the reader at some emotional distance. The professional man "hails" a professional reader. Yet the three different ways of referring to himself also suggest that no single representation is adequate or complete. In fact, the inclusion of personal material sometimes nuances and complicates our interpretation of the identity performed on the home page.

While most of the textual space of the home page is devoted to Dr. Bontis's professional persona, on the menu bar a link to "Family" occupies the top left corner. English, as with most Western languages, is based on a left-to-right reading pattern. We read home pages the same way, from left to right and from top to bottom. Therefore, whatever is placed on the top left corner of the screen is given high priority, as the author can assume that most will read that section first. This is where the "Family" button is located. When we click on it, we find brief narratives about Nick Bontis's wife and infant child, his sister, his parents, his dog, and the extended family on both his own and his wife's side. Kress and Van Leeuwen note that objects that appear on the left of a page function as a "Given" (i.e., that which is already known or assumed by the reader or viewer) whereas material on the right side of a page functions as the "New" (i.e., that which is to be learned or is potentially at issue) (*Reading* 186–202). In a printed visual text, this arrangement would suggest that the positioning of the "Family" material marks a known backdrop, a secure context, from which the professional man emerges. The "Given" would be the relationships between the author and family members, both those with whom he is close (wife, child, siblings, and parents) and those who are more distant (ancestors); the "New" is the working man on his own. In a hypertext document, the spatial arrangement of elements is more complicated than this model would permit; nevertheless, the inclusion of significant and carefully placed elements that refer to family members does suggest a context against which the individual can be seen. The question of their importance, however, as well as their specific roles in shaping the self performed here, invite further commentary.

Included in the "Family" section are several photographs. Unlike the small photos that appear on the main page, some of these photographs are large, close-up photographs of Nick Bontis's wife, child, sister, and parents. The size and near-professional quality of the photographs is striking. In particular, the close-up photos of his wife and sister, both young and attractive women, look like model shots in magazines and advertisements. What do we make of such provocative pictures? Read one way they suggest the author's admiration of these women, his closeness to them, his regard for them. Read another way they could be interpreted as one more accomplishment or achievement in this man's successful life.

In the photographs of his wife and sister, the subjects looks directly at the camera. In such photos, the subject solicits the viewer's gaze. According to Kress and Van Leeuwen's theory of reading visual images, these are "demand" pictures, which seem to call upon the viewer to enter into an imaginary relationship with the subject (*Reading* 121-30). By contrast, self-portraits of the author are less close up and do not necessarily depict him alone or engaging the viewer's look. Images of Dr. Bontis connect him to worlds of action (professional and sport) and are generally taken from a long-shot perspective. One prominent picture on the first page depicts him with eyes averted. This would be an "offer" picture, in Kress and Van Leeuwen's terms: it offers the subject to the viewer as an object of information, but does not invite an imaginary relationship with him. In this particular photograph, the camera angle is from slightly below the subject's head, which suggests that the viewer must "look up to" the subject. The author's self portraits are more objective, more focused on his position within an external world of school, work, and sport, interpretations that once again conform to the conventional ideology of masculine identity. These "offer" photos suggest that he is presenting himself for scrutiny and evaluation, but also keeping his inner self hidden and at a distance.

There is little humour or irony in this home page. Little play with identity. Little introspection, although there are presentations of the past and of the younger self. Such lack of irony and self-scrutiny is perhaps disappointing given the subversive possibilities of the medium. In fact, what the home page *Bontis.com* speaks to is the incredibly powerful ideology of masculinity that continues to shape male identity in the first part of the twenty-first century. And this despite the insights generated by several decades of theoretical work in gender studies. Here is a presentation of self that is all too familiar. Here is the confident, active, intelligent, competitive, professional man who unabashedly proclaims his many successes. Here is the man who keeps his emotional life hidden. Readers of autobiography have encountered this kind of autobiographer countless times before.

And yet, that is not all there is to be said. Let us not forget or ignore the fact that this author also connects himself not just to immediate family members but also to ancestors. The genealogical diagram links the individual to an extended familial context and reinforces an important fact: this man is the son of immigrant Greek-Canadian parents. This point sheds additional light on the presentation of self. Immigrant families often expect—indeed count on—their children to succeed in social terms. Such families tend to value very highly their children's education, which, in turn, leads to successful professional careers. They also tend to prioritize heterosexual marriage and the reproduction of the nuclear and/or extended family. Depending on the culture of the original country, these demands are often felt acutely by sons. Perhaps the author is performing for his family, as well as for his colleagues and students.

We must also remember that the home page is not entirely self-made, as it incorporates images (videos, for example) that have been made by others. Nor is the portrait of the self isolated from others—students, colleagues, family members, and members of the soccer team are all part of the author's identity. While the author is certainly ready to put himself forward, he also clearly links himself to other people, as well as to organizations, institutions, and groups that are a significant part of the context through which his identity has been formed. The home page, then, while clearly serving a professional function, also at least partly serves a personal one: it emphasizes the multiple contexts in which the individual exists and that contribute to his self-formation. Furthermore, it introduces tensions and paradoxes that require careful analysis. The self presented here conforms to the script of the academic and corporate man, and yet the emphasis put on family and other communities of belonging complicates that self-representation. Another paradox is that those photos of Dr. Bontis keep something hidden from the viewer and do not invite a personal relationship, while the home page as a whole seems to be remarkably detailed and revealing. Digital life writing facilitates the inclusion of a wealth of materials drawn from an individual's life. At the same time such texts can exaggerate certain performances of identity while rendering others more ambiguous. It could well be that the technical and creative possibilities afforded by new media encourage authors to be more self-revealing than they even want to be. Although it is difficult to generalize from one home page when there are tens of thousands of them on the Internet, it could be that the genre of the personal home page actually invites exaggerated performance of certain aspects of the self. My own experience demonstrated that old anxieties about being under scrutiny are still with me; indeed, my home page is probably more interesting in terms of its silences and omissions than in terms of its offerings—even though in the photograph I do engage the reader's gaze!

Personal home pages and other genres of digital life writing are perfect occasions for the kind of "backyard ethnography" Smith and Watson (*Getting a Life*) and others have begun. Along with Ryan, I suggest that it is time to stop making general pronouncements about identity in cyberspace and to turn our attention to producing detailed analyses of particular artifacts made in digital media. Critics of autobiography are well positioned to produce nuanced interpretations of digital life writing because they are trained to analyze the self as a performative and textualized construction in a given cultural and historical context. While the generic resources and discourses of selfhood that shape autobiographical identities in Western cultures still generally structure selves performed on the Internet, the creative and technical resources that are available to authors of digital texts open up additional interpretative paths. These multimodal and interactive texts require analytical paradigms and strategies drawn from disciplines outside of and in addition to literary studies. Only when these have been developed and put into extensive practice will we have a fuller sense of how to read and understand autobiography on the Internet.

NOTES

1 I am grateful to Andrew McMurry and Gabriele Helms, both of whom offered theoretical and technical help in the early stages of this project.
2 Early enthusiasm for the postmodern potential of online identities has given way to more sober second thought. See Turkle, Bolter, and Landow as proponents of a general argument that cyber identities represent a realization of a multiple, fragmented, decentered, and contingent self, and Wynn and Katz for a trenchant critique of that argument.
3 See Poster's chapter 5 for a fuller discussion.
4 Since at least the 1980s, scholars of autobiography, particularly feminist scholars, have attended to the ways in which authors who lack social status use autobiographical forms (often unconventional) to shape and affirm their subjectivities (see Personal Narratives Group and Anne E. Goldman, for example). Computer technologies have also assisted in the soliciting and archiving of such life stories. In England, the *Mass-Observation Archive* contains papers generated by the original Mass-Observation social research organization (1937 to early 1950s), as well as material collected since 1981. In France, Lejeune and others have founded *Autopacte*, a similar archive of life writings by "ordinary" French people.
5 Theories of genre understood in terms of rhetorical and social action have gained increasing currency in recent years. Carolyn R. Miller's work is seminal. See also the collection edited by Coe, Lingard, and Teslenko.
6 For a useful discussion of the history of blogs (which began to appear in the mid-1990s) and the development of the genre, see Paquet.

7 Mary G. Mason first brought the feminist theory of women's identities as relational specifically to the field of autobiography studies in the essay she published in Olney's influential 1980 collection, *Autobiography: Essays Theoretical and Critical*.

8 Timothy Dow Adams and Marianne Hirsch (*Family Frames*) have produced important scholarly works on visual media and autobiographical narratives. See also Egan, especially chapter 3, and Smith and Watson's collection *Interfaces*.

GABRIELE HELMS

....

REALITY TV HAS SPOKEN
AUTO/BIOGRAPHY MATTERS

Television has brought life stories into our homes for a long time through newsmagazine programs, talk shows, and documentaries. In fact, I would agree with Laura Grindstaff that "the attempt to highlight shared experience or lived reality has been one of the guiding principles of news and documentary production since the advent of television itself and, before that, cinema" (*Money Shot* 46). Reality-based television genres that focus on practices of self-representation are not new then. The development of reality-based programming can be traced quite specifically to *Candid Camera*, which first aired on American television in 1948, *An American Family* (1973 on PBS), and MTV's *The Real World* (1992), but the shows associated with the genre of reality TV in North America today, which regularly make newspaper headlines, have gained prominence only since the first airing of *Survivor* on CBS on 31 May 2000. Producers quickly took advantage of the low production costs of reality TV shows and have created dozens of other reality TV programs since then, many of which did not, however, last beyond their first season. From applauding the exceptionally high ratings of these reality TV shows, or dismissing them because of their lack of complexity and the dumbing-down of audiences, to crying moral panic over the way reality shows display and legitimize the decline of traditional values, popular journalism has found many reasons for engagement. Academic attention, however, has been limited even though media critics, such as Jon Dovey, have spoken in recent years of our age as the "first-person media era" (*Freakshow*), which suggests that the representation of subjectivity has been recognized widely as a contemporary concern. In some academic disciplines, resistance may not be directed so much at reality shows but at television in general as too trivial for analysis. In fields that focus on non-fiction television programming, including media and cultural studies, the challenge may have more to do with the difficulty that Frances Bonner simply describes as "trying to find a way to approach the material" (2).

Reality television, a term originally used to describe programs based on emergency-service activities such as *Rescue 911*, *Cops*, and *America's Most Wanted*, is most often described today as a hybrid television genre that combines elements of drama, especially soap opera, with documentary and game-show elements, and thus combines the primary purpose of entertainment with information. Generally thought of as part of factual rather than fictional entertainment, reality TV's hybridity is foregrounded in alternative terms such as "reality soap," "infotainment," or "tabloid television" (Dovey, "Reality TV" 134). Bonner uses "ordinary television" as her umbrella term to describe shows characterized by "their lack of anything special, their very triviality, their very ordinariness" (2). Definitions vary, however, and may range from drama that uses topical events as source material (such as *Law and Order*, NYPD *Blue*, *The X-Files*, *The West Wing*) to tell-all talk shows (such as *Jerry Springer*), game shows (such as *Who Wants to Be a Millionaire?* and *The Weakest Link*), food programs (such as *The Naked Chef*, *Emeril*, *Two Fat Ladies*), fly-on-the-wall observation shows (such as *The Osbournes* and *Real World*), and lifestyle programs (such as *Changing Rooms*, *Extreme Makeover*). Dovey may be accurate in saying that "the different kinds of programme described as 'reality TV' are unified by the attempt to package particular aspects of everyday life as entertainment" ("Reality TV" 135). In spite of this commonality, I will limit my discussion to programs such as *Big Brother*, *Survivor*, *The Amazing Race*, *The Bachelor/ette*, *Joe Millionaire*, *Paradise Hotel*, and *Temptation Island* to avoid overgeneralization; these reality TV programs are prime-time reality game shows that place ordinary people in contrived situations, framed within a range of confessional modes of speech, to observe their actions until one person remains who wins a prize. The "time-travel" reality shows aired by PBS (e.g., *The 1900 House*) and the History Television channel in Canada (e.g., *Pioneer Quest*) also appear to belong here; but they complicate this category, for they seem to combine equally the three functions of information, education, and entertainment, known as the Reithian concept of public broadcasting. These programs warrant critical analysis in the future especially for the ways that they engage history and connect locale with national mythology and identity, but this task lies beyond the scope of this paper.[1]

Debates about the relationship between representational media and reality are neither new nor limited to television. While it is the television's capacity for liveness (i.e., its ability to render realistic audio and visual representations in real time, as in sports broadcasts) that separates it from other representational media (cinema or even the computer), what I have defined as reality TV has little to do with this kind of liveness ("live to air"). Many consider the phrase "reality TV" a contradiction in terms because rarely do viewers see "reality as it happens." While the scenarios they watch are admittedly contrived, the words spoken and some of the action are usually considered unscripted. Cameras may be positioned in multiple places and run 24/7, but what the audience sees on television is a highly mediated and edited version of events in one-hour or half-hour segments that have taken place at an earlier point in time. As Mark Andrejevic explains, "cast members live in a kind of panopticon—not everything they are doing is taped and watched, but they have to live with the knowledge that at any moment, their words and actions could be taped for broadcast" (260). Plot devices familiar from literature shape the shows' development and highlight their high level of mediation, leading Bill Nichols to describe the conventional story format of reality TV shows as "a perversely exhibitionistic version of the melodramatic imagination" (53). Episodes tend to work toward a climax, such as the campfire vote on *Survivor* or the rose ceremony on *The Bachelor/ette*, or they conclude with a teaser familiar from serials that build suspense. As James Friedman observes in *Reality Squared*, it is not the form or content of the reality programs that represent a significant shift in the television landscape, but "the open and explicit sale of television programming as a representation of reality" (7).

I argue that this representation of reality depends on the auto/biographical performances of the shows' participants and that, following Friedman, it is the open and explicit sale of this auto/biographical discourse that accounts, at least in part, for the success of reality TV. Low-cost production may explain the appeal of reality TV to television stations, but it does not explain why viewers continue to tune into these reality-based programs. Reality TV is part of what Dovey has described as the evolution of a "social practice that demands a grounding in the personal, the subjective and the particular" (*Freakshow* 22). Auto/biography studies provide us with the critical concepts and questions, in effect the tools, to examine this social practice closely because scholars of auto/biography focus on the very elements basic to reality TV: individual and collective lives, everyday experiences, ethics, authorship, identity, embodiment, (self-) knowledge, audience, and authenticity. In the last decade, auto/biography scholars have turned to an increasingly broad range of media, such as painting, theatre, oral history, photography, film, and most recently the Internet,[2] recognizing that the telling and receiving of life narratives happens not just in published auto/biographies, long the predominant object of study but also in the auto/biographical practices that permeate our everyday lives. And yet, when it comes to television, the sole focus of auto/biography scholars has been on genres of confession, especially talk shows (Janice Peck, Cynthia J. Davis). With the exception of John Dovey (*Freakshow*) and Kate Douglas, the latter also a literary critic, media scholars do not usually rely explicitly on categories or questions informed by auto/biography studies even though their work frequently speaks about the same issues.

What can the auto/biography scholar contribute to the discussion of reality television? I believe that the popularity of some of the most highly rated reality TV shows results exactly from their focus on auto/biographical performance. To understand the shows' popularity, we need to recognize them as auto/biographical practices and see them as part of a long tradition of such practices in a wide range of media. They are not simply "the end results of the explosion in visual technologies," without contexts and without history, as Bilge Yesil reminds us (6). Attention to how auto/biographical elements function in these shows, in combination with an analysis of the hybrid formats they employ, may also help, at a later point, to assess the differences between the wide variety of reality-based programs. What is more, approaches developed in auto/biography studies can help us to examine the relationship between reality TV and the cultures in which we live. Are the lives represented on these shows, and the ways they are represented, reflections of contemporary understandings of self and identity? Do they in turn shape the way we live and represent our lives? These questions may be particularly important if we consider that the demographic (fourteen to twenty-five years old) most attracted to reality TV is otherwise least interested in news television, but most interested in the construction of identity (G. Turner 379). Finally, reality television may make us "revise how we understand the autobiographical" and re-examine our literary theories of auto/biography that may not be adequate for the analysis of practices in non-print media (Smith and Watson, "The Rumpled Bed" 13); the pervasiveness of reality TV urges us to examine the interplay between the "technical resources and the ways in which we experience and express our lives" (Zuern, "Online Lives" xxi). The immediate purpose of this paper is not to present detailed analysis of individual programs, however. What follows are observations that suggest productive points of intersection between auto/biography studies and media studies. Rather than detailed arguments in and of themselves, these observations are intended to spark further theorization and critical study of reality TV as auto/biographical practice.

PARTICIPANTS PLAY THEMSELVES

The main appeal of reality TV as auto/biographical practice is that participants are not professional actors. They play themselves. Viewers are expected to assume an identity between the participants' off-stage selves and the personae they portray on the program. In fact, as part of the application process, participants vouch for their authenticity as they agree, among other things, to background checks, which can include a credit and criminal check, but also interviews with family members or employers.[3] Such a "contract of identity" is, of course, reminiscent of Philippe Lejeune's autobiographical pact, which describes the identity of the author and narrator/protagonist ensured by the proper name. This promise of identity informs, for example, the way that the names of participants were provided in a web description of *The Surreal Life*, a show that followed seven pop-culture celebrities in a shared house for two weeks (spring 2003). Each full name was followed by the appropriate self-reflexive pronoun (e.g., "Corey Feldman—Himself"), insisting that these celebrities would play who they "really" were.[4] For producers, the reliance on people who play themselves rather than actors constitutes one of the main ways they reduce production costs. When every single actor on a sitcom such as *Friends*, which portrayed the lives of six thirty-somethings in New York, could demand one million dollars per episode, the grand prize of a million or half a million dollars awarded to a single participant at the end of a whole season of a reality show must appear like small change. But where lies the attraction for viewers?

Audiences derive, as Jane Roscoe suggests, some pleasure from seeing people like themselves (479). At the same time, viewers of reality TV, not unlike readers of auto/biographies, enjoy "try[ing] on the experience of another" because their own identities "crave the confirmation of like experience, or the enlargement or transformation which can come from viewing a similar experience from a different perspective" (Conway 6). In fact, I believe that these processes of auto/biographical identification and separation inform all audience engagement with auto/biographical practices regardless of medium. And yet, what makes auto/biographical performances on TV particularly appealing seems to be the sense of immediacy and promise of accuracy conveyed by visual representation.[5] Viewers see "real" people whom they could meet and recognize on the street tomorrow.

However, representation is never unmediated, and performances of identity are mediated in particular ways on reality TV programs. Locales on reality TV shows are often exotic (especially on *Survivor* and *Temptation Island*); contexts and occasions are artificial (e.g., contestants in the Big

Brother house have no contact with the outside world and do not go to work for up to three months; the Bachelor dates twenty eligible women at the same time). Participants agree that their actions be recorded by open or hidden cameras and microphones twenty-four hours a day. Not only do they perform for the cameras, but what audiences finally see has been heavily edited by the shows' producers. As Mark Burnett, producer of *Survivor*, explains, "for every hour of television broadcast, over a hundred hours of tape will be edited down" (14). Often show participants reflect on the tensions between their selves "on and off stage." For instance, Jun Song, the winner of *Big Brother 4*, says on the show's website that her biggest fear about joining the house was "being portrayed inaccurately or unfairly. I would like to pick up my life post-BB4." Jun's worry highlights her awareness that who she "really" is may not match how she will be perceived by viewers, and that this discrepancy could negatively impact her life after the show is over. In other words, participants may not actually be in control of their own representation (Bonner 90); authorship of their subjectivity may only partially belong to them. We can observe a similar reflexivity of participants when they comment on their behaviour as being required by the game rather than being an accurate representation of who they are. Richard Hatch, for example, winner of the first *Survivor* show, said just before the jury voted, "I wouldn't change anything I did, and I hope you recognize that was what I had to do to play the game" (qtd. on CBS's *Survivor* website, in "Survivor Profiles: Richard"). The goal of winning the (half) million dollars at the end of the game thus works to justify actions that are "out of character." Eliminated participants in particular make that distinction between who they "really" are and how others perceive them in order to explain why they were voted out. However, ultimately participants have no recourse to correct possible misconceptions. Participants usually acknowledge in writing as part of their application that the show may ultimately represent them in a way they may perceive as inaccurate. The eligibility requirements that contestants for *The Bachelor* have to sign, for example, state explicitly under point 12 of the form available on the program's website that "applicants acknowledge, understand, and agree that Companies [*sic*]…use or revelation of Personal Information and Recordings as defined in these Eligibility Requirements may be embarrassing, unfavorable, humiliating, derogatory and/or portray The Bachelor and/or the Bachelorettes in a false light. Each applicant agrees to release, discharge and hold harmless the Companies from any and all claims." In other words, not only do reality shows rely on carefully constructed scenarios and staged situations, but the auto/biographical performance that viewers see has also become a collaborative production of the participant and producer.

Reality shows throw into sharp relief concepts such as subjectivity, identity, reality, honesty, and authenticity. On the one hand, they ask viewers to believe that participants are authentic because they play themselves. On the other hand, they acknowledge the artificiality of their performances, including the participants' frequent self-reflexive commentary on whether their actions are in keeping with who they "really" are. Reality TV invites us to examine how these concepts are modulated by the medium of television and to what extent the play with identity construction and representation in reality TV is consistent with the manipulation of identity performance that we can observe in other contemporary auto/biographical practices such as Internet blogs and chat rooms.

If participants on reality TV shows are not actors but ordinary people, it should be possible for anyone to be a participant. What Grindstaff calls "professional ordinary guests," that is, "people who make a habit of going on talk shows out of a desire to get on TV" and thus "compromise the aura of authenticity that guests are supposed to convey" (*Money Shot* 172), do not pose a problem for the programs discussed here since participants are usually rendered ineligible if they have appeared on other prime-time reality or game shows. Moreover, some programs provide guidelines on their websites about what kind of participants producers would like to involve. The *Survivor* team, for instance, looks "for a diverse group of men and women who represent a broad cross-section of American society," with the following traits: strong-willed, outgoing, adventurous, physically and mentally adept, and adaptable to new environments; producers seek contestants with interesting lifestyles, backgrounds, and personalities. *The Amazing Race* requires that contestants "be adaptable to various living and working situations and...enjoy working and living in close proximity with others of varied age, sex, race, background, and experience." In a way, then, these reality-based programs hold out the great promise of democratizing television and by extension the world in which we live. Individual differences could be celebrated, and viewers may seek to engage with such differences, realizing that our way of being is far from fixed and stable. In this "ethical move," as Gay Hawkins puts it, "that documentary can sometimes invite us to make, the self is responding to difference rather than judging and classifying it" (421). It seems, however, that participants on the programs examined here ultimately form a remarkably homogeneous group in spite of some diversity in racial background. Most contestants are young, hip, attractive, and heterosexual. If someone does not share these characteristics—and happens to be over fifty, overweight, gay, deaf, or a breast-cancer survivor, examples that have been drawn from *Big Brother* and *Survivor*—their difference immediately becomes a topic for discussion and is used as an opportunity to assert tolerance: their difference really makes no difference. Or so everyone claims. Such insistent categorization and invocation of equality may tell us more about the identity and moral superiority of the classifier than about those participants who are being singled out. At times, however, it seems to be the person her/himself who insists that s/he is to be treated differently, complicating any one-way directionality. Does reality TV serve the purpose of democratization or normativity? Close analysis of individual programs will be required in future studies to test these preliminary speculations.

REALITY PROGRAMS CREATE PERSONAL CRISES

A crisis often constitutes a radical change in someone's life that will provide the motivation for auto/biographical writing.[6] In much contemporary auto/biography, unresolved crises will lead to generic experimentation to find suitable forms for their expression and exploration, as Susanna Egan has shown in *Mirror Talk*. While in these cases crisis may lead to auto/biographical representation, the auto/biographical moment of the reality show leads to personal crisis. Or, to put it differently, reality shows create crisis situations to test the abilities or limits of the participants so that they can determine a winner. It is not usually enough to bring together groups of people whose daily activities we watch unless we are dealing with the Osbourne family; the audience wants to see how people will react in what Hawkins calls "simulated ethical crises" (413). In these moments of crisis—when participants are tempted to cheat on a spouse or are asked to form alliances to oust another member—they are expected to reveal the most about themselves, to show their true selves. It is also in these moments that they may be most emotional, which explains why reality TV is often referred to as "emotion television" in the Netherlands. And for what purpose? It appears that viewers like to witness how participants struggle with such ethical conflicts. Struggle and conflict make good television because they lead to high ratings and profits. Perhaps even more striking, however, is the fact that so many participants speak of their show experience as a unique opportunity to learn about themselves and others. Even when they don't win, they are grateful to have participated. Consider two comments made by *Survivor* participants as representative examples: "The last few days have taught me a lot about not only my strengths but more importantly my weaknesses. I kind of feel invincible at times and *Survivor* has been a big reality check for me"; "I feel really good about myself...I have learned so much and I'm a completely different person because of it. I'm so glad I had this opportunity" (qtd. in Douglas). Self-knowledge comes from crisis, and reality TV becomes the generous provider of such crises and by implication of self-knowledge.

Hardship, deprivation, and conflict become accessible to the audience vicariously through the participants' crises. Viewers may initially experience exhilaration, disgust, or shock, but ultimately a crisis that may be truly startling, bizarre, or emotionally intense in one's own life is given "an offhand and commonsensical ring" on the show (Nichols 45). Crisis is rendered banal, part of a game. Ethics themselves are trivialized since the main goal is to keep the audience interested regardless of the impact the crises may have on the participants and their families and friends. Viewers are supposed to be entertained by such crises; they are not encouraged to explore what kinds of responses would seem ethically appropriate. Do they feel empathy? A desire to help? Do they think about the longterm effects that such crises may have on others? As Bill Nichols suggests, "there is no 'aha' on reality TV" (61)—I would add, there is perhaps only an "oh no."

IDENTITY IS CONFIGURED IN TERMS OF WINNERS AND LOSERS

Given the game-show framework of reality TV, the self-knowledge gained and sense of identity developed from such crises will be limited. In the short period of time that participants are part of a show (ranging from a few hours to a few months), the main purpose is to learn about who they already are, not to examine how they became that person or how they could change through retrospection—a process more often associated with written auto/biography. Auto/biographical performances on a reality show do not seek to understand the development of identity: they are interested in taking stock of it in the moment of performance—of crisis. The crises ultimately lead to winning the prize, which limits the models of identity available on reality-based shows: one becomes either a winner or a loser.

This focus on crisis and winner/loser identities shapes the narrative plots available on these shows since all events throughout the season lead to the final moment of determining the winner. We do not usually find the alternative narrative emplotments we know from other auto/biographical genres, such as the journey of self-discovery, conversion, or a call to action.[7] What we do recognize as audiences of drama and prose, however, is the pattern of exposition, rising action, climax (being voted off or evicted—or winning) and denouement, a pattern that characterizes each installment of the reality TV shows discussed in this paper. In its focus on the lived moment, ideally a moment of crisis, reality TV thus seems continuous with lived life—that is, it remains unpredictable—within a predictable plot line that seeks to identify winners and losers and that thrives on the participants' anxieties to belong to the former rather than the latter category.

The cult of the individual, on which these identity models seem to rely, is oddly enough paired in most reality TV programs with the need to be a team player. Over two decades ago, feminist critics, such as Susan Stanford Friedman (writing on women's auto/biographies) and Carol Gilligan (developing a psychoanalytical model of gender differences), drew the attention of auto/biography scholars to how identities were constructed relationally rather than autonomously or independently. Paul John Eakin's study of the relational life, *How Our Lives Become Stories*, reminds us of the interdependence of the story of the self and the story of the other in auto/biographical genres. If only the engagement with others allows the auto/biographical self to develop a sense of identity, if the autonomous self is, in other words, an illusion, then reality TV's focus on the relationships between participants seems more than appropriate. And yet, the ultimate goal of this relationality is predetermined by the identity models available: you win or lose. It is no surprise then that manipulation, deception, humiliation, and alliance-building are among the strategies of choice as participants position themselves within groups and vis-à-vis the television audience. The success of the participants in turn justifies these types of behaviours and legitimizes them as characteristic of relationality. As Tony Tremblay points out, programs such as *Survivor* suggest that "society is best served when individuals fend for themselves" (51). If "competitive conniving" appears natural and inevitable, part of one's survival instinct (53), and if the only desirable identity available on reality TV is that of the winner, then compassion, honesty, and altruism are undesirable and ultimately self-destructive.

CONFESSION IS THE MODE OF CHOICE

The confessional has become one of the most easily recognizable auto/biographical modes in reality-based programs. In its long tradition that extends back to St. Augustine's *Confessions* (c. 397–400) and Jean-Jacques Rousseau's *Confessions* (1782-89), confession, whether religious or secular, describes a private discourse in which a person speaks in retrospect about a past experience that requires explanation, justification, or atonement. Usually, confessional narratives are a record of some kind of error and frequently of its overcoming; embedded in the confession often lies the desire to reaffirm values previously transgressed (Manganiello 2001). It is addressed to an interlocutor who listens, judges, and sometimes has the power to absolve.

On reality TV, the confession has become public—millions of viewers are watching it. It has also become ritualized in new ways. The "diary room," for instance, is an essential element of *Big Brother*; in this room participants are expected to record their feelings, frustrations, and thoughts, and their nominations of who should be evicted from the house. By using the term "diary," the program relies on the audience's familiarity with the basic characteristics of the diary genre: for instance, its insistence on immediacy, daily or at least periodic coverage of events, and lack of foreknowledge (Cottam) but also its "potential for confession" (McNeill 7). The TV program then extends the diary genre by designating a physical space for it in the house and changing the medium from the written word to oral delivery. The program thus institutionalizes an opportunity for reflection and retrospection in the auto/biographical performances of its participants.[8] Often confessions on reality TV shows are connected with the process of elimination; participants who have just been voted off/out are given a chance to speak about their experience and their feelings of regret or misgivings. On *Survivor*, for instance, the voted-off participant goes to a separate location close to where the tribal council was held, known as the confessional, where s/he says his/her parting words directly to a camera. The confession is played over the closing credits of the episode. On *The Bachelor/ette*, the participant who has not been chosen returns to the limousine in which s/he arrived; as s/he drives off, s/he speaks directly to the camera. The confessional address on *The Bachelor/ette* delays the arrival of the winner; while the viewer knows at this moment who has won, the confession nevertheless creates suspense before the final encounter with the winner. In both examples, the confession is used as a strategy to externalize the production of identity for the audience. If truth is a quality of inner consciousness, then one way of accessing the true selves of participants is to let them talk about their experience and emotions.

What is the role of the viewer who becomes a witness to the participants' disclosures? The confessional statement places each viewer in a privileged position, an authority point of view (Douglas; Dovey, *Freakshow* 106), even if that viewer is one among millions. Through the use of direct camera address, the confession creates the sense of immediacy and urgency needed to establish a special "live" relationship between speaker and audience, one that remains unattainable in the written confession. In the case of *Survivor*, Kate Douglas argues, the confessionals work to excuse certain "'betrayal behaviours' in the spirit of positive experiences and game playing." The viewer may not be expected to provide absolution in these instances, but by witnessing the participants' awareness that they have violated social norms, the audience is reassured that those norms are still in place. In the case of *The Bachelor/ette*, the rejected participants do not usually confess extreme or inappropriate behaviour; instead, they voice their disappointment (often amid tears in the case of women), reflecting on what the bachelor/ette has lost by not choosing them, and pointing to their lives beyond the show, either emphasizing how difficult it will be to move on or how they will continue to thrive in spite of the setback. Here the confessional statements authenticate the idea that being on the show has deeply affected the life of the participants beyond the show. While confessions on these reality programs ensure further self-exposure of the participants, one cannot lose track of the fact that they are manipulated carefully by the shows' producers: they are heavily edited and strategically placed. We will need close analyses of specific examples to show how they are used to construct participants' identities and elicit desired audience responses (such as empathy or disbelief).

VOYEURISM AND EXHIBITIONISM CREATE A THEATRE OF INTIMACY

Consider that over thirty cameras and sixty microphones monitor the *Big Brother* house, including bedrooms; thirteen housemates live there. Consider that *Temptation Island* focuses on the possibility of making participants cheat on their partners. That *The Bachelor/ette* publicizes one person's search for a spouse. In their focus on self-disclosure and the audience's witnessing, reality TV shows make accessible to public view private spaces, family life, and intimate details, thus completing the externalization of participants' inner lives. In the process, reality TV repeatedly flirts with the taboo and forbidden, especially with the possibility of intimacy revealed (Nichols 46). The primary activities of the audience are onlooking and overhearing (Corner). Recent auto/biography scholarship has increasingly focused on questions of ethics in the production and reception of auto/biographical texts.[9] What are the consequences of such public exposure of family secrets? Comparative analysis of written auto/biography and reality TV may enable future scholars to determine whether the medium of self-representation impacts the cultural limits to self-revelation. One of the *Big Brother 4* episodes made the headlines, for example, when Amanda and Dave were seen to have sex while the cameras were rolling, but descriptions of sexual relations in a written auto/biography may no longer seem offensive. Has the boom in trauma narratives, which often focus on incest, rape, illness, or other forms of extreme suffering and have become popular in North America since the 1990s, prepared contemporary audiences to feel both entitled to learn about and prepared to deal with the sometimes shocking revelation of private lives on reality TV shows? Does voyeurism lie at the heart of audiences' engagement with all auto/biographical practices, not only those of reality TV? If so, one could argue that the differences in audience responses to auto/biography are differences in kind, not category; for instance, while it could be argued that the voyeurism of auto/biography readers serves educational or therapeutic purposes, audience responses to reality TV do not seem to be driven by education or catharsis, but by the basic pleasure of watching and listening.

While the act of observation is completely legitimate when it comes to the reality-based programs I have mentioned, since all contestants agree to continuous surveillance and the airing of such footage, an element of guilty pleasure remains on the part of the viewer, who is learning about someone's private life without having to reciprocate. Such "vicarious pleasures," Joanna Gill suggests, may be inherent to any confessional text. In the case of reality TV, an element of secrecy remains as viewers can watch anonymously in the privacy of their homes without being seen.[10] At the same time, viewers gain knowledge about the participants that other contestants usually do not have (Gabe), providing the kind of dramatic irony that keeps audiences interested. By observing others from a position of omniscience, viewers can live vicariously and can engage without having to take responsibility or consider ethical implications; they can move between attraction and revulsion without consequences for themselves. The desire to watch others is certainly not new (Yesil), but it is more easily available and accessible through the technologies that bring us reality TV; an average of over twelve million viewers tune in to the most popular reality TV programs.[11]

To speak of voyeurism is to speak of only half the equation, however. The other half is the desire of ordinary people to be watched. Over 6,000 applicants responded to the first casting call for *Survivor* (Burnett 10). The most common reasons why participants want to be on these shows are to win the money, to become famous, and to be part of a unique experience.[12] In exchange, they are prepared to make their most private lives public. Not unlike online diaries, which make "confessions widely available but still anonymous, impersonal, separate from diarists' offline lives and identities," reality TV enables participants to maintain "the illusion of anonymity necessary for 'full' self-exposure" (McNeill 27). In "the theatre of intimacy" that is reality TV, the public performance of intimate details satisfies both the voyeuristic curiosity of viewers and the exhibitionist greed of participants desperate for an audience.

While fame and celebrity status have long been associated with auto/biography genres—in fact, celebrity auto/biography could be considered a sub-genre of its own—it used to be the case that one had to be famous to enter the auto/biography market. With reality TV, one becomes a celebrity (of sorts) by performing one's auto/biography, not the other way around. Fame is now within reach for the ordinary person. At times, the celebrity status achieved through auto/biographical performances on television later translates into the auto/biographical practice of the written text as has been the case with Bob Guiney's *What a Difference a Year Makes* (2003). Guiney had been one of the unsuccessful bachelors on *The Bachelorette*, which aired on ABC in January and February 2003. His book, a chronicle of how participation on the show changed his life, appeared in October 2003 in the middle of the second season of *The Bachelor*, which featured Guiney in the leading role; the auto/biographical spinoff thus ensured personal financial gain for Guiney.

What are the implications of such desire to become famous through surveillance? Grindstaff argues that self-exhibition validates one's existence ("Trashy"). The kind of surveillance exercised on many reality TV programs may help participants boost their self-confidence and thus becomes linked with self-knowledge and self-expression. In the process, reality "becomes dependent on perpetual surveillance, which is presented as the antidote to artificial interactions—to 'acting'" (Andrejevic 261). Surveillance thus no longer appears threatening in an Orwellian sense, but promises authenticity and the "democratization of publicity *as* celebrity" (268). It has become "a harmless instrument of the public good" (T. Tremblay 60). We may be left with the troubling implication that such belief in the advantages of surveillance also suggests that any fear of self-disclosure could be interpreted as an admission that there is something to hide. If you do not want to reveal all, there must be something wrong with you. To borrow Grindstaff's question ("Trashy"): is this democracy or social control internalized?

IT IS ALL ABOUT THE AUDIENCE'S ANXIETIES

If the predominant concerns of contemporary North American, maybe Western, culture have to do with self-knowledge, autonomy, privacy, and security, then reality-based programming seems to respond on all fronts.

It does not seem to heighten these anxieties; instead, in its focus on auto/biographical performance, the intimate personal experience, it provides (preliminary) answers to the chaotic, uncertain, fragmented, disengaged world in which we live. In reality TV shows, coherence, closure, and knowledge (of self and others) are possible. While television as a form may tend towards uncertainty and openness, may in fact provide "a relatively safe area in which uncertainty can be entertained, and can be entertaining" as John Ellis argues (82), reality TV programs paradoxically manage to create a sense of certainty through their reliance on auto/biographical and formulaic narrative structures even though they work most closely with the "reality" of a world characterized by information overload, empathy fatigue, and failed grand narratives.

Reality TV shows contribute to the process of what Ellis calls "working through," a concept he has borrowed from psychoanalysis to describe the role of television in "processing the material of the witnessed world into narrativized, explained forms" (78). Television is constantly engaged in the process of making and remaking meanings, attempting explanations. It places the audience in the position of witness and enables viewers to see others navigate their realities and define their own sense of self. Viewers seem to gain control over the content of the television program when it becomes "real" exactly because it could be their own reality (Andrejevic 261). Viewers recognize, I believe, a shared material world on reality TV, which is exactly what they connect with and what confirms their perception of reality. Given the "disappearance of an unproblematic belief in the idea of true selves" (Smith and Watson, *Getting a Life* 7), reality TV seems ideally suited for the contemporary cultural moment in which "we're left with the politics of the self to keep us ideologically warm" (Dovey, *Freakshow* 26).

NATIONAL IDENTITIES MATTER IN A GLOBAL CONTEXT

In the ongoing debates about globalization and the role television, and media more generally, have played in forming a worldwide system without national distinctiveness, reality TV programs can be used as examples to challenge the extent of such proposed cultural homogenization. At first glance, the fact that so many reality TV shows have been imported to so many countries seems to support the argument for a globalized culture. Take *Big Brother*, for example. The program was developed by Endemol Entertainment in the Netherlands, but it is seen today in at least twenty countries.[13] While the show's format always includes the surveillance of a group of people in a house removed from the outside world, the model is adapted in each country using specific technical and textual innovations as well as local contexts. Roscoe explains, for example, that the Australian version of the show emphasized fitness and outdoor activities both in the design of the house and in the contestants; challenges, she argues, also led to different group dynamics than was expected from the US version. In such national adaptations, Bonner argues, television networks "localize" the program by adjusting the elements that make it ordinary: participants, settings, language use, etc. (176–86). Her analysis of the British program *The Antiques Roadshow* and the Australian *Burke's Backyard* reveals that ordinary television, in combination with sports and news programs, "plays a substantial role in the production of an assertively national television system" (210) because it provides the very evidence audiences need to imagine the kinds of communities one may want to call nations.

In the case of *Survivor* and *Temptation Island*, such evidence is established through the very absence of the immediate national context. The exotic locations chosen for these programs reinscribe familiar oppositions of civilization, knowledge, and self-discipline (associated with America) on one hand and wilderness, primitivism, and temptation (associated with Africa, Thailand, South America, or remote islands in the Caribbean or South Pacific) on the other. *Survivor*, in particular, exploits "the common subconscious ideal of island life" as it appropriates elements from cultural anthropology and religious rituals in its creation of a castaway experience (Burnett 12). Reminiscent of colonial narratives in their structure, use of stereotypes, and language, these shows ultimately reinforce the participants' sense of Americanness through their displacement to a foreign locale. In fact, Tony Tremblay argues convincingly that "the idea of America" is nowhere more pervasive than on *Survivor* (48). A closer examination of the relationships between individual auto/biographical performances of show participants and the construction of national identities will enable us to explain how these programs develop notions of belonging and patriotism and, by adding a cross-cultural perspective, why particular shows have different success rates in different countries (why, for example, *The Bachelor* is a huge hit in North America but not in Germany, and why *Big Brother* has been successfully adapted in at least twenty countries).

AUDIENCE INTERACTIVITY CREATES NEW COMMUNITIES

As reality TV programs play with new genre formats on screen, producers have also taken advantage of the increasing convergence of technologies to create interactivity, that is, involvement of the viewer, usually in terms of direct action, with the shows they watch. Websites not only support the television program through basic materials such as pictures of participants, background information, and episode summaries, but also provide extras that move beyond what is available in the typical one-hour slot by improving the quality of access to information and creating interactive forums. They provide previews, archives (of stories and videos), and, most importantly, live video streams.[14] Viewers also find online polls (e.g., "Who played the game the best?" on the *Survivor* website), quizzes (e.g., "Can you be tempted?" on the *Temptation Island* site), message boards, and chat rooms (sometimes with evicted show participants). All of these activities ask the audience to respond to the program. Their input will impact the way that participants are perceived in public; moreover, they provide opportunities to connect with other viewers. Finally, websites usually offer related merchandise such as shirts, sunglasses, or bags that will identify the wearer as a member of the show's audience. In some cases, audience adjudication allows viewers to participate directly in the programs they are watching. Viewers of *Big Brother*, for instance, were initially invited to interact with the show by telephone vote to determine which house guest was to be evicted. In some locations, sets have become accessible to visitors, and televised live shows are orchestrated around evictions or around final celebrations of winners. Closer to home, some viewers have moved from solitary viewing to mass gatherings in bars, etc., often betting on the shows' winners, just as they gather to watch sports events. The activities described here turn viewers into co-producers of the life stories they watch; they become consumers of others' auto/biographical performances and of their own performances in the process. Guarding against the temptation to idealize such community-building, Sean Rintel and Sue McKay point to its limitation: "by co-opting (or perhaps pre-empting) the tools of fan communication, television network websites are promoting the idea of community, but creating only pseudo-community—group connections without ongoing commitment except to the products of the mediasphere."

ON-AIR REALITY HAS OFF-AIR CONSEQUENCES

Participating on a reality TV show no doubt impacts the lives of contestants beyond the programs themselves. In addition to the emotional impact on their lives, including feelings that may range from excitement to regret and humiliation, and possibly strained relationships with family and friends, some show contestants achieve exactly the kind of fame they were hoping for. That auto/biographical practices have effects that reach beyond the limits of their medium is not unique to reality TV. The extent and pervasiveness of these off-air consequences, however, remains unprecedented as a result of the mobilization of multiple media. Television networks benefit from bringing participants on morning or late-night talk shows and having them make cameo appearances on other shows, but some participants benefit more immediately from their new-found fame when their participation on reality TV leads to other career opportunities, especially in show business. Alida Kurras of the second *Big Brother* house in Germany, for example, has not only become a radio and TV moderator there, but has also released a CD and created her own perfume.[15] *Playboy* has repeatedly made much-publicized offers to reality TV participants.[16] In 2001, the pop group Destiny's Child won the MTV Video Music Award for Best R&B video for their song "Survivor," which shows them in leopard-skin loincloths walking through a forest reminiscent of the settings chosen for *Survivor* programs. The Pulau Tiga Resort, whose expansion was facilitated by the arrival of the CBS production crew of the first *Survivor*, now uses the island's TV history as a marketing strategy. The intertextuality generated by popular reality-based programs has also shaped contemporary language use. Phrases like "the tribe has spoken" have become commonplace in everyday conversations and advertising.[17] Recognition of such intertextual references creates another sense of community and belonging, one deeply seated in the world of reality-based programming.

OUTWIT, OUTPLAY, OUTLAST

Auto/biographical performances are at the heart of today's reality TV popularity. If we want to understand what John Corner has called our "post-documentary culture," in which the function of the documentary has shifted to diversion, i.e. "popular factual entertainment,"[18] we need to examine the ways in which selfhood functions in everyday auto/biographical practices across a wide range of media. We can draw on traditions of auto/biographical practices to understand more fully the connections between the forms chosen and the contexts out of which they emerge and in which they operate. The interplay between the low-cost production of reality TV and the public desire for personal stories certainly begs further exploration. In spite of frequent claims over the last couple of years that the reality TV craze is almost over, the audience's desire for reality TV and its focus on auto/biography appears to be far from satiated. Not only do millions of viewers continue to tune into the latest hit shows, such as the ninth season of *Survivor*, which opened to just over twenty million viewers, or the second season of *The Apprentice*, which attracted over sixteen million viewers with its first episode (both in September 2004), but the television industry has also validated reality TV programming by creating distinct categories for its Primetime Emmy Awards: Outstanding Reality Competition Program and Outstanding Reality Program.[19] Rather than argue that the popularity of reality TV will lead to a backlash against auto/biography any time soon, I believe that the demand for the personal story is here to stay.

In fact, the pervasiveness of auto/biographical practices across a wide range of media may renew interest in the long history of auto/biographical genres. One of Canada's daily newspapers, *The National Post*, for instance, began including short daily entries from Samuel Pepys's *Diary* in its "Arts & Life" section in late September 2004, introducing its first entry as follows: "Before Bridget Jones, there was Samuel Pepys. A naval administrator and first secretary of the British Admiralty, he kept a detailed and now-famous diary through London's turbulent 1660s. What follows is his description of daily life 343 years ago." The point of connection between the popular-culture reference to *Bridget Jones's Diary*, the successful 2001 movie based on Helen Fielding's novel (1996) by the same name, and Samuel Pepys is, of course, the diary as a prime example of auto/biographical practices. Pepys, Jones, and reality TV—my intention is not to equate the three but to suggest that they occupy different places on the continuum of auto/biographical discourses, each one emerging out of specific sociohistorical contexts. If, as I have argued, reality-based shows insist on the importance of personal identity and auto/biographical discourse, then it is about time that auto/biography scholars take reality TV seriously because it has much to tell us about the construction and performance of identity in the twenty-first century.

NOTES

1 While PBS's *The 1900 House* (which first aired in June 2000), *1940s House* (November 2002), and *Manor House* (April 2003) were set in Britain, *The Frontier House* (April 2002) and *The Colonial House* (coming soon) are set on the American frontier. History Television's *Pioneer Quest* (June 2000), *The Quest for the Bay* (February 2002), *Klondike: The Quest for Gold* (February 2003), and *Quest for the Sea* (January 2004) were all set in Canada.

2 See, for example, T. Dow Adams, Gale and Gardner, Hirsch (*Family Frames*), Man, Smith and Watson (*Getting a Life* and *Interfaces*), as well as Zuern.

3 Background checks often include psychological screening to determine whether applicants fit the profile of people wanted for a particular show. For instance, one of the conditions for participating on *Temptation Island*, in which unmarried couples travel to an exotic locale to test the strength of their relationships, is that participants do not have children. When during the first season (winter 2001–02), Taheed Watson and Ytossie Patterson referred to their child during the taping of the show, they were kicked off the show (on camera) for having misrepresented information about their background. In March 2001, the

couple filed a lawsuit against the producers, claiming defamation of character and seeking damages. Watson and Patterson insisted that they had mentioned their child during casting, but that they had been told not to bring it to anyone's attention. Another casting "mishap" occurred when it turned out that groom-to-be Rick Rockwell on *Who Wants to Marry a Multi-Millionaire* had a restraining order against him from his former girlfriend.

4 One of the seven celebrities on the show was Jerri Manthey, a former participant on *Survivor 2*. See <http://www.tvtome.com/tvtome/servlet/ShowMain-Servlet/showid-12331>.

5 The same is true, of course, for auto/biographical practices on stage, but television reaches a much wider audience.

6 Starobinski observed, initially over thirty years ago, that "radical change" seems to act as a motivating factor for autobiographers (78). For recent studies that explore crisis as a reason for auto/biographical writing, see Thomas Couser's work on illness and disability (*Recovering Bodies*) and Leigh Gilmore's exploration of trauma narratives (*The Limits*).

7 *The Amazing Race*, which first aired in 2001 on CBS and has completed its fifth season, explicitly draws on the travel narrative plot as it sends twelve teams of two people "racing" around the world, dealing with various challenges along the way, for a cash prize of one million dollars. It won the Primetime Emmy Award for Outstanding Reality Competition Program in 2003 and 2004.

8 The "Diary Room" on *Big Brother* also provides participants a private space for consultations—a sort of confession?—with professional psychologists if requested. While these conversations are taped, participants are assured that they will not be aired (Roscoe 477).

9 For explorations of the connection between ethics and life writing, see the co-edited volume by Adamson, Freadman, and Parker as well as Couser (*Vulnerable Subjects*), and Eakin (*Ethics of Life Writing*).

10 Roscoe suggests that the unique set-up of the Australian *Big Brother* house heightens this sense of secrecy and guilty pleasure, since visitors can look inside the house from the outside without the participants in the house being able to see them (479-80).

11 We find an extension of this kind of voyeurism on the many "voyeur sites" available on the Internet, where visitors can watch people in their own homes all day long thanks to webcams that allow real-time transmission of images. Often these sites feature people engaging in sexual activities, raising questions about the line between voyeurism and pornography. While this discussion goes beyond the scope of this paper, I believe that the voyeurism/exhibitionism enabled and encouraged by reality TV needs to be examined in the context of similar contemporary trends in other media.

12 Of the thirteen housemates on *Big Brother 4*, six say on the show's website that their main reason for being on the show is to win the money, two name money and fame, and five give other reasons. <http://www.cbs.com/primetime/big-brother4/>.

13 According to the Endemol website, these countries include the following: Argentina, Australia, Belgium, Brazil, France, Germany, Greece, Hungary, Italy, Mexico, the Netherlands, Norway, Portugal, Romania, South Africa,

Spain, Sweden, Switzerland, UK, and the USA. <http://www.endemol.com/format_descriptions.xml?id=1>.

14 These video streams are not, however, available for free. In 2004, the *Big Brother* website offered a package at US $24.95 per season.

15 Alex Johlig of the first German *Big Brother* house recorded a couple of songs and is the only guest from that house who has remained a celebrity in Germany.

16 Some women have accepted the *Playboy* offers, such as Jerri Manthey of *Survivor 2* who appeared in the September 2001 issue (US) and Alida Kurras who appeared in March of the same year (Germany).

17 Tony Blair borrowed Anne Robinson's game-show phrase "you are the weakest link, goodbye" to attack Conservative opposition leader William Hague in Parliament in December 2000 (Gibson).

18 Corner summarizes "three classic functions" of documentary forms: 1) "the project of democratic civics," usually funded by official bodies; 2) "journalistic inquiry and exposition"; and 3) "radical interrogation and alternative perspective." He proposes "diversion" as a fourth function that has slowly developed in recent times.

19 In 2003, the Emmy award for "Outstanding Special Program" was renamed the Emmy for "Outstanding Reality Competition Program." The Academy of Television Arts and Sciences thus recognized the dominance and popularity of reality TV programs in the current TV landscape.

SHERRILL GRACE

PERFORMING THE AUTO/BIOGRAPHICAL PACT
TOWARDS A THEORY OF IDENTITY IN PERFORMANCE

Acting and autobiography go hand in hand....The concept of persona...is central to autobiography, and its dynamics are best understood by way of its functioning in drama.   — Evelyn J. Hinz (200-201)

How can we (or should we?) articulate the specificity of theatre as something performative...? How can the liveness of theatre performance reveal performativity?   — Jill Dolan (431)

PERFORMANCE, AUTO/BIOGRAPHY, AND THEATRE

Despite increasing attention in recent years to the rich multidisciplinarity of auto/biographical practices, prose forms of narrative published as books still receive the bulk of popular attention. Many specialists in auto/biography studies, however, have recognized what artists have long understood—that auto/biography exists in film and in photography, that portraiture (portraits and self-portraits) is closely related to the auto/biographical, and that plays can be auto/biographical.[1] To date, however, few auto/biography specialists have explored a range of auto/biographical plays or examined what actually happens to the auto/biographical when it takes the form of a play performance.[2] If I may be allowed a theatrical trope for a moment, I would suggest that in the wings at stage left, the auto/biography experts are rehearsing their performance and performativity lines, while in the wings at stage right, the theatre studies experts stand about waiting for their cue. Downstage centre, a play has just begun (an *auto/biographical* play), so I want to insist, from my side of the proscenium arch, that both sets of players get out there onto centre stage and into the act.

But if auto/biography theory stands ready (in full costume) to enter stage left, just what is happening at stage right? The view from that side of the disciplinary divide between theatre and literary studies (where auto/biography most commonly resides) suggests that very few theatre specialists even seem to be aware of auto/biography theory and of the connections between narrative, visual, and dramatic auto/biographical practices, let alone the potential synergies to be discovered by bringing the two acting companies together.[3] Since the early 1990s, specialists in theatre studies have been calling (and with good reason) for a repatriation of terms like performance and performativity (see Diamond, Dolan, Gale and Gardner, and Worthen), and if they were listening to the folks on the other side of my metaphoric stage they would certainly hear these terms constantly invoked, as even a glance at Sidonie Smith and Julia Watson's *Interfaces: Women/Autobiography/Image/Performance* demonstrates. In her 1993 article, "Geographies of Learning: Theatre Studies, Performance, and the 'Performative'," Jill Dolan invites us (and I include scholars from both sides of the stage) to see if we can locate ways in which live theatre performance can "*reveal* performativity" (431), and she challenges us to look for theatre performances that show, "with gestic insistence, that we are not...self-same individuals" (435). To my ear, this is the cue for auto/biography theory because, when Dolan asks me to look for theatre performances that will demonstrate that a self is not "self-same," I understand her to be invoking key markers of auto/biography—subjectivity and identity. However, what Dolan's geographical map does not include are the coordinates of auto/biography, and yet these are precisely the coordinates that I believe will help us see what is happening (up there on centre stage) in specific auto/biographical plays.

For some time now, in my work on Wendy Lill, on plays about Tom Thomson and Emily Carr, on Sharon Pollock, and Sally Clark, and on certain long monologue plays (see Grace and Rebeiro), I have been picking away at the issues raised by auto/biographical plays, and I remain troubled by the view still held by some theorists of autobiography, that autobiography is generically defined as a written and read narrative. For example, in his 1998 study, *Memory and Narrative: The Weave of Life-Writing*, James Olney traces a through-line from St. Augustine to Rousseau to Beckett, but, when he comes to Beckett, he discusses the novels and plays together as if they were all novels, and he makes no substantive acknowledgement of the fact that the plays are theatre and exist most fully in performance. When he considers *Not I*—the play that serves as his touchstone for Beckett's obsessive, futile life writing—he both dismisses the *actress's* ordeal as "Mouth," and he fails to address the gender shift required by the play and what that shift could mean for Beckett's handling of his life story in this play or for the performance of the play and its reception by an audience.[4] More importantly, Olney's determined literary and stage left approach to Beckett and his refusal to address these questions of performance directs my attention stage right to Dolan, who complains that the adoption of theatre terms as mere metaphors by scholars in other disciplines allows them to devalue or simply ignore the theatre. But what about the play? At centre stage that auto/biographical play is now under way, and I need all those actors waiting in the wings to help me *see* it. What's more, I suspect that the performance of such a play can, to quote Dolan again, "*reveal* performativity," and that one strategy for such revelation is what I will provisionally call performative auto/biographics.

In *Le pacte autobiographique*, Philippe Lejeune describes a tripartite relationship as the central core—the pact—of autobiography. The participants in this pact are the writer, the narrated subject (Lejeune combines two participants here—the narrator and the character), and the reader.[5] While this pact works well to describe the cathexis of auto/biographical prose, it does not get us very far (nor was it intended to) with non-prose media. Nevertheless, I take this pact as one of my givens, a starting point from which I want to argue for a different kind of pact. I want to ask what happens to the pact when auto/biography takes place on stage because I do believe that (as with prose narratives) we must agree to a pact.

To pursue this inquiry, I will also need to query the common and overused terms "performance" and "performativity" (in Judith Butler's sense) to see if they can be salvaged to describe what happens in plays. Finally, I will adopt—and adapt—Leigh Gilmore's term "autobiographics" to highlight the ways in which theatre produces identity because I find Gilmore's concept and term extremely useful, not least for the stress it places on process and practice, instead of on genre, and on a set of strategies and sites for producing and locating self-representation, which help me identify the auto/biographical in plays. Moreover, I will suggest that one useful way to think about the auto/biographical pact in drama is through *performative auto/biographics*—the practice of creating a life story in a script and on stage that *becomes* a version of that life, whether the story is autobiography, biography, or, as I think may often happen, a hybrid: auto/biography. When I use the term auto/biography I put a slash between the *auto* and the *bio* in order to indicate two quite distinct conditions: first, that we can have plays that are *auto*biographical or *bio*graphical and, second, that plays frequently draw on both. Indeed, even biographers are coming to see the importance of the autobiographical within biography and theorists of autobiography have long recognized the role of the biographical within the autobiographical (see Eakin; Egan; Olney, *Memory and Narrative*; and Ty).

Underlying my discussion are several assumptions—that prose auto/biography is intimately linked with, though different from, theatre performance; that auto/biography lives forcefully on stage; that studying representative examples of auto/biographical plays will help return concepts of performance and performativity to the theatre; and that attention to these plays will expand the parameters of auto/biography studies and, hopefully, make us think about the popularity and practice of auto/biography in new ways. I start from Evelyn J. Hinz's provocative and illuminating suggestion in her 1992 essay "Mimesis: The Dramatic Lineage of Auto/Biography" that *drama*, not prose, is "the sister art" of auto/biography. But I will end, I hope, by answering Jill Dolan's questions.

THE A/B PACT, OR WHO SIGNS WHAT?

Before I can reframe the debate about the auto/biographical pact, I must go back to Philippe Lejeune who, in his well-known and often-cited essay "The Autobiographical Pact," argues that autobiography relies on a specific "contract" between the author and the reader. This contract is crucial for the reader who accepts the narrative he/she is reading as historical and personal truth because of the signature on the narrative (Lejeune, *Le pacte* 22–23). By signing (more precisely reproducing typographically) his/her "proper name" on the title page, the writer first guarantees the *identity* of the author with the narrator (and the character—Lejeune's *personnage*) and then the *truth* of the story as written and read. Lejeune's signed contract involves three parties—the writer, the narrator (and character), and the reader. Underlying this auto/biographical pact is Lejeune's constant comparison of life writing with the novel, which differs from life writing insofar as it is never bound by such a contract, not even when the fiction is first person and, thus, uses the "I" that grammatically reads as identical with the "I" of the autobiographer (see Lejeune, *Le pacte* 27–30).

I am indebted to Lejeune's concept because it foregrounds specific challenges for my work on drama, while forcibly reminding me that a pact nonetheless exists: first, the tripartite nature of the pact excludes other potential players (for example, an editor, a publisher, a translator, not to mention an unreliable or lying author), and, therefore, has no room for all the inescapable collaborators in a play production; second, the assumed primary analogy of an auto/biography with a novel and, thus, with the private act of reading precludes the volatile dynamics of live public performance; and, third, auto/biography's appeal to truth-telling, historical facts, authenticity, a verifiable reality (of person or events) that exists or existed before and outside of the narrated/performed/re-presented story flies in the face of the patently illusory world of theatre.[6] The shortest way to grasp the implication of Lejeune's pact is to say that we (the reader/watcher/listener) believe what the autobiographer tells us to be true, and if we discover that it is not true, we feel cheated, deceived, and manipulated. But theatre is by definition illusion, make-believe, never to be mistaken for reality— unless we want to look as foolish as the country bumpkin who leapt on to the stage to rescue little Nell from the leering villain.

When thinking about auto/biography as drama, then, the pact must be expanded. Five co-signatories to the pact are the minimum I would allow for plays in performance: the author and the artist-as-playwright are there, and I am on the scene—watching, reacting, interpreting. But at minimum two others are there with us: the actor (character) and the director. Whether the actor (character) is the playwright (as has happened with Joy Coghill, Linda Griffiths, Sharon Pollock, R.H. Thompson, and Guillermo Verdecchia, to name just a few examples), or a stranger to the story, we still have a distinct, additional co-signator to the pact. The director, who is rarely a *character* on stage, is nevertheless everywhere, and I include under the signature of the director both the physical space and the staging (set design, lighting, sound, costumes) required to mount a play performance. The auto/biographical pact in theatre performance has at least five names on the bill.

Many theorists have articulated the constituent elements of performance; some have tried to tease out the distinctions between *performance* and *performativity*. Regardless of what angle they take, all recognize the basic relation of both concepts to each other, and the equally complex relations internal to each. In his article "Posing: Autobiography and the Subject of Photography," Paul Jay argues that "visual memory" (as distinct from temporal memory) is central to auto/biographical writing and to photography, and he claims that "a creative, constitutive relationship exists between image and identity in autobiographical writing" (191). Adopting this description of visual memory (as it pertains to photographic images), I would like to extend it to my role at play performances because when Jay describes "posing [as] a form of self-representation" (194), he enables me to see my attendance at the theatre as a mode of self-representation, as a learned role that I perform. This concept of posing closely resembles Butler's theory of performativity; thus, my theatre-going is a socially sanctioned and learned identity role that I take on, a role scripted by aspects of class, race, education, profession, and economic status. But the performative can be pushed further. In "Performative Acts and Gender Constitution," Butler herself re-examines the close analogy between theatre and performative acts as she described these in *Gender Trouble*, and she locates a common ground for theatre performance and performativity in the speech-act theory that influenced her development of the concept. However, in the final analysis, Butler insists that theatre performance is always grounded on prior models of gender identity in the sense that the gender performed on the stage is merely a performance (an illusion) because the actor has an already established gender, untouched by the performance, to which he or she reverts the minute the curtain comes down (271).

In a sense, of course, this is true. As an actor, playwright Sharon Pollock has more than once played the role of Lizzy Borden (a childless spinster, and likely patricide, involved in a lesbian affair) in her play *Blood Relations*, but in *real* life, off-stage, she remains the heterosexual mother of six and daughter of a father who died of natural causes.[7] However, I think (as does Dolan) that Butler narrows the possibilities too much and allows theatre performance far too little creative and re-creative energy and complexity. Indeed, Butler comes closer to fully appreciating this potential when she writes that "Just as a script may be enacted in various ways, and just as the play requires both text and interpretation, so the gendered body acts its part in a culturally restricted corporeal space and enacts interpretations within the confines of already existing directives" ("Performative Acts" 277). By this I understand Butler to be allowing the potential for stage performance of identity (gendered or any other kind) to be performative and, thus, capable of exposing essentialism as false (as a role) and of challenging the scripts that prescribe our identity acts.

The point of performing performativity may not be to change the gendered identity script of the actor in real life, but it most certainly may be to show an audience member how to do so. Elin Diamond puts it this way: "As soon as performativity comes to rest on *a* performance, questions of embodiment, of social relations, of ideological interpellations, of emotional and political effects, all become discussable....Performance is precisely the site in which concealed or dissimulated conventions might be investigated" (5). I believe that this performance site is all the more open to discussion *as performative* when the subject of the play is auto/biographical because in these kinds of plays self-identity is performed, whether by the author as actor or by another actor, before both the author and the audience (understood as both individual and collective). I have come to agree wholeheartedly with W.B. Worthen, who resists the notion that today, in the West, "the performance of plays is *residual*, a mode of production fully inscribed within a discourse of textual and cultural authority" (1094). By contrast, Worthen argues that a performance is the ultimate citation, rather than a performance *of* some pre-existing thing (a script, a published text), and that it reconstitutes and produces the text (1097-98).[8]

PERFORMING AUTO/BIOGRAPHY ON STAGE

There are many plays in the Canadian repertoire that can be usefully considered auto/biographical, but there is a considerable degree of variation among them. They can be monologues but they can also have two or many characters. They can be narrowly autobiographical—primarily and closely focused on the individual performing self—or they can be multifaceted, splitting the autobiographical self into many selves. They can focus primary attention away from a single individual's life story to the telling and performing of others' life stories, to biographical selves, and these plays can—indeed, I suspect they often do—perform what John Eakin calls relational identity: the constitution of "I" through relations with others.[9]

I do not want to generate a typology here, but some examples from contemporary Canadian plays will suggest the range of auto/biographical possibilities on stage. In *Fronteras Americanas*, for example, Guillermo Verdecchia tells us aspects of his autobiography by embodying and performing them himself. Moreover, the identity he performs is multiple and shifting; it is a *dialogized* (a term I use deliberately) identity that we watch him learn how to perform and that we gradually realize he is performing, strategically, *at us*, in relation to us.[10] Although this is a one-character piece, performed at its premiere and in several other performances and readings by Verdecchia himself, the character of "Verdecchia" is multiple, and his most ironic alter ego is called Wideload, an other self with which "Verdecchia" often argues and an irrepressible persona who frequently upstages his more earnest, sensitive self.[11] The following brief exchange provides a representative example of how a single playwright/performer can produce performative auto/biographics on stage that capture his sense of relational identities.

Here, "Verdecchia" is telling "us" about his first day at school, when the teacher could not pronounce his name, and then Wideload interrupts:

> VERDECCHIA: Miss Wiseman forces her mouth into shapes hitherto unknown to the human race as she attempts to pronounce my name. "Gwillyou—ree—moo…Verdeek—cheea?" I put my hand up. I am a miniscule boy with ungovernable black hair, antennae and gills where everyone else has a mouth. "You can call me Willy," I say. The antennae and gills disappear.

It could have been here—but I don't want to talk about myself all night.

WIDELOAD: Thank God. I mean I doan know about you but I hate it when I go to el teatro to de theatre and I am espectin' to see a play and instead I just get some guy up dere talking about himself—deir life story—who cares? Por favor....And whatever happened to plays any-way—anybody remember plays? Like wif a plot and like a central character? Gone de way of modernism I guess and a good thing too. (317)

At its most obvious, this exchange illustrates several degrees of relation-ality (immigrant child with Anglo-Canadian teacher, same child negotiat-ing identity through linguistic dissonance, adult "Verdecchia" reliving his traumatic childhood experience, and adult "Verdecchia" interacting, liter-ally jockeying for centre stage and our attention, with his dismissively Latin American and not-to-be-repressed other self) all of which rely on the auto/biographical pact as performed in relation to a live audience.[12]

Lorena Gale's *Je me souviens*, an extended monologue play in which Gale recalls and recreates multiple selves in dramatic, developing rela-tion with each other and with the voices of others whom she *impersonates*, has many of the same performative qualities as Robert Lepage's *The Far Side of the Moon*, which he claims is different every time he performs it. While I can imagine someone else performing these parts, I think the result would be quite different—not necessarily deficient, just different— because in each play, indeed, in each performance of each play, it is the author (character) who performs her/his identity for her/himself in rela-tion to the audience. The theatrical illusion of identity between playwright and performer, and thus the pact with us, is both illusory and actual: it really is Lorena Gale playing "Lorena Gale" and Robert Lepage playing "Robert Lepage." Moreover, she and he play a different self to a different audience every time. If I stay with the single-character play, written and per-formed by the same person, for a moment longer but turn to Linda Grif-fiths' *Alien Creature* or Kristen Thomson's *I, Claudia*, then new possibili-ties present themselves. In performance, *Alien Creature*, gives us *both* Linda Griffiths and Gwendolyn MacEwen; Griffiths stresses this point in her "Playwright's Notes" when she warns us that "only both of us can speak" (10). To some degree then, Griffiths is performing herself as she creates Gwen and Gwen's biography in the first-person voice and pronoun of the autobiographer. In *I, Claudia*, a deft use of masks allows the performing child "I" to dramatize her own and her parents' story, thereby performing both her *auto*biography and their biography. This young, traumatized self is looking for herself in relations with others whom she must, as it were, perform or stage herself. This concept of a performed relational self is especially clear and poignant in the figure of her alter-ego Drachman.[13]

In plays with several characters, there is an equally rich range of difference and possibility. Sharon Pollock is her most overtly (to date) auto/biographical in her 1984, prize-winning play *Doc*, where she tells her own story by telling her version of her parents' story—and no biography can be anything else but the biographer's version shot through with the biographer's *autos*. The *autos* in *Doc* is divided between the child (Katie) and the grown woman (Catherine, the writer), and we are asked to consider how this child relates to, grew up into, this woman. To answer that question, the woman must first confront her living father and conjure her dead mother, who will tell her own life story. The woman (both Sharon Pollock and Catherine) is proud of her father and identifies with him—he is a success, not a self-pitying victim (like her mother). "I always felt close to him," Pollock has said (qtd. in Knelman 74). And yet, she has also expressed caveats, noting that "once the play is created it becomes something apart from the real event or the people who were used as its material" (74), and even something apart from personal, ethical concerns: "I have to hope they see that I've used them to tell a story that's larger than our personal story. I have to trust that the love and affection with which I've used very personal material is apparent" (74).

Doc is, at every level, the very personal story of Pollock's own family in which her mother was an alcoholic who killed herself, leaving her child (Katie in the play) alone at a young age.[14] The father, Ev (based on Pollock's father, Dr. Everett Chalmers), is a demanding, self-confident, and domineering general practitioner who always puts his practice ahead of his family and his wife's growing frustration and despair. The motivation for the play rests with the daughter (Catherine), who fled the parental home as soon as she could (Pollock left hers at eighteen) but has been tormented and haunted by the family past ever since. Her father's failing health provides her with an excuse to return, but instead of a happy reunion, the two, who are very much alike, argue over what did or did not happen and who was to blame, and Catherine confronts the ghost of her own childhood in the form of Katie, who bitterly blames her mother for abandoning her. This child inhabits Catherine, who speaks for her adult and child self (and for Pollock) when she says, "For a long time I prayed to God. I asked him to make her stop. I prayed and prayed. I thought, I'm just a little girl. Why would God want to do this to a little girl?" (7).

Slowly, as the play proceeds, we move more and more deeply into the memory play-within-the-play of Catherine's return and, as we do, various moments of crisis and confrontation are re-enacted and remembered. The more distant past buried in the child Katie's life and remembered by Catherine involves another suicide that hovers over and haunts the child's experience, the father, and the adult Catherine. This first suicide was the grandmother's, Ev's mother, who walked onto a train track to be killed by a train.[15] This woman left a letter behind, and when the play opens we find the elderly, ailing Ev sitting by an open trunk holding the *unopened* letter from his mother. At the end of the play, Ev and Catherine will decide to burn this letter because it no longer seems necessary for either of them to read it. I find this decision disturbing, but most critics agree that the burning of the letter releases father and daughter into a forgiveness and reconciliation that lays the ghosts from the past (see Wasserman, "Daddy's Girls"); in a sense, they do not have to open and read the letter because they already know why Ev's mother killed herself. In exploring her own role in this family trauma, Pollock seems to be implying that she, like Katie and Catherine, identifies with the father—Katie cries, "I'm like you, Daddy. I just gotta win—and you just gotta win" (124)—and that while she regrets and deplores the suffering of her mother and grandmother, she will refuse to be a victim and a loser in life.

However one interprets this ending—and each production can shift the interpretation—the notion that Sharon Pollock has faced aspects of herself (her own ghosts and her living father's influence) in this play and decided that winning, or surviving, is worth the cost to others is unsettling. The play, of course, is not that simple. Pollock is also assessing the father's commitment to the larger social good of his community, where sick and dying people need him more than his family does (or so he feels), and she is presenting all too clearly a child's sense of anger over a mother's abandonment, first through drink and then through death. Describing her childhood trauma, Pollock has said, "For years I disliked my mother intensely. Her drinking embarrassed me....When she died we found bottles secreted all through the house. She drank everything—even perfume. I remember once when I was about 11, I poured a bottle of rum down the sink [*Doc* 114]. My mother couldn't believe it....I was 16 when she died" ("Families" 48). She described the events following her mother's death in a 1983 interview with John Hofsess: "Then came the funeral: my father was weeping, my brother was weeping, my grandmother—who didn't forgive my father for years, she was convinced it was all his fault—was weeping....As soon as I could, I left home and went to Toronto. I plunged into a completely ill-advised marriage and had five children with a man I wouldn't even give the time of day to now" (Pollock, "Sharon Pollock"). Understanding of the mother's gendered and class position, which requires that she stop work and leaves her isolated in her house with little to do and no sense of self-worth, is touched upon, but it is not the focus of the drama. Pollock's mother's story would have to wait for another play.[16]

In *Moving Pictures*, Pollock splits the auto/biographical "I" into three characters, but the performance of this multiple, shifting self is incomplete without its relations to others' stories. Here Pollock functions as a biographer who researched and tells Nell Shipman's story through her relations with her parents, her husband and lover, her son, her animals, and the movie moguls who control her life (see Grace, "Creating the Girl"). *Angel's Trumpet*, her most recent play, also involves a biographical act on Pollock's part, and like *Moving Pictures* it incorporates complex subtextual aspects of Pollock's own autobiography. In both plays, the woman artist struggles to perform herself against the roles defined for her by men, and only through performance (artistic performance as filmmaker/actress/writer/dancer) can she hope to redefine and become herself.

This redefinition-through-performance of self is powerfully clear in Joy Coghill's *Song of This Place*, where one artist must learn how to embody another by living through key moments in that other artist's auto/biography. To become Emily Carr, the Actress (played by Coghill in the play's 1987 premiere), must merge her *autos* with Carr's *autos* in a performance that moves beyond mere biography—a play *about* Carr—to become doubly auto/biographical (Grace, "Writing the Self"). In *The Lost Boys* and *Billy Bishop Goes to War*, we have two more plays that take the lives of real people performing in real events—the theatre of war—as the basis for staging biography, but that is where the similarity with Coghill's play begins to shade into difference. R.H. Thompson's *The Lost Boys* is closer to Coghill's than to John Gray's *Billy Bishop* because here one actor (character), played by Thompson in the premiere, creates through memory and letters not only his family's history but his own resemblance to his dead uncles; in a sense, he discovers aspects of his autobiography by conjuring theirs. *Billy Bishop*, while based on the real air ace's own autobiography, maintains a distance between the historical Billy and the actor (Eric Peterson) who performs "Billy," as well as the other characters. Compared with Thompson's or Coghill's plays, *Billy Bishop* is always *about* the real man, and we are not asked to sign a pact promising any degree of identity between the actor and the character he plays.

PERFORMATIVE AUTOBIOGRAPHICS

As I hope these examples illustrate, auto/biography is very much at home in the theatre, but that home is not the armchair in which I read a memoir, a biography, or a novel. The experience of a performance is public, and it is orchestrated for us by others besides the author or character. To a degree not paralleled by a memoir or biography (although they require a publisher and possibly an editor), the ephemeral staging of a performance conditions and produces the experience of the play. When the subject of the play is auto/biographical, then it is identity itself that is being performed. This *thing*—the self, the subject of auto/biography, the *self-play* (to coin a term)—only exists in performance and is new each time a performance is mounted.

As performance, plays necessitate ongoing change and re-siting in physical space in what amounts to a process of translation (see Godard 338-40). Moreover, when auto/biography takes place on stage, the range of signators to the pact must be expanded; where one can stop meaningfully with three (as Lejeune does) for the reading of a prose narrative, it is impossible to see a play without several other mediators and a physical, public space in which the show is mounted. What I cannot capture verbally is the *process* of mounting and watching the performance and, therefore, the inescapable fact that when the lights come up *nothing* remains except the remembered experience or, perhaps, a static photographic trace, in a production photograph, which is only a fragmentary simulacrum of the real thing and all too often represents a scene, shot, or configuration that is never actually seen in the play as staged. This is why I call the process *performative* auto/biographics. These plays tell life stories. They do so in terms of their medium and genre-specific conventions.

Most importantly, they must be performed to exist, to be experienced, to work as auto/biography. In some of them—*I, Claudia*; *Doc*; *Fronteras Americanas*; and *Je me souviens*, for example—performance enacts the performative in that the performer changes, adjusts, and modifies identity and life story in the process of playing the part, and we are able to watch and possibly learn that identities need not be prescribed, interpellated, and fixed. Performance and performativity can be taken back to the theatre after all, and with some very interesting results. If Robert Lepage must perform his auto/biographical monodrama, *The Far Side of the Moon*, differently every time he does it because he is playing *to* and *off* the audience and because he himself changes over time, then an auto/biographical play can indeed "*reveal* performativity" for the actor's (character's) identity and, potentially, for ours.[17] In the last analysis, I believe, perfor-

mative auto/biographics returns agency to the theatre by producing identities for all who sign the theatrical pact.

NOTES

1   For discussion of auto/biography in film and photography, see T.D. Adams,
    Egan, Hirsch (*Family Frames*), Jay, Kaplan, and Smith and Watson (*Interfaces*);
    for analysis of the relationship between portraiture and the autobiographical,
    see Brilliant, Hubert, Lejeune ("Looking at a Self-Portrait"), Rideal, and Yang;
    and for specific consideration of dramatic texts see my references in note 2.

2   In "Performing Lives," Susan Bennett considers the work of Canadians like
    Linda Griffiths, who has created monodramas from the biographies of other
    artists or public figures; in chapter three of *Mirror Talk*, Egan examines drama
    as an autobiographical genre; Hinz argues convincingly that drama, rather
    than the novel, is a more appropriate generic ancestor for autobiography; Har-
    ris explores the boundaries between self and role in a number of solo post-
    modern performances; see also Grace, "Creating the Girl from God's Country"
    and "Writing the Self." I am also intrigued by the challenge contemporary
    biographers face when dealing with the lives of theatre people, and I wonder
    if the life and art of such a subject affects the biographer's craft—but this is a
    large topic for another occasion, albeit one that has received, to my knowl-
    edge, almost no critical attention.

3   In "Between Performative and Performance," Barbara Godard points to yet
    another puzzling gap in our appreciation of the "relation between dramatic texts
    and performances" (331). Although Godard does not discuss auto/biographi-
    cal plays or draw on autobiography studies, she does make a major contribu-
    tion to our understanding of a play performance as performance and of the com-
    plex processes of identity production that take place on stage. By examining
    the role of theatre semiotics (both as language and as gesture), the impact of
    cultural scripts that constrain translation in theatre, and the function of what
    Richard Schechner has called "twice-behaved behaviour" (qtd. in Godard,
    328), she argues that the performing arts play "with behaviour to produce
    social effects" (329).

4   For Olney's use of *Not I*, see section three of his book, called "Not I," and in
    particular his comments on pages 232-33, 242, and 248. For a thorough discus-
    sion of audience reception, see Susan Bennett's *Theatre Audiences*.

5   In his original 1975 study, Lejeune speaks of three co-signators to the pact
    with the reader as follows: "L'autobiographie…suppose qu'il y ait identité de
    nom entre l'auteur…le narrateur du récit et le personnage dont on parle"
    (23-24). I have shifted this basic paradigm slightly to place greater participa-
    tory stress on the reader who must also, as I see things, sign on.

6   For further discussion of Lejeune and his influence on subsequent theorists,
    see Gilmore, *Autobiographics* (75-78) and Smith and Watson, *Reading Autobiog-
    raphy* (8-9). Lejeune himself has addressed critiques of his pact in "The Auto-
    biographical Pact (bis)" and has revised or qualified some of his earlier state-
    ments. Far from finding fault with his original concept, I find it extremely
    productive for my own rethinking of what takes place in auto/biographical

plays. There is, of course, another crucial challenge to the pact that I have not yet explored, and it is the relationship between the auto/biographical pact itself and the far larger generic pact entered into by a play-going audience.

7   Pollock first played the role of the infamous Lizzy in the 1976 premiere of the early version of the play, called *My Name is Lisbeth*, at Douglas College. By the time of its 1980 premiere with Theatre 3 in Edmonton, the work had undergone major revisions to become the play-within-the-play we know as *Blood Relations*, and in 1981 Pollock played the role of Miss Lizzy in the Theatre Calgary production.

8   Worthen makes this claim from the position of performance studies. Clearly, the author who publishes her play and has her name reproduced on the title page will have a somewhat different view of the matter. At times, Worthen's privileging of performance echoes postmodern assertions that the author is dead.

9   See Eakin's discussion of relational identity in chapter two of *How Our Lives Become Stories*. Among other sources, Eakin is drawing upon influential feminist work on women's identity as constructed—and represented—through their relations with others (their fathers or mothers, their husbands and children, for example), but he agrees with Susanna Egan, Nancy K. Miller, and Shirley Neuman that relational identity can, and should, be tracked across gender boundaries (see Eakin, *How Our Lives Become Stories* 56-57). Without question, the auto/biographical plays I examine defy any attempt to limit relational identity by gender. Eakin's notion of autobiography's story about the story (59-61) may prove a useful concept for understanding those auto/biographical plays that foreground the playing of roles within the play itself, and I am exploring this idea (and its possible link with Schechner's notion of "twice-behaved behaviour" [see Godard 328-31]) in my current work on Sharon Pollock.

10   I have long argued that Bakhtin's concept of the dialogic applies to drama, his own demurrals on this point notwithstanding, but the most cogent argument I know of for the practice of dialogism in the theatre is the study by Knowles.

11   The play premiered in January 1993 at Tarragon Theatre's Extra Space, where it was directed by Jim Warren, with sets by Glenn Davidson. Verdecchia performed it later that year in Montreal and again on Tarragon's main stage in October 1993.

12   I have been fortunate to watch (I am tempted to say participate in) more than one performance of *Fronteras Americanas* by Verdecchia, from the 1994 high-tech production at the Vancouver Playhouse to several dramatic readings before small, intimate groups. Each time, the performance is the same and different; each time, the performer relates differently to his audience; each time, the selves being performed change. These differences constitute theatre as a public, live performance in a particular space and under specific social, temporal, and material conditions. The play has been performed by other actors (for example, in Edmonton, Halifax, and Australia), and it would be interesting to compare Verdecchia's performance of "Verdecchia" with these other interpretations. One question I would ask in such a comparative study would be— what happens to the autobiographical pact?

13 To perform the role of Drachman, Thomson/Claudia uses the mask of an older male and she creates the voice of an immigrant janitor who works in the school's boiler room. Drachman is both *impresario* and narrator; he introduces the play and watches over the young girl and, through his own storytelling, he explains hers: "Reflected on the surface of her grief she saw herself" (22).

14 Pollock has acknowledged the autobiographical nature of this play in many interviews, but the full extent of the play's auto/biography (for it is, indeed, her story, but also her brother's and her parent's) has yet to be documented—a task in which I am currently engaged. When the play was performed at Fredericton's Theatre New Brunswick in 1986, with her father and her hometown neighbours in the audience, she agreed to change the title to *Family Trappings*, which generalizes the situation as if to draw attention—and possibly blame— away from the father. The shift in title back to *Doc* after the Fredericton performance refocuses the play on her father and his profession, which provides context, if not excuse, for his neglect of his family.

15 It is popular lore in Fredericton to this day that Dr. Chalmers's mother committed suicide on the railway bridge that still crosses the St. John River in Fredericton.

16 In her interview with Hofsess, "Sharon Pollock: Writing for the Illegitimate Theatre," Pollock states that "As I grow older…I understand my mother better. I see now what a difficult position she was in" (3). Her mother's story is, to some degree, revisited in *Getting It Straight*, a monodrama in which a mad woman's rantings disclose the madness and violence in our contemporary, patriarchal society. The importance of Pollock's mother for her biography and her art has not been explored, but I have come to think of this relationship as central to my approach to Pollock's biography. Neuman's discussion of the absent or repressed maternal body (see "Your Past") sheds light on the figure of the mother in several of Pollock's plays, not only in the overtly auto/biographical *Doc*.

17 Lepage describes this changing relationship to self and audience in his comments in the Vancouver Playhouse Playbill for the September 2002 production of this performance piece.

KATHY MEZEI

DOMESTIC SPACE AND THE IDEA OF HOME IN AUTO/BIOGRAPHICAL PRACTICES

THE DOMESTIC EFFECT

In making biography and autobiography live, domestic spaces play a crucial yet often unacknowledged part. While writers and scholars have unquestionably recognized the role of place in the formation of identity,[1] and although artists have always paid tribute to the house and home in the location of self,[2] less attention has been paid to domestic space and to what we might call the domestic effect. Is this perhaps because of the personal, private, everyday quality of the houses, homes, gardens, and material objects that constitute domestic spaces?[3] Certainly, as geographers Béatrice Collignon and Jean-François Staszak observe, "where research on public space has flourished within Social Sciences, private space has received as yet little attention, despite its obvious importance in our everyday lives."

Interdisciplinary in approach, recent studies of domestic spaces may incorporate feminist theory, cultural studies, sociology, anthropology, geography, architecture, history, philosophy, art, film, and literature, and have expanded beyond traditional ideas of home to include, for example, scientific laboratories and prison cells. While the field of domestic space focuses on the material, psychological, spiritual, and social aspects of house and home and garden, it also draws upon the everyday[4] and human relationships within and beyond the house.[5] Moreover, because domestic spaces are the product of a society, they express and reinforce its norms, social practices, and ideologies.[6]

Early feminist critics noted the dailiness that characterizes women's autobiographical writings, ruefully observing that diaries, journals, and memoirs by women, which recorded the private, the routine, the interrupted, the fragmentary, the domestic, and the personal, consigned both the genre and the gender to the margins of literary canons.[7] However, because women's writing and auto/biographical practices have begun to achieve their due recognition over the last few decades, it is important to review domestic spaces as sites of epiphany, revelation, personal interaction, and change, to investigate these "domestic effects," and to recognize the domestic as monumental rather than merely incidental, ornamental, and marginal in the life writing of both men and women. Revisionary and critical attention to gendered space by contemporary feminist scholars (Shirley Ardener, Daphne Spain, Nancy Duncan, Doreen Massey, Linda McDowell) and to gender in/and architecture (Debra Coleman, Elizabeth Danze, and Carol Henderson; Beatriz Colomina; Dolores Hayden; Jane Rendell, Barbara Penner, and Iain Borden; Lynne Walker) has facilitated this (re)turn to the domestic. Studying the effect of the domestic on and through auto/biographical practices thus deepens our knowledge of how selves are imagined, constructed, and represented. Interior domestic spaces (furniture, rooms, doors, windows, stairs, drawers—familiar, everyday objects) which have and could be perceived as banal and ordinary, and hence insignificant, are vital to the shaping of our memories, our imagination, and our "selves."

As a consequence, domestic spaces present writers and characters with provident venues for dreaming and for locating and constructing an "emerging interior self" (Rybczynski 36). In *The Poetics of Space*, Gaston Bachelard famously observes how the house, its secret rooms, and its private corners shelter and protect the daydreamer and inspire reveries, preparing the ground for artistic creation. The house becomes an "embodiment of dreams" (6, 15): "not only our memories but the things we have forgotten are 'housed'…And by remembering 'houses' and 'rooms' we learn to abide within ourselves" (xxxvii). In another iteration of this link between home and imagination, Jean-François Lyotard comments how "it is impossible to think or write without some façade of a house rising up, a phantom to receive and to make work of our peregrinations" (275). Thus, autobiographical fictions like Proust's *A la recherche du temps perdu*, or memoirs like Mary Gordon's *Seeing through Places* and Dionne Brand's *A Map to the Door of No Return* associate private domestic spaces and experiences, as recalled from childhood, with the evolution of inner consciousness. Writers frequently scrutinize their characters and their selves through the literary representation of domestic ritual and the recollection and description of home in the "most social *and* the most inward and private of moments" (Romines 14). For example, in *Home: American Writers Remember Rooms of Their Own* (Fiffer and Fiffer), which pairs each writer with a specific domestic space from the porch to the storm door, we encounter Henry Louis Gates, Jr. remembering his childhood living room and the centrality of the TV, which he describes as functioning "like a fireplace in the proverbial New England winter" and as a "ritual arena for the drama of race" (48), or Jane Smiley meditating on bathrooms as the core of the house and the "eternal now of physical life" (115). These reflections illuminate not only the role of domestic space in the evolution of a writer's identity, but also the imaginative possibilities of ordinary spaces.

Narrating the home accordingly offers a convenient and familiar medium for investigating self and subjectivity by means of the intersection of space and time through memory and the histories and generations of the house's inhabitants and of space. While poems, novels, and auto/biographies can be envisioned as constituting a "dwelling place," domestic spaces are themselves "fictional constructs…stories the telling of which has the power to create the 'we' who are engaged in telling them" (Bammer ix). As Alice Munro aptly puts it, a story is "like a house. Everybody knows what a house does, how it encloses space and makes connections between one enclosed space and another and presents what is outside in a new way….So when I write a story I want to make a certain kind of structure…I've got to build up, a house, a story, to fit around the indescribable 'feeling' that is like the soul of the story" (224). Home is also a place *in* and *from* which one writes—Emily Dickinson's private bedroom at The Homestead; Jane Austen's tripod table in the midst of domestic busyness at Chawton Cottage; Virginia Woolf's room of one's own out in the garden at Monk's House; Gordon's beloved house in Truro on Cape Cod; and Brand's isolated house in the northern Ontario countryside, far from the sea, light, and warmth of Trinidad, her birthplace.

Attentiveness to the domestic "effect" implies noting the effects of the house, its exterior façade and surroundings, its interior decoration and arrangements, and its material objects on the individual's identity and on the composition of the written or visual text; in other words, it invokes the symbiotic relationship between structures that symbolize and determine the self and their narrative expression. As Fredric Jameson suggests, built space can be understood as a kind of language where nouns would seem to be rooms, and corridors, doorways, and staircases, spatial verbs and adverbs (261).[8] The idea of home, which incorporates not only a sense of physical place, but also a web of personal relationships and the weave of experience, memory, and the process of remembering, can thus be thought of as "an enacted space within which we try and play out roles and relationships of both belonging and foreignness" (Bammer ix). It is a common narrative strategy for auto/biographies to begin and follow a personal trajectory by locating the self in relation to home or specific spaces within the home. Mary Gordon opens her *Seeing Through Places* with the Proustian "some days I would be left at my grandmother's house" (14); the diasporic *Lost in Translation* by Eva Hoffman and *A Map to the Door of No Return* by Dionne Brand commemorate loss and dislocation not only through journeys into the unknown, but also through memories of childhood homes where the seeds of dislocation and the impossibility of belonging or return were already relentlessly germinating: Eva in her bed in Cracow listens to the hum of traffic, her parents speaking, the maid cleaning up the kitchen; Dionne in her living room in Trinidad listens to the BBC, the news from away, and the sound of the sea that brings from away and takes away.

THE AUTOBIOGRAPHICAL HOUSE

Is one's house or home *in itself* an autobiographical act and practice? That is, do the design, possession, inhabitation, and decoration of the house articulate and display the self—and which aspects of the self? And if so, in what ways do they signal the outward, material expression of the self and/or offer a shelter for the cocooning and introspective self? Conversely, do auto/biographical narrative and the positioning of the self inscribe domestic space, specifically the house and the concept of home? How do different dwelling places differently embody the self, shape narrative, and offer points of reference for the location, evolution, and expression of the self?

C.G. Jung and Sigmund Freud have been enormously influential in determining how we approach these questions, underpinning, for example, the writings of Gaston Bachelard, Anthony Vidler, Clare Cooper Marcus, Bettina Knapp. In his memoir, *Memories, Dreams, Reflections,* Jung recounts how his concept of the collective unconscious emerged from Freud's attempt to interpret his house dream:

> I was in a house I did not know, which had two stories. It was "my house." I found myself in the upper story, where there was a kind of salon furnished with fine old paintings....Descending the stairs I reached the ground floor. There everything was much older....Everywhere it was rather dark....I came upon a heavy door, and opened it....I discovered a stone stairway that led down into the cellar. Descending again, I found myself in a beautifully vaulted room which looked exceedingly ancient [Jung descends another stairway of narrow stone and steps into a cave where he discovers two human skulls]. (158-59)

While Freud obsessed about the significance of the skulls that Jung had discovered in the cellar of his dream house, insisting that they represented Jung's death wishes concerning his wife and mother-in-law, an increasingly irritated Jung decides instead that the house represents the psyche, his psyche. For example, the salon symbolizes consciousness, while the lower floors—and cellar—depict levels and layers of unconsciousness.[9]

Subsequently, it has become commonplace to interpret houses (in dreams, memories, literature, and art) as settings for an emerging interior life (Rybczynski 36), and as extensions of self as in the psyche and body. Compartments of the house—doors, hallways, stairs, attics, cellars, closets, and caves—signify aspects of the conscious and unconscious self and body parts (rooms as wombs, drawers and boxes intimating a hidden psychological life). When Freud discovered that one of the meanings of *heimlich* (belonging to the house or family) was its opposite—"something hidden and dangerous…so that '*heimlich*' comes to have the meaning usually ascribed to '*unheimlich*'" (226)—he proposed that the uncanny (*unheimlich*) might be "something which is secretly familiar [*heimlich-heimisch*] which has undergone repression and then returned from it" (245), thus linking self, home, haunting, and narrative, and offering generations of readers a map of the inner, secret spaces of being and house.[10]

With this fusion of obsession, home, and memory, it is understandable how houses become stories and narratives of hauntings by memories, ghosts, and traces of selves and others. Conversely, stories are haunted by lived and imagined houses, which frequently mimic the psyche and bodies of their inhabitants as well as the social practices and political ideologies of the nation; a "house" and its (dysfunctional) practices can at times be seen as a microcosm of a nation or of a minority culture within a nation. For example, Winston Churchill apparently claimed that Jan Struther's humorous representation of an upper-middle-class British home and family, *Mrs. Miniver*, published just after the outbreak of war in 1939, and the subsequent film adaptation (1942), had done more for the Allies than a flotilla of battleships (qtd. in Grove xi); the very different example of Marilyn Dumont's depiction of her "old schoolhouse" home, encircled by white judges, in her collection of poems *A Really Good Brown Girl*, is emblematic of the embattled Métis nation in contemporary Canada (11).

DOMESTIC SPACE AND THE LOCATION OF AUTO/BIOGRAPHICAL IDENTITY: SOME EXAMPLES

The following examples deliberately range across very different forms of life writing—biography, photographic art, and the memoir—and across continents, time periods, gender, class, race, and sexuality.[11] Proffering tentative responses to questions posed earlier, they attempt to expose the often subliminal but potent effect of domestic spaces in the study of lives and the formation of identity by "seeing through places."

Figure 1. Jane Austen's dining room. Reproduced from Nigel Nicolson's *The World of Jane Austen* (1991) with permission.

Jane Austen's Dining Parlour

Figure 1 is a photograph of Jane Austen's dining parlour at Chawton Cottage, where Austen lived from 1809 to 1817, the year of her death; this uninhabited space is redolent with meaning. This black and white photograph was taken by Stephen Colover for Nigel Nicolson's book *The World of Jane Austen* (1991). With its glossy photographs, drawings, paintings, and large format, Nicolson's book is directed to a generalist audience and seeks to situate Austen within her historical and geographic space in an accessible and appealing manner. Nicolson opens his book by stating, "this book is not a biography of Jane Austen, although it outlines the chief events of her life. Its main purpose is to discuss and illustrate her houses—the houses she lived in and visited, and the houses she invented for her novels" (11). In studying the photograph, we experience not only the image of a room in which Jane Austen lived and wrote and which plays a part in the formation of her writing identity, but also the biography of this now monumentalized domestic space, Chawton Cottage. The room and its furniture have assumed a symbolic and legendary quality, for Austen apparently wrote her novels at the small tripod writing table in the communal space of the dining room. Remembering that personal privacy is a recent (nineteenth-century) concept, we should not be surprised by Austen's lack of privacy in this busy, noisy house. The famous anecdote of the door with a deliberately squeaky hinge, which alerted Austen to intruders and at the sound of which she quickly hid her papers, signals the blur between public and private spheres. This blurring is further enacted within the dining room itself. The public and transparent space of the dining-room window emits light and offers a point of observation for the writer, and the Austens can observe arriving visitors; conversely, visitors can peer into the interior and view the family seated at the table on display: "A gentleman passing by in a coach reported seeing the family 'looking comfortable at breakfast'" (Bowden 6). As we examine the photograph, we too participate in this gaze and configure the space in many ways: perhaps we insert ourselves into the room past or present; perhaps we envision Austen herself seated at the table; or, as in my case, perhaps we remember trailing two young children through this small and echoing space several years ago amid a clutch of American tourists. Then and now, a private domestic space is transformed into a public spectacle, and the *unheimlich* infiltrates the *heimlich*.

The dining-room table, set with the family's Wedgewood dinner service, connotes middle-class domestic rituals and relations, and a gathering site for family intercourse and meals. In its arrangement of furniture and as manifested by the two tables, the dining-room represents a combination of domestic and work space, emblematic of women's writing lives: lack of privacy, interruption by others and domestic duties, surveillance, and secrecy on the one hand; grounding in the rich fabric of domestic and family and private life on the other. This interior domestic space has become an apt metonym of Jane Austen and her fiction—miniature, domestic, contained, and constrained, yet open to the outer world and intimating concealment and secrets. Like the gentleman passing in his coach, our glance into this room has drawn us into the writing and private life of Jane Austen, and by means of this photograph we can begin to imagine the domestic effect on Austen, her writing process, and her novels. As a still life and as a monument to the early nineteenth century, reconstructing the past yet empty of human figures (including the phantom present-day tourist), this photograph displays a simulacrum of Jane Austen's domestic and writing "world."

American Dream Home

Figure 2 offers a more contemporary perspective on domestic space and the interrogation of the subject, its location, and focalization. This photograph, "Fox and Fence" (1991), was created by Gregory Crewdson, an American photographic artist who is fascinated by the uncanny, the American vernacular, and domesticity. He has mounted or participated in exhibitions on this subject, such as the 1991 "Pleasures and Terrors of Domes-

Figure 2. Gregory Crewdson, *Untitled, 1991*. C-print, edition of 10 with 2 APs 20 x 24-inch paper size. Courtesy of the artist and Luhring Augustine, New York.

tic Comfort" show at the Museum of Modern Art in New York, and the 1999 "Threshold: Invoking the Domestic in Contemporary Art" show in Sheboygan, Wisconsin. Probably a photograph of Lee, Massachusetts, a favourite subject of Crewdson, the American dream of a single family detached suburban house with white picket fence and laundry on the line is here rendered uncanny through the unusual perspective of the outsider fox, the insects, the disturbing absence of people, and the subtle creation of an uneasy atmosphere. The space enclosed by the picket fence in the middle ground resembles a family plot in a graveyard, while the slats in the foreground are eerily reminiscent of tombstones.[12]

Thus the *unheimlich* that lurks within the *heimlich* is uncovered as the American dream and domestic idyll are stalked by death and threatened by unsettling perspectives. Traces and hints of the life of a house, community, and family are signaled by everyday domestic objects, like the laundry hanging on the clothesline, and through what is hidden, absent, and distorted. In this representation of domestic space, the perspective and position of the subject and how it perceives house and home, the enigma of a reliable perspective, and the unsettling of foreground, middle ground and background raise the spectre of uncertainty. Who or what is the subject? Whose perspective is it? What are we meant to be seeing? Our gaze is drawn to the fox, who is foregrounded and who, along with the white fence slats and insects, is in focus, while the rest of the objects—

houses, laundry, distant hills—are blurred and slightly out of focus. The fox's prominent staring eye and illuminated head capture our attention and direct our gaze towards the shadowed house, although it is distracted by the enormous insects and a soft evening light in the distance. When we perceive the familiar and the homely from another and unfamiliar position—that of the fox, butterfly, or bug—they suddenly metamorphose into the uncanny and grotesque, i.e., fence slats into tombstones. We feel the spectral sense of the presence of "some*one* as some*one other*" (9) proposed in Derrida's logic of hauntology. Because of the focalization and narrative composition—the defamiliarizing perspective of the foregrounded and enlarged fox and insects and butterflies—the effect of the domestic is to disturb and disrupt accepted representations of home and community. As with Jane Austen's dining room, the experience of viewing is voyeuristic in relation to the auto/biographical subject and to the private and domestic. Peering, unexpected and uninvited, into someone's private room or backyard, and thus trespassing on the intimate lives and spaces of others, forces the spectator to face, apprehensively, his/her own subject position. The eye, the gaze, and the subject (fox) and object (domestic scene) are disturbed, and the viewer's position as spectator/subject or as object of the returning gaze of the photograph is disrupted, for we gaze into the photograph via the "view from aside" (the fox's one-eyed stare). As Slavoj Žižek, referring to Lacan's discussion of the antinomic relation of eye and gaze, comments, "the eye viewing the object is on the side of the subject, while the gaze is on the side of an object" (109). Although Žižek is discussing pornographic films, a similar unsettling of the viewer's position and the redirection or awryness of our gaze occurs with this photograph, suggesting how the angle of the gaze can transpose the home into the unhomely. Similarly, memoirs by Mary Gordon and Dionne Brand uncover the unhomely in domestic spaces and objects through their quirky angles of narrative focalization.

Memoir 1: Mary Gordon's Seeing through Places

The memoir of American novelist and journalist, Mary Gordon, *Seeing through Places: Reflections on Geography and Identity* (2000), obviously links the formation of her identity with specific places houses. Her opening chapter, "My Grandmother's House," fixes a moment and a place in her childhood and in her quest to locate her self. By the act of entering the physical space of this house (and as she writes later there were three ways to enter this house: the front porch, the side porch, and the kitchen) Gordon embarks on a journey back through her life story and forward into the recognition of the construction and creation of a writing self. The house literally provides the entry into the self, a self frequently presented as *unheimlich*. But Gordon has ambivalent relations with the houses in her life; she longs for some, resents others. And, as she admits, her focus on place is an (unsuccessful) attempt to circumvent people in her life story.

The signposts along this journey include Gordon's parents' apartment, her grandmother's house (which becomes her widowed mother's house), the summer house in Cape Cod ("the only house I have ever really loved" [209]), and a cherished university apartment in New York, though one wonders how Gordon will "remember" the apartment later from a more distant and contingent time and space. By "seeing through these places" and articulating her ambivalence towards some of these places, she constructs the narrative framework of the memoir, for, as Fredric Jameson remarks, physical trajectories through buildings can constitute virtual narratives or stories (244). Gordon's travels through different houses and rooms constitute the stages of her life story and the mechanism to uncover her selves; objects in her grandmother's house, her intimidating aunt's quarters, and the porch where her uncle slept for many years trigger memories and family anecdotes as she pieces together the puzzle of her origins.

The memoir's first sentence, "some days I would be left at my grandmother's house" (13), with its implications of loss, dislocation, and the spectral presence of "some*one* as some*one* other," announces the preoccupations of the memoir. The child's dislocation operates not only at the level of unpleasant or conflicted memories, but also at the level of language (the grandmother uses "commode" for "toilet" and "pantry" for "kitchen shelves") and of domestic objects like the frightening pictures that "were not about pleasing the eye" (*The Shroud of Turin*, Christ pointing to his sacred heart like a pimento or tongue, and a *trompe l'oeil* that, depending on how you looked at it, suggested Christ at the Scourging at the Pillar, Crowned with Thorns, or his Agony in the Garden) (25). The *trompe l'oeil* is a conspicuous *mise en abyme* of Gordon's own narrative strategy since her life story depends on how she looks at it and from what place and time, the narrative angles she chooses, and the perspective with which she "sees through places." Domestic objects and rooms become touchstones for memory, self-reflection, evasion, and a double-voiced positioning of the self who, writing in the present, narrates the past. To Gordon, her grandmother and the house that embodied her represent a rigid morality and sense of duty, a guilt-ridden and repressive Catholicism, and a bourgeois mentality against which her imaginative and literary spirit rebelled: "My grandmother had no interest in having a good time…and her house proclaimed this....Her house was her body, and like her body, was honorable, daunting, reassuring, defended, castigating, harsh, embellished, dark" (15). Moreover, the grandmother's house exerts agency, possessing a life of its own: "The house demanded strength, but did not give it. It was not a loving house; it was a house that required service from a devoted lover...we failed the house and it punished us and we, like whipped creatures, huddled against it, trying simply to survive" (48). To rephrase Jameson, houses can constitute narratives or stories.

After Mary Gordon's father's death, mother and daughter move into the grandmother's house, and after the grandmother's death, they continue to live there. With its smells of cleaning and baking, its daunting attics and inhabited porches, this uncanny house where she was once a curious and reluctant visitor becomes home. The house begins to mimic the dysfunctional relationship between the increasingly alcoholic mother and rebellious teenage daughter; Gordon reflects in retrospect that it was not good for her, her mother, or the house that her mother, after a drawn-out lawsuit, was awarded (43):

> My mother and I destroyed the house....We let things pile up. Every surface was covered with papers, some many years old, and we couldn't imagine how to begin to get rid of them....The living room became uninhabitable, so dusty that I was overcome with asthmatic attacks if I tried to sit there. So we didn't sit there. We stayed in the kitchen, where we would clear a space on the table large enough for two plates. Not two together, one plate for my mother, then some papers, then an opening for a plate for me. Upstairs in my pink bedroom, the pink that age had darkened to the color of a particularly feminine bad luck, I allowed chaos to overcome me. (44–45)

This house personifies the women's loneliness and unhappiness, and unravels the idea of home as a sanctuary and family abode.

For Gordon, weekends cleaning house with her grandmother and mother instead of playing like other children led to a phobic dislike of housework (37). Indoctrinated into rituals of domesticity, and conceding the *effect* of order and cleanliness, Gordon in the present cannot step away from her guilt or rage, her sense that there is a conflict between domesticity and creativity, and that her "self" must oppose the meaning of an orderly house. From her study in the New York apartment where she lives at the time of writing her memoir, she confesses, "I see the creation of domestic order as time taken away from reading, writing, talking, being with friends or in the world, and although I am sometimes choked with regret and shame at not maintaining a beautiful abode, I do not change my ways" (249). Like Alice Munro, who compares writing stories to building houses, Gordon establishes symbiotic relationships among the configuration of the house, the practice of writing, and the fabrication of a self.

The "enclosed spaces" and the connections between them described by Munro also characterize the structural frame of Gordon's memoir as she moves from house to house, delineating rooms, furniture, domestic objects, and housekeeping or its deficiency. The symbol of house as mother, house as symbol of self, house as the dwelling place of the writerly imagination permeates her memoir. We witness the effect of the idea and materiality of the home in the construction and positioning of Gordon's auto/biographical self. The domestic effect is both negative, as she turns away from the grandmother's house, imagining it antithetical to her independent and writing self, and salutary, as she mourns the loss of the house in Cape Cod with which she identifies, recalling "the time in the house when only it and I were awake, when I was dreaming, reading, writing" (216). Describing the attachment between a place and writing happily and well, Gordon recalls "it is only when you come back from this kind of writing that you are grateful to the place that has gone on being the same while you were out of it; the desk, the chair, the floor, have not rearranged themselves while you were rearranging the universe in words" (212). By navigating the reader (and herself) through her life in houses, she links specific places—domestic spaces—to her conflicted identity, an identity shaped and haunted by the spectral presence of her mother and grandmother and the house they shared.

Memoir 2: Dionne Brand's A Map to the Door of No Return: *A Note on the Door*

In this memoir of dislocation and notes to belonging, Dionne Brand focuses on the effect of a specific aspect of the house, the door, in the formation of the identity of a writing self and of a people, descendants of African slaves in the Caribbean. The epigraph, "door of no return," refers to the "door" in slave castles along the west coast of Africa, through which Africans were forced to depart as slaves: *"But to the Door of No Return which is illuminated in the consciousness of Blacks in the Diaspora there are no maps. This door is not mere physicality. It is a spiritual location. It is also perhaps a psychic destination. Since leaving was never voluntary, return was, and still may be, an intention, however deeply buried. There is as it says no way in; no return"* (n.pag.). Unlike Gordon, whose "homes" were all located in New York State, Brand experiences global migration and exile: origins in Africa, a childhood home in Trinidad, invasion in Grenada, an apartment in Toronto, travels to Europe and Africa and across Canada, and a house in northern Ontario. How, she asks herself, can she map these impossibilities, a set of changing locations, the migration of her people (Africa, the Caribbean, North America), her own "undwelling" (215), and her "marooned" self (216)?[13] Brand and her text wander from place to place, reflecting on her readings and her encounters with travellers, friends, and family, and relating her search for maps and the absence of maps. The memoir's brief sections mirror Brand's peripatetic existence and her writing back into her forgotten history; their resistance to chronology and linear narrative exemplify the troubled migrations of her people. In this dislocated and dislocating narrative, she jumps around in time and space, thus initiating the reader into a similar dislocation by means of fragments of and fragmented memories, places, experiences, and encounters.

Like Gordon's grandmother's house, the "door" for Brand unleashes memory, forgetting, and, in Brand's case, the history of the African diaspora: "The door is a place, real, imaginary, and imagined...It is a place which exists or existed. The door out of which Africans were captured, loaded onto ships heading for the New World. It was the door of a million exits multiplied. It is a door many of us wish never existed. It is a door which makes the word *door* impossible and dangerous, cunning and disagreeable" (19). In alerting us to the danger and the *unheimlich* of a familiar domestic object, Brand, too, questions the meaning of the everyday language of home and the effect of this language on the formation of identity and belonging. Her memoir opens with dislocation and the absence of name and naming, and the words to locate a place of origin: although Brand's grandfather claims he knew "what people we came from" (3), to the disappointment of the thirteen-year-old Brand he never remembers. Their mutual disappointment gathers into estrangement and opens a small space inside Brand that she carries with her (6) as if she were haunted. Out of this fissure between past ("having no name to call on was having no past" [5]) and present, Brand resurrects the "Door of No Return," a place emptied of beginnings, a site of belonging and unbelonging (6), a domestic space which ridicules any idea of home, return, and comfort. In its very denial of return, the door of no return invokes Freud's image of the obsessive return of that which is repressed or concealed within the *heimlich*. Brand's obsessive desire to learn the names of the people she came from and her grandfather's equally obsessive forgetting set the stage for the repeated and returning image of the door as a symbol of unimaginable horror, trauma, and repression. But this door also offers a kind of opening—to origins.

Brand's subtitle, "Notes to Belonging," reminds readers of the inevitable connection between home, writing, and belonging. In its literary and visual representations, the door suggests a liminal space separating outside from inside; the act of opening, closing, locking, and unlocking doors, and leaving doors ajar symbolizes secrecy, privacy, invitation, and the protection or violation of the self. As intermediary between enclosed spaces and between inside and outside, the door serves as a structural device of passage, entrance, and departure, and of invitation into a physical or metaphysical space. While Georg Simmel ("Bridge and Door") and Bachelard invoke the door in its possibility as connection between the world and a separate existence, and Bachelard suggests that the "door is an entire cosmos of the Half-open" (222), to Brand the door stands for the impossibility of return. However, the home, the place where she "came" from, has at last been named and imagined; it is a point of beginning and belonging.

NOTES

1 The range of studies include such classics as Martin Heidegger's "Poetically Man Dwells…," Gaston Bachelard's *The Poetics of Space*, Yi-Fu Tuan's *Topophilia* and Homi K. Bhabha's *The Location of Culture*. See also the special issue of *Biography and Geography* edited by Miriam Fuchs.

2 A random sampling would include Emily Dickinson's "The Homestead," Edgar Allan Poe's "The Fall of the House of Usher," many of the novels of Edith Wharton, Henry James, and Virginia Woolf, Evelyn Waugh's *Brideshead Revisited*, V.S. Naipaul's *A House for Mr. Biswas*, Marilynne Robinson's *Housekeeping*, and Louise Bourgeois and Tracey Emin's installations.

3 Roderick Lawrence proposes that "the concept of home is ambiguous, and therefore, it cannot be taken for granted. In particular, the common association between domestic space and home is contentious," although, unfortunately Lawrence does not here elaborate on this contentiousness (53). Indeed, distinctions between house and home are the subject of ongoing debates, as is the meaning of home. For our purposes here, I suggest that "house" is a built form with a fixed location in which a constellation of people dwell; and home is an idea or concept rather than a material form, an idea that is fluid, ranging from a built dwelling place to cyberspace homepages to homelessness.

4 The idea of the everyday and its relation to auto/biographical writing that I am trying to articulate here differs from that explored in the articles collected in Sidonie Smith and Julia Watson's *Getting a Life: Everyday Uses of Autobiography* in that my emphasis is on the "domestic effect" rather than on the various aspects of everyday auto/biographical practices.

5 I wish to here acknowledge my collaborator in the study of domestic space, Chiara Briganti, with whom I have developed these concepts. See Chiara Briganti and Kathy Mezei, "House Haunting: The Domestic Novel of the Inter-War Years" and Mezei and Briganti, eds., "Domestic Space Forum." The domestic

space website, <www.sfu.ca/domestic-space>, has a selected and ongoing bibliography.

6 Similar to Bourdieu's notion of *habitus*, houses, gardens, and domestic interiors mirror and generate dispositions of national and local social practices and ideologies (Bourdieu 53).

7 The word "diary" originates in the medieval Latin *diarius*, which means "daily."

8 In her essay "The Hidden Rooms of Isabella Valancy Crawford and P.K. Page," in *Mosaic's* special issue *Literature and Architecture*, Wanda Campbell quotes a similar analogy by Diane Favro: "architecture is as much about words as about actual buildings" (69).

9 See Clare Cooper Marcus's elaboration of this concept in *House as a Mirror of Self*.

10 It is worth noting that in French *hantise* carries the connotation of an obsession or a nagging memory, whereas in English one of the meanings of "haunt" is a "place or abode that one frequents"; its origins lie in the Old English *hamettan*, to provide with a home or house.

11 See, for example, Beatriz Colomina, ed. *Sexuality and Space*; Aaron Betsky, *Queer Space: Architecture and Same-Sex Desire*; Marjorie Garber, *Sex and Real Estate: Why We Love Houses*.

12 I thank Dr. Ann Davis, curator of the Nickle Arts Museum for this observation.

13 Marooned is a powerful adjective referring not only to abandonment but also to the Maroons, slaves in the Caribbean who escaped from their plantations and rebelled against the plantation owners.

SUSANNA EGAN

THE SHIFTING GROUNDS OF EXILE AND HOME IN DAPHNE MARLATT'S *STEVESTON*[1]

Exile implies an originary home that is no longer accessible, a place of belonging to which there can be no return. Where exile may involve continuous wandering, or, at least, a sense of rootlessness, home is permanent in the imagination, like Paradise, lost but unchanging. These distinctions are so commonly recognized that narratives of exile and home tend to define one in relation to the other. Therefore, when Daphne Marlatt, from Australia and Malaysia, describes herself as "at home" in Vancouver, she disrupts my common-sense reading of perpetual migrancy, particularly because she is a writer who has contributed so much to specifically Canadian literature. "This is the only place that I feel I really belong," Marlatt told George Bowering. "I'm a local writer, I'm a west coast writer" ("Given This Body" 32). Drawing on her personal experience of two nostalgias in her family, for England and for Penang, and her own eager adoption of this final home, Marlatt has repeatedly created the Vancouver region as the point of entry for a woman's story, the situation in which losses can be assessed and, as in *Ana Historic*, new directions can be chosen. In *Steveston*, I will argue, she has also situated herself within a web of migrations (generic, historical, and geographical) in such a way as to make migration or exile a perpetual and therefore permanent condition—like home.

Smaro Kamboureli's praise for *Steveston* on the back of the 2001 edition comments on Daphne Marlatt's "recognition that language is larger than the individual writer, that the body is the threshold of the personal and the cultural, that our memories are not just our own but belong to history as well." Kamboureli's thorough implication of Marlatt in *Steveston*, both as woman and as writer, supports my own desire to read this long-poem cycle as auto/biography.[2] However, *Steveston* is not about Marlatt's life but about a place and a community to which Marlatt has never belonged, which makes my desire suspect if not actually perverse. Given neither authorial claims beyond use of the first person nor any other conventional markers for auto/biography, I have to ask myself how and why this poem invites or enables such a reading, what kind of auto/biography I am finding, and just what I contribute to understanding of this poem or of auto/biography when I find Marlatt "herself" at the heart of the text?

My answers begin with Marlatt's treatment of Steveston, the place, as geographically and historically impermanent, as always temporary for every kind of settlement and therefore as a suitable location for exploration of migrancy. They continue with Marlatt's own theoretical work, the permission she seems to provide, for example, when she describes her documentary perspective as necessarily personal: "yes, the voice in most of my work is subjective and individual rather than universal," she tells Brenda Carr. "It's marked by my gender as well as my history, class, national identity, race, all those things. *Steveston* has often been called a documentary but the writing doesn't assume that there is an unmediated objective position. I put myself in there, recording all the sexual baggage I carried as a woman on the dock" (Marlatt, "Between" 103). Marlatt is very evidently part of the ninth poem in the cycle, "End of Cannery Channel," presenting herself as chatting, notebook in hand, with men raising their starboard pole, and in the eleventh poem of the cycle, "Work"; in both cases she is simultaneously the perceiving subject and the object of sexual banter. I understand her subjective stance also to include her actual participation in the poem's explorations so that she (and she includes her reader) becomes the "we, our, us" to be considered, as in:

> It's not linear:
> > the stainless
> steel lines going down in the Gulf echo other trollings, catch
> in the mesh of a net we refuse to see, the accretion of all our
> actions, how they interact, how they inter/read (intelligence),
> receive, the reading the sea, a vanishing marsh, a dying river,
> the mesh we are netted in, makes of *us*. (*Steveston* 46)[3]

Marlatt's presence in this poem as perceiver, participant, and analyst of the human condition will be important to my reading of this work as auto/biography. That willful entanglement in "the mesh of a net we refuse to see" aligns the poetic act with fishing and anticipates that "(intelligence)" will produce not just a catch but maybe new or unexpected materials in what it "makes of *us*." Poetry becomes the means for hauling in both speaker and reader in search of suspected but deeply hidden selves.

In "Self-Representation and Fictionalysis," Marlatt expands these possibilities of her auto/biographical presence to consider the role of language in self-representation: "Autobiography is not separable from poetry for me on this ground i would call fictionalysis: a self-analysis that plays fictively with the primary images of one's life, a fiction that uncovers analytically that territory where fact and fiction coincide" (124). She qualifies her opening claim, that autobiography is not separable from poetry, by specifying the presence of self-analysis, a foundational function of autobiography, and of "the primary images of one's life," which are simultaneously personal and abstract, capable, that is, of resonance in the lives of others. That "mesh of a net we refuse to see" includes not only "all our / actions, how they interact" but also the language (that can seem transparent in documentary) in which they are caught and which makes and interprets *us*. Both Marlatt's perspective and her "primary images" encourage me to look for Marlatt in this poem.

My questions about *Steveston* as auto/biography also find answers in the ways in which other people have read *Steveston*, in the history of the poem as documentary, and, above all, in the poem's identification of human experience (personal, political, economic, gendered) as part of its ecosystem. Curiously, my quest for auto/biography began in Steveston's ecosystem, in particular with the river and the salmon, which have served as an icon for the Pacific Northwest since the earliest days of human settlement. Only after struggling with the role of the salmon in the text did I turn to Marlatt and her critics for guidance. Just maybe, if the narrative form presents human experience (individual, social, cultural, interrelational) as deeply embedded in its environment, it also overrides or complicates distinctions between perceiver and perceived ("I, you") and the abstractions that follow (that pertain to "one"), enabling Marlatt's "primary images" to troll, like radar or sonic scan, for the invisible catch that "we refuse to see." Marlatt invariably pushes difficult or original meaning through an innovative form crafted to accommodate it, so my sense of "herself" (historian, poetic speaker, woman in time and place), thoroughly integrated with the meanings of these people in this place, may not, after all, be "outlandish." On the contrary, if Marlatt's "self" or her story is *here*, then it resonates precisely with land—and water and other forms of life—an auto/biography determined by place.[4]

Both Marlatt's choice of place and her identification of her own experience of the place are important. Yet her focus is outward, on the Japanese community. Maybe, I speculate, Marlatt as an immigrant to Canada was attracted to the immigrant community of Japanese-Canadian fishers in Steveston.[5] In her 1984 essay "Entering In: The Immigrant Imagination," Marlatt describes the importance in her life of Strathcona, an immigrant neighbourhood in Vancouver where she lived for six years, discovering both the communities of immigration, so different from the isolation of her own family, and the connections these communities have with the old worlds from which they come. "I lived in it for six years," Marlatt writes, "and felt completely at home, felt as if part of me had been returned to a whole i'm still discovering" (21). Diana Relke has discussed the paradox of home and homelessness in Marlatt's work and Marlatt's "internal necessity of untangling that paradox" (45). Shirley Chew associates the dark vision of *Steveston* with Marlatt's childhood experience of the Japanese during the war in and around the Pacific (her own family leaving Penang for Australia in expectation of Japanese invasion), experiences that are central to Marlatt's novel *Taken* and to her personal history in "Entering In."[6] Listening to Marlatt herself, I must recognize these possible associations and the radical differences between herself and the people she met in Steveston, as well as her own understanding that "you can only locate by putting yourself in the context of all the relative points that surround you" (Marlatt, "Given This Body" 63). Locating the self, maybe in particular a migrant self, involves finding one's bearings in specific social and geographical locations and then relating these locations both to one's social and to the individual imaginary.

Nonetheless, in terms of auto/biography, I am stuck with the literal fact that Marlatt enters Steveston, the place, as an outsider, records and writes about histories other than her own, and leaves. Given that *Steveston* does not, in any literal sense, include Marlatt's history, my exploration of this possible auto/geography begins with a few guiding questions. How does Marlatt position herself in this history, and with what effects? How does her narrative serve her own history in relation to the place and the community she records? Does the repetition of this story, from *Steveston Recollected* to three editions of *Steveston* over a period of nearly thirty years, simply document the popularity of these projects, or does it also contribute to my understanding of auto/biography made resonant in relation to time, place, and text?

MARLATT AS HISTORIAN

In 1975, the Provincial Archives of British Columbia published an "aural history," *Steveston Recollected: A Japanese-Canadian History,* edited by Daphne Marlatt. "Authentic" experience, vouched for in photographs and quotation, and the comparative informality and immediacy of narrative produce a vivid documentary of the "recent past" in this specific place and its local culture, quite precisely foregrounding as the subjects of their own narratives those whom official histories tend to marginalize and objectify. Their interviews involved Kaya Koizumi as primary interviewer and translator, addressing the Japanese community in Japanese.[7] Robert Minden and Rex Weyler took photographs, and the text also includes historic photographs by Philip Timms and F. Dundas Todd. Daphne Marlatt assembled these materials, provided a secondary translation, and inserted what the copyright page refers to as "written sketches."

Marlatt is present in the editorial choices that combine verbal and visual information about places and people and in the combinations of information.[8] Verbal text includes, for example, such documents as union minutes, anonymous diary entries, historical information from several sources (drawing on a bibliography provided at the end), and sociological and technical information in appendices. *Steveston Recollected* is therefore multi-generic documentary, combining interviews with researched information, citations from sources, and editorial commentary. Marlatt is also present in the choice of oblique and overlapping but generally chronological historical survey, which includes the wartime evacuation of Japanese Canadians to the interior, their postwar return, and the contemporary scene. Marlatt's inclusion of photographed documents such as the notice "to male enemy aliens" "to be posted in a conspicuous place," and a letter in English to "Spud Matsuchita," prisoner of war, from his friend Ken, substantiates, in explicit documentary fashion, the episodic information obtained in interviews. Marlatt is also present in the secondary translation of the interviews from Japanese. Most pronouncedly, she is present in the written sketches with which the work begins and ends and which provide a coda to many chapters.

Such interventions are all in the day's work for documentary history, especially when the historian is conducting interviews and therefore participates in a live exchange. Distinctively, however, Marlatt positions herself and her responses to people and place quite explicitly within the documentary. Marlatt engages the reciprocal "I/you" relationship that Benveniste has described as foundational to subjectivity in language, which positions the historian within her history and necessarily affects its possibilities. Acknowledging feminist theories of auto/biographical identity as relational, Paul John Eakin also notes "the dialogic play of pronouns" which "tracks the unfolding of relational identity in many registers...teaching, again and again...that the self is dynamic, changing, and plural" (*How Our Lives* 98).[9] By such means, among others, Marlatt positions herself in the text "in many registers," as Eakin puts it, as observer, as participant, and as subject. For example, Koizumi's interview with Asamatsu Murakami, rendered in English under the chapter title "Boat Boss to House Boss," positions Marlatt in the scene and includes her speculations and interpretation: "He is 88, says Maya in English, turning to include me, and he has 17 grandchildren! (How would it be to be 88, living in your son's house, which is quiet and smells of good food, caring for the garden slowly, reflecting occasionally on old friends—who's dead, who's dying—the old boat, the old days....) Mr. Murakami grins at my impressed 'oh' and says something to Maya, who translates, laughing, 'You're very young'" (*Steveston Recollected* 12).

Not only does she rely on her translator but her relationship with the old man also mushrooms from very little information into her own speculations about his inner life. Such speculations are also internal to her, not represented in her "impressed 'oh.'" Murakami's amusement that she is very young, responding to her "oh," the spoken and the unspoken, merely intimates what Marlatt has described as "the whole of what is being said" (Curran and Hirabayashi 114). This "whole" includes the white spaces of the page, in which silence, or the juxtaposition of one voice with another, one angle with another, suggests a deceptively spare or understated narrative with significantly expandable possibilities for the poetry that follows this history. Here Marlatt is the outsider, the visitor, expanding her history by means of her explicit but unvoiced effort of sympathetic identification. Between them, she and Murakami have also engaged in a curiously direct "you/you" exchange in which they do and do not recognize each other: living in your son's house—you are very young. Marlatt's more direct, apparently unmediated records also include shifts and slides in pronoun use, implicating her as listener in indirect speech. In each instance, her language avoids appropriation because it foregrounds her interpretive role and the presence of her reader, but it also indicates the imaginative move she is making from documentary to poetry.

Where the documentary produces people with their voices and memories and their narratives that both present and interpret such objects and episodes as the canneries, the boats, the nets, the wharves, the strike, the fire, and the evacuation—the substance, in other words, of historical records—the historian's participation in documentary moves her history from remembrance of things past into dynamic, body-perceiving possibility. *Steveston Recollected* holds in tension the information that, once produced, is finite, and Marlatt's processes of discovery that are open-ended. Where more information for this history or a subsequent volume could be produced, the historian's own processes of discovery evolve and change in ways that specific information cannot. Marlatt's interpretive role in this text therefore releases the history of Steveston from its finished state as documentary into its role in her life, her imaginative relations with these people and this place, and therefore, by degrees, into the possibilities of a mythic role for exploration of migrant identity, the situation and the experience that the poet shares with the people of Steveston.[10] This last possibility, at the heart of my reading of *Steveston* as auto/biography, emerges from this particular historian's identification with people in place and time (people reflecting occasionally on old friends—who's dead, who's dying—the old boat, the old days). It develops with the very reflexivity that positions her (she's very young) in a history of people with whom she cannot even speak. It pushes past the limitations of document (as all auto/biography eventually must) in her poetic reworking of what matters to her about what she has found.

HISTORIAN AS POET

Even before *Steveston Recollected* appeared in print (1975), Talonbooks had published the first edition of Marlatt's long-poem cycle, *Steveston* (1974). Marlatt has described the transition from documentary to poetry first as including the women of the community and second as working with the profound abstractions to be drawn from the material of the documentary. She and her colleagues had "approached Steveston as a fishing community. Fishing is done by men....Later, when Robert [Minden] and I were working on our own on *Steveston*, we talked about how Steveston's women seemed invisible and I realized that what I wanted to make surface through the obvious ring of that town's fishing activity were the women, the women you didn't see on the streets, you didn't see on the docks because they were at home, or they were in the cannery" (Marlatt, "Between" 103). *Steveston*'s project, then, is to reverse the male focus of *Steveston Recollected*. She does so not simply by means of attending to those invisible lives but also in terms of what she calls a "figure/ground reversal" (103). Much as the documentary had produced as subjects those members of the local culture whom official histories tend to marginalize and objectify, so poetry now shifts perspective again, producing characters and their situations in the network of their ecosystem. Because the invisible cycles of female experience are repeated in the cycles of the land, the ocean, the delta, and the river, they subsume the fishing community into their larger meaning. Chronology gives way to chronotope, or the reading of time and space in relation to each other.[11] As Marlatt tells Carr, "It's part of the ecological vision in *Steveston*, trying to shift that ground which is usually background for the figure so it becomes foreground" ("Between" 103). The characters of Steveston are so vividly present in the poem cycle that one cannot describe this ground as simply altered but must recognize the intersection between people and place, and their interdependence. Further, these shifting perspectives of figure and ground and the border between them constitute the narrator's imaginary, her "primary images"; this imaginary effects the feminizing of the landscape and the blending of the female figure with it. Accordingly, these shifting perspectives situate her as auto/biographer; the woman who has been an historian, working with her team, becomes part of this landscape, blending and merging her experience with her perception of the world around her.[12]

Opening with the challenge from poet to reader to "Imagine: a town," *Steveston* draws on the documentary information of *Steveston Recollected*, including direct quotation, but shifts the "I/you" relations from those established in the history. The inhabitants of Steveston become "he/she," their lives still central, but the poet's voice now moves into the first person and invites the reader, as "you," to become "we." If "we" imagine this town, we will see it "running before a fire/canneries burning" (11). "Do you see the shadow of charred stilts/on cool water?" the speaker asks, pushing that word "imagine." And then, "do you see enigmatic chance standing/just under the beam?" Chance invokes the card game that Harold Steves refers to in *Steveston Recollected*: "apparently they were gambling or something, one of their card games, somebody upset the coal oil lamp and started the fire. It just happened that morning there was a very heavy west wind blowing, going about 25, 30 mile an hour. It just took right through, nothing could stop it" (40–41). However, Harold Steves, named and photographed in *Steveston Recollected*, becomes an [not "and"] unnamed "he" in the poem Steveston, his information layered within the dense suggestibility of poetry: "(A hall? A shack. / they were all, crowded together on top of each other" (11), presumably like the cards and the cans of fish lost to the fire. The edge of the table becomes "the edge / where stilts are standing, Over the edge of the / dyke a river pours, uncalled for, unending," invoking the edge of land and of continent, which water separates from another continent, another edge (11). From a particular and terrible event, Marlatt abstracts the chance, the high risks, of migration (for fish and for gambling men), and the inexorable nature of loss and death. At this level of profoundly shared experience, though not, of course, at the level of personal or familial association with the actual fire, Marlatt explores her own imaginary. For instance, she has spoken about dreams with George Bowering, the two of them likening dreams to poetry in that both dreams and poetry tell stories that only become accessible in times of focused attention. During the writing of *Steveston*, she tells him, she had recurrent and frightening dreams of the sea: "They always took place either where the sea joins the land, as on the shore, or in the sea within sight of the shore. They were filled with corpses, with dead bodies" (47), suggesting to her, in her fascination with the constant interaction of river current and sea tide, that the work she was doing had to do with death.

No sooner is the reader invited to "imagine" than the town (people running from fire) merges with the river pouring, and the chance (of people's lives, of cards, and of fire) "lurks / fishlike, shadows the underside of pilings" and then "flicks his tail & swims, thru" (12). Steves has described the wind as taking "right through," but no road goes through. Steveston the place is at the end of the road, and only the elements of life and death move through, powerful as homing salmon in their pursuit of meaning:

> "At the end of the road," she says
> Steveston is. At the mouth, where river runs under, in, to the
> immanence of things. (*Steveston* 53)

With this translation of history into poetry, Marlatt expands the material specificity of place (a town, canneries, a river, a wharf) and episode (crowds, a card game, an oil lamp, a fire) in order to abstract "chance" as this death ("bodies of men & fish corpse piled on top of each other"), this labour that the "trucks of production" also drive "thru," and the movement of fish at the river mouth. On land, "this marshland silt no graveyard can exist in," which merges with water, which "swills, / endlessly out of itself to the mouth," river and ocean meet at the delta, and the people who come here for the chance of fish share with fish the chances of life and of death.[13] However, when Marlatt's vocabulary is dense with suggestion, the sources of death are also capable of renewal in life. So, for example, that "mouth," which Marlatt describes as "such a powerful word" ("Given This Body" 49), is both that of the river, which swallows—fish, human lives, silt—and of the poet who inhales or consumes this world and produces the breath and the language in which it is new-made.

The specificity of poetic language both expands the possibilities of meaning and condenses multiple possibilities into the single word or phrase, which in turn allows an abstraction rich enough to encompass the speaker and her audience. If the river that pours (uncalled for, unending) calls up the town running before a fire, it is also unending both in its own rush from the lakes and streams of the interior to the sea and in the story it evokes of a fishing community poised on this delta for the return of the fish to their source. Poetry renders human habitation, the hall, the stilts and pilings, and the dyke, not just subject to disaster as in the case of an accidental fire but, more seriously, permeable or shifting in relation to the unending flow of time across this place. "Residue"—of human lives or fish lives, of water or of blood, is time that rings (or "circuits" or "environs") the mouth of the river and creates the delta that is neither land nor sea. Abstracting from the particulars of history, Marlatt opens parentheses that she does not close, closes those that she has never opened, and suggests the juxtaposition of the struggle for survival of this one community at this one time with the flow of antediluvian time (creating the delta from river-born silt) and the movement of fish from their source in the interior out across this delta into the open sea as well as their necessary return up the river to their source.[14] Exploring Marlatt's feminist poetics in 1986, Laurie Ricou explains these parentheses and supports my search for auto/biography in this poem when he describes precisely the large agenda with which the poem alters the ground of the documentary. Ricou sees "the labyrinth of unclosed parentheses" as a key technique in *Steveston* because "Daphne Marlatt is the absent woman recording, who would be in the poem if the parenthesis ever closed and the text returned to its main subject" ("Phyllis Web" 207). Not only is the poet's life deferred by her use of language, but she, like the other migrants of this poem, from the Japanese community to the fish, the land, and the water, is present only in transition, or in exile from permanence. Refocusing of figure and ground may alter the relations of human subject to ecosystem, but neither the men who go fishing nor the woman who positions herself in this community have therefore ceased to be present; they are part of what is significantly implied in this poetic revision.

Where *Steveston Recollected* locates information in chronology, *Steveston* as poem cycle locates human experience within the cycles of land, water, and the fish that bring these people to this place. Such location of the human in the natural world still engages with individual history, hence the voices of characters interviewed for the history, and hence, too, the poet's observation of hard and sometimes hopeless lives. However, the individual (humorous, courageous, resourceful), and the episode (vivid in living memory), become part of a movement much larger than the specific, part of cycles and necessities beyond their control, and therefore capable of becoming emblematic. Not least, the source being sought is not the point of origin, as in a linear concept of identity, but a point in the cycle that includes both life and death and is therefore neither singular nor final. Further, the cycles of repetition and return provide neither ends nor beginnings but the continuities to be found in disruption. They map the individual, contemporary experience onto that which is both historical and antediluvian.

Steveston, the place, lends itself particularly well to this kind of exploration. Geographers note that the "legacy of the Fraser Glaciation and, to a lesser extent, some of the preceding glacial episodes, is written clearly in the local landscape" (Slaymaker et al. 21). Similarly, though so much more recently, human habitation in its many episodes, marks the landscape with its human histories. When Marlatt concludes her first two editions of *Steveston* with the poem entitled "Steveston, B.C.," she is providing what has been at one time an adequate postal address as well as a reference to the times preceding any human history that she can tell. Her chronotope produces a felt simultaneity of present and past, and raises, therefore, rather more comprehensive questions about people in place than can be raised by means of the felt presence of this poet among these people at this time as in the documentary project.

In *Steveston*, the personal sketches and meditations that situated Marlatt in her documentary now expand to include the largest questions about survival amidst constant dislocation, about dislocation as neither isolated nor disconnected, and about the urgencies of movement and change. Further, this continuous flux that the poet identifies in Steveston provides the emblematic capacity to convey her own experience of belonging in movement, of exile as central to human experience because originating in the environment. When the specific becomes emblematic, it takes on mythic proportions, privileging meaning over information and not requiring the specific match of narrative with historical event in order to carry auto/biographical import.

WHY THIS PLACE?[15]

Steveston as geographical location and as multiple communities determined by geography and by socio-economic histories gives Marlatt the material and imaginative "grounds" for her poetic evocation of *Steveston*. Combining geography and history, Marlatt relates individual and communal identities (including, I suggest, her own) with the place in which she finds them. Perceiver and perceived share a site or situation that shapes them and shapes in turn the world around them; the intense layering of meaning in these poems, in which words that are repeated acquire new meanings by virtue of new context, supports my understanding of such inextricable relations. *Steveston* as poetry seems to enact Doreen Massey's theory that places, like identities, are articulated at their points of intersection with each other ("Double Articulation" 118).

Massey has complicated the relations of community and place by indicating that one locality can contain several communities (as Steveston most certainly does) and that communities are not necessarily place-bound ("Double Articulation" 110) (as those in Steveston most certainly have not been). She describes the identity of a place as therefore unfixed, with no single historical or essential past because the relations that shape it are dynamic and changing (115). In the case of Steveston, even the recent relations between river and ocean, between water and wind and land have altered the relative shapes of water and land and their possible uses for fish and for people. (Similarly, Edith Turner notes, Wakayama is a "conglomerate of small islands joined through years of time by delta formation at the mouth of the Kinokawa River"). Human habitation has also been dynamic and changing, involving seasonal migrations for native fishing followed by trans-Pacific migration for work and for trade. These human uses, in turn, have altered the very lie of the land with rather more than ditches and dykes, ramshackle canneries and housing and then, increasingly, mechanization, industry, paved roads and dense housing; historians note that "the Steveston waterfront has Chinese sand as well as sand from the Fraser River" because windjammers in the 1890s used to travel from the far East loaded with sand as ballast, which they dumped and replaced with fish for the return journey (Stacey 2). Ironically, the very constituents of place have migrated across the Pacific like the people and the fish. The edges or borders of Asia and North America are implicated in the drifts of people and fish, water and land.

In relation to these larger movements, the plight of the particular immigrant community, or the particular immigrant, is both specific and necessarily resonant. Massey writes of place as a source of stability in these circumstances: "When time-space compression is seen as disorienting," she observes, invoking the chronotope that Marlatt uses in poetry though not in documentary, "and as threatening to fracture personal identities (as well as those of place) then a recourse to place as a source of authenticity and stability may be one of the responses" (*Space* 122). For Massey, as for Marlatt, and as for most immigrants, place may be simultaneously a memory, a desire, and a current location. What works so exceptionally well for *Steveston* is the capacity of this place, by virtue of its very instability and its relation to other places (like words in a poem), to both contain and suggest the haunted, the desiring, and the situated identity in one time and one place. Precisely because the flux and instability of human experience resonate with the flux and instability of this place, and constitute the relations of social and geographical place, the poem may evoke and interpret identities in terms of place without fixing them. Rather, these identities, in this place, repeatedly invoke the struggle for survival and the inevitability of change.

Enacting her exploration of place through time, Marlatt's distinctive long lines are tidal, reaching across the page, withdrawing, and returning. According to Marlatt, they push time, which she understands not as linear (which must end and so foreclose future possibilities) but as cyclical ("Long" 317), creating the chronotope that maps relations. Both the long line and the cycle begin with the poet locating herself in an unfamiliar world and entering the rhythms of time and place, of river and tide, of men (in the beginning) and fish. However, such rhythms extend, even in this particular situation, beyond the local to include distinctions between the local and the remote (the "here" of Steveston and the distant "there" of Japan or Penang), evoking the time over which people have repeatedly moved and settled, the generations of migration (for this fishing community and for Marlatt herself). Marlatt's long line pushing time, and her cycles circling place, together locate the poet and her Steveston population in time and place that are not limited but include all the possibilities of each.

Marlatt herself identifies the image of "a network, the ways in which all of the poems & all of a poem's parts, as all of us & where we live, are interconnected....It moves around & around its own end where the river disappears, & it ends," like the river of Kwakiutl legend, "when it can go no further, where it dives back in to the heart of things" ("Long" 317). Certainly, the nets and webs that recur throughout the cycle map the network of the delta. Similarly, the heart of things echoes Marlatt's "source," the headwater to which salmon must return, like the poet locating herself in body and in imagination in order to generate a new journey in the text. Tropes of heart and head and body return to the physical woman as "source" of experience and of narrative.

These journeys are also sexual and procreative in activity and in relations, associating life and death, generating the generations of repetition and return in contrast to the stasis and end incurred by (asexual) disassociation. In the nineteenth poem, for example, the speaker's particularized experience connects memory and desire for a curious moment of sexual harmony:

> We've come to generations, generation, Steveston,
> at the heart: our death is gathering (salmon) just offshore, as,
> back there in this ghostly place we have (somehow) entered (where?)
> you turn & rise, gently, into me. (50)

The new poem that Marlatt added for the 2001 edition begins "generation, generations at the mouth" (61), and connects human refusal of interrelations with a natural world turned void and finite, though it concludes with the suggestion that the "clans of the possible...gathering, the chinook,/ the coho rivering just offshore are us" (62). "What *is* the body's blueprint?" the speaker asks, and "what is the mouth of the river now?" (62). Generative interrelation requires migration both literal and imaginative. At a profoundly biological level, the body's blueprint, human experience, like that of the salmon, whether guided by stars, the riverbanks, or the magnetic pole, knows the rhythms that move and connect across distance and time and that require this narration.

From the specific to the metaphoric, these poems enact the drive of masculine desire: the poet herself, young Western woman, is propositioned on the float by Japanese fishermen struggling to raise their starboard pole; in broader terms, the masculine adventures of travel and trade cut the water, matching in their drive the seasonal urgencies of salmon. Nonetheless, the movement of the whole, from specific to metaphoric, genders the world of *Steveston* female. The boats (she/her) are tenderly beloved, intimate partners for seafaring men. The woman who waits for the fish to arrive, or who moves as with sea legs across her kitchen floor, shares her rhythms with the spring melt, which brings the rivers in flood out to the sea with their silt deposits and their young salmon that will travel up the western seaboard and out across the Pacific until their year of return. These rhythms, too, are both tidal and cyclical, connecting experience to language, and connecting river and ocean and land at the river's mouth, spaces of incoming / outgoing flow. In *Salvage*, Marlatt revisits this theme of gendered movement, concluding with the "allure of the current she / rides their rushing out, her and the words all / uvial" (25). Because these connections are shifting and continuous, this female gendering structures the poem cycle and absorbs and carries with it those aspects of experience that depend on fixed or permanent markers.

For example, in the poem beginning "Pour, pour," Marlatt reiterates the urgency of the fish re-entering time and locates their journey very specifically in what Ricou describes as "oral mapping" (*Arbutus* 32). He notes Marlatt's mingling and blurring of the spatial and the temporal as place names work in her syntax to describe the migration of the salmon "wood-ward" to "graves" and "end,"

> past any tidal reach (renew) fish
> seek their source, which is, their proper place to die (*Steveston* 15)

The urgency of this migration depends less on place (temporary settlements found only on specialized maps [Ricou, *Arbutus* 32]) than on the purposes of life and death that these place names serve to articulate. Marlatt's "source" is also moving, given as proper names, themselves the signs of temporary settlement, or as the seed head on marsh grass in backwater eddies, or the forgotten life "glimpsed from behind tatter windowhanging" (16), or as the source of work and cash. The source of life is also the source of death, and Marlatt connects the varieties of both in the rhythms of this place. On the one hand, she is attentive to the ground on which she stands as a map that is both historical and geographical, and, on the other, she reads that map for all the ways in which it can locate the self so standing, both watching and participating in movement.

Curiously, because this delta enacts the repeated displacements of human migrations, it is preferable to alternatives of enforced settlement. In terms of documentary information, Marlatt draws on the evacuation of the Japanese to internment camps, Japanese experience "salted always with their evacuation and return" (32), the Hastings Park transit barracks and the mountains of New Denver both "seeming to / go nowhere" (36). In contrast, the dead-end (Gravesend?) road of Steveston situates the ecological imperatives of change, of loss, and of hoped-for renewal. The meeting place of Marlatt with her material includes the displacements of land and water, of the Japanese fishing community, and of her own migrant history, just as it records the abundance and now the loss of fish.

George Bowering, in his interview with Marlatt, expressed his surprise that the seventeenth poem, "Intelligence (as if by radio?" associates narrator and reader not with fishermen but with fish. Marlatt's response demonstrates once again how she uses the particular in order to generate the larger picture: "Chance is part of it, but the nets or the web, they're synonymous, what we're actually caught in. It can be as huge as the electromagnetic currents of the earth. It's what the environment is." When Bowering asks whether the very act of living catches us in these webs, Marlatt responds, "Right. It's relationship, & how tremendously interwoven all of our lives are with all of these other lives around us, as well as what we step on daily, the earth. What we move in, the air. What we move in also in terms of history. We move in an accretion of time, which we don't recognise" (Marlatt, "Given This Body" 81). *Steveston* operates as a series of recognitions. Marlatt's association, and the association she establishes for her readers, depends on identification not simply with human characters and situations but also between these and the patterns of life and death, of journey and return, of struggle and change and loss evoked by this place. Her foundational environmental image, the life cycle of the salmon, describes both the nature of this place, once known as "Salmonopolis," and of the people, including the perceiving and participating self, situated in place, which does not itself stay still.

REPETITION AND RETURN

Quoting Toni Morrison on "The Site of Memory," Marlatt writes about how "memory and imagination conspire. Morrison stresses terrain as the very stuff of memory. The immediate "siting" imagination leaps to, as if context were everything (and it is). Are we who we are because of where we've been? Does place...actually stage identity so that identity takes its shape from it?" ("Perform[ing]" 202). I have been exploring the ways in which Steveston the place provides the immediate siting for Marlatt's own imaginative recognition of migrant identities. I suggest that she sees migrant identities as far more than the result of socio-economic forces or the situation of minorities struggling on the margins of what others enjoy as stable lives. In contrast, *Steveston* presents migrant identities as subjectivities sharing the rhythms of the natural world, rhythms of movement and change that locate the migrant in continuous process. In this way, this "context" maps an identity that holds memory and desire in continuous balance. Further, Marlatt situates her perceiving "I" not at some fixed point of apparent authority but in the heart of the movement with which she identifies.

Whereas actual revisions to *Steveston* have been minimal over the years, each edition, the last most dramatically, incorporates changes that refuse closure. The documentary is closed, but the poem continues. As Marlatt puts it in another context, "Try again. Repeated attempts to articulate the problem of naming and the inexhaustibly unnameable contradictions of a self writing her way through the cultural labyrinth she finds herself in. Does she? Find herself?" ("Preface" i). To read *Steveston* as I have done is to connect it with Marlatt's theoretical writing and her novels, *Ana Historic* and *Taken*, both of which mirror the narrator and her subject in each other. Repeatedly, Marlatt's work locates the personal experience, with all its specificity, within large repetitions of historical dislocation and conjunction, loss and change. If Marlatt here is creating resonances between auto/biography and all that she demonstrates place to mean, then she may also be trolling for profound commonalities in experiences of migration, commonalities that can be overlooked in the contemporary study of auto/biography when it focuses on political and geographical specifics. For if this poem cycle includes self-discovery, it does so in gendered terms that override markers of permanence and therefore division. She also replaces the loss, as in "exile," with the repetition and return of the migrant—at home in a world that reflects her auto/biographical condition.

My reading of Marlatt, against the grain of the narrator's explicit subject matter, has most likely developed from those deep instinctual reactions that poetry provokes, so the question must be whether it has any implications for autobiography studies more generally. Whereas poetry is more likely than prose to fuse the factual with the metaphorical, this poem reminds me that autobiography in either genre develops its purposes and meanings from both documentary evidence and a longer reach after more resonant meaning; that all written text belongs in the world of language, and therefore of references that can be endlessly elaborated or deferred; that autobiographical narrative, implicit in this case, or explicit, as is more commonly the case, belongs in the evolving body of thought of the autobiographer's other works (in this case Marlatt on Marlatt as in a hall of mirrors); that the autobiographer is necessarily absent from her text, but that she can return herself to her text by means of association and recognition; and not least, that relational identity, commonly understood in terms of human relations, can also be configured, and read in terms of eco-relations—that is, both the natural world and the relevance of human relationship with it.

NOTES

1 My thanks to Manuela Costantino, Shana Hugh, Elizabeth Maurer, Joy Dixon, Michael Egan, Sherrill Grace, Laurie McNeill, Laurie Ricou, and Edith Turner for quite varied kinds of inspiration and support.

2 I use the virgule in auto/biography to indicate the close interaction between writing about the self and writing about others. Note that even if *Steveston* is Marlatt's own story, it is also quite emphatically the stories of other people.

3 Page numbers for *Steveston* refer to the Ronsdale edition of 2001.

4 For sustained and influential work in this area, see Pierre Nora, Slawomir Kapralski, and Miriam Fuchs.

5 In Appendix A in *Steveston Recollected*, Marlatt suggests that the terms "emigration" and "immigration" are misnomers for the Japanese migrations to North America given that the peasants, fishermen, and labourers who left Japan did so for work and expected to return. Their constantly extended time in Canada effectively stopped their journeying back and forth across the Pacific like the salmon they came to Canada to fish. Edith Turner's information from Steveston Museum indicates that Gihei Kuno was the first Japanese immigrant to Steveston. He came in 1887 from Mio Mura in Wakayama Prefecture and wrote home "telling of the abundant fish here and encouraged others to come. Agriculture was failing in Mio Mura causing economic stress. Emigration was the hope of a better life, especially for the young people. Eventually half the village came here."

6　In *Ghost Works*, Marlatt includes both her return to Penang, perhaps, given the title, in appeasement of her dead mother ("Month of Hungry Ghosts"), and her journey to England ("How Hug a Stone") with her son, Kit. These auto/biographical treatments of places, relationships, and identity would make for interesting comparison with my present reading of *Steveston*.

7　The project seems to have begun with Koizumi and then developed into the book project involving Marlatt and the photographers (see Marlatt, *Steveston Recollected* xiv).

8　Jeremy D. Popkin, among others, has located the historian in the writing of history, but I am not suggesting here that all documentary is, by default, auto/biographical. Rather, I argue that Marlatt is uniquely present in this work, and that she develops her presence in the transition from documentary to poetry. Further, as relations between verbal and visual texts shift from edition to edition, Marlatt's poem cycle stands increasingly clear of visual referents.

9　See *How Our Lives Become Stories*, where Eakin refers specifically to the work of Mary Mason, Domna Stanton, Susan Stanford Friedman, Bella Brodzki and Celeste Schenck, Joy Hooton, Carol Gilligan, and Nancy Chodorow (47–48).

10　Discussing Marlatt's use of the Kwakiutl myth of the ocean as a river that runs into the underworld and the rape of Kore/Persephone, Christina Cole suggests that "this mythic level underlies everything about which she writes in *Steveston*" (12).

11　For the uses of dialogism in auto/biography, see William L. Andrews, Betty Bergland, Susanna Egan, Mae Gwendolyn Henderson, Françoise Lionnet, and Kirsten Wasson. My use of the term chronotope here points to the interdependence of time (which is history) and space (which is social). Recognizing Mikhail Bakhtin's understanding that individual and society evolve together, I am here adding an ecological dimension to suggest that individual and society evolve in close relation with their environment.

12　Marlatt and Minden have both described how they went their separate ways and met to compare notes or to show each other their findings. I am focusing here on the poetry but do not underestimate either the beauty or the importance of Minden's photographs to this text. Most notably, however, in the 2001 edition they no longer face the poems as if their purpose were documentary (as in the 1984 edition) but form their own photographic experience of Steveston in a separate section. See "On Distance and Identity: Ten Years Later" in *Steveston* 1984, 92–95. The Ronsdale Press edition includes head shots of both Marlatt and Minden from the 1970s on the final page of the book and current head shots on the back cover, foregrounding the dual authorship of this work and the personal presence of both authors.

13　Slaymaker et al. describe the Fraser River as draining an area of about 230,000 square kilometres, or more than one quarter of British Columbia: "It is one of the great rivers of North America. Its delta meets the sea along a perimeter of 50 kilometres, and its active western delta front extends south for 37 kilometres from the North Arm" (29–30).

14　In his history of the sockeye salmon, Robert L. Burgner describes very consistent schedules for an annual migration of some 3,700 kilometres, coming home to rivers like the Fraser. Armstrong suggests that these migrations have taken place for about a million years ("Unclean Tides").

15 Chris Hall describes *Steveston* as "a topography of the human mind, its concerns and emotions, above all, its quest for fulfillment" and writes of "the mediation of place" (156).

CHERYL SUZACK

LAW STORIES AS LIFE STORIES

JEANNETTE LAVELL, YVONNE BÉDARD,
AND *HALFBREED*

Realism locates its language within the postcolonial condition...lived experience does not achieve its articulation through autobiography, but through that other third-person narrative known as the law.

— Sara Suleri, "Woman Skin Deep" (766)

This chapter explores how legal texts inform and complicate our reading of the life stories of Aboriginal[1] women, in order to claim legal texts as an overlooked discursive arena within which to recover the historical and cultural formation of Aboriginal women's social subjectivity and agency in the Canadian nation state. It also argues for a consideration of legal texts as an under-represented yet necessary context in the formation of autobiography studies. The essay begins with a series of court cases that track the legal claims by Jeannette Lavell and Yvonne Bédard to retain their status as First Nations women following their marriages to non-Native men, and the subsequent silencing of these women through the legal process. These legal texts, I suggest, serve as an important material background against which to read Maria Campbell's *Halfbreed*, in that the conditions of production represented by the court cases complicate literary/critical approaches to the text that privilege an idealized reading of Campbell's life story and that construct Campbell as an agent in her own self-transformation. Such readings, I propose, overlook the social and cultural conditions that constrain Aboriginal women in society and that provide an important condition of production for Campbell's life story. In claiming the discourse of law as a complement to the discourse of Aboriginal women's life stories, I suggest that reading the generic conventions of law and autobiography together can interpret life stories to different political ends and articulate a politically committed Aboriginal feminist practice that facilitates a politics of needs.

THE REINSTATEMENT CLAIMS OF JEANNETTE LAVELL
AND YVONNE BÉDARD

In the winter of 1973, Jeannette Lavell and Yvonne Bédard captured the interest of Aboriginal communities across Canada when their challenges to the membership provisions in Indian Act legislation appeared before the Supreme Court. Born Jeannette Vivian Corbiere of Indian parents at the Wikwemikong Reserve on Manitoulin Island, Lavell appealed the removal of her name from the Wikwemikong band list following her marriage to David Mills Lavell, who was neither Indian nor a member of an already existing Indian band (Re Lavell *Ontario Reports* 1, 391). Her appeal first appeared in the York Judicial District County Court, where her lawyer argued that the removal of her name from the band list constituted discrimination against her on the basis of sex. Under the terms of the band membership provisions in section 12(1)(b) of the Indian Act,[2] Lavell lost her status as an Indian woman because of her marriage to a "non-Indian man." Band membership provisions for Indian men, however, did not impose the same penalty for Indian men who married non-Indian women.[3] Counsel for Lavell claimed that section 12 (1)(b) of the Indian Act deprived Lavell of "equality before the law" (390). According to the Canadian Bill of Rights, counsel claimed, this section was "rendered inoperative" because it violated the equality provisions stipulated under part 2 of the bill.[4] Her lawyer contended that Lavell should therefore be reinstated as a member of the Wikwemikong Band in light of the discriminatory provisions enacted by Indian Act legislation (393). Judge Grossberg disagreed. He stated that because Lavell "entered into a voluntary marriage," her "status" as a married woman "imposed on her the same obligations [that it] imposed on all other Canadian married females." Through marriage, he continued, Lavell enjoyed "the same rights and privileges as all other Canadian married [women]" (394). Given her preferential status as a married woman, Lavell was not "deprived of any human rights or freedoms contemplated by the *Canadian Bill of Rights*," and, accordingly, could not claim to have been denied "equality before the law" (394, 393). Judge Grossberg dismissed the appeal by Lavell and upheld the decision by the Registrar of the Department of Citizenship and Immigration to delete Lavell's name from the Wikwemikong band list. In concluding his remarks, he noted that "if s. 12(1)(b) is distasteful or undesirable to Indians, they themselves can arouse public conscience, and thereby stimulate Parliament by legislative amendment to correct any unfairness or unjustice...s. 12(1)(b) of the *Indian Act* is not rendered inoperative under the *Canadian Bill of Rights*" (395-96). Following the court's upholding the termination of her band membership, Lavell appealed the decision to the Federal Court of Canada.[5]

Yvonne Bédard was born of full-blooded Indian parents on the Six Nations Reserve in Brant County. She married a man of non-Indian inheritance and lived with him and their two children off-reserve for a number of years. When she returned to the reserve after her separation from her husband, the Council of Six Nations notified her that subsequent to her fourteen-month residency she was expected to dispose of the property bequeathed to her in her mother's will and quit her occupancy of the house and the Six Nations Indian Reserve (*Bédard v. Isaac et al.* 393). Bédard's case appeared before the Ontario High Court of Justice, where her lawyer argued that the request to quit the Six Nations reserve and the removal of Bédard's name from the Band Register constituted "actions that discriminate against her by reason of her race and her sex" because her right to occupy band property was contingent upon her status as an Indian woman (394). Bédard's lawyer contended that under the provisions of section 1(a) of the Canadian Bill of Rights, Bédard had been denied her "right to the 'enjoyment of property, and the right not to be deprived thereof except by due process of law'" (394). Her lawyer filed an injunction to restrain the Council of Six Nations from expelling Bédard and her two infant children from the reserve, and sought a ruling on the prevailing interpretation of race and sex distinctions in Indian Act legislation (391).

The Bédard/Lavell cases became linked after Judge Osler in the Supreme Court of Ontario invoked as legal precedent the decision by the Appeal Division of the Federal Court to reinstate Jeannette Lavell as a member of the Wikwemikong Band. The appellate court voted unanimously in Lavell's favour to "set aside the decision of Judge Grossberg" and to "refer the matter back to him to be disposed of on the basis that the provisions of the *Indian Act* are inoperative to deprive the applicant of her right to registration as a member of the Wikwemikong Band of Indians" (Re Lavell *Criminal Law Quarterly* 241). Following the reasoning established by the appellate court, Judge Osler stated in the Bédard decision that not only did the *Indian Act* "discriminate by reason of sex with respect to the rights of an individual to the enjoyment of property" (*Bédard v. Isaac et al.*), but it also, he claimed, produced "a different result with respect to the rights of an Indian woman who marries a person other than an Indian" than it did for "a male Indian [who] marries a person other than an Indian, or an Indian who is a member of another band" (396). Setting aside the "larger question" of "whether virtually the entire *Indian Act*...may be said to be a valid exercise of the powers of Parliament and may remain in force despite the *Canadian Bill of Rights*" (396), Judge Osler declared section 12(1)(b) of the Indian Act inoperative under the Canadian Bill of Rights and invalidated "all acts of the Band [Council] and of the District Supervisor" in revoking Bédard's status and rescinding her right to occupy property on the reserve (397). Bédard was granted an injunction to restrain the Council of Six Nations from expelling her from her home, and an order was passed overturning the resolution by the Band Council that Bédard dispose of her property (397).

The reinstatements of Lavell and Bédard to band membership and the Supreme Court of Ontario's recognition of Bédard's right to occupy property on the reserve did not go uncontested. In January 1973, both women appeared before the Supreme Court of Canada as respondents in an appeal launched by the Attorney General of Canada in Lavell's case and representatives from the Council of Six Nations in Bédard's. The Supreme Court allowed the reasoning established by the High Court of Justice in the Bédard decision and considered both cases together (*A.G. of Can. v. Lavell— Isaac v. Bédard* 1352). Intervenant status was granted to several organizations and individuals who, because of their political dispositions with regard to Indian Act legislation, appeared before the court either as intervenants on behalf of the reinstatements of Lavell and Bedard or in opposition to them. Support for the women's claims thus coalesced in opposition to the discriminatory provisions of Indian Act legislation. The following associations challenged the act's validity: the Native Council of Canada, a national organization established on behalf of Métis and Non-Status Indians, which argued that "Native rights…should be derived from one's racial and cultural organizations rather than from the discriminatory provisions of the *Indian Act*" (Factum of the Native Council of Canada 4); the Alberta Committee of Indian Rights for Indian Women Incorporated, an advocacy group representing several women's clubs and individuals, which contended that "if the *Indian Act* is for the protection of Indians as is alleged, then that protection…should be afforded equally to both sexes" (8); and the Anishnawbekwek of Ontario Incorporated, which claimed that "those sections of the *Indian Act* which were applied by the Registrar to effect the deletion of the name of the respondent from the Band List solely because of her marriage to a non-Indian, create [a series of] inequalities…based upon classifications of race…[and]…sex…'to which federal legislation must respond'" (Factum of the Anishnawbekwek of Ontario 7, 12).

Opposition to Lavell's and Bédard's reinstatements privileged the membership provisions of Indian Act legislation yet articulated these regulations as "special status" that protected the "customs of the Indian" and the practices of Indian communities (Factum of the Treaty Voice of Alberta Association 3). Support for Indian Act legislation issued from the Treaty Voice of Alberta Association, which claimed that "the customs of the Indian people are exactly the provisions set out in the *Indian Act*" (2); from national and provincial Indian organizations, which disagreed with the "present status system in the *Indian Act*," but nevertheless supported the Attorney General of Canada's proposal that "any such revision [to Indian Act legislation] is properly the task of Parliament" (Factum of the Indian Organizations 2); and from the Council of Six Nations which, in addition to asserting their legal standing as the "duly constituted governing body of the Six Nations Band and Reserve pursuant to the provisions of the *Indian Act*, R.S.C. (1970)" (Factum of the Appellants 3), also stated that "the provisions of the *Indian Act*, R.S.C. (1970) c. I-6 and particularly Sections 12 (1)(b)...are paramount and must prevail in the event that such provisions are held to be inconsistent with the provisions of the *Canadian Bill of Rights*" (11).

The court's authorization of intervenant status to several political organizations disavowed recognition of Lavell's and Bédard's claims to racial and sexual discrimination under the terms of the membership provisions in Indian Act legislation and realigned their challenge to these provisions as a conflict about the constitutional validity of Indian Act policy in relation to the Canadian Bill of Rights. This realignment created a dilemma for the Supreme Court of Canada. To uphold the women's claims to Indian Act identity, the court had to acknowledge the problem of racial discrimination in British North America Act legislation. To deny the women's claims to Indian Act identity, the court had to recognize the sexual discrimination provisions in Indian Act legislation. In a paradigmatic move that disavowed the sexism of official state policy and sustained the race politics of Indian Act legislation, the Supreme Court upheld the appeals by the Attorney General of Canada, the national and provincial Indian organizations of Canada, and the Council of Six Nations. Jeannette Lavell and Yvonne Bédard lost their status as Indian women and were forced to leave their reserve communities.[6]

ABORIGINAL WOMEN AND THE PROBLEM OF INTERSECTIONALITY

The failed attempts by Lavell and Bédard to appropriate the judicial system to secure legal recognition of their status as First Nations women in order to live as legitimate members within their Aboriginal communities expose how legal discourse renders visible a decisive intersection between lived experience and social power. These court cases[7] also enumerate how legal texts engender life stories. In what follows, I argue for an analysis of the intersections between race and gender determinations in social and legal discourse in order to explain how indigenous women are positioned at the intersection of race and gender discourses within the nation-state. Understanding the "intersectionality" (Crenshaw 140) of indigenous women's experiences makes clear Aboriginal women's socio-cultural status as racialized subjects, and, together with a conceptualization of colonial state power, illuminates the process through which state policies authorize and perpetuate the life struggles of Aboriginal women within Native communities at the same time as they abrogate Aboriginal women's socio-cultural empowerment through legal, legislative, and political means. Such an analysis discerns the doubling process of subject-constitution engendered by state legislation such as the Indian Act. On the one hand, this legislation attributes the idea of *autonomy* to Aboriginal women in their claims for equal treatment with Indian men in order to disavow the historical dimensions of their gendered experiences. On the other, it privileges an undifferentiated interpretation of Aboriginal identity in legislative policies such as the British North America Act to secure a homogeneous vision of Aboriginal communities by denying the gender differences of Aboriginal women's racialized subjectivity. Kimberle Crenshaw's theorization of "intersectional experience" as a form of analysis that "is greater than the sum of racism and sexism" (140) provides one approach to understanding this complex social and political process, for it shows how "crosscutting forces establish gender norms and how the conditions of [race] subordination wholly frustrate access to these norms" (156).

In what follows, I undertake a form of race and gender intersectional analysis, focusing on the devaluing of Aboriginal women's identities by the state. Rather than affirm Crenshaw's proposal that gender is subordinated to race in affirmative action analyses of racism (161), I wish to ask instead if "the paradigmatic political and theoretical dilemma created by the intersection of race and gender" that Crenshaw explores, in which "Black women are caught between ideological and political currents that combine first to create and then to bury Black women's experiences" (160), represents an "impossible choice" (J. Scott, "The Sears Case" 172) in the assessment of race and gender intersectionality for Aboriginal women. I draw here on Joan Scott's recognition that "equality-versus-difference" presents an "oppositional pairing" that "misrepresents the relationship of both terms" and produces a "double effect": "it denies the way in which difference has long figured in political notions of equality, and it suggests that sameness is the only ground on which equality can be claimed" (174). This pairing, according to Scott, represents "an impossible choice" for feminist critics, since it implicitly claims that because "women cannot be identical to men in all respects, they cannot expect to be equal to them" (174).

The problematic identified by Scott through the oppositional pairing of interests occurred, I would contend, during a climate of political and cultural uncertainty for Aboriginal communities during the formation of national Indian political associations in the late 1960s and early 1970s. In that historical moment, in the interplay between the goals of state citizenship and the formulation of egalitarian principles by the state, the constitutional future of Indian communities was thrown into uncertainty by the federal government's decision to revoke the constitutional basis of the Indian Act and to terminate the relationship between First Nations communities and the Crown. The subsequent formulation of Aboriginal rights as requiring a choice between *equality versus sexual difference* envisaged Indian identity at the political level, which depended upon the strategic deployment of gender identity at the community level. I argue that the social and political context of debates about the 1969 *Statement of the Government of Canada on Indian Policy* (White Paper) and the subsequent disenfranchisement of Lavell and Bédard is an important condition of production against which to read Maria Campbell's life story *Halfbreed. Halfbreed* was written during this time of political transformation within Indian communities, when questions about the value of identity politics and equal rights, and their relationship to competing interpretations of Aboriginal identity, were widely debated.

Read as an intervention in social debates of its time, Campbell's life story illuminates her political engagement with a discourse of equal rights that is founded on the erasure of difference. My purposes in reading Campbell's narrative for its engagement with dominant political narratives of Aboriginal identity are twofold: first, I illustrate how this life story portrays the limitations of a discourse of equal rights that is founded on the erasure of difference; and second, I demonstrate how the interplay between identity and politics is recast by Campbell's narrative in the service of a coalitional vision of Aboriginal women's identity. Ultimately, I argue that Campbell's life writing, in its assertion of identifications with other disenfranchised members of society, urges feminist critics to conceptualize Aboriginal women's political and social identity through an invigorated notion of *relationships* and *needs* rather than solely through a discourse of equal rights.

I am also concerned here to intervene in the critical scholarship on Maria Campbell's *Halfbreed* by illustrating how the social conditions of the text's production complicate our understanding of its interventionary politics. In the emerging canon of criticism on Native literatures, *Halfbreed* has been recognized as a groundbreaking text by both First Nations and feminist literary critics. First Nations critics have claimed the narrative as resistant for its articulation of race and gender identities that inhere in Native communities. Kateri Damm, for example, privileges its "truthtelling qualities" and polemical style, which, she argues, "presents a more honest or 'true' depiction of 'what it is like to be a halfbreed woman in our country'" (98). However, this approach to the political implications of the text does not take into account how Native identity is embedded in discourse as a signifying system in which ideological positions are simultaneously inscribed and disavowed (de Lauretis, "Feminist" 12). *Halfbreed* is read for its ideological transparency. Critics render visible racialized and gendered subjectivity, but fail to provide a politically informed critical apparatus. Such approaches assert the autonomy of Campbell's text without situating it historically.

In a similar manner, feminist literary critics such as Gretchen M. Bataille and Kathleen Mullen Sands, whose critical practice recuperates American Indian women's autobiography for its expression of "a fully detailed account of life experiences centering on the personal growth of the individual, incorporating family histories and tribal context" (23–24), claim *Halfbreed* as a "confessional and personal account" through which Maria Campbell not only "f[inds] her niche in the politics of her people" but also "survive[s] the personal struggle" so that "she is ready to work to make life better for all her people" (125). This reading of Campbell's life writing is also problematic because it advocates an interpretation of Native subjectivity and women's identity that privileges the rugged individual as an agent in her own transformation and that valorizes victimization as an enabling condition in society.[8] Such an analysis disavows the material conditions that existed when Campbell wrote her story. These conditions emerged in the courts and complicated any transparent conceptualization of agency for Aboriginal women, as my analysis of Lavell's and Bédard's cases illustrates. Moreover, such a reading fails to account for the overwhelming sense of cultural, social, and political disempowerment that Campbell asserts when she describes the material conditions that prompted her to write her life story. In an interview with Doris Hillis, she states,

> I didn't sit down to write an autobiography. I didn't sit down to write a book. I didn't think I was a writer. When I wrote *Halfbreed*, a few

months before, I had been on a job that had meant a great deal to me, and I was fired because I was accused of being Communist....I was starting to have a political awakening....I was very vocal. I was the only woman in the organization, within the executive, and during that time, women—especially Native women—didn't speak out like that. So I was fired from my job....For the first few months after I was fired, I didn't have a job and my money ran out. The only job that I could go back and do was wait tables, which paid $2.50 an hour, or something. I had a friend who...told me..."If things get so bad, and you've got nobody to talk to, write yourself a letter." And so *Halfbreed* came. (Campbell, "You Have to Own Yourself" 44–45)

Writing, for Campbell, enables her to recognize how her subjectivity was materially and socially determined by the economic and political possibilities that delimited opportunities for Aboriginal women.

To argue the need to reconsider Native literatures in the context of their historical and material realities is to begin the important work of examining the ethnocentric assumptions that predominate in colonial relations and that appear as normative in literary/critical discourse. One of the characteristics of criticism on Native literature is a tendency to represent Native writers as preoccupied with a choice to either "assimilate or vanish" (Fee 169). This representation serves a double purpose in literary criticism: it recentres the hegemony of the dominant culture as an inescapable theme of Native writers, and it disavows the recognition of Native writers' attempts to construct cross-cultural affiliations so as to articulate their place in history and to assert a form of social resistance. As a "normalizing discourse" perpetuated by the dominant ideology "whose work," according to Mary Louis Pratt, "is to codify difference, to fix the Other in a timeless present where all 'his' actions and reactions are repetitions of 'his' normal habits" (139), such criticism disavows the complicated material histories and cultural locations that Aboriginal/Indigenous peoples occupy as subjects within the nation-state and as colonial objects of legislative processes. Following postcolonial feminist critics like Chandra Talpade Mohanty, who argues that feminist critics need to be vigilant in "uncover[ing] how 'ethnocentric universalism' is produced in certain analyses" ("Under Western Eyes" 55), I suggest that a politically committed critical practice attends to the ways in which it can simultaneously occlude and defuse the oppositional politics of a text by taking for granted the interventionary politics of its own approach.

Yet, conceiving the agency of the subject as it is simultaneously constructed within and limited by the discursive narratives of political and social discourse, and producing counter-narratives in the service of an emancipatory politics, remain difficult tasks. These tasks are troubled further by the tendency of Aboriginal critics to construct the field in terms of its "absolute difference" from other literary practices. For example, Lee Maracle in "Oratory: Coming to Theory" argues that the theoretical language of Western discourse displays and perpetuates the colonizing impulses of Western culture: in order to gain the right to "theorize," Native peoples must "attend their institutions for many years, learn [to use] this other language, and unlearn our feeling for the human condition" (10). Maracle argues against the appropriation of literary critical language to a reading of Native literature and proposes instead that Native literature be understood as a storytelling practice in a culture-specific Native context (3). Thomas King in "Godzilla vs. Postcolonial" suggests a similar impasse in the relationship between postcolonial theory and Native literatures when he argues for the cultural autonomy of Native texts (12). While it is important to recognize both Maracle's and King's points about the developmental logic within the field of postcolonial literature that reorients texts around a single binary opposition of the colonizer versus the colonized, it is equally imperative, I argue, to resist representing the field of Native literatures in terms of its absolute difference. If it is the case that Native literature is completely separate from an imbrication with other cultural narratives of a shared past and conflicted present, then the question arises as to why literary critics within the dominant culture should attend to the issues that Native writers address. Why read Native literature and why argue for its importance as a field of cultural production? To phrase this question somewhat differently, in the terms set out in Satya P. Mohanty's cogently argued essay, "Us and Them: On the Philosophical Bases of Political Criticism," "If the relativist says that everything is entirely context-specific, claiming that we cannot adjudicate among contexts or texts on the basis of larger, evaluative or interpretative criteria, then why should I bother to take seriously that very relativist claim?" (128). A partial response to this problematic in the field of Native literatures is to argue that the literature needs to be understood within the context of its material histories with an eye to critiquing the ethnocentric assumptions and strategies of appropriation at work in dominant critical practices. One approach to this problem is to formulate a critical reading practice that can attend to the imbrication of identity politics with political and legislative discourse. David Scott suggests such an approach, arguing for a postcolonial project that "rethink[s] the idea of the subject in relation to social and political identity" and "reproblematiz[es]" the "normative concepts of citizenship and community" (153) that are articulated for us by the modern nation-state.

GOVERNMENTALITY AND ABORIGINAL POLITICS

In "The Aftermaths of Political Sovereignty," David Scott locates a problem for contemporary colonized subjects who seek to advance their claims to "citizen-subject" identity by appropriating "seemingly attractive positions" (149) that appear to offer "a normative vocabulary [for expressing their] social and political hopes" (134). For Scott, this vocabulary does not express our political will but rather recontains our "rational autonomous agency" (152). This new vocabulary reflects the defining feature of our postcolonial present in which "resurgent liberalism" abounds and remains unchallenged (145). For Scott, the lack of a political alternative to the liberal nation-state produces a dilemma for colonial subjects who seek "through the democratic revolution" a "wider field of choice" that "carries with it the new possibility of freedom and agency" (152). For Scott, however, the appropriation of normative concepts to produce a subject "as the source of 'free will' and rational autonomous agency" (153) carries with it an ideological problem. Scott defines the dilemma:

> Modern power, and its political embodiment liberal democracy, constitute a regime in which power is inscribed within a *new* field of functionality (that of the social), in relation to a *new* target (the government of conduct), and in relation to new guiding or normative concepts (among them, freedom, procedural justice, legal equality, representative government, and public opinion)...one has then to read the inscription of the modern into colonial space not as the emergence of an "empty space" or of an "indeterminate" power but as a governmental *reorganization* of the existing institutional and political space such that by a certain number of transforming arrangements and calculations the conduct of the colonized is constrained or urged in an *improving* direction. (152-53)

In the system of governmentality that Scott describes, colonial subjects are "urged" in an improving manner that reinscribes their political claims within a "new field of functionality" to contain their political platforms within a terrain that has been arranged for them on behalf of the modern nation-state.

This system represents precisely the form of government representation extended to national and provincial Indian associations during the controversy in Aboriginal communities over the White Paper. The 1969 *Statement of the Government of Canada on Indian Policy* has been regarded by some historians as a minor occurrence in Canada's political landscape. Yet its importance as an impetus for political organizing within Native communities cannot be overestimated. Drafted as a response to the growing frustration of Native communities with systemic racial discrimination that restricted their rights as citizens and disempowered them, the federal government's White Paper proposed to end racial discrimination against First Nations peoples by removing their special status with the Crown and by terminating the Indian Act (Weaver 132). As Sally Weaver explains, "the white paper described the Indian as a person 'set apart' in law, in government administration, and in society generally. These undesirable conditions were attributed to 'the product of history' [which, it argued] had nothing to do with [Indians'] abilities and capacities...[but rather] with their colonial status as a distinct society" (166). Rather than recognizing the historic relationship between First Nations peoples and the Crown, the White Paper premised its model of citizenship on the eradication of difference. It stated, "This Government believes in equality. It believes that all men and women have equal rights. It is determined that all shall be fairly treated and that no one shall be shut out of Canadian life, and especially that no one shall be shut out because of his race" (Statement 6). The White Paper conceived of the problem of "Indian citizenship" as an issue that conflated structural racism with the problem of race and that proposed the idea of a political future for First Nations peoples that depended on the elimination of the social and cultural distinctiveness of First Nations communities. It forged a vision of Native identity that disavowed history and that legislated limited interpretations of legitimate Native identity.

First Nations communities recognized in the withdrawal of the Indian Act the removal of the legislative basis for their distinct status. In rallying to oppose the federal government's proposal, however, they confirmed legislated definitions of Native identity. Under the terms of Indian Act legislation, only status Indians had the right "to be and remain an Indian" (Canada, Indian and Northern Affairs 1). Despite historic rights to legal/national recognition, other Aboriginal peoples—those who identified as Métis, non-Treaty, or enfranchised—remained unrepresented. The National Indian Brotherhood, in their proposal *Citizens Plus*, constructed Native identity according to the terms imposed by the federal government, and thus appropriated a system of identification that disavowed the social complexities of Indian identity. For this reason, when the question of racial discrimination surfaced as a problem in the courts, the National Indian Brotherhood could only rely on their recognition of the Indian Act as representative identity in order to repress the threat of the atomization of its provisions within the courts. In spite of their acknowledgment that the Indian Act discriminated against women, they refused to support the reinstatement claims of First Nations women and thus foreclosed the possibility of reconfiguring the dominant paradigm of Native identity and community.[9] The widespread social uncertainty in Aboriginal communities prompted by the case and the rearticulation of the Aboriginal women's claims as a struggle between "Indian rights versus women's rights" impelled the publication of Maria Campbell's *Halfbreed*.

RECONCEIVING RIGHTS: MARIA CAMPBELL'S *HALFBREED*

For Métis women in Canada, the project of articulating the histories and struggles of "many different kinds of women" has been driven by political as well as cultural considerations. Until the passage in 1982 of Canada's Constitution Act, Métis people remained unacknowledged federally as a distinct group of Native people with their own socio-cultural identity (Peterson and Brown 4). While the lack of federal recognition of Métis people shows how dominant assumptions constitute the narrative of the nation "Canada," the arbitrary cultural narratives that form the fabric of the national culture indicate the problem of overdetermination in the construction of "Métis" identity. This narrative circulates as the sign of difference in cultural discourse and attempts to obscure the "heterogenous histories of contending peoples, antagonistic authorities, and cultural locations" (Bhabha, "DissemiNation," *Nation and Narration* 299). Jacqueline Peterson and Jennifer Brown identify the multiple determinations that attempt to secure a heterogeneous Métis identity as "corrupt"; Métis identity, they observe, is neither the privileged "white" identity of the dominant settler culture nor the authentic "red" identity of the First Nations peoples, but rather, is often pejoratively referred to as 'halfbreed,' 'breed,' 'mixed-blood,' 'métis,' 'michif,' or 'non-status Indian'" (4).

Although the dominant culture uses these designations to belittle Métis identity, Métis scholars and political activists appropriate the terms to illustrate how they may be employed resistantly as individual sites for reinscription and decolonization. Janice Acoose, for example, connects the name "Halfbreed" to a system of matrilineal family practices and communal identities that remain unrepresented in historical accounts of the Métis community.[10] Howard Adams retains the label "Halfbreed" to manipulate social conventions that would privilege the term "Métis" as a more "polite" identification. In Adams' usage, the term "Halfbreed" indicates its origins in the system of economic exploitation out of which the name developed. Recognizing the historical structures of racism and economic exploitation out of which Métis communities developed, Adams identifies how the name "Métis" emerged as a more polite term used by white settlers who considered the name "Halfbreed" a vulgar expression for referring to those people of part-Indian, part-white origin. "Halfbreed," according to Adams, was the name given to Métis people "by white traders in the early fur-trading years" (ix). Adams, in what has been referred to by Janice Acoose as a "gesture of defiance" (150), continues to refer to himself publicly as a "Halfbreed" (7). Métis scholars have attempted not only to forge relationships with each other through cultural discourse but also to build coalitions at the political level. In 1996, the Métis National Council, in conjunction with the Bloc Québécois, proposed an act to instate Louis Riel as a "founding father" of Canada. They wanted to recognize the common ground and communal identity embodied in the notion of "Métis" in order to destabilize the dominant historical narrative of Canada's beginnings that positions the Métis people as a band of criminal renegades committed to overthrowing the country.[11] I identify the interventionary politics of Campbell's writing by positioning her within a community of scholars who have attempted to politicize Métis identity and by illustrating how Campbell's articulation of gender identity participates in the political practice of decolonization. In Campbell's life writing, gendered identity is inscribed not only as a geopolitical social location that articulates Métis disempowerment but also as an imaginative site of social and historical transformation that enables gender reconstruction.

In *Halfbreed*, Campbell disrupts the dominant narrative that the "only good Indian" (Cardinal 1) is a status Indian with a vision of Aboriginal history and identity predicated on the recognition of difference. Her narrative of lived historical memory and subjectivity interrupts what Homi K. Bhabha calls the "transparent linear equivalence of event and idea" ("DissemiNation," *Nation and Narration* 292-93). Working through historical memory to restore an ideal of community, Campbell writes the story of the Halfbreed people into the landscape of the Canadian nation. She states, "My people fled to Spring River which is fifty miles north-west of Prince Albert. Halfbreed families with names like Chartrand, Isbister, Campbell, Arcand, and Vandal" (7). The recognition of women's place is at the centre of this narrative event: "Great Grandma Campbell, whom I always called 'Cheechum,' was a niece of Gabriel Dumont....She often told me stories of the Rebellion and of the Halfbreed people....Grannie Campbell was a small woman with black curly hair and blue eyes. She was a Vandal, and her family had also been involved in the Rebellion....Grandma

Dubuque was a treaty Indian woman, different from Grannie Campbell because she was raised in a convent...My Mom was very beautiful, tiny, blue-eyed and auburn haired....I was born in early spring...Maria" (11-15).

Campbell's narrative of her family history challenges the rationalized narrative of the modern nation, which permits only one representation of Aboriginal identity, by asserting the value of the personal and communal in recognizing the lives and relationships of Aboriginal women. Yet she cannot undo the colonial encounter that produces the differences of Aboriginal subjectivity. Grandma Dubuque remains a treaty Indian, Grandma Campbell a member of the Halfbreed people. Rather than dismiss these identities as rhetorical difference, Campbell asserts that Aboriginal identity is materially and historically produced by colonial dispossession. She writes, "In the 1860's Saskatchewan was part of what was then called the Northwest Territories and was a land of free towns, barbed-wire fences and farmhouses. The Halfbreeds came here from Ontario and Manitoba to escape the prejudice and hate that comes with the opening of a new land....fear of the Halfbreeds.... along with the prejudice of white Protestant settlers, led to the Red River Rebellion" (3). Unlike the strategy of the National Indian Brotherhood, whose claim to Indian identity affirmed a racist colonial structure, Campbell's narrative illustrates how colonization disrupts Aboriginal identity to displace an ideal of community with an imposed structure of naming and difference. Indeed, Campbell's description of the systematic racism of impending settlement and Indian Act legislation points to the dispossession of Halfbreed people from their property in Red River and to their relocation along the road allowance land allotments. The resulting loss of cultural cohesion and personal dignity that Campbell describes echoes tellingly with the sexual discrimination and colonial legislation that the National Indian Brotherhood enacted when they opted to dispossess Lavell and Bédard of their status as Native women.[12]

The resonances between Campbell's narrative and the court record emerge even more forcefully when she attempts to theorize the relationship between the atomization of identity and its production of a discourse of rights. During a childhood encounter between herself and a game warden, an encounter that the narrative seems at pains to recuperate as a funny childhood story,[13] Campbell describes how betraying her father to the game warden for a candy bar resulted in severe poverty and starvation for her family during his imprisonment. She illustrates how an imagined ideal community—represented by the dominant society—whose rights must be protected from the undisciplined rights of the subordinated individual becomes embodied in an abstract notion of social justice. She writes, "The Law will do many things to see that justice is done. Your property, your family, the circumstances, none of it matters. The important thing is that a man broke a law. He has a choice, and shouldn't break that law again. Instead, he can go on relief and become a living shell" (61). Campbell recognizes that a rights-based discourse depends on an abstract notion of the individual in relation to the good offered by society.[14] As Joel Bakan argues," rights are not just inert tools that can be used by social movements to advance their causes through litigation; rather, they actively structure the very nature of political struggle. Moreover, rights discourse is an important and unique political language because of its universal form and presumptive validity in liberal-democratic societies" (118). In a culture in which a discourse of individual rights predominated (Trudeau 358), Campbell's narrative articulates the dangers for subordinate communities of appropriating a discourse of rights to community ends in a colonial society. Her critique emerges most persuasively in her description of Treaty Indians who refuse to remain in solidarity with the politically uncompromising position of Métis organizations out of concern for risking their Treaty rights (182).

In perhaps the most compelling moment when her narrative resonates with the court record, Campbell describes her recognition that the community work she has undertaken on behalf of the provincial government divides her from the Saddle Lake Indian community and destroys her friendship with Marie Smallface (180). The sense of betrayal and self-reproach that Campbell experiences propels her to recognize her complicity with the racist structure of representation put forward by the provincial government. In a final critique of the idea that individual rights occur at the expense of community rights, Campbell articulates a future vision of community when she says, "I believe that one day, very soon, people will set aside their differences and come together as one. Then together we will fight our common enemies. Change will come because this time we won't give up. There is growing evidence of that today" (184).

As I have argued, one of the most interesting features of Campbell's text is her critique of the representation of community rights versus individual rights. Campbell's story also articulates how social and political discourses intersect to facilitate her disempowerment along axes of race and gender identity. For Campbell, this relation emerges through recognition of the Métis community's location at the intersection of material and social organizations of space that prohibit their economic empowerment. In Campbell's narrative, the Métis represent neither members of the white settler population with access to land as homesteaders (12), nor "Treaty Indians" with land available in reserve allotments (26). Instead, the Métis occupy the border zone of expendable land that parallels the road lines, thus earning them the name the "Road Allowance people" (16). The recognition of this geopolitical space allows Campbell not only to locate the Métis community within a historical narrative of economic exploitation, but also to show how the multiple intersections of race and gender produce the indeterminacy of the border zone that enables oppositional political consciousness.

I do not ascribe the oppositional politics of Campbell's text to her individual agency as a writing subject in an uncomplicated manner. Rather, I understand Campbell's text to participate in a broader political project of writing back to the national narrative by appropriating a standpoint perspective that articulates Métis history and identity from an invested position, which begins with a conceptualization of the "people." Second-wave feminist critics have theorized the standpoint for this perspective as "a feminist politics of location" (Rich 210). This critical approach emerged out of debates in feminist theory between subjective notions of identity formation that privileged experience as the basis for knowledge production (C.T. Mohanty, "Feminist Encounters" 74) and theoretical approaches to feminist practice that demanded a feminist epistemology as a site for grounding feminist critique (Felski 38). These tensions have important consequences for analyzing Native women's discursive practices. As Emma LaRocque has noted, "Native scholars, particularly those of us who are decolonized and/or feminist, have been accused of 'speaking in our own voices,' which is taken as 'being biased' or doing something less than 'substantive' or 'pure' research" (LaRocque 12).[16] To avoid the reductionism of arguing that Native women have unmediated access to their subjective reality and to recognize how Native women writers critique the material and social systems of inequality, I read Campbell's narrative of gender identity for its production of "a multiple, shifting, and often self-contradictory identity, a subject that is not divided in, but rather at odds with, language; an identity made up of heterogeneous and heteronomous representations of gender, race, and class, and often indeed across languages and cultures; an identity that one decides to reclaim from a history of multiple assimilations, and that one insists on as a strategy" (de Lauretis, "Feminist" 9). To situate Campbell's writing as an articulation of Métis identity that is "multiple, shifting, [and] self-contradictory" is not to overlook its interventionary politics in creating a stable representation of identity formation, a stability that critics have valorized for its life storytelling possibilities as "Campbell's autobiography" (Acoose 139; Grant 126). Rather it is to identify how Campbell's writing participates in a critical approach to social reality, an approach whose political purpose is to intervene in political discourse that constructs the narratives of the nation-state.

For, in Maria, Campbell constructs a protagonist who is not only outraged by the poverty and economic disparity within the Métis community but also dissatisfied with her socially regulated gender identity as a Métis woman. To escape from the poverty of her family, Maria dreams of becoming "Cleopatra" and fleeing from her community (18); she rebels against her father when he replaces her with her brother for the baseball game (33); and she believes in the promises of Jim Brady that the Métis people will unite to demand justice from the government and be delivered from their economic hardships (65). In a pivotal scene during Maria's early socialization as a young woman, Maria's great-grandmother Cheechum takes her aside and beats her with a willow switch for accusing her parents of not providing for the family (47). This moment of indoctrination propels Maria to believe she is capable of rescuing her siblings from the social services people: she marries a man she barely knows just to keep her family together (106). When this decision leads to disaster after the man abandons her in Vancouver, Maria finds herself abandoned socially and economically and begins prostituting herself to maintain a drug habit (106, 124). Even though each of these experiences indicates Maria's growing recognition of how her subjectivity is constrained by socio-economic restrictions and social expectations, each event also distinguishes the tension in Campbell's storytelling between the desire to celebrate her Métis identity, to satisfy her friend's request that she make her narrative a "happy book" (13), and her intention to articulate the systemic poverty and oppression that plague the Métis community in order to create an oppositional consciousness and site for social recognition. Campbell's life story suggests that, ultimately, identity can be a site for initiating political change, history can be a narrative open to re-signification, and discriminatory discourses can be points of departure for inscribing political consciousness.

Thus, Campbell pledges her book to "my Cheechum's children" to acknowledge a matrilineal inheritance alongside her recognition of Louis Riel's importance to the Métis people (11). She retells the story of Riel's campaign on behalf of Métis rights not only to insert a narrative of origins that begins with the Canadian government's colonizing practices but also to insist that her beginnings are forged by Riel's activism and by her great-grandmother Cheechum's resistance to the early Canadian settlers (15). Campbell's narrative renders the story of a life as it emerges at the intersection of race, gender, and history. It also recounts the history of those women who have been omitted from historical accounts of the Métis people in Canada.[16]

Campbell's inscription of an oppositional consciousness enables a more complicated feminist analysis of the politics of location, one that recognizes how Métis women are positioned in society through the intersections of race, class, gender, and historical discourses. Such an analysis provides an important point of departure for considering how our external social subjectivities have been produced at odds with our internal self-conceptions. Campbell's story thus constitutes a revisionary critique of Métis identity and of personal sacrifice. Her commitment to writing this personal history represents an obligation to social transformation that demands alternative forms of feminist politics and identity.

In keeping with the community-based ideal of political praxis that Campbell's text invokes, it is important to consider an alternative approach for conceiving a "Native" subject of feminist discourse, one that shifts the project of feminist politics from women's rights to a reconfiguration of these rights as women's needs. The life stories of Aboriginal women as they are represented through legal texts and autobiographies advocate a crucial critical perspective for undertaking this work. A politically committed feminist practice does not have to conceptualize these claims solely in terms of equal rights for Aboriginal women. Representing a politics of needs as well as a politics of rights is an important way of both reconceiving Aboriginal feminist practice and articulating the provocative interventions of Campbell's text.

As I have been arguing, the continuities between Campbell's life story expressed in autobiography and the life stories of Lavell and Bédard represented in case law disclose the shifting boundaries between political, economic, domestic, and personal spheres that illustrate the limited, relative social power of Native women in society. To address these limitations, feminist politics would have to return to explaining how gender identity gets constructed through institutionalized patterns of representation. Nancy Fraser argues convincingly that "needs are markers of major social-structural shifts in boundaries separating what are classified as 'political,' 'economic,' and 'domestic' or 'personal' spheres of life" and that "needs talk is a moment of self-constitution of new collective agents" (171). To challenge hegemonic patterns in the representation of Native women, we need to take seriously Fraser's recognition of our role in creating "bridge discourses," "linking loosely organized social movements with the social state" (174). In so doing, we would reprise our feminist positions as "the oppositional wing of an expert public," connecting "extra-academic social movements" with an "emergent pedagogical countercul-ture," and we would reappropriate our responsibilities as "critical public intellectuals," knitting together "new hybrid publics" with "arenas of social struggle" (11). The urgency with which Native women voice through writ-ing their problematization of the issue of "*who* gets to establish authorita-tive thick definitions of people's needs" remains, as Fraser argues, "a polit-ical stake" (164). Our job is to attend to these voices and to interrupt where possible the continued devaluing of Native women's claims.

ACKNOWLEDGMENTS

I would like to thank the editors of this collection, Marlene Kadar, Susanna Egan, Jeanne Perreault, and Linda Warley, for their excellent suggestions which have benefitted me enormously in the revision of this work. I am also indebted to the anonymous reviewers for Wilfrid Laurier Press who urged me to clarify my thinking on the relationship between a politics of needs and the politics of Native women's writing. Finally, I would like to thank Stephen Slemon and Mary Elizabeth Leighton for their unfailing support and encouragement of my work.

NOTES

1 Terms such as "Aboriginal," "Indian," "Native," "Métis," "First Nations," "Indigenous," "status," and "non-status" are problematic in view of what Con-stance Backhouse describes as the "historically impermanent, social construc-tion of the concept of 'race'" (7). This is especially so when exploring a wide range of legal and legislative material. Where possible, I have attempted to follow conventional usage within the text discussed. Needless to say, the most important names are those we call ourselves as First Peoples even when they are tied to the impositions of a colonial heritage.

2 Under the terms of application for section 12(1)(b) of the Indian Act of 1951, the following persons were not entitled to be registered as Indians: "a woman who is married to a person who is not an Indian" (R.S.C. 1951, c. 149 indexed in Venne 319). As Kathleen Jamieson argues, however, women who "married out" represented not the exception to repealed band membership but rather the rule. Jamieson notes that in the revised legislation passed on 17 May 1951, the "enfranchisement and membership sections were greatly elaborated upon and altered," thereby significantly "increas[ing] the disadvantages for women who 'married out'" and further emphasizing "the male line of descent" as the "major criterion for [band membership] inclusion" (59–60). The membership provi-sions, though contradictory, remain sweeping in their effects, for even as they articulate membership through the "male line," they dispossess women in sys-temic ways. One of most significant amendments for Indian women, known commonly as the "double mother" rule, stipulated that persons ineligible to be

registered included the following: "(iv) a person born of a marriage entered into after the coming into force of this Act and [who] has attained the age of twenty-one years, whose mother and whose father's mother are not persons described in paragraph (a), (b), (d), or entitled to be registered by virtue of paragraph (e) of section eleven [of the Indian Act], unless, being a woman, that person is the wife or widow of a person described in section eleven" (Venne 319).

3 The band membership provisions in Indian Act legislation exhibit what Constance Backhouse refers to as the "unabashed male chauvinism" that "makes Indian status pivotal to one's relationship with an Indian man" (21). The provisions declare under Section 11 that a person is entitled to be registered if that person "*(c)* is a male person who is a direct descendant in the male line of a male person described in paragraph *(a)* or *(b)*;" "*(d)* is the legitimate child of (i) a male person described in paragraph *(a)* or *(b)* or (ii) a person described in paragraph *(c)*;" "*(e)* is the illegitimate child of a female person described in paragraph *(a)*, *(b)* or *(d)*, unless the Registrar is satisfied that the father of the child was not an Indian and the Registrar has declared that the child is not entitled to be registered;" or "*(f)* is the wife or widow of a person who is entitled to be registered by virtue of paragraph *(a)*, *(b)*, *(c)*, *(d)* or *(e)*" (Venne 319).

4 Section 2 of the Canadian Bill of Rights dictates that "Every law of Canada shall, unless it is expressly declared by an Act of Parliament of Canada that it shall operate notwithstanding the *Canadian Bill of Rights*, be so construed and applied as not to abrogate, abridge or infringe or to authorize the abrogation, abridgement or infringement of any of the rights or freedoms herein recognized and declared" (*Ontario Reports* at 392).

5 Judge Grossberg's evaluation of Lavell's case signals the much more systemic problem of prejudice against her. Much of this bias is represented in his commentary with regard to Lavell's appeal. In his judgement, Judge Grossberg points to the "*dubious relevance* of the legal point [he has] to decide;" stresses that "*with no disrespect to her*, [he is] unable to accept her assertion that she cannot retain her Indian culture, heritage and customs and inculcate these in her child or children if she so desires" (394, emphasis added); and underscores the "appellant's *emotional and militant evidence*" (395, emphasis added). Judge Grossberg's interpretation of Lavell's appeal exposes the added dimension of race discrimination that she experienced before the court, for not only did Judge Grossberg rule against her claim in arriving at his decision, but he also exposed her to the humiliation of disavowing the legitimacy of her concerns for the retention of her family and culture. Lavell glosses the problem of court bias in an acceptance speech she gave in 1990. In it she states that "Judge Grossberg made some very nice comments in the courtroom about how I should be happy to no longer legally be an Indian and glad that marriage to David took me away from the terrible reserves. He also said that I wanted to have my cake and eat it too. That was my introduction to the Canadian justice system" ("Award Address" 22). One of the advantages of reading the earlier decision next to the later cases is to recognize how subsequent judgements *narrow* the perspective of the court to the legal question at hand so as to eliminate the level of affective subordination that minority groups experience as a result of their appeal to the judiciary for resolution of their claims.

6   The court's disenfranchisement of Lavell and Bédard fails to register the enormity of losses that Indian women suffer as a consequence of their exclusion from band membership through Indian Act legislation. As Kathleen Jamieson argues in *Indian Women and the Law in Canada: Citizens Minus*, the disadvantages to Indian women traverse their social, political, economic, and civil rights (1). Jamieson states, "the consequences for the Indian woman of the application of section 12(1)(b) of the Indian Act extend from marriage to the grave—and even beyond that. The woman, on marriage, must leave her parents' home and must dispose of any property she does hold. She may be prevented from inheriting property left to her by her parents. She cannot take any further part in band business. Her children are not recognized as Indian and are therefore denied access to [the] cultural and social amenities of the Indian community. And, most punitive of all, she may be prevented from returning to live with her family on the reserve, even if she is in dire need, very ill, a widow, divorced or separated. Finally, her body may not be buried on the reserve with those of her forebears" (1).

7   For an examination of the cases that explores their contribution to political and judicial issues through questioning the "legitimacy of the administration of native peoples in Canada" and as providing an "opportunity to explore the constitutional value of equality" (28), see John D. Whyte, "The Lavell Case and Equality in Canada." For an analysis of the cases as a challenge to the "kinship character" of Indian Act legislation (409), see Douglas E. Sanders, "The Indian Act and the Bill of Rights." It is surprising to read Sanders' scholarly assessments of these cases, not only because he legally represented the Indian Associations in their opposition to the reinstatements of Lavell and Bédard, but also because his analysis of their claims *as* Indian women infantilizes them as politically unsophisticated based on a notion of Aboriginal communities as "underdeveloped" because of their "absolute [cultural] difference" from non-Native communities. In answer to the rhetorical question, "Can we anticipate a women's movement within Indian communities comparable to that found in the larger Canadian society?" Sanders responds, "There seem to be two possible views. The first would argue that the Indian communities, as culturally different collectivities, may not be drawn into such concerns. In this view the *Lavell* case was an attempt to impose norms of the dominant society on a culturally different minority, and was, no matter how well motivated, just another piece of cultural imperialism. A second view suggests that the preconditions of the women's movement do not yet exist in Indian communities" ("Indian Women" 672). My concerns with this interpretation of the case are that the first view represents bad history and the second betrays cultural ethnocentrism. These views represent precisely the dismissive attitudes towards Native women's experiences of historical disempowerment by the state that Lavell's and Bédard's challenges were designed to address.

8   Gayatri Spivak articulates this problem by illustrating how Western intellectuals remain inattentive to the important relationship between social subjectivity and political analysis. Spivak claims that these intellectuals reinscribe the "sovereign subject" of Western humanist discourse as the normative subject of oppositional consciousness" by "leaving unexamined the forms of ideological

subject-constitution within state formations (275), and by reinscribing the "oppressed subject" as a "knowable object," and thus effacing the task of transforming political consciousness (277). Spivak suggests that the postcolonial critic undertake a program of investigation that renders visible the mechanism through which the "Third World" is made "recognizable" and "assimilable" to a first-world audience (292). This program would examine the "assumption and construction of a consciousness or subject" in order to expose how this process of "subject-constitution" enables the domestication of the "other as self" within Western imperialism (295).

9 The position adopted by the National Indian Brotherhood (NIB) in their support of the Attorney General of Canada against Lavell and Bédard was not without a sense of enforced compromise. As Harold Cardinal explains, the alarm raised by the "Corbiere-Laval (*sic*) case" at the mid-1972 meeting of the NIB in Edmonton prompted the Indian Association of Alberta to claim that "there had to be an intervention by Indian people against Mrs. Laval (*sic*)" (110). Cardinal states, "We realized when we decided to intervene that we would, of course, alienate the feminist movement, and that we would also lose some of our traditional public support. It proved one hell of a mess to get into, because no matter what we did, everyone got mad at us, and it was difficult to maintain a sane and rational discussion on the issues involved. We had one other problem that few white people ever appreciated, and that was trying to cool tempers on the reserves where this was a big emotional issue. It seemed that everyone on the reserves had come into personal contact with this problem: it had affected mothers and fathers who had had to make decisions about their daughters; people who had to decide whether or not to leave the reserve to marry someone off the reserve; old people who had had to make decisions about grandchildren. *This was one issue that had touched everyone personally at one time or another*" (111, emphasis added). Cardinal concludes by claiming, "There was an extremely strong feeling on the reserves that a decision had been made by the women involved [presumably Lavell and Bédard], and that they were going to have to live with that decision" (111).

My interest in the complexities of the problem of "marrying out" and my critique of the political approach adopted by the Indian associations emerges not from a desire to assign blame to these organizations for failing to recognize the political and community concessions they were forced to make. Rather, my concern is to understand how the manipulation of concepts and definitions by the parties involved participated in what Joan Scott calls the "implementation and justification of institutional and political relationships" (172). Following from Scott's analysis of the dichotomous pairing of identity and difference in the Sears Case, my understanding of the importance of the lessons of history is fuelled by a desire to "articulate a critique of what happened that can inform the next round of political encounter" (172). Since the issue of reinstatement has not been resolved nor gone away (see Danylchuk), it remains crucial to understand how these compromises occur and what stakes are involved in continuing to affirm an interpretation of Aboriginal community at the expense of Aboriginal women.

10 Janice Acoose's "Campbell: An Indigenous Perspective" provides an analysis of Maria Campbell's attempts in *Halfbreed* to recover the life stories of those women who have been overlooked in historical accounts of the Métis people. Acoose's thoughtful analysis of the intersections between sexism and racism in Campbell's life story illuminates how these narratives have converged to obscure and silence the roles of women in Métis communities. Janice Acoose's family refer to themselves as "Halfbreed" in spite of the current popularization of the term Métis (150).

11 The Act, identified as Bill C-297, reads, "Whereas not withstanding his conviction, Louis David Riel has become a symbol and a hero to successive generations of Canadians who have, through their governments, honoured and commemorated him in specific projects and actions" (Canada, *House of Commons* 3).

12 Janet Silman begins her extraordinary as-told-to account of the Tobique women's political struggles for social and cultural equity, as well as reinstatement, with a chilling reminder that during the legal battles of Lavell and Bédard, "Organizations such as the National Indian Brotherhood mounted a lobbying campaign against [them]" (13).

13 Campbell's telling is both poignant and painful, allowing the reader to experience at one level the author's childhood innocence and at another her abject sense of shame and responsibility for her father's capture.

14 I invoke here a complementarity between Campbell's illustration and Wendy Brown's assessment of rights discourse in late-twentieth-century politics as "necessarily operat[ing] in and as an ahistorical, acultural, acontextual idiom" within which "rights operate as a political discourse of the general, the generic, and [the] universal" (97). For Campbell, the abstract promise of legal rights works in conjunction with the Christian ethos of the nation-state to require her recognition of the value of these rights even as she is forced to assimilate her social position as unworthy of them through the state's moralizing institutions. Campbell writes, "One of my teachers once read from St. Matthew, Chapter 5, Versus 3 to 12: 'Blessed are the poor in spirit for they shall inherit the Kingdom of Heaven.…I became very angry and said, 'Big deal. So us poor Halfbreeds and Indians are to inherit the Kingdom of Heaven, but not till we're dead. Keep it!' My teacher was furious[,]… and I had to kneel in the corner holding up the Bible for the rest of the afternoon.…I used to believe there was no worse sin in this country than to be poor" (61).

15 At issue for LaRocque in these arguments is the manner in which academic work by Native scholars is dismissed as unacceptable in Western-controlled education systems because of the use of experience as a foundation for knowledge production.

16 See, for example, Sylvia Van Kirk's *Many Tender Ties: Women in Fur-Trade Society, 1670–1870*. Campbell's autobiography also invokes an important historical connection between Indian women who cared for Europeans during fur-trading times even though they were eventually abandoned by these men, and the Métis women of the community who are outraged when Métis veterans return from the war with British "war brides" (22). The implications of this passage

suggest that while the contemporary narrative of national independence equates pride with masculine identity, this narrative continues to depend on the devaluing of Native women. Christine Welsh's "Women in the Shadows: Reclaiming a Métis Heritage" provides a moving analysis of how these dismissals resonate for those who come after as "ghostly" relations haunting the gendered silences of the historical record.

JEANNE PERREAULT

....

MURIEL RUKEYSER

EGODOCUMENTS AND THE
ETHICS OF PROPAGANDA

"This is the war imagination made; it must be strong enough to make a peace."   — Muriel Rukeyser, 1940

Muriel Rukeyser is known as a leftist poet, a feminist, an activist against the war in Vietnam, and a supporter of politically oppressed writers. She is not known as an employee of the United States government's World War II propaganda machine. Looking at Rukeyser's papers held at the Berg Special Collections at the New York Public Library and in the Library of Congress, I found documents from her time as a propagandist for the American government. I was disconcerted—how does a radical socialist artist reconcile herself to serving not only a governmental but a military purpose? In seeking the answer to that question, I learned a great deal about subversion, about the possibility of bringing the principles of racial equality and social justice into an arena of militaristic politics. As well, I expanded my apprehension of what can be understood as life writing. In addition to the usual materials in which the "I" asserts itself, Rukeyser's papers contain forms, memoranda, and so on. These inform and reveal much about the person and as such are "egodocuments."

In 1942, Rukeyser went to work in Domestic Operations, Graphics and Printing Division, in the Office of War Information (OWI), under the Office of Emergency Management, part of the Executive Office of the President. The form hiring Muriel Rukeyser reads:

> War Service Indefinite Appointment, Reg. V. dated Dec 9, 1942, issued by Office of War Information, NYC. File: DWX;PLK:DV EO 9063.
> Visual Information Specialist, $3,800 per annum.

This bureaucratic little item is an "egodocument." Jacques Presser, a Dutch autobiographical theorist, developed the term in the 1950s (Dekker 8). He determined that the materials enabling an understanding of a life need not be restricted to specifically self-focused or self-authored materials. The wide range and disparity of materials we currently gather as auto/biographical life writings or practices may be considered egocuments—from the familiar, like diaries, letters, and journals, to the less familiar: wills, recipes, medical histories, and portraits. In this paper, I examine the documents produced by and surrounding Rukeyser's work for the American government, finding in the term "egodocuments" a way to articulate life writing that may have an objective or intention uncontained by the usual issues of "ego"—that is, some kind of self-aggrandizement or gratification that may not involve others. As auto/biography flows over, under, around, and through barriers that genre limitations impose, it may be useful to give some thought to why readers are so eager to see writings and texts of all sorts as life or self writings. Susanna Egan describes the unruly auto/biographical genres that "become moments of reality and knowing" (28). Her concern, beautifully, is with the genres that "like water, show us the movement of wind" (28). The egodocument will not likely satisfy the hunger for that degree of insight; yet consideration of the more mundane documentations of a life, the productions that are instrumental, may offer a way to assess that life, to see the writer as a worker in the world, and to imagine the effort of imagination and language required to have an impact on the world. The artist's words will find their way to ears that can hear them. Egodocuments, on the other hand, will likely have a more determined target. To treat the egodocument as auto/biography is to accept that self will stir the surface of life wherever it can. In Rukeyser's case, the memoranda, the FBI files, and the marginal notes are the tracks of her time as a propagandist for the American government.

As a functionary in the Office of War Information, Rukeyser asserted her poet's imagination and sensibility, irritated her superiors, and initiated propaganda that affirmed an egalitarian and democratic America. She would also affirm her identity as a principled person. Reading her files—which she, herself, selected and saved, another manifestation of identity—brings dry documentation into the larger context of the life; the egodocuments become a kind of signposting of the subject's interior. This matters, in part, because the unfolding of a nation's history is so often read through its official and unofficial documents. When these texts can be read as egodocuments, the life of a nation can be seen as one part of the life of a person, and, conversely, the person's life can offer insight into the shaping of a nation. When an ethics of justice (rather than a desire for power or personal interest) informs the life, the egodocuments may support a world view, as well as a world, in which justice can be imagined.

Rukeyser's own history is reasonably familiar. From a comfortable New York Jewish family, she attended Vassar and Columbia University, graduating in 1932. She demonstrated her belief in fundamental civil rights early. Abuse of working people enraged her, and the scandal surrounding the Union Carbide silica mine in Gauley Bridge, West Virginia, inspired "The Book of the Dead," her long prose poem using medical, legal, and scientific documentation in its exposure of the ruthlessness of industrial capitalism. This poem offered Rukeyser a "chance for intervening in, and shaping, the popular imaginary of the masses," which, Walter Kalaidjian argues, was one of Rukeyser's deepest passions (68). This desire to have an affect on public consciousness and values shaped Rukeyser's sense of the possibilities in the OWI. Rukeyser's awareness of the rapid growth of fascism in Spain, Italy, and Germany made the US's non-interventionist policies intolerable. Appalled by anti-Semitism and isolationism at home, horrified by Nazi propaganda, disgusted by inequality in American society, and eager to resist imperialist forces, Rukeyser supported the military (rather than economic) engagement of the USA in the European and Pacific wars.

Of course, Rukeyser was not alone in her views. Many leftists, however, insisted that the real war was a class war and that neither the Allies nor the Axis forces supported class revolution. Big labour unions, along with America Firsters, as they were called, including wealthy and powerful newspaper families, and even writers like Hemingway who had been thoroughly disillusioned by the manipulations of propaganda during World War I, all stood against American participation in the European war.[1] When the Pearl Harbor attack eliminated debate about the US joining with other anti-fascist nations in the war, some undercurrents could rise to the surface. The huge international forces at play seemed to be poised on a single sharp edge, fascism against democracy, but at home definitions of democracy were changing as corporate values gained authority over American principles.

The history of the OWI provides some unusual insight into that internal conflict over values. In October 1941, poet Archibald MacLeish was placed at the head of Roosevelt's newly formed Office of Facts and Figures (OFF). MacLeish held the view that propaganda and truth need not be contradictory and committed the OFF to disseminating as much war news as possible. While this ambition might not seem dangerous to US interests, in the eyes of the FBI and Martin Dies, then-Chairman of the House of Un-

American Activities Committee, MacLeish was suspect, having chosen for the staff of OFF mainly individuals fingered as intellectual communist sympathizers. The conservative government agencies thus kept close watch on MacLeish's agency.[2] This hostile view was reinforced by the deeply suspicious right-wing public, which saw both MacLeish and Roosevelt as war mongers and tools of a Jewish conspiracy. At the time, war news and propaganda were blurred in that two not always compatible standards were in place: the news must be true, and the news must not give aid and comfort to the enemy. In an effort to make propaganda and war news more coherent, early in 1942 MacLeish suggested the establishment of a unified, interdepartmental committee to coordinate the dispensing of information. This was the Office of War Information. On 17 June 1942, with MacLeish as assistant director, Elmer Davis was appointed director of the OWI. Davis was very clear about his own intentions: "It is the job of OWI not only to tell the American people how the war is going, but where it is going and where it came from—its nature and origins and what (besides national survival) our Government hopes to get out of victory" (Davis and Price 13–14). The OWI continued to draw fire from the right, which saw it as a swarm of fellow travellers. Alongside the OWI, the Office of Security Services—which later became the CIA—claimed a shaping hand in domestic propaganda. The OSS supported the militaristic exclusive concern for victory, in contrast to the OWI's ideological battle against fascism (Laurie 3).[3]

It was in the beleaguered nest of the OWI that Muriel Rukeyser worked to find a place for her own specific principles and concerns, and where she produced the materials I am calling egodocuments. In the late 1930s, Rukeyser was writing poetry and working for the leftist press, but unlike many other leftists—those more committed to international communism and class war—she urgently wished that the United States would join Britain and its allies in the war in Europe. She had long been involved in leftist activities and a writer for socialist journals like *The Daily Worker* and *The New Masses*. Like other writers and artists, Rukeyser found a place in the new Office of War Information taking a position in the Graphics Division.[4] Her work involved developing poster campaigns for domestic distribution to encourage Americans to support the war effort with rationing, buying war bonds, conserving rubber, and so on. As well, her office developed propaganda urging Americans to see themselves fighting with European allies against German and Japanese fascism. The Graphics Division produced visual and verbal images of the enemy as well as of allies and loyal Americans. For Muriel Rukeyser, this responsibility was an opportunity to help shape Americans' ideas about who they were and what they valued.

Rukeyser's files, notes, and memoranda, some longhand, others typed carbon copies, articulate the values she brought to the OWI. These unpublished egodocuments offer insight into the effort Rukeyser made to shape her language into a form acceptable to government authorities while presenting her vision of democratic America to the public.

One document consisting of five numbered, typed pages is of particular interest as it indicates the process Rukeyser went through as she composed an argument suitable for institutional consumption.[5] In these pages, Rukeyser outlines her plan for developing a kind of propaganda specific to a democratic America, critical of current practices and intense in its sense that America must be of a piece. That is, she attempts to persuade the wartime bureaucracy that its goals must reflect the America the war is protecting, not merely manipulate the public's will to win over a demonized enemy. The first page, dated 1 December 1942, and included here in whole, has Rukeyser's ink notes at the top of the page and contains sentence fragments and isolated words. I will indicate Rukeyser's longhand with italics. The typed pages sound the poet's sensibility as Rukeyser struggles for the right words:

> *by a tremendous and total effort, our civilization can grow in every part so that it can forever crush the fascist threat of brutalizing? Whatever good we have gained, and [?killing?] a great part of both good and evil.*
>
> Somehow, the words for surpassing, the word for a tremendous spiritual effort that will bring our total culture through, discarding and refining as it strengthens—that word is needed.
> I look for a line of encouragement to surpass oneself.
> I am not able to tell a people of endurance and courage to Endure, to Offer; but if I could tell them, from a desk as completely as I would with a dying word, that I know the great effort of growth will win wars as it wins land, as it wins love, I would do that. I would say it in every way I can: in poems, in pictures, in posters, in my life.
>
> Surpass. v.t.—To exceed; to excel. Gainsay—gaindo
>   Outdo, outdistance—>outlive, survive
>   Outgrow, expand
>   Raise to another power, scale up

Rukeyser is trying on a rhetoric of persuasion, mouthing phrases like "by a tremendous and total effort" and "forever crush the fascist threat." For her, however, the ready-made language of policy propaganda does not flow freely. She seems to lose control of the sentence with the phrase "fascist threat of brutalizing," and she interrupts herself with a question mark and starts over. The next line contains an illegible word, but any imaginable substitute for the illegible word leaves that line a fragment. She seems to be thinking aloud, as it were. Her thoughts outweigh and outclass the available language of propaganda. Propaganda rarely attempts to introduce whatever common elements "a great part of both good and evil" share, and Rukeyser in this egodocument is not able to yoke the complexity of her understanding with the language of conventional propaganda. Rukeyser approaches the problem of drawing the American people into support for the war the way she might approach a poem and from her experience as a poet. She knows what is needed: an expansive and substantial language. She seeks the "words for surpassing," "the word for tremendous spiritual effort," and "a line of encouragement" for herself and for others that will form the matrix of imagination and belief and faith necessary to encourage and to inspire. The repeated presence of "I" suggests how forcefully her personal will shapes her argument. Who she imagines herself to be gives the whole passage its force and reveals how much personal authority she brings to her task. What she says the people require, and what she offers and asks of them, is very much what she demands of herself as a poet and a person.

On the second page of this OWI document (typed on flimsy green draft paper, not quite onion skin—it looks military, like office walls), Rukeyser moves into bureaucratic voice. Her semiotic register leaves figurative language behind (though she cannot quite subdue the "I") as she describes and explains the necessity of vivid presentation:

> 2. WRITERS AND POSTERS [this paragraph is crossed out in ink with large X]
>
> Writers can be used for two functions in relation to OWI posters. They can be invited to suggest plans and main images for campaigns, and they can be called in to write specific captions for posters in process. But, since this sort of writing depends on a sense of imagery and conciseness in regard to it, I suggest that the writers we approach will form a group that has little relation to books or formal writing: people who have worked with film and radio scripts, certain political and city columnists, a few poets and

Rukeyser begins again:

> The writer can approach the planning of posters only in terms of imagery. His secondary function, the writing of captions after the poster is in process, depends to a large extent on the image, as well.[...] The writers called in to work on OWI posters need first of all to be familiar with this effect of reinforcement <u>of the image</u>.

Rukeyser is drafting her initial thoughts and correcting as she goes. The second paragraph is more precise and more assertive than the first, which she deleted. She omits the tentative phrasings: "can be invited to suggest," "this sort of writing," and "I suggest that writers." In the revised paragraph, Rukeyser emphasizes the role of the writer as a rather subtle one, not merely duplicating the message of the figure. The writers' words must show that they are aware of the effect the image will have. To ensure that this aim is met, she recommends a careful selection of writers from various media—film, radio, and poetry:

> Planning will require only those people with a challenging and vivid sense of imagery. Caption writing can use writers who have worked, in one way or another, with images which can be translated into visual terms.

Rukeyser envisions her own role as engaging with specific writers on specific campaigns, planning specific posters. For her, no mass-produced or convenient image or text would suffice; at the same time, no creative effort would be wasted and her intention to build a useable "fund" of ideas shows the economy of her planning. This argumentation also indicates that Rukeyser expects to have to fight for her ideas.

> As I see one of the possibilities of my position, it will be part of work [*sic*] to reach writers whose suggestions would be valuable in specific campaigns, work with them and with the artist in planning specific posters and in relating whatever writing goes on in the poster to its purpose and picture.

For her, the position offers "possibilities": her active participation in every level of the work, ensuring that her values would not be countered by anything her office produced.

In the next section of this five-page document, Rukeyser outlines her basic principles, particularly her insistence that the US develop a mode and method of propaganda that does not employ fundamentals established by the Nazis. Adolf Hitler, conversely, laid the fundamentals of effective propaganda at the feet of the British, calling the German propaganda effort in World War I "Inadequate in form, psychologically wrong in essence... inadequate" (Hitler 178). He saw in British propaganda a "fearful" weapon, of which Germany had to gain control. Hitler's articulation of how propaganda must work reveals attitudes consistent with any right wing agenda. His contempt for "the masses" is matched by his loathing of the "blasé little gentlemen" who comprise an intellectual elite. In his view, effective propaganda must work "chiefly on the feelings and only to very limited extent on the so-called intelligence" and "must keep its intellectual level to the capacity of the least intelligent" (180). Hitler goes on: "The great masses' capacity to absorb is very limited, their understanding small, and their forgetfulness is great. For these reasons any effective propaganda must be confined to a very few points" (181). Hitler's final (often repeated) point is that "Propaganda must limit itself to saying a very little, and this little it must keep forever repeating....Only thousand fold repetition of the simplest ideas will finally stick in [the masses'] minds" (184–85). Nazi propaganda emphasized emotional manipulation, repetition, and simplicity.

Figure 1. Emphasizing the difference between American and Nazi values and freedoms

Rukeyser observed that American propaganda methods relied upon the Nazi model and she claimed this as a failure of imagination. She insisted that the US must make a different kind of propaganda from that of the Nazis, and she outlined the ways that difference could be achieved:

A BASIC ATTITUDE
Because of the direct appeal and propaganda strength which the Nazi methods have had, and because of the wide appeal of *Mein Kampf*, with its unmistakable challenge to many instincts—and because of certain flaws in imagination of the defending side in any struggle, until it assumes the initiative—many of our propaganda methods have had a direct relation to Nazi propaganda and to *Mein Kampf*....

I believe that it is up to us to assume the imitative in propaganda— that is, on every side of the war. Our imaginations have been forced to the necessity of understanding such aspects of the military scene as total war, the new air power, the changed social community, but our propaganda methods still wait on Nazi initiative. I suggest that...a continual challenge to our people to keep the purposes of this war among their weapons...be given to them through this [OWI] division.

Rukeyser was repelled by the militaristic, sentimental, and demonizing direction of much propaganda. Like MacLeish, who asserted that "campaigns of personal hatreds, of hatred for whole nations of human beings are disgusting" (qtd. in Bredhoff 28),[6] Rukeyser wanted to distinguish between the forces of fascism and the forces of democracy without denying humanity to the enemy.

For Rukeyser, the purpose of the war was not merely to win but also to affirm the best of American values and the worth of the human spirit. She wanted to make Americans recognize the plurality of "purposes of this war," and that required extricating American propaganda from Nazi methods. To achieve these goals would take intense thought and imagination from the propagandists. She furthered her argument with examples and detail:

> There is not much sense in using a good many of the ground-impulses of the human being in our propaganda; for not in these ways do we differ from the Nazis or the Italian fascists or the Japanese. Recently, in a poster competition, the prize-winning entry showed a soldier kissing his little son goodbye. I would quarrel with the choice and distribution of that poster. The main image is so deep a human gesture that it has nothing in it to distinguish us from the enemy; undoubtedly, the love of children is true for both sides of our age's struggle. There is a wide area of meaning and feeling which is common to both sides of the war: each side feels it is necessary to win, to build the state in its way, to prepare the entire world for a certain way of life. It is not in this area that our propaganda must lay [sic]. It is in the part of our lives which is not shared by the enemy. That is, in <u>purpose</u>, in an attitude toward the <u>present</u> as <u>part of the future</u>.

Two aspects of Rukeyser's argument stand out: first, Rukeyser will not demonize the enemy, although she names the German and Japanese fascists "enemy." To acknowledge the humanity of the opponent has rarely been the position of any warring nation, but to assert that "a wide area of meaning and feeling...is common to both sides of the war" and to accept that each side feels it is *necessary* to win would likely outrage conservatives in the war office. Here, too, Rukeyser insists on the personal authority of "I" as bedrock legitimation of her argument. But Rukeyser is firm in her argument that real differences exist and that American propaganda will be stronger if it works on those differences rather than relying on either sentimentality or aggression. Her views bring the forces of intelligence, thoughtfulness, and will into the discussion. Her own emphasis indicates that she sees fascism as an "end justifies the means" way of life in which the present is cut off from the future. America, in contrast, must see the integral reality of the present in its purposeful vision of the future. Rukeyser moves from this rather abstract declaration into possibly mundane examples:

> Our posters should, I feel, deal with the possibilities that are still open to us, from which the fascists have cut themselves off, systematically and irrevocably, by their own statement and action....By adopting this program, we can keep our war aims and peace aims continually before us, working out at the same time a basic plan of propaganda which shares none of the drives of fascist propaganda, but which will appeal to any of the fundamental, healthy and fighting instincts.

What Americans have are "possibilities" from which the Nazis have "systematically and irrevocably" cut themselves off; the connection with imagination is merely implicit here (perhaps considered too ephemeral for this document). Only later, in *The Life of Poetry*, do we get a vivid sense of Rukeyser's meaning when she says, "We [Americans] are cut off from large areas in ourselves...less and less do we imagine ourselves and believe in ourselves" (44). She uses the same figure of amputation (cut off from) in referring to both Nazis and Americans, and she names what is being denied: "the dynamic character of our lives," time, possibility, and "the human spirit" (44). All these aspects of humanity rely upon the imagination, which is not only individual but shared: "The impoverishment of imagination affects our society, our culture, deeply" (44). Imagination is not a merely aesthetic force. Rukeyser claims for Americans "fundamental, healthy and fighting instincts," which include a will to fight for social justice and the common good, as well as for basic survival, and the imagination to realize their common connections.

Rukeyser believed that successful propaganda would use the skills of professional writers and artists, but imaginative power, she argues, is not limited to the contributions of professional artists. She added to the list of useful contributors defence workers, farmers, and schoolchildren who could provide valuable captions to go with the visual images on the posters. Rukeyser's aim here was to show that the war effort was not the property of the government or the military but resided in the common or social imagination:

> As for the "non-writing" writers who will be useful for work on posters, I propose to find them, too: defence workers, the letter-writ-

ing farm hands, school-children who may contribute not only reactions, but slogans. I imagine that the slogans themselves will come from these people and the forces rather than from desk workers, and I should like to try to work accordingly, planning and writing captions in the office, but looking among the "non-writing" people for the slogans themselves.

Figure 2. Encouraging American participation in WWII

Rukeyser also showed that she was sensitive to region and to local issues, and she revealed that antiracism and concern for diversity was an issue for some white writers in the 1940s:

> I think particularly of what work we may be launching. If, for example, we do something about regional discrimination against Mexicans in the Southwest, it may be most useful to call on members of the writers' group in Santa Fe....I shall make myself responsible for a national coverage of writers—however thin this may need to be buttered, for our work.

> The widest participation will be the most stimulating, since this work is, in the most profound sense, a venture in the imagery of war and purpose, as well as a perfectly definite program for poster work.

This statement concludes Rukeyser's enthusiastic and energetic five-page statement. At the bottom of the page, she typed her name and the date: 14 December 1942. Her papers give no indication of what her intentions were for distribution or readership. However, for an insight into her view of what the Graphics Division of the OWI could and should attend to, document is significant. And as an egodocument demonstrating the process of articulating selfhood in varying registers, it is invaluable.

There can be no doubt that, in her early days with the OWI, Rukeyser saw war propaganda as an enormous opportunity in the struggle to influence the attitudes and values of Americans. Her "most profound sense" of the "imagery of war and purpose" becomes clear as Rukeyser's later notes show. Her optimism about what the OWI could achieve was high, but for only a very short time. In early February of 1943, Rukeyser provided a detailed account of the ways the Graphics Division could be useful to the work of the Bureau of Intelligence. In that memorandum, she made particular note of the attention that should be paid to local race relations and to problems between labour and management. A few of her suggestions are especially telling:

> Boston Region: Poster on shortages (re-open use of Kollwitz picture or some other picture, with some variant of the "ask the women and children of starving Europe" idea)

> Atlanta Region: Manpower poster (now ready) [Rukeyser includes this uncited passage in quotation marks] "large bomber plant near Atlanta begins production...local recruitment to avoid problems of immigration. Special attention should be paid to role of Negroes in such planning. In Alabama, now, there is much friction between the races, which is attributed to the activity of political reactionaries who are creating race issues, 'nigger baiting,' to develop hostility against the national administration and its domestic policies"

> [Rukeyser comments that a paragraph] "like this is the strongest evidence of the immediate need for all sorts of graphic material"

> Dallas Region: Race posters (Negroes, Mexicans particularly) (In preparation, poster—The Future of the American Negro is the Future of American Democracy)

Through views such as these, Rukeyser pushed the morally and socially significant dimensions of what the OWI could achieve with its poster campaign and continued to work at establishing an effective group of artists and writers to further the OWI's aims.

While Rukeyser was expressing her belief that the best propaganda must show Americans what their country can look like *after* the war, the OWI structure was changing and the Graphics Division with its associated writers was increasingly pressured by an model of performance based on the intensifying art of advertising. Rather than basing their position on the MacLeish/Davis "information" view of propaganda, which held that Americans are intelligent enough to make responsible decisions if they are given sound and substantial information, new propaganda advisors argued that domestic propaganda (for conserving rubber, for example, or planting gardens) would have to rely on self-interest and private advantage to get the population to undertake the necessary steps to support the war effort. One of these new advisors was Lieutenant Commander Price Gilbert, former vice-president of Coca-Cola and a naval officer suspected of being charged with the task of clearing the radicals out of the War Office. Gilbert was the occasion of a particularly engaging example of the irritation felt by artists in the Graphics Division, who took seriously the four essential human freedoms Roosevelt named: freedom of speech, freedom of worship, freedom from want, and freedom from fear (Winkler 5). Ben Shahn and others are said to have made up a poster on which the Statue of Liberty was shown with four arms, each holding aloft a bottle of Coca-Cola. The text reads, "The War That Refreshes: The Four Delicious Freedoms" (Winkler 64; Burlingame 215). Frances K. Pohl gives a different version: "[They] took a poster depicting soldiers with raised bayonets and replaced the guns with Coca-Cola bottles," the texts reading, "Try Our Four Delicious Freedoms" and "The Cause that Refreshes" (123).

Rukeyser's exchange of letters with Gilbert shows her position as well as her exasperation, and clearly reveals the gap between the new authorities and the writers and artists originally hired to work in the OWI. On 12 March 1943, Rukeyser submitted a memorandum to Price Gilbert critiquing present practice and outlining her own ideas about a new series of posters on "the nature of the enemy": "The inquiry into the nature of the enemy has taken several forms: industrial cartoons will select Nazi or Japanese types, brutalize them, and set them up as targets; the big advertising campaigns will present scenes of horror, done in six colours, and will leave the meaning of these scenes hanging—out of inability to answer them." Rukeyser begins her pitch with a critique of previous poster campaigns and their reliance on bestializing racial and ethnic types and on graphic scenes that evoke revulsion. Her sharpest barb relates to the lack of understanding by the creators of the posters, who "leave the meaning of these scenes hanging." The scathing implication here is that propagandists have little comprehension of the significance of the war to their own people. Rukeyser goes on to put forward the new series the Graphics Division is offering:

> This series is the first planned series which the Graphics division has submitted as a treatment of the nature of the enemy. It isolate[s] a set of characteristics—suppression, starvation, slavery, torture, murder—as the parts of the nature of the enemy, illustrates them in a series of sharp and moving images, and stamps across the face of each the official answer of the American people—UNCONDITIONAL SURRENDER.

The effect of such a series is more direct. There is no point in showing material destruction, even the destruction of churches, by the enemy, now that ["our" is xxxed out] the bombers of the United Nations are answering the destruction of the Axis.

Rukeyser's argument is consistently grounded in the differences between the fascist forces and the allies. The brutal behaviour of the Nazis and other fascists (Italian, Japanese) is to be directly faced. American isolationism, Rukeyser implies, will have to give way before the direct exposure of Axis treatment of invaded peoples and the violation of democratic principles. Her honesty foregrounds the fact that destruction, "even the destruction of churches," is no marker of distinction, and like demonizing the enemy, is inadequate as effective propaganda. Her ideas reveal that she has no doubt that the allies offer a real alternative to the totalitarian forces and that, in keeping with American policy, compromise with fascism is impossible, and only unconditional surrender is acceptable. Her argument continues: "The Graphics Division has shown to the American people—working at home to back up its armies—what happens under Fascism to the people of Axis and occupied countries, the qualities we fight against, and the one answer which these qualities must receive." Ruykeyser goes on to describe five posters that would focus on specific aspects of the "nature of the enemy" and the effects of fascism:

> The five posters…—from the Millman head of the man gagged under Nazism, with its humiliation and broken protest, to the Perlin head of young death—from the protest of the tortured Kuniyoshi back to the protest of the Shahn man in the concentration camp, giving us in his look, suffering and responsibility—to the universally-moving image of the Kollwitz children holding their bowls up to empty space for food—these are all personal and deep-cutting images of civilian life under an enemy rule, a rule which in the nature of its qualities is hateful to the American people.

The images Rukeyser describes avoid the demonized, racist caricatures of bestialized subhumans. The focus, instead, is on the lived experience of people under fascist domination. The artists she names are of interest in their own right: Yasuo Kuniyoshi was Japanese-born, living in America from the age of six years but categorized as an enemy alien; Ben Shahn was a well-known labour activist and leftist; and Käthe Kollwitz was an honoured German artist, driven out of her country by the Nazis. These artists embody Rukeyser's stated position on distinguishing the principles and practices of people from their heritage or nationality.

Figure 3. Emphasizing the difference between USA and Nazi actions

In this memorandum to Gilbert, Rukeyser makes her opposition to the presence and policies of the "advertising men" clear. Pushing always for a complicated and intelligent presentation to the American public, she urges Gilbert to recognize the existence of "questions" the war brings to the surface. Her view was a direct challenge to that of O.W. Riegel, propaganda analyst for the OWI, who stated that "the function of the war poster is to make coherent and acceptable a basically incoherent and irrational ordeal of killing, suffering, and destruction" (qtd. in Bredhoff 29). Rukeyser wrote, "It is high time that we in our posters raised many of the questions which the advertisers have not been able to raise; high time that the government produced its own series of graphic answers to the challenge of the enemy." Rukeyser's tone shifts and she becomes less rhetorical and more hectoring: "It is high time" suggests that her patience is stretched, and her exasperation seeps out from under her reasoned, principled polemic. While Rukeyser did not articulate the questions she has in mind, presumably she was referring to the kind and quality of democracy that will meet Americans when the war is over. This concern, too, is implied in her reference to the "challenge of the enemy." Rukeyser was less concerned with military challenge than she was with the ideological challenge to elemental American values. The posters she describes cover a range of wartime suffering, each sufficiently specific to invite a particular response; whether that response was outrage or compassion, the viewer would be inspired to resist the effects of fascism.

Rukeyser's penned note at the bottom of the page may be her musing on further arguments or simply her own reminder to herself about her task:

we fight to destroy fascism—we fight to build the world—which provides a positive base—a starting point for our answer to the enemy, and for all of our posters calling for everyday sacrifice and resistance

Gilbert's response to Rukeyser's memorandum was an undated note of only a few lines, the most relevant containing a snide little rap on the knuckles to counter Rukeyser's careful argument. Gilbert says, "We must get across to the American public the idea that 'In union there is strength.' Our hope of victory will be greatly increased if we quit squabbling among ourselves and put up a united front to the enemy."[7] To Gilbert, the urgent questions of principles and practices that are crucial to Rukeyser are merely "squabbling" and must be suppressed for the sake of victory.

More than a month after her long argument supporting the poster series on the "nature of the enemy," Rukeyser offered Gilbert a more direct critique of OWI propaganda and suggested yet another take on the divergence between advertising aims and appropriate, responsible propaganda. The following is a memorandum dated 20 April 1943, sent to Price Gilbert, with copies to Elmer Davis, Archibald MacLeish, Gardener Cowles, Jr. (a conservative appointed by Davis), and others, signed by Rukeyser, Ben Shahn, and Betty Chamberlain (another leftist in the war office):

> To Lieutenant Commander Price Gilbert
> From Muriel Rukeyser
> Subject: A Poster Program for Identified Groups
>
> Government posters have not tried to use the best and bravest of advertising methods, but they have instead set themselves up as <u>another form</u> of advertising, using the same space and employing the same methods as any commercial advertisement. Posters are now set up alongside of other ads, and give the effect, often, of competing with those ads....
>
> In expanding the field of posters, it must be remembered that to speak of the war in terms that do not differ in any way from the terms of a toothpaste ad is to offend the groups in our country that have already shown themselves to be vitally concerned with the war. In total war, these groups are bound to grow during the war until the entire country takes its place among them. To present the facts of the war accurately and in proper proportion...to present the everyday reminders and orders in terms of the large issues of the war itself [is our responsibility].

To these urgent words, Gilbert replied, "There is no reason why noble sentiments should not appear in government posters." His tone is arch and ironic, and he reduced Rukeyser's concern for the "proper dignity" of the government's message to "noble sentiments." While Rukeyser, Shahn, and others were deeply engaged with the issues at stake in both the OWI and the nation, Gilbert ignored serious ideological differences and seemed to see no more than "squabbling" in Rukeyser's passionate belief in the fight for democracy against fascism. These exchanges offer a microcosm of the conflict that drove so many talented people out of the OWI.

Later, in *The Life of Poetry*, Rukeyser articulates her frustration with the lost opportunity to make American propaganda meaningful:

> During the war, an attempt was made to use writing with the work of some of the painters.[8]...Advertising men came in, telling the administration that ideas were their field, that the government needed their techniques. The advertising men made it clear that there were two ways of looking at ideas in a war against fascism. Those of us who were working on the project believed ideas were to be fought for; the advertising men believed they were to be sold. The audience, those at home in wartime, were not "citizens" or "people." They were "customers." No such ideas as ours were to be executed. The advertising men won, with those who decided that this was not a war against fascism, that it was a war to be won, and the meaning worked out afterward. (145)

By including this analysis of her view of the work she did with the OWI in her autobiography, Rukeyser clearly shows that she saw the official political stance she took as part of her "life in poetry." Her anxiety about the "meaning" and the methods of American propaganda persisted through the years following the war and the "advertising men" remained emblematic of the failure of opportunity the OWI represented.

The OWI, however, was always beset by internal conflict, largely based on the resistance of internal workers such as Rukeyser to the adoption of slick advertising methods designed to manipulate the American public. OWI workers continued to insist that presenting the truth about the war effort was its fundamental task and that they were degraded by the "selling" of patriotism as though it were soap suds. Fifteen members of the staff resigned in frustration in late April of 1943.[9] An editorial report in *The New Republic* suggested that the deep malaise expressed in Rukeyser's memorandum was not the only reason fifteen members of the staff resigned, although staff members stated that the "activities of the OWI on the home front are now dominated by high-pressure promoters who prefer slick salesmanship to honest information" (qtd. in "Editorial" *The New Republic* 551). Elmer Davis attempted to refute this charge, claiming that the OWI "deal[s] in one plain commodity—the facts the people of this country need to win the war" (551).

Rukeyser did not resign with this group, although her letter to Gilbert shows how disappointed and frustrated she was. Her commitment to the values of egalitarian democracy kept her in the fight a while longer. In a letter dated 23 April 1943, Archibald MacLeish thanked her for letting him see a copy of her memorandum to Gilbert and says "Of course, I think you are dead right to stay on in the job you are doing." MacLeish's reply functions as yet another egodocument in Rukeyser's life, suggesting how close she was to leaving with the others, although she herself, in the materials we have, did not threaten to leave. Despite MacLeish's encouragement, even Rukeyser, however, was finally exhausted by the fruitless efforts to influence the direction of the OWI, and she resigned on 1 May 1943. While Rukeyser worked in the OWI, the domestic right wing kept up a constant barrage of attacks, with anti-Soviet feeling increasing after revelations that Russia had slaughtered 15,000 Polish Army Officers during the Nazi-Soviet conquest of Poland in 1939. Laurie cites congressional charges that the OWI was "pro-Communist," that it sheltered "aliens, radicals, and subversives," and that "the agency harboured radicals, and Communists, and was heavily influenced by 'international Jewry'" (175). The anti-Semitism of Republican congressmen was buttressed by the statements of members of the Office of Security Services, who argued that the problem was not that Communists were spies within the OWI but that "it is full of international left-wing Jews" and that its "Jewish saturation makes its voice un-American in the Western ear" (175). As a Jew and one fully aware of Nazi anti-Semitism (although not yet aware of the Nazi "final solution" agenda), Rukeyser would have found these attacks not only repellent but also ironic given the similarity of these views to Nazi thought.

The accusations of a communist presence in the OWI were met directly by Elmer Davis, who announced that after exhaustive investigation of the 2000 employees of the OWI, only six Communists had been found. Congress was not satisfied with this, nor was the FBI. Hoover undertook an enthusiastic investigation of the OWI, and Muriel Rukeyser, already listed in their files as a leftist, was inevitably one of their suspects. *The New York Times* found Rukeyser among the most interesting of the 1,300 New York City OWI employees, and reported that "Poetess in OWI Here Probed by U.S. as Red." The column refers to her as a "well-known young poetess…alleged to have mixed considerable left-wing politics with her iambic pentameters" and it describes her writings in *The New Masses* as "violently partisan." As demonstrated in her own writings, however, Rukeyser was hardly a partisan of any totalitarian ideology; rather she held conventional and constitutional American ideals central to her beliefs.

Rukeyser's document of resignation simply states that she was leaving for "policy reasons." The FBI, however, chose to record a different source, surprising in its mundane publicness. FBI File No. 100-27, dated 21 December 1944 cites the University of California's "Current Biography," published in 1943: "On May 1, 1943 she resigned from the Classification Division, Office of War Information six months after she had been engaged to plan poster campaigns because she said most of the posters had been rejected through a policy of down with the world or through fear of these issues" (6).[10] The readable (that is unexcised) sections of Rukeyser's FBI file does not indicate that there was further speculation or information forthcoming about her reasons for leaving the OWI.

The FBI file on Rukeyser, not large, I imagine, by FBI standards, is about two inches deep. On 31 October 1942, the Office for Emergency Management (the umbrella office under which OWI existed) requested that Mr. John Hoover, director of the Federal Bureau of Investigation, provide a "summary of the information in your files concerning Miss Muriel Rukeyser." Responding with alacrity, Hoover sent the information on 4 November, indicating that Rukeyser had been a subject of interest since 1937 when she published articles, all detailed in the FBI report, in *The New Masses* and *The Nation*. The FBI cites the Dies Committee as the source of information: she "was reported in 1938" as being a member of the John Reed Club, named after an American Bolshevik; she was signatory to a letter (11 January 1939) that "defends the work of the WPA Federal Arts Project"; and she was organizing a mass letter-writing protest against the dismissal of 1,526 Project workers. She was a member of the League of American Writers, "said to possess Communistic tendencies and…to closely follow the Communist Party line." Further, the FBI reports, she spoke against the embargo on Spain for the American Student Union, "an alleged Communist front organization." This summary of her activities was enough to provoke a request for a full-bodied FBI investigation for the Office of Emergency Management.

While the FBI provided a thorough accounting of the newspapers she wrote for, the speeches she gave, the classes she taught, and the company she kept, Rukeyser was not overtly harassed or blacklisted. However, the FBI did keep close track of her and knew for certain how and when she obtained a library card at the University of California at Berkeley (7 February 1945). Although Louis Budcz, the infamous ex-communist who informed on hundreds of fellow travellers, claimed that Rukeyser was a communist, she was not called before the House Committee on Un-American Activities (HCUA). The FBI closed its file on Rukeyser on 1 November 1949, but after Budez named her as one of the "400 Concealed Communists," on 20 December 1950, her file was reopened. Its notes indicate that

"MURIEL RUKEYSER sponsored or was a member of numerous organizations which had been cited by HUAC as Communist Front organizations."[11] Rukeyser's file appears inactive after September 1955, when the Special Agent in Charge informed the Director of the FBI that Rukeyser "does not meet the standards [of the Security Index]" and her file was closed.[12] Rukeyser requested and got access to her file through the Freedom of Information-Privacy Acts. The file came with a letter explaining that the excisions were made (subsections of Title 5, Section 552 of United States Code) when disclosure would "reveal the identity of an individual who has furnished information to the FBI under confidential circumstances or reveal information furnished only by such a person and not apparently known to the public or otherwise accessible to the FBI by overt means."[13] Rukeyser has amended her FBI and SAC files (Bu 77-27812; SAC 100-102441) with marginal notes contradicting or agreeing with its specifics (but that is another topic). The FBI was scrupulous in protecting its sources, and Rukeyser would have learned little about its investigation of her as an OWI employee.

The brief period she spent working in the centre of a bureaucratic power structure was a critical moment in the life of Muriel Rukeyser. Although she continued to fight throughout her life for domestic and international social justice with words and non-violent actions, the Office of War Information provided her with a microcosm of the conflict between social democracy, with its humanitarian ideals, and corporate capitalist democracy, whose goals are inescapably materialist. Rukeyser's articulation of self in the egodocuments presented here—memoranda, letters, autobiographical writing, and investigative reports—reveals much about her sense of self and of nation. The egodocuments provide insight into the person as she strives to influence her world. As supplementary to modes of life writing based on introspection and directed towards an interested readership, egodocuments give readers a more remote perspective while allowing an inference of intimacy. Rukeyser hoped that the Office of War Information would be part of an American twentieth century characterized by democracy and social justice. She continued to work and write for her vision of America and the world, while the OWI eventually devolved into the Central Intelligence Agency. Muriel Rukeyser—along with her colleagues in the Office of War Information—offered a vision of America and its place in the world that today seems unimaginably remote.

ACKNOWLEDGMENTS

I gratefully acknowledge the support of Social Sciences and Humanities Standard Research Grant, which allowed archival research; the librarians at the Library of Congress and the New York Public Library's Berg Special Collections; the able research assistance of Sarah Schwartz and Jude Polsky; and helpful readings from Jude Polsky, Marlene Kadar, Susanna Egan, Linda Warley, and, as always, Pauline Butling.

NOTES

1 See Scott Donaldson (333-37) and Clayton Laurie (29-44) for detailed accounts of Americans' positions.

2 The American Communist Party was established in May 1921 and became the Communist party of America (CPUSA) in 1929. In June 1930 the House Un-American Activities Committee was assembled. Martin Dies became Chairman in 1938 (Barson and Heller 14, 23).

3 Laurie provides an extended account of the conflict between the OWI and the OSS (166-91).

4 The following references are to Rukeyser's papers held at the Berg Special Collections, New York Public Library, and at the Library of Congress.

5 This document is held at the Berg Special Collections, New York Public Library.

6 Bredhoff attributes these words to MacLeish, giving the date 7 June 1942. I could find no reference to a speech on that date in MacLeish's papers registered at the Library of Congress.

7 Rukeyser papers, Berg Collection.

8 Rukeyser here reiterates the grievous loss of the poster series: "In a workshop where Shahn, Perlin, Koerner were among the painters. I served as writer and many artists were called in; work was commissioned and planned. Welders by Shahn were to be used to remind us of our mixed birth; a head by Shimin, the head of a young Negro boy;...the starving children of Käthe Kollwitz. None of these was ever used" (145).

9 See Burlingame for a more detailed account of the crisis, which ultimately led to the destruction of the Domestic Branch of OWI (214-20).

10 All material referred to from the FBI files is contained in Box 52 of Muriel Rukeyser Papers, Library of Congress.

11 Document dated 22 April 1952.

12 In November 1963, it seems that the FBI asked SAC, New York, to locate someone named ROKEYSEE at 790 Riverside Drive, NYC. SAC reports that they could not find ROKEYSEE at 790 Riverside Drive "or anywhere else in Manhattan." They did, however, find a listing in the telephone book for a MURIEL RUKEYSER at that address. A provocative memorandum from SAC to the FBI, dated 20 August 1973, lists "'WOUNDED KNEE'" as a caption. The paragraph to which it is a caption is completely excised.

13 Letter to Rukeyser, dated 7 March 1979.

BINA TOLEDO FREIWALD

GENDER, NATION, AND SELF-NARRATION

THREE GENERATIONS OF DAYAN WOMEN IN PALESTINE/ISRAEL

The essence of the nation...is a matter of self-awareness or self-consciousness.   — Walker Connor (104)

Central dimensions of the roles of women are constituted around the relationships of collectivities to the state...[and] central dimensions of the relationships between collectivities and the state are constituted around the roles of women.   — Floya Anthias and Nira Yuval-Davis (1)

I, YOU, WE (?)

To enter the discursive universe of autobiography is to enter a linguistic space shaped by the signs of the deixis—the contingencies of person, time, and place—and their subject-forming function. This space is ultimately an existential and ethical one. The autobiographer cannot but say (however obliquely) "I," and "here," and "now," and in so doing makes a subject emerge who claims a particular location in the world. In the autobiographical act, a self and its other(s) are named, a community (a "we") and a place of belonging are invoked, histories (both individual and collective) are fashioned. To say "I," the linguist Emile Benveniste contends, is always already to say "I am": an act of self-engendering. But this subject-constituting act is also inextricably embedded in a system that (re)presents three principal modes of the self's relation to the other. These modes—which autobiographical practices foreground and, in turn, allow us to investigate—alert us to what is at stake, epistemologically and ethically, in the construction of individual and collective identities. Benveniste identifies two axes along which the relationship between self and other can unfold: the axis of subjectivity (the I-you relationship, reversible by definition) points to the possibility of dialogue and mutuality between subjects; and the axis of personality (which distinguishes between I/you as persons, and he/she/they as non-persons) is the paradigmatic mode of exclusion and othering. The third modality, whose relation to the axes of subjectivity and personality forms my theoretical object of investigation here, is exemplified by the first-person plural: the affirmation of collective be(long)ing through a discursive feat by which an "I" wills a "we" into being. If, as Walker Connor and Benedict Anderson argue, the essence of the nation is self-consciousness—born of those cognitive and affective acts by which subjects effect a shift from "I" to national "we"—then self-narratives can serve as privileged sites for both the construction and interrogation of the nation.

Any reflection on nation that has as its focus Palestine/Israel[1] is inevitably carried out in the shadow of the difficult and complex realities that have marked the region for over a century now. These realities, and the contesting narratives that have been an integral part of them, heighten one's sense of the inescapably partial character of the language we use to represent self and other. In an earlier version of this paper, I identified myself as an Israeli belonging to the first generation born after Independence: a generation born to refugee parents and greeted with the promise of an end to a millennia-old history of persecution and genocide,[2] the promise of a homecoming and the long-awaited Ingathering of Exiles. But I am, of course, also an Israeli born in the aftermath of what has been inscribed in Palestinian memory and historiography as the catastrophe or *al-Nakba*, the "traumatic events of 1947–49, which cost the Palestinians their majority status in Palestine and their hope of controlling the country, and cost half of them their homes, land, and property" (Khalidi 178). I have since made another home for myself in the calmer but by no means uncontested national space that is Montreal/Québec/Canada (Freiwald "Nation"), but for the Jewish and Arab inhabitants of Palestine/Israel, daily reality continues to be shaped by the disastrous consequences of an inability to reconcile respective national aspirations, a failure to engage in an "I-You" relation of reciprocity (Buber 58).

While the present essay deals with autobiographical writings by Jewish women in Palestine/Israel, I would like to frame my discussion with the voices of two Israeli Palestinian[3] contributors to *Calling the Equality Bluff: Women in Israel* (Swirski and Safir). What their observations suggest— beyond the shared concerns of Palestinian and Jewish women as women in patriarchal societies—is the critical and emancipatory potential of the perspective of those whose gendered position places them in an oblique relation to the nation. Nabila Espanioly, a Palestinian from Nazareth, reminds us that Women in Black, a group that includes both Jewish and Arab women, was one of "several women's peace groups that organized in the wake of the *intifada*, as women were the first to respond" (148).[4] Her essay concludes with this expression of hope: "If Israeli Jewish women perceive the connection between Israeli Palestinian women's struggles for peace and equality and their own efforts, the two circles will come closer together" (151). Mariam Mar'i, a Palestinian from Acre, insists in an interview with the Jewish Israeli reporter Bili Moskona-Lerman that "a Palestinian state is the only solution to the problem," but she also acknowledges that "you see the PLO [Palestinian Liberation Organization] as we once saw Zionism" (44). The interviewer notes that Mar'i's other concerns are "about tradition, religion and extremism—Arab as well as Jewish" (44). As I listen to these voices, I think of a recent commentator on the Arab-Israeli conflict who urges us to adopt the principle of mutual personhood (between individuals as well as groups) as a foundational moral imperative (Bornstein vii), and I think of Virginia Woolf's compelling demonstration, in *Three Guineas*, that violations of this principle begin inside the patriarchal home and inevitably lead to the deadly battlefields of the nation, with their "ruined houses and dead bodies" (162). What I hear in the first-person accounts of Espanioly, Mar'i, and (to varying degrees) the Jewish women autobiographers discussed below, is both an affirmation of the right to collective identity (for oneself and for the other), and a critique—born of an intimate knowledge of inequalities *within* the nation—of the injustices that can be perpetrated in its name. What such a critique can enable is the creation of what ethnographer Ayala Emmett describes, in her study of Jewish and Palestinian women's peace activism, as a discursive "transnational territory" (48): not a final destination, but a potential site of solidarity and resistance to different forms of oppression. Gender, Emmett concludes, can provide a ground for reimagining the nation, as such peace groups "deploy gender solidarity to participate in imagining nation-ness indivisible from justice" (183).[5]

This essay examines the life writings of three women—Deborah Dayan, Ruth Dayan, and Yael Dayan—who represent three generations of one of Israel's most public families. Spanning over a century, their life histories allow us insights into the making of the imagined community that is contemporary Israel. The Dayans, one should however add, have been an integral part of the Ashkenazi (of European ancestry) "labor elite" whose moral, social, cultural, and political authority has shaped present-day Israel (Sternhell 4–5). The voices heard here, then, while marginalized by gender, come to us from the centre of power and privilege. It will be the task of the larger project of which this essay is a part to bring into the discussion the experiences and perspectives of other segments of the national population, most notably those of Mizrahi (Oriental) subjects (of North-African or Middle-Eastern origin) whose ethnically marked experience within the nation has been one of cultural, socioeconomic, and political inequality (Hever et al., "Epistemology" 17).

Benedict Anderson's brief but astute observations about Zionism and Israel provide a helpful point of entry into a discussion of those founding narratives of the Jewish nation-state within and against which the Dayan women's own self/nation-narratives emerge. Anderson sees the Zionist project as a response to that particular form of racism that is anti-Semitism, an ideology that in the age of nationalism has made the Jew the nation's Other: "Jews, the seed of Abraham, [are, for the anti-Semite,] forever Jews, no matter what passports they carry or what languages they speak and read" (149). For Anderson, the significance of the emergence of Zionism and the birth of Israel lie in that "the former marks the reimagining of an ancient religious community as a nation, down there among other nations—while the latter charts an alchemic change from a wandering devotee to local patriot" (149). Two popular Hebrew expressions of the pre-state era capture the centrality to the national narrative of the elements evoked by Anderson: the dream of escaping a perpetual condition of otherness; the desire for sovereignty and a measure of control over one's collective destiny; and the foregrounding, in the expression of that collective identity, of a relation to the homeland that draws on, but also secularizes, a biblical connection to the territory. This is the spirit of the famous exhortation by Theodor Herzl, one of the founders of political Zionism: *im tirzu ein zo hagada* (if you [plural] will it, the dream will come true); and of the rallying cry of the pre-state *Yishuv* era: *anu banu hartza livnot u'lhibanot ba* (we have come to the land of Israel to build and be rebuilt in her).

Nations and nationalism, Walker Connor has noted, "are 'the stuff that dreams are made of,'" in part by virtue of their appeal to a myth of common descent—a particularly compelling form of group identification (210). But the very principle around which notions of nation and homeland are built, other theorists remind us, "is a pattern of select inclusions and exclusions" (George 2). Thus while the early Zionists felt a historic connection to the land, the territory they longed to build and be rebuilt in was, of course, neither empty nor "unbuilt." Adding gender to the critical perspective through which nation is examined further foregrounds the dual sense in which exclusions are constitutive of the nation: overt exclusion is the principle by which group membership is established and belonging is determined; but a pattern of occluded exclusions also marks the nation from within. As Anderson points out, one of the senses in which the nation is an imagined community is that "regardless of the actual inequality and exploitation that may prevail [within the nation]...the nation is always conceived as a deep, horizontal comradeship," a "fraternity" (7). The very language used here suggests one kind of inequality the nation not only naturalizes but indeed exploits; in the patriarchal blueprint for the nation as a masculinized fraternity, women become its absolute—yet absolutely necessary—binary Other. Recognition, Ernest Gellner has suggested, is the operative principle in the (internal) constitution of the nation: "Two men are of the same nation if and only if they share the same culture...[and/or] recognize each other as belonging to the same nation" (7). But how do Woman/women (de Lauretis, "Feminist" 5) figure in this originary reciprocal gaze? The present essay thus approaches the three Dayan autobiographies with the following questions: how have these women seen their contributions to *binyan ha'aretz*, the building of the national home? Were they indeed rebuilt in her? How did their (gendered and other) experiences transform their understanding of the nation and of nation-ness? And how can their writings help us rethink the dynamics of exclusion and inclusion, of recognition and misrecognition, that are constitutive of one of the most potent forces in our contemporary world, that of (ethno)nationalism?[6]

THREE LIVES: AN OVERVIEW

A brief overview of the three lives is in order before broaching these questions. Deborah Ztolovsky was born in Ukraine in 1890 and came to Ottoman-governed Palestine in 1913, leaving behind family, an interrupted university education, and socialist activism. She lived through the years of the British Mandate in Palestine and died in 1956, eight years after the founding of the Jewish state. In Palestine, she married Shmuel Dayan, and had a daughter and two sons. Her oldest, Moshe Dayan, would become one of Israel's most recognizable military and political figures. She lived to mourn the death of her youngest son, Zorick, killed in the War of Independence, but was spared her daughter Aviva's suicide years later.[7] A *halutza* (woman pioneer) of the wave of Zionist immigration to Palestine commonly referred to as the Second *Aliyah* (1904–1914), Deborah Dayan is in many respects an exemplary Founding Mother. She lived and worked in Degania (the first *kvutza* or collective village) and then in Nahalal (the first *moshav* or cooperative village), experiencing the many hardships of those years.[8] She was active in the Women Workers' Movement, and was an editorial member and writer for its journal *Dvar Hapoelet* (Voice of the

Woman Worker) for twenty-two years. In 1953, Deborah Dayan was named Mother of Israel. Her autobiographical volume, *B'osher u'veyagon* (*In Happiness and in Sorrow*), appeared posthumously in 1957. The volume, edited by her husband Shmuel Dayan, is comprised mainly of her columns for *Dvar Hapoelet* but also includes selected letters (mostly addressed to her husband during his travels), as well as Shmuel Dayan's diary entries from the last days of her life. An abridged English translation of the volume was published in 1968 under the title *Pioneer*. At 152 pages compared to the original's 400, the English translation is not only highly selective but also clearly slanted and unreliable (and will thus not be used in this essay). The choice of the English title is already telling, for *Pioneer* celebrates the myth but gives little indication of the complex life the original volume reveals: Deborah's ambivalence towards the national project, arising from her experience as a *woman* pioneer (in sections like "The Woman's Part"); her clear-eyed view of the monumental challenge involved in turning an ethnically diverse population of immigrants (herself included) into a national citizenry; and her grappling with the personal cost of a collective dream that left her, as her grandson would put it, a bereaved mother with "mourning permanently lodged in her eyes" (Gefen 30, my translation).

Ruth Shwartz (b. 1917), like Moshe Dayan, was born in Palestine. She lived from the ages of two to nine in England, where her parents were posted, acquiring English as her first language. She met and married Dayan in 1937 (they divorced in 1971; shortly thereafter he would marry Rahel Rabinovich, his lover of eighteen years). Her autobiography, *And Perhaps...The Story of Ruth Dayan* (1973; written with Helga Dudman and published simultaneously in Hebrew and in English), takes us from the late 1930s in Nahalal through the social and military upheavals of the next four decades, touching on issues and conflicts that still remain unresolved today. As a text that reflects on both the private life and a lifetime of national service, Ruth Dayan's autobiography, like Deborah Dayan's, speaks directly to the question of the woman's part in the national dream (and its darker underside), aptly taking its title from a poem by Rachel (a celebrated pre-state poet): "And perhaps these things never happened at all.../.../Was it real? Or did I dream a dream?"

The third autobiography discussed here is by the daughter of Ruth and Moshe Dayan, Yael Dayan (b. 1939). The autobiography was published in English in 1985 and translated by the author into Hebrew in 1986. The title and dedication alone tell a good part of the private story. Entitled *My Father, His Daughter*, the autobiography is dedicated to "my mother, who loved, understood, and tolerated us both"; and there was much to tolerate: the married Moshe Dayan would, for example, invite his daughter to meet his lovers at a separate apartment he kept. Interwoven with this charged familial story is a public narrative that voices the preoccupations of a society well past its pioneering days: a society marked by a succession of wars and constant threats to its existence; transformed by the experience of becoming an occupying force; and grappling with internally divisive issues of religion, class, and ethnicity. Like her grandparents and parents, Yael Dayan has been involved in public national service, serving as a member of the Knesset (Israeli Parliament) in its thirteenth session (representing Labor), fourteenth session (representing One Israel), and fifteenth session (as a member of Labor-Meimad).

THE MASTER NARRATIVE

In their introduction to a collection of essays entitled *Woman-Nation-State*, Nira Yuval-Davis and Floya Anthias examine the ways in which women figure and participate in ethnic and national processes. The broad areas they identify provide a helpful grid with which to approach the Dayan autobiographies. Women, they note, figure as symbols in national discourses, and although they participate in national, economic, political, and military struggles, they are often seen as occupying supporting and nurturing roles in relation to men. Among the areas in which women's participation is crucial, Yuval-Davis and Anthias list the following: women are "recruited" as biological reproducers of members of the ethnic collectivity, but also as reproducers of the boundaries of the ethnic/national group; women are not only socializers of small children, but also participate centrally as transmitters and reproducers of the collectivity's culture and, in the case of a multi-ethnic collectivity, the ethnic symbols and ways of life of the dominant group. I want to begin by looking at the gendered national script against which the lives and life narratives of the three women unfold.

The ideological inscription of women as absent from the valorized public sphere and as idealized keepers of the patriarchal familial/national hearth is nowhere more evident than in Moshe Dayan's massive autobiography, *Moshe Dayan: Story of My life* (1976). Women are all but absent from this narrative in which the political and military saga of an emergent nation and Dayan's own life story become practically interchangeable. The autobiography's framing prologue and epilogue, however, are telling. The prologue takes us back to the first days of the Six-Day War, and the visit by Moshe Dayan (the war's greatest hero) to the Wailing Wall. He writes "[leaving it] I had noticed some wild cyclamen of a delicate pinkish mauve sprouting between the Wall and the Mograbi Gate. I plucked a few to bring to Rahel [his second wife]. I was sorry she could not have been there that day" (3). A fine sentiment, if one chooses to disregard the insidious gender ideology underwriting the familiar troping of women as delicate flowers,[9] or overlook the fact that, as Moshe Dayan would have well known, *no* woman could have been there. Indeed, what makes this scene— of a male soldier at the site of the ancient Temple—a particularly reso- nant national tableau is the convergence of two patriarchal ideologies that have been constitutive of the Jewish nation-state: an orthodox Judaism that excludes women "from full participation in the public sphere while subordinating them to male authority in the private sphere" (Raday 19), and a masculinist militarism reinforced by the realities of the Arab-Israeli conflict and the perceived imperatives of "national survival and national identity" (Sharoni 96). To draw again on de Lauretis's terms of analysis, in Dayan's prototypical narrative of the nation, women—"the real histor- ical beings who cannot as yet be defined outside of those [patriarchal] dis- cursive formations"—are absent, but Woman—that "fictional construct, a distillate from diverse but congruent discourses dominant in Western cul- tures…the other-from-man (nature and Mother, site of sexuality and mas- culine desire, sign and object of men's social exchange)" ("Feminist" 5)— does make a brief but crucial appearance. In the epilogue, we find Moshe Dayan, in the aftermath of the Yom Kippur War (the war that will turn him from hero to villain), seeking solace in his favorite activity, amateur arche- ological exploration. Roaming the Negev desert, he discovers a cave which he imagines housed a family "some two thousand years before our Patri- arch Abraham" (516). These are the autobiography's concluding lines: "It was an extraordinary sensation. I crouched by the ancient hearth. It was as though the fire had only just died down, and I did not need to close my eyes to conjure up the woman of the house bending over to spark its embers into flame as she prepared the meal for her family. My family" (516).

In Dayan's national and personal narrative, the men are patriarchs, his- tory's shakers and movers who, like Abraham, have proper names and identities; the women, while crucial as legitimating symbols of national con- tinuity (by Jewish law, maternity determines the identity of the child), remain anonymous and faceless as they prepare the family meal. Further, the slippage from "her family" to "my family" is particularly revealing, as it naturalizes (by literalizing) the reigning trope (myth) of the nation— which is also that of traditional autobiography—the trope of blood and/as belonging. The nation, Connor writes, is "a group of people who *feel* that they are ancestrally related. It is the largest group that can command a person's loyalty because of *felt* kinship ties; it is, from this perspective, the fully extended family" (202, emphasis added). Rooted in the trope of the patriarchal family, the national narrative depends on—and is thus invested in naturalizing and perpetuating—its gendered script. Moshe Dayan's autobiography clearly illustrates the multiple ways in which women's gendered discursive position as the eternal maternal-feminine serves the national narrative: it functions to erase history—the plural, discontinuous histories that have taken shape over the intervening millennia—allowing a unified, continuous story to be told (more on this, as seen though Yael Dayan's eyes, later in the essay); it serves to legitimate a collective claim through an appeal to a biological relation, arguably the most basic form of human kinship; and it invokes (in the figure of the mother/land) a particularly powerful affective bond (given the historically gendered division of labour in which women have been the nurturers of infants and young children) between members of the collectivity.

In form, Moshe Dayan's hegemonic self/nation-narrative follows the model of his beloved scriptures. The narratives of the Hebrew Bible often "begin with ancestry" (Lewis 33), and are rarely interested in exploring character as a "locus of conflicting emotion…[or] internal tension" (Davies 14). It is perhaps not surprising, then, to find in women's counter-narratives of the nation the very traits—conflicting emotions and internal strife—shunned by the dominant national paradigm. Such inner turmoil can be seen as the direct result of a contradiction at the heart of the nation-building project, for while Zionism proclaimed equality for all, "in practice, neither the early settlers nor the second wave of immigrants at the turn of the century had transcended the patriarchal norms of their home communities in Europe" (Feldman 30–31). In *The Founding Myths of Israel*, Zeev Sternhell makes the broader claim that as a form of "nationalist socialism" and an ideology based on the idea of the nation as an extended family, Zionism subjected social concerns (such as class and gender equality) to "the principle of the nation's primacy," and reinscribed traditional bourgeois gender roles (7-8). Thus while women were there from the very start, the story of their immigration and settlement is just beginning to be told, for their experiences, actions, and struggles have been "either ignored, or put on a 'pioneering pedestal,'…In neither case were women's own voices heard" (Bernstein 1-2).

DEBORAH DAYAN

One voice that has come through to us, loud and clear in its ambivalence towards the hegemonic national script, is Deborah Dayan's. Here is her own take on the woman-in-the-primordial-kitchen fantasy so beloved by her son.

In the following passage (dated 1935) from the autobiography, Deborah reflects on the symbolism of an inscription in a work-log found from the early days of the *Yishuv*: "There is something symbolic about this page, with only two words inscribed on it: 'Kitchen: Sarah.' That's all it says. As if to remind us that this has been our lot since the Biblical days of Sarah to this day: 'in the beginning there was the kitchen.' We rebelled against the weight of this tradition, refused to be trapped in it…and when asked about the work we wanted to do, cried out: 'anything but the kitchen'" (89).[10] Deborah's sentiments and critique here resonate with other testimonies of women who were part of the three waves of immigration known as the Second, Third, and Fourth *Aliyot* (Freiwald, "The Subject"). Their auto-biographical writings document their extensive participation in the national struggle, but they also reveal another struggle. Writing of the settlement experience in the 1920s, Rahel Yanait (later married to the second president of Israel, Yizhak Ben-Zvi) is forceful in her indictment: "In the thick of that passionate movement toward the land, the women workers suddenly found themselves thrust aside and relegated once more to the ancient tradition of the house and the kitchen" (109). Similarly, Chuma Chayot, writing in 1932, denounces the prevalent gender ideology of the *Yishuv* and makes a range of demands whose foresight is truly impressive, calling for changes in the socio-economic conditions necessary to pave the way for women's economic independence: a fair share for women in the labour market and in traditional male occupations; pay equity; more training and education; and daycares to accommodate working mothers (222–23).

Deborah Dayan's autobiographical volume opens with a selection from a speech she gave in 1954—when I was three—in Petach-Tikva, my hometown. The occasion was the fiftieth anniversary of the Second *Aliyah*, that turn-of-the-century wave of immigration that was so instrumental in shaping the nascent nation-state. This short text (hereafter referred to as the Petach-Tikva speech) captures the principal threads of the life that unfolds in the pages of *In Happiness and in Sorrow*, but it also reveals—as much through what it says as through its silences—both the dominant national topoi that her generation would pass on down to mine, and a more complex vision of the individual and the collective than the one offered by the official state narrative. I will speak of the silences first. In the climactic conclusion to her speech, the rousing national rhetoric celebrating the "conquest of the [uncultivated, empty] land" is belied by the Arab place name (Um-Djuni) that Deborah uses to refer to their first settlement in the Galilee (later given the Hebrew name Degania): "Just as we had faith in that first breaking of the ground in Um-Djuni…so we will have faith in the freshly turned furrows in the hills of Jerusalem, in the Galilee, in the ploughed expanses of the Negev" (n.pag.). The effect of putting the Arab presence on the land under erasure here is all the more poignant when one is reminded that Petach-Tikva—founded in 1878 and celebrated in the Zionist narrative as the first pioneering Jewish village in Palestine—was the site of one of the first conflicts, in 1886, between Arab *fellahin* (tenant farmers) and the Jewish settlers the *fellahin* saw as dispossessing them (Khalidi 99).

Alan Dowty has suggested a number of explanations for the failure of the early Zionists to meaningfully recognize the presence of the local Palestinian population (46-50). Among these is the suggestion that the hostile reaction of the Palestinian Arabs to the Jewish settlers simply led the latter to revert to a familiar pattern developed over a long history of persecution: "Increased threat usually forced Jews to bond more closely together, with tradition as the glue that held them together and ensured their survival" (89). The writings collected in *In Happiness and in Sorrow* demonstrate just how precarious that personal and collective sense of self was for the early settlers. In the opening of her Petach-Tikva speech, the sixty-four-year-old Deborah Dayan recalls her younger self aboard the *Princess Olga*, the ship that took her to Palestine. She was, Deborah writes of that other self, "a young woman who uprooted herself from school and everything held dear, for those fires that had once kept her alive now appeared alien, and in the distance new bright lights beckoned." But as the next sentence reveals, what lay ahead felt no less alien than what was being left behind; shifting to the first person, she writes, "I came to an unknown land, not knowing where to turn in this homeland" (n.pag.). The focal sentence in the speech, from which the volume's editor (Shmuel Dayan) might have taken its title, captures the affective centre from which all the writing flows: "In happiness and in sorrow one thought accompanies me: you are not alone, you belong to a greater collective, to a collectivity creating a homeland" (n.pag.). Throughout this speech and the volume as a whole, Deborah's voice vacillates between a sense of profound aloneness and not-belonging, and a fierce desire to find/make such belonging for herself and the other immigrants by creating the "greater collective." As the speech suggests and the rest of the volume amply documents, belonging remains elusive, undermined, on the one hand, by the realities of gender inequality, and on the other, by the inherent difficulties of a "diaspora nationalism" (Gellner 106) that seeks to turn an Ingathering of Exiles from many lands into a national populace. Deborah tells her audience, "After a while I could write to my friends in Russia that I was happy, that I arrived at the source, my roots—that I belonged now to the great family of workers at Degania"; but in the next paragraph she recalls the need to confront the men in her agricultural collective with the "particular problems of the working woman," due in no small part to their attitude towards her. She cites the difficulties of reconciling work with the familial duties expected of the women in the settlements, and the isolation experienced by young mothers with no familial or community support. The ethnic diversity of a predominantly immigrant population posed other problems. One of the great accomplishments of the early women settlers, Deborah tells her audience, was the absorption of immigrants from all corners of the world. But, she cautions, there is still much to be done to bring about integration and national unity: "with a prayer in our hearts we hope for the day when the people will become one, when divisions between the ethnic groups [*bein eda l'eda*] will fall away" (n.pag.).

The writings collected in *In Happiness and in Sorrow* flesh out the affective and ideological dimensions of the subject's relation to the nation so suggestively captured by the Petach-Tikva speech. Immediately following the speech, a short personal narrative entitled "My Mother" (dated 1936) recreates an originary scene of lack and dispossession that is both historically specific and existential in scope. The speaker recalls a state in which "it seemed that in the whole world there remained only the three of us—mother, myself, and my little brother...now we are one body, but perhaps we don't really exist. Only she exists—mother" (3). In the beginning, for the emergent subject, there is the longing for the gaze of the other to confirm one's own existence. But for this subject the plea is to remain unanswered: born to the only Jewish family in the Ukrainian village, there is no community to embrace the child and claim her as their own. The gendered matrix of the family breeds further isolation: a father who locks himself in his study, and a distraught mother who tearfully sings a plaintive Ukrainian song bemoaning a woman's bitter lot in life. Outside the home, other betrayals await the youngster. An undated text entitled "My Name" (4–7) speaks of young Deborah's great attachment to the Russian people and culture and the painful experiences of rejection communicating to her her alien status. Nor is there relief once she reaches the shores of the promised land. The volume documents her continued experiences of alienation in Palestine: her fellow comrades in the kibbutz, regarding her as too urban and bourgeois, reject her application for membership: "finally I understood that they were talking about me [she can only follow their conversation with difficulty since her Hebrew is rudimentary]: 'she has come to us from a different culture, our [communitarian, rural] ideals and ideas are foreign to her.' I covered my ears, I could bear it no more. To get up and leave—but go where?" (264).[11] She moves with her husband to a less communitarian settlement, but her gendered marginalization and the isolation imposed on her as a mother leave her with a sense of "total, desperate, loneliness" (84). There was no escaping this condition of gendered otherness for the women of Deborah Dayan's generation, for it was enshrined in the very terms of the national vision as it was articulated by two of its founding fathers, Theodor Herzl and David Ben-Gurion (Israel's first prime minister). Reacting against a European racializing discourse that figured Jews as morally weak and emasculated, Herzl's vision "rested on the reification of a dichotomizing bourgeois gender system" and hailed the birth of a masculinized New Jew (Bunzl 83). It was women's "special mission" and ultimate obligation, Ben-Gurion would declare, to (re)produce the New Hebrew: "[women] should enjoy the same rights and responsibilities as the men, except where motherhood is concerned" (Ben-Gurion 375).

As the writings in *In Happiness and in Sorrow* demonstrate, Deborah Dayan sought her personal salvation in the project that would also become the nation's lifeline: "the national task of absorbing new immigrants" (Dowty 63). In a conclusion to a text dated 1950 and included in the section entitled "In the Immigrant Villages," Deborah adopts and adapts the *mode ani* prayer, the first dawn blessing recited by observant Jews in gratitude to the Creator for restoring the soul after the night's sleep. Replacing the prayer's religious referent with a national(ist) one, Deborah gives thanks "to the people for allowing me to observe the *mitzvah* [commandment] of absorbing immigrants" (168). Yael Dayan comments on the work that her grandmother and mother dedicated much of their lives to, the monumental task of absorbing, settling, and training new immigrants: "Women from old established *moshavim* [plural of *moshav*] volunteered to work with new immigrants, initiating them into a style of work and life they had never known. My grandmother Dvorah had been doing it for a while already, and my mother joined in, going every day to the *moshav* not far from Jerusalem to which she was assigned" (74–75). This life work too, however, would ultimately prove a precarious route to collective belonging. Spanning many decades, Deborah's writings demonstrate a profound longing to embrace and be embraced by the national collectivity, a longing that is continuously frustrated by the many divisions—ideological, ethnic, gendered—within the nation. From the beginning, she challenges the oppressive gender ideology of her (Ashkenazi) pioneering comrades, and later she denounces the oppression and abuse of women within other immi-

grant groups (235); she is equally disheartened by manifestations of rejection and hostility between the different (Jewish) ethnic groups, resulting
in "another kind of exile within the nation: a Jew rejecting a Jew!" (228).
More muted is Deborah's critique of the way in which the Jewish establishment (of which she was a part) handled the absorption of immigrants from
what she calls the "developing countries" (Arab and Muslim countries)
(182). As recent scholarship has reminded us, these immigrants were sent
to live "in remote locations, usually near disputed border areas, lacking in
the necessary infrastructure for subsistence, and excluded from the socio-
economic and political centers of power" (Kemp 65). Although Deborah
does acknowledge "serious mistakes in the planning of these villages, discrimination in matters of housing and infrastructure...problems regarding social programs, the condition of schools, the future of the youth"
(182), one will have to turn to the narratives of these subjects themselves
for a fuller understanding of both their subjection (partly through an Ori-
entalizing ideology) and their modes of resistance to emerge.

RUTH DAYAN

Two generations removed from the pioneering world of Deborah Dayan,
Yael Dayan recognizes the significance of her grandmother's and mother's
contributions to the national project of absorbing immigrants, but feels a
greater affinity with (and indeed admiration for) the military and political world of her father. In sharp contrast to the proto-feminist critique
that animates Deborah Dayan's writing, the granddaughter's narrative—
with the famous photographs from the Six-Day War on the covers of the
English and Hebrew editions, showing father and daughter in military
uniform and poses that bespeak both camaraderie and intimacy—naturalizes the patriarchal family structure that dictates that "Mother" could
pursue her work, but only as long as "she was always home in the evenings,
to settle our quarrels, look at our school reports, or engage in the social
activities my father's position required" (75).[12] Without much evidence
of a (self-)critical perspective, Yael Dayan writes of her parents, "By nature
and upbringing, my father was a patriarch....My mother's lack of confi-
dence and natural humility served both of them well....They both knew that
his needs, his desires and comforts and plans would come first with her"
(75). Ruth Dayan's own narrative, however, tells a different story, as she
reflects on the seductive lure that the patriarchal family first held for her,
and her subsequent realization of its oppressive grip.

In the household of Deborah and Shmuel Dayan, Ruth writes, she
initially saw her dream come true (it was a dream constructed, in part,

out of the Russian novels so beloved by both Deborah and Ruth): "I fell in love with this Russian family....This, I thought, was what I had been dreaming of; this was exactly the way I wanted my own life to be. The way they all sat down together for meals...with Shmuel presiding like a patriarch, was a joy to me" (10). When she gets her wish, however, that fate proves less than joyful. As the narrative reveals, Moshe Dayan, like his father, extolled the virtues of agricultural work on redeemed native soil but was hardly interested in it himself. Joining the Haganah (precursor to the Israeli army) and leaving Ruth and their young daughter Yael to fend for themselves on the farm, he preferred the battlefields to the cornfields, and in later years the company of his many lovers to that of his wife and children. Ruth's narrative throughout reveals an ambivalence that is never fully addressed. At times, she loudly proclaims her willing participation in the gendered script of the family (but this might be, at least in part, in self-defence against accusations that she worked outside the home while the children were still young): "Building my life around my family was what I wanted; and it was what I did until circumstances changed our way of life. Yael was certainly never left alone at Nahalal. I did not work outside the home—or join the Haganah—in the years before Yael was born, because all that I wanted was to be with Moshe" (151-52). Elsewhere, her critical perspective recalls Deborah's, as when she speaks of the Haganah men getting "all the fun and glory" while she was left behind "dutifully cleaning out sheep dung" and feeling "very much on the fringe of things" (46). When their first child, Yael, is born, Moshe is away, and she is left "alone with a crying baby, growing increasingly bitter about the Haganah, feeling out of the mainstream" (60). Ruth's ambivalence towards the gendered script of the nation is most clearly articulated in her tribute to Deborah Dayan: "Though I admired Devora tremendously, I did not understand until afterwards how much she had given up to come to Nahalal, and how much she continued to give up. With her mind and education she could have been one of the country's leaders. Instead she remained at the farm, holding the family together, driving herself physically with the hardest chores" (10).

Ruth recalls that, as a young married woman watching her mother-in-law "hold the farm together while Shmuel was so often at Zionist meetings," she resolved to "never repeat Devora's pattern of life" (62). While the pattern would repeat itself in the early years of Ruth's marriage, both Deborah and Ruth devote much of their autobiographical writing to documenting their involvement in what they perceive to be women's great contribution to the building of the Jewish nation-state, the absorption of immigrants. Ruth makes the case eloquently: "All the fighting," she writes, "all the deaths and tragedies, brought us our state. With the state came newcomers—displaced persons from camps in Europe and refugees from Arab countries. For me, the state of Israel began not with the War of Independence, but with the newcomers. The war was the price that had to be paid to build a nation that would absorb immigrants" (122). For Ruth, her life work in the service of the nation is a direct continuation of the mission undertaken by the pioneer women of Deborah's generation:

> During this period [early 1950s] Devora asked me if I could help her in her work. She was in charge of the *moshav* movement's program of women volunteers who went from veteran settlements like Nahalal to help immigrants being organized into new *moshavim*....*Moshav* women were performing one of the most important tasks in the country: showing families who came from the Arabian desert and European camps how to live in their new homes as Israelis. Under Deborah's direction wives left their comfortable *moshav* farmhouses to live in the new villages, often for as long as a year,...This was a form of national service. (128)

Ruth's contribution to this form of national service would eventually turn into an original and significant project. Visiting villages of Bulgarian and Yemenite immigrants who were failing as farmers, Ruth notices traditional crafts in their houses and recognizes that "Here was something unexpected. If rats and water shortage made agriculture impractical, why not do something with this talent?...suddenly, leaders in other places discovered handicraft talents....It became a craze" (128). By 1973, the craze would become a large-scale home industry supplying an extensive chain of stores called Maskit and defining a new Israeli style in jewelry and weaving.

The vision that emerges from the nation-building work of women like Deborah Dayan and Ruth Dayan, unlike the hegemonic vision articulated by Moshe Dayan, is pluralistic and profoundly ethical. Integrating immigrants, Ruth recognizes, is a two-way process, as she finds herself "learning about customs and beliefs and ways of life totally foreign to those of us who grew up in Israel" (136). As a national-scale project that brought together Palestinian Arabs and Jews from different ethnic backgrounds in the creation of arts and crafts that combined traditional skills with modern designs, Maskit was premised on a recognition of the plural character of the population inhabiting the territory of the state. It was driven by both (historically oriented) respect for those differences, and (future-oriented) faith that these cultures could meet and converge in productive aesthetic and ideological ways. Recognizing that immigrants often have more in common with the non-Jews of their countries of origin leads Ruth to conclude, "I always feel uncomfortable talking about 'racial purity': there is no such thing; our world is too mixed up" (131). This vision, Ruth writes, gained particular importance after the Six-Day War: "Once the fighting stopped and the new situation permitted open contact with our former enemies, I realized that I did have a real job. It started with handicrafts, through my travels for Maskit, and led to friendships. War and peace, I know perfectly well, are made by military men and politicians. But all sorts of things are possible when people learn to understand each other and realize that such understanding is in their interest" (211). She calls for the creation of a climate where Jews and Arabs "can sit down and talk together" (220), and adds that "until the Palestinians unite to form their own state, I do not see how the problem can be solved permanently" (221). Ruth's foresight here is all the more striking when one recognizes that "until 1992 the women's peace and coexistence position [a position that began to be publicly articulated only after the 1982 Lebanon War] seemed utopian" (Emmett 2).

One of the closing passages of Ruth Dayan's autobiography suggests some of the issues at stake for contemporary Israeli women as citizens of a nation-state that continues to negotiate the terms of its existence both from within (with respect to the secular/religious rift, for example), and from without (with respect to the Israeli/Palestinian conflict). As is often the case in autobiographical writing, this passage illuminates larger collective concerns while focusing on intensely felt personal experiences. The passage sets side by side two episodes involving an exchange of rings. In the first, Ruth recalls a meeting with Theresa, an Arab-nationalist friend to whom she offered a Maskit ring as a gift. Theresa responds with ambivalence, but also with her own gift to Ruth, a gift of (mutual) recognition offered not in the spirit of forgetting (or forgiving) historical grievances, but of reaching out in spite of them; she tells Ruth, "more than twenty years ago my husband was sentenced to death by the Haganah. He escaped. I swore then that I would never wear a ring until our rights were restored. But because this ring is from you, I will wear it around my neck, on a chain" (231). In the very next sentence, Ruth writes, "Rings also play a painful part in a Jewish divorce. The woman must remove her wedding ring and all other rings she may be wearing…under the searching eye of the presiding rabbi…nobody has warned me of this" (231). What follows is an account of the humiliating yet hilarious experience of the divorce ritual at the house of Rabbi Goren, chief rabbi of Tel Aviv at the time, who presided over the Dayans' divorce. "There is little dignity in many of the customs we preserve" (233), Ruth observes of the ritual of "casting out" the woman. In the domestic space of the Gorens' living room, however, the procedure gets somehow transformed. When the ink on the *Get* (divorce) document would not dry, the Rabbi's wife thinks of a solution: "she brought out her electric hot plate and we put the document, with its age old terminology, on the hot plate and plugged it in. This worked very well" (232).

For things to "work very well," these anecdotes seem to suggest, what is needed are the perspectives and interventions of those who think of people as well as "the people." Countering a monolithic and past-bound national narrative of origins, Ruth Dayan offers a forward-looking vision based on mutual recognition and the negotiation of differences. The very last page of her autobiography, listing entries from her appointment book, is emblematic in this regard. The list includes appointments with Maskit personnel, with a friend's daughter having romantic complications, with a group of Arab women from Bethlehem about doing work for Maskit, with Rabbi Darai of Jaffa about a group of Jews from Ethiopia, with Jewish and Arab students at Haifa University, with a new immigrant from France who makes handbags, with a unit of border police, mostly Druses, in Gaza, and lastly, "With a friend, an expert in these things, to plan the garden of my new [post-divorce] home" (236). The list stands as a defiant response to the injunction "Sara: Kitchen"; as an acknowledgment of the multiple and complex strands that run through "I" and "we" in (post-1948 and then post-1967) Palestine/Israel; and finally (echoes of *Candide* here), as an expression of hope in the simple prospect of a peaceful existence (sadly, yet to be realized in the region).

Helga Dudman opens her foreword to Ruth Dayan's autobiography with these observations: "you can divorce a husband, but not a legend. In this case there was not the slightest reason for saying good-bye to the legend. A long love affair with a force of history may be easier to maintain than a marriage" (xi). Ruth Dayan's own narrative registers (however obliquely) a more ambivalent relation to the force of history—the particular vision of the nation—represented by Moshe Dayan. "My love affair with my husband," she writes, "was part of my love affair with my country" (170), but then she adds, "the price of living with a legend can be too great" (176). It is in the daughter's narrative that we find both the most explicit critique of the legend and the clearest evidence of the price it can exact.

YAEL DAYAN

As the narrative of a favoured, father-identified daughter of a nationalist patriarch, Yael Dayan's *My Father, His Daughter* exhibits the problematic dimensions of patriarchal nationalism as they play out on both the affective and ideological levels. Within the family, Yael's self-positioning reproduces the familiar triangulation: the daughter both devalues the mother[13] and, considering her a rival, fantasizes about taking her place.[14] The father in such a scenario, Jessica Benjamin has noted, becomes "a figure of excitement" representing "freedom, the outside world, will, agency, and desire" (86). Moshe Dayan is indeed such a figure in his daughter's life-narrative: she recalls being taken along with him on military excursions in the desert where she was, she writes, "the only female, the only child around, and I felt honored, as if allowed a glimpse of the world of giants" (79). She associates him with "a sense of freedom" (78), with "mobility...speed" (82), and liberties taken with the law and morality: stealing chickens from a *moshav* nearby (82), "indulging in extramarital affairs" (82), treating as his personal property millennia-old artifacts he finds on his amateur archeological digs. In thrall with such power, what the young Yael learns and internalizes from a father who allows her exceptional access to the privileges of patriarchy is a model of subjectivity that valorizes autonomy and separation at the expense of what Benjamin calls "intersubjectivity," the recognition of the subjectivity of the other and the limits on one's freedom such recognition ethically entails (93). Her creed becomes a demand for "total freedom and independence" (124), as she sides with her father (and against the mother) in vowing "not to be slaves to the confining dictates of family routine" (100).[15]

Espousing the father's creed of unfettered individualism (qualified perhaps only by his devotion to the soldiers under his command), with its indifference to the needs and rights of others, ultimately disables a more critical perspective in the daughter. In many respects, Yael Dayan's *My Father, His Daughter* follows the model of her father's autobiography, a volume she helped write and edit and which she describes as composed of "a series of peaks, with the personal and the national drama intertwined" (146). In Yael's narrative (as in her father's), the highest peak is the victorious ending of the Six-Day War, representing a convergence of personal and national high points: her father's greatest military accomplishment; her own most intense experience of national service (as a war reporter); and meeting her husband-to-be, an army officer many years her senior. "It wasn't mere coincidence," she writes, "that the nation's and my father's finest hour, which was also a turning point, produced my own happiest moments and days" (194). Written to a large extent in defence of her father and his vision, *My Father, His Daughter* is marked by the autobiographer's blind acceptance of her own privilege, and her lack of critical awareness of the inequalities and injustice that characterize the domestic and national worlds surrounding her. In the domestic sphere, her response to her father's many infidelities is disgust, not with him but with the women he chooses, for their "vulgarity" (167). Her response to Ruth's decision to seek divorce is condescending disapproval: "[we] were strongly opposed to it...[the family] felt that if she had managed all these years, perhaps with our help and encouragement she could go on" (204). Politically and ideologically, Moshe Dayan's bedtime stories of "our ancestors who walked this desert" (80) continue to colour the adult daughter's perception. Even in retrospect, there is little thought given to the Arab owners of the "deserted houses" in Jerusalem taken over, after 1948, by the "Custodian of Absentees' Properties" (69), or to the owners of "deserted fruit orchards" in the "deserted Arab villages" around Jerusalem (72). Relocating to Jerusalem after the War of Independence, the family would enjoy frequent visits to these orchards; "each of these wild, overgrown, unattended 'bustans' was like a new Eden" (72-73), Yael recalls. The autobiographical narrative does eventually register Yael's critique of some of the consequences of her father's vision, but to the extent that such a new understanding is experienced as a fall from grace, nostalgia continues to exercise its powerful hold.

It could well be that it was the father's personal betrayal—Yael's narrative is framed by the account of how Moshe Dayan left his children out of his will, clearly choosing his second wife over the preferred daughter—that made it possible for the daughter to shake off the bonds of "ideal love" (J. Benjamin 79) and gain a measure of critical distance. As *My Father, His Daughter* moves towards closure, the autobiographer's voice assumes a new perspective. This perspective is not only critical of an imperialist national mindset emerging after the Six-Day War—"people quickly assumed the role of occupants in the territories, dismissing the possibility of ever returning them....Israeli society as a whole underwent a change for the worse, because it lost the strength to resist the chance of an easy life" (205-206)—but more broadly interrogates the vision of the nation exemplified by Moshe Dayan. In its recognition of the explosive plurality of the nation, Yael's challenge to the dominant homogenizing and totalizing nationalist dream of her father is ultimately congruent with her grandmother's and mother's shared vision. Referring to Moshe Dayan's *Living with the Bible*, Yael writes: "[it is] a perfect juxtaposition of life in biblical Israel and Father's own life as it related to it....*What was lacking was a whole dimension of Judaism which he failed to relate to*....The vast depths of Jewish morality, the gap in time when the people had the Book without the land and survived on faith alone, the heights of ethics the prophets demanded of the people, the post-biblical writing, the Talmud and the Mishnah, without which self-preservation would be impossible—he did not relate to" (251-52, emphasis added). And pausing to reflect on Moshe Dayan's image of the pre-biblical woman bent over her cooking for her (and his) family, she adds, "His family was not exterminated in Dachau; it did not worship in secret in medieval Spain or fight in the Warsaw ghetto. His family did not derive strength from the Hasidic tales of an Eastern Shtetl or hide in caves in the Atlas Mountains. His family did not joke in Yiddish or read the Bible with a guttural Sephardic accent...The betterment of society, the ideological foundation of egalitarianism and socialism—of which the world of his parents consisted—the spiritual concerns of our revived civilization were not dominant in his priorities" (252).

MAY THERE BE PEACE (?)

Yael Dayan's concluding reflections enact the tension between "the pedagogical and the performative" that Homi Bhabha sees as endemic to the construction of the nation (146). Her evocation of a national space defined by the "heterogeneity of its population" (Bhabha 148) gives the lie to her father's totalizing narrative "of the 'social' as homogeneous" (146). But even such a pluralistic vision of the nation, for all its concern with social justice, cannot escape the dark shadow of the always potentially violent division between Self and Other that is the very condition of national identity. The normative national Subject, Israeli scholar Hannan Hever has suggested, is a "living dead"; constituted in opposition to a threatening Other, the national Subject is "either dead with a live [memorialized] national existence or alive as a person who has interiorized death [who lives with anticipation of dying for the national cause] and is dead within life" (133). It is indeed under the sign of death that the self/nation-narratives of both grandmother and granddaughter open. Sitting in the cemetery in Degania and contemplating those fallen in the service of the nation, the bereaved mother Deborah Dayan observes in herself a mixture of gut-wrenching anguish and strange calm; she is puzzled at first, then finds a name for it: "this is the feeling of homeland [*moledet*]! The feeling of homeland?—And I thought that we only knew the value of homeland, our duty to her. But no! Here we have earned the *feeling* of homeland" (34). In an early chapter of her autobiography entitled "Before Memory," Yael Dayan seeks to reach deep into that which sustains collective identification. What surfaces are figures of loss and bereavement: "the roots are where the home is, where the grave is, where some of the children are to live and be buried" (25). Although not recognized as such by the autobiographers themselves, their maternal subject position produces a distance from the script of national subjectivity and a third term—they are neither the dead nor the living dead, but their mothers—that disrupts the repetition of a Self-Other binary wherein "the question of the cost of individual death is obscured" and the figurative borders between the dead and the living are blurred (Hever 126). In these autobiographical narratives, death does not simply belong to "the people"; it is literal and literalized, its cost made horrifically particular.

The specificity of nationalism, Liah Greenfeld has argued, is that it "locates the source of individual identity within a 'people,' which is seen as the bearer of sovereignty, the central object of loyalty, and the basis of collective solidarity" (3). Three principal imperatives, directed at individuals as members of the national collectivity, follow from this grounding of the nation in ideas of sovereignty, loyalty, and solidarity: one is called upon to privilege one's own people, showing loyalty to them above all other people (or values); one is called upon to manifest that loyalty, in the first place, by doing whatever is necessary to safeguard the nation's (primary) right to sovereignty; and one is called upon to espouse solidarity, that is, disregarding evidence to the contrary, to regard the collectivity as "fundamentally homogeneous, and only superficially divided by the lines of status, class, locality, [or] ethnicity" (Greenfeld 3). The self/nation-narratives examined here help us query and trouble the assumptions that underlie these imperatives. And beyond their value in dramatizing the disruptive intervention of the performative inside the exclusionary and homogenizing space of the nation, they also urge us to continue asking: how/can the nation be a feeling and a duty not to die and kill for, but to live and let live by?[16]

NOTES

1 I use this designation in order to encompass a range of referents that include both the Jewish and Arab Palestinian narratives of this contested geopolitical space. Palestine is both the name used for the region during the Ottoman regime and the British Mandate of 1918-1948 (before the founding of the Jewish state of Israel), and the Palestinians' name for their national homeland.

2 At the risk of contributing to what one commentator has cleverly named the "'gevalt syndrome,' or doomsday mentality...the deep-seated pessimism and anxiety rooted in the vicissitudes of Jewish history" (Dowty 25), here is a par-

tial list of the historical record that the events of World War II made all the more difficult to forget: "the eleventh-century Crusader slaughters, expulsion from England in the thirteenth century, from France in the fourteenth, from Spain in the fifteenth, the 1648–49 Chmielnicki massacres in the Ukraine (leaving tens of thousands dead), the pogrom in Uman (in 1768, again in the Ukraine), the pogroms throughout southern Russia in 1881. The twentieth century brought the Kishinev pogrom of 1903, the more general Russian pogroms of 1905, the pogroms in the Ukraine leaving approximately another 100,000 dead in 1919–20, and finally the murder of six million Jews by the Nazis" (Cohen 43).

3 In *Palestinian Citizens in an Ethnic Jewish State*, Nadim Rouhana suggests that a more accurate term for this collective identity would be "'Palestinian in Israel,' a phrase that reflects the political realities and helps Arabs cope with the complexities and paradoxes of the political system of which they are formal, but not belonging, citizens" (150).

4 *Intifada* refers to the Palestinian uprising in response to the Israeli occupation of territories resulting from the 1967 war.

5 See Sharoni for another study that seeks to demonstrate that "Palestinian and Israeli-Jewish women's struggles for gender equality and for a just resolution of the Israeli-Palestinian conflict" has resulted in the creation of a "space for new interpretations of peace and security" (152).

6 I adopt here Walker Connor's understanding that all nationalism is ethnically predicated, so that one would need to employ a different term, such as patriotism, to refer to civic identity or civic loyalty.

7 Aviva's son, the writer Johnathan Gefen, sees in his mother yet another casualty of the Zionist revolution. Gefen's ironically titled auto/biography *Isha Yekara* (literally Dear Lady) explores the impact on his own life of his mother's depression, a condition that indeed cost him dearly and which he sees as a symptom of a national malaise. Gefen writes of the generation of his grandparents Deborah and Shmuel Dayan: "they did not love themselves, only that reflection of themselves they sought in their high ideals and ideology, and so could not love their children" (189–90, my translation).

8 David Ben-Gurion, Israel's first prime-minister and a contemporary of Deborah Dayan's, describes the bitter "birth pangs of farm settlement in Israel": "plagues of nature, the desolation of the terrain, Arab enmity, corrupt Turkish administration, antagonism from the zealots of the 'old *Yishuv*' in Jerusalem, the agricultural ignorance of all but a few settlers" (36).

9 Mary Wollstonecraft's undoing of this trope still stands, over two centuries later, as a fine example of a counter-narrative: "The conduct and manners of women, in fact, evidently prove that their minds are not in a healthy state; for, like the flowers which are planted in too rich a soil, strength and usefulness are sacrificed to beauty; and the flaunting leaves, after having pleased a fastidious eye, fade, disregarded on the stalk, long before the season when they ought to have arrived at maturity" (7).

10 All citations from Deborah Dayan's autobiography are from the Hebrew original, in my translation.

11 In the narrative, Deborah Dayan turns to A.D. Gordon, a towering figure among the pioneers of the Second *Aliyah*, hoping to find an answer to her

predicament: "how to pull up roots from a distant and foreign land, and put them in a new soil, telling them: 'be nourished, and live'" (264). Although they find a common interest in the European culture they share (they speak of Isodora Duncan), Gordon can ultimately only reiterate the collectivist nationalist ethos, "speaking not of us [as individuals], but of the nation as a whole" (265). For an illuminating discussion of A.D. Gordon and the ethos of nation-building see Sternhell 47–73.

12   Reflecting on her years of feminist activism in Israel, Marcia Freedman writes, "the fear and hostility that feminism aroused in widening circles lasted throughout the seventies and into the eighties" (50). Yael Dayan, she recalls, rejected the women's movement, claiming that "she was already liberated, she wrote in a mass-circulation woman's magazine, and she hadn't needed the help of a movement" (51).

13   Yael Dayan makes the briefest mention of her mother's work accomplishments, and when she does, they are always framed by reminders that Ruth was, first and foremost, a wife and a mother who willingly did what was expected of her. Condescending comments—such as "My mother was famous for her lack of self-confidence" (29)—often accompany the few references to the mother in the narrative.

14   Throughout the narrative, Yael Dayan makes references to her father and herself as making "a good-looking couple" (167).

15   The mature autobiographer does question, however, the moral legitimacy of her (married) father's claim to such freedom from all domestic obligations (100).

16   This essay is dedicated to the memory of David Solomonov, twenty-one, who was killed on Yom Kippur, 6 October 2003, on the Israel-Lebanon border.

CHRISTINE CROWE

GIVING PAIN A PLACE IN THE WORLD
ABORIGINAL WOMEN'S BODIES IN AUSTRALIAN STOLEN
GENERATIONS AUTOBIOGRAPHICAL NARRATIVES

This history of resistance punctuated by cruel repression is *marked on the Indian's body* as much as it is recorded in transmitted accounts....In this sense "the body is memory." It carries, in written form, the law of equality and rebelliousness that not only organizes the group's relation to itself, but also its relation to the occupiers.

— Michel de Certeau, *Heterologies: Discourse on the Other* (277)

The body must be regarded as a site of social, political, cultural and geographical inscriptions, production or constitution. The body is not opposed to culture, a resistant throwback to a natural past; it is itself a cultural, the cultural, product. — Elizabeth Grosz, *Volatile Bodies: Toward a Corporeal Feminism* (23)

For many colonized peoples, representations of the tortured, maimed, and exiled body have become important sources of communal and cultural memory as well as tools for political leverage in negotiating compensation for colonial atrocities. Many Aboriginal women in Australia employ descriptions of their own tortured bodies—as cultural products of government assimilation policies—to achieve political change through the writing of their autobiographies; they approach first-person narratives as a way of educating non-Aboriginal audiences about government policies that have exiled Aboriginal people from their own cultures, histories, languages, and bodies. These texts serve two purposes: to document the lives of Aboriginal women through the representations of gendered and racialized bodies affected by experiences of Australia's policies of removal (resulting in what is now commonly called "The Stolen Generations") and to create a dialogic space in which non-Aboriginal audiences are encouraged to engage with and respond to such representations.

Autobiography has been a frequent choice for Australian Aboriginal women who wish to transform social attitudes because the genre provides a space for both resistance and dialogue. Carole Ferrier, Jennifer Sabbioni, and Anne Brewster have all argued that resistance of some form or another has often been the primary motivation for the development of Australian Aboriginal women's autobiographical narratives. However, as Rey Chow warns, agency must be found simultaneous to the act of textual creation rather than before or after it, and resistance must include more than just a one-way reaction (51). Indeed, to read Aboriginal women's autobiographical narratives solely as texts of resistance not only ignores the didactic motivations that underline these narratives but also effaces the dialogic possibilities of autobiographical narratives as mediums for social and political transformation.[1]

When an Aboriginal autobiographer makes a truth-claim, the implicit question that follows that claim—"Do you believe me?"—creates a critical dialogic site between the author/narrator and the reader within specific historical and political contexts. By addressing their narratives to non-Aboriginal readers, Aboriginal women implicitly invoke Paulo Freire's theory of witnessing as a political and "dynamic" process whereby society both receives and is altered by the testimony: "Witness is not an abstract gesture, but an action—a confrontation with the world and with men—it is not static. It is a dynamic element which becomes part of the societal context in which it occurred; from that moment, it does not cease to affect that context" (178). The dynamic aspect of the witnessing act affects those who receive such testimony by introducing the "relay" function of such narratives: those who listen in the "second person" become charged with the responsibility of carrying on the story and ensuring its continued transmittal. For those in the "first person"—the Aboriginal women who have lived to tell the story—the transformative possibility of this "confrontation" between writer and reader starts with a re-evaluation and reinterpretation of their relationship to their own racialized bodies. Such a positive reinterpretation empowers Aboriginal women as witnessing subjects by legitimizing both the subject and object of their autobiographical expression.

The assertion of the role of the witnessing subject carries strong political and social implications because, in many cases, witnesses dare to challenge the metanarratives of accepted and dominant versions of history. Indeed, as Shoshana Felman has noted, there is a certain risk of alienation related to the act of witnessing "since the witness is a dissident by definition, since the witness can, by definition, have no ally" (185). While such a risk may haunt the witnessing act, the desire to "be believed" and reunited in dialogue after a history of being alienated through silence drives many Aboriginal women's acts of autobiographical witnessing. In anticipation of political resistance and to provide incontrovertible witness to the abuse they have suffered, Aboriginal women foreground their exiled and tortured bodies in their autobiographical narratives. The dynamic presence of these narrated bodies and their importance in the achievement of these dialogical goals is best illustrated by two recent Stolen Generations narratives: Carmel Bird's collection of oral testimonies from the *Bringing Them Home* report called *The Stolen Children: Their Stories* (1998) and Rosalie Fraser's *Shadow Child: A Memoir of the Stolen Generations* (1998). These texts, among others, clearly represent the ways in which Aboriginal women work within the dialogic intersection between the author/narrator, the reader, and the gendered and racialized body.

BODIES IN CONTEXT: THE 1997 *BRINGING THEM HOME* REPORT

Since Theresa Clements's *From Old Maloga: The Memoirs of an Aboriginal Woman* (1954), over fifty autobiographical narratives by Aboriginal women have been published in Australia. The most recent surge of publications took place in the decade after the Australian government's creation of the Council for Reconciliation in 1991.[2] This surge is not surprising, considering that the political environment from 1991 onwards encouraged the engagement of non-Aboriginal readers with the Stolen Generations testimonies of both Aboriginal individuals who were removed from their communities and the Aboriginal communities affected by the removal of children from their midst.

For the first six years of its existence, the Council for Reconciliation largely focused on the local, grassroots level. Then, in 1997, the Human Rights and Equal Opportunity Commission published *Bringing them Home: Report of the National Inquiry into the Separation of Aboriginal and Torres Strait Islander Children from their Families* (otherwise known as the *Bringing Them Home* report).[3] This report provided many non-Aboriginal Australians with their first exposure to cultural genocide in Australia. As a result, it held widespread implications for ways in which those in the "second person"—readers, critics, and citizens of the world—valued and approached Aboriginal autobiographical narrations of history as the narratives confronted, altered, and subsequently became an integral part of the societal context in which they occurred (Whitlock, "In the Second Person" 199).

Penny van Toorn has argued that the acts of witnessing found in the *Bringing Them Home* report altered the Australian political landscape because of "unprecedented public demand" for the stories. This demand, in turn, has transformed the narratives into "both a lucrative commodity and a potent moral and political force in the Australian community" (259). The commodification of the stories from the *Bringing Them Home* report highlights this contradictory "desire" of Australians to engage with, understand, and reconcile events that both horrify and fascinate. Taking into account the ways in which these Stolen Generations texts may satisfy current political needs, several questions then arise: how do autobiographers play on this "desire" in order to create a dialogic space within their narratives, through which they attempt to transform such environments? How do Aboriginal bodies function politically, socially, and discursively as witnesses in Aboriginal women's autobiographical narratives? And why is the representation of the abused and tortured body specifically used to create this space? Such questions invite consideration of the corporeal aspects of witnessing acts, the literal embodiment of narrative, and the role of "real" bodies in constructing the "bodies of evidence" invoked in the *Bringing Them Home* report.

BODIES OF EVIDENCE: THE ABORIGINAL BODY AS WITNESS

Despite the proliferation of articles and books providing critical commentary on the *Bringing Them Home* report, discussions of the physical body, the racialized body, and the gendered body have been strangely missing from these discussions. Critics have been so focused on placing witnessing narratives within the discursive realm of analysis that these stories have been, quite stunningly, disembodied at a time when bodies in Aboriginal Stolen Generation narratives have become increasingly important as carriers of community memory and as tools for resistance against the Australian government's attempts to silence such narratives.

One of the methods of control used by Australian officials during the time of the Stolen Generations was the refusal to listen to or take seriously complaints of physical abuse. Currently, the Australian government's refusal to apologize to Stolen Generation victims along with its chosen attitude of "what's done is done and can't be undone" keeps open the wounds that were perpetuated by earlier governments; as Deborah Bird Rose explains, "Aboriginal people are subjected to double injury, and each injury is perpetuated through denial as well as through violence [insofar as] the injuries of colonisation which stand as concrete evidence of a violence are denied or trivialised by conservative settler ideology....Practices of suppression—distance, denial, and disablement—generate pain; pain generates more suppression, which generates more pain. As the powerful seek to insulate themselves from any relationship to the pain of others, their very actions continue to open and exacerbate the injuries" (112). Bird Rose's discussion makes clear the dynamic relationship between silence and violence: denying the legitimacy of an expression of pain relegates that narrative to silence. Indeed, for the narrator, the experience of being silenced after telling the story of abuse may cause more mental anguish and emotional strain than the physical abuse itself because the social devaluation of an act of personal expression renews and, in some cases, compounds the initial feelings of powerlessness and voicelessness suffered during the abuse.

Such recorded attempts of communication by victims and the silencing of the same by officials fill the *Bringing Them Home* report. In her testimony for the inquiry (subsequently published in *The Stolen Children: Their Stories*), Evie defines the "saddest times" as those during which victims were silenced: "The saddest times were the abuse. Not only physical abuse, the sexual abuse by the priests over there. They were the saddest because if you were to tell anyone, well, the priests threatened that they would actually come and get you. Everyone could see what they were doing but were told to keep quiet" (qtd. in Bird 39). Like Evie, Millicent connects her memories of abuse with the silence, exile, and denial surrounding her attempts to make her experiences of abuse known and legitimated. In fact, her suicide attempt derives from her physical and social exile and the lack of acknowledgment of the abuse rather than from the physical pain of the actual rape:

> Then I had to go back to that farm to work....This time I was raped, bashed and slashed with a razorblade on both of my arms and legs because I would not stop struggling and screaming. The farmer and one of his workers raped me several times. I wanted to die....When they returned me to the home I once again went to the Matron. I got a belting with a wet ironing cord, my mouth washed out with soap and put in a cottage by myself away from everyone so I couldn't talk to the other girls....They showed me no comfort which I desperately needed. I became more and more distant from everyone and tried to block everything out of my mind but couldn't. I ate rat poison to try and kill myself but became very sick and vomited. This meant another belting.[4] (qtd. in Bird 30)

At the time of their abuse, these women make desperate attempts to stop the violence, only to be punished in return for daring to speak out loud. Now, through their testimonies, they choose another means by which to expose their abusers and the systems that empowered those abusers. Although the compulsion to be believed and the struggle to make the story meaningful to both narrator and listener may result in the feeling that "no amount of telling seems ever to do justice" (Laub 78), for many Aboriginal women autobiographical narratives provide an opportunity to refuse the injury caused by silence; the stories act as resistance against and proof of "histories of the gendered and racialized body that has been placed under surveillance, disciplined, silenced" (Brewster 5). To be silenced is, in essence, to be derived of meaning-making practices. Autobiography, in contrast, with its relationship between self, identity, and narrative, encourages those meaning-making practices. Aboriginal women's autobiographical narratives thus derive from "a desire that the body not be lost to meaning"; accordingly, they continue the "ever-renewed struggle of language to make the body mean, to struggle to bring it into writing" (Brooks 22–23). According to feminist theory, the body acts as a source of self-meaning, but it also acts as a fluctuating site of gendered and racial identity as others "read" and negotiate it within social discourse. Colonial situations foreground these negotiations, since at the heart of assimilation "was the surveillance and management of the sexuality and reproduction of black women" (Whitlock, *Intimate* 168–69).

Stories of such management of Aboriginal women's sexuality and further instances of Aboriginal women negotiating identity through their bodies—bodies that become sites of shame, denial, and fear—proliferate through Stolen Generations narratives. As a result of her abuse, Carol develops a sense of herself as a sexual object without agency: "I grew up knowing that our private parts were evil, yet missionaries could touch us when they felt like it. That is why when I grew up that I automatically thought when a man wanted sex that I had to give it to him" (qtd. in Bird 61). Like Carol, other Aboriginal women were taught at a very young age that their bodies would and could be used against their will by men in positions of authority and power. Ruth Hegarty remembers that on the first night of her new life as a domestic servant, the older Aboriginal women in the dormitory had instructed her to protect herself: "Even though I hated being closed in, I pushed the dressing table against the door" (103). This attempt to avoid penetration into her private living space reflects the wider struggle of Aboriginal women to avoid sexual penetration by force. Unfortunately, many Aboriginal women lost this particular battle, and

Hegarty identifies the high rate of teenage pregnancy as another legacy of the institutionalization of Aboriginal women: "I'd come home from work pregnant and so gone the way of most other girls from the dormitory. I was painfully aware that our lives were beginning to mirror those of our mothers" (126). By the time she carries her second child, her despair at being caught in the cycle begins to affect her sense of identity: "By this time my perception of myself was down to zero" (128).

These narratives foreground relationships among gender, sexuality, self-esteem, and identity through descriptions of the female Aboriginal body being abused, raped, or maimed. One of the punishments mentioned in several Stolen Generations narratives relates to the shaving of female heads or the cutting of hair. In *When the Pelican Laughed*, Alice Nannup tells a story about this type of punishment often used in the Moore River Settlement in Western Australia: "There was this beautiful girl named Linda and she was as fair as anything. She had long curly, wavy hair, right down her back. She had a boyfriend named Norman and they used to see one another....[One day] they ran away together, but they were caught. They brought Linda to the middle of the main street right in front of the office. They made her kneel, then they cut all her hair off. It was falling down in big long tresses and we were made to stand and watch"[5] (Nannup, Marsh, and Kinnane 74–75). The practice of cutting off the hair of Aboriginal children and women represents the surveillance of sexuality Whitlock mentions. Long hair acts as a signifier of femininity, so to cut off a woman's hair at once reinforces her gendered identity while at the same time destroying her own pleasure in that identity. In these instances, the hairless woman becomes symbolic of the attempt by officials to control what they perceive as the wild and savage sexuality of the Aboriginal woman.

The silencing of Aboriginal women illustrates the ways in which authorities recognize and avert potential threats to their power and control. As Elaine Scarry notes, those who hurt others physically or mentally often only exert power over their victim when they feel threatened or insecure; to silence someone is to belie one's own fear of what they may reveal, what secrets they have to tell (18). Judith Butler calls these attempts at silencing "operations of foreclosure" and identifies such operations "in those instances in which we ask: What must remain unspeakable for contemporary regimes of discourse to continue to exercise their power?" (*Excitable* 139). Aboriginal women perform acts of witnessing through their texts in order to oppose these "operations of foreclosure" and, in so doing, challenge those "regimes of discourse" that would prefer to have their stories remain unspoken and the scars on their bodies hidden from sight.

ROSALIE FRASER'S *SHADOW CHILD: A MEMOIR*
OF THE STOLEN GENERATIONS

Rosalie Fraser's autobiographical narrative, *Shadow Child: A Memoir of the Stolen Generations*, offers an excellent example of the way in which an Aboriginal woman uses her scarred and abused body as a site of authority from which to perform her acts of witnessing. Published in 1998, *Shadow Child* documents Fraser's removal from her family on 13 March 1961 when she was just over two years of age. As she explains, "on that day, my brothers and sisters Terry aged eight, Stuart aged six, Karen aged four-and-a-half, Beverley aged eight months, and myself, were all made Wards of the State through action taken by the Child Welfare Department of Western Australia" (10). At this time, Fraser and her sisters, Karen and Beverley, were separated from their brothers and sent to live with a foster family.

Fraser's memoir illustrates how the abused body becomes a rhetorical device for acts of witnessing. In her narrative, she gives graphic descriptions of episodes during which she suffers both mental and physical abuse in order to make an impact on her reader and thereby elicit a response.[6] In her description of bath time with her foster mother, Mrs. Kelly, Fraser calls on the narrative authority offered by spoken words, bodily reactions, and the psychological legacy of the experience to frame and anticipate the reader's horrified response:

> Bev and I both remember her language and actions as though it were yesterday. She would say, "Get undressed, you bastards, and get in that fuckin' bath." While we were trying to get undressed she would stand there and push our heads against the wall, hit us and slap us about, all the time shouting at us to hurry up. Once we were in the bath, sometimes she would put her hand over my face, pushing me backwards until I was lying under the water [and] she would hold me under the water until I could no longer struggle….Then it would be Bev's turn. I would have to sit in that bath and watch Bev being drowned, and the whole time I was watching I would hold my breath for her, as though if I did so she would be okay. The terror I felt then, I can still feel today. (16)

In another incident, she describes a particularly disturbing punishment for playing outside in the mud with her sister, Bev: "My foster mother dragged me by the leg, screaming, out from under the bed and down the passage into the kitchen. She laid me over her knee, ripped my pants off, forced my legs apart and pushed something long and sharp inside me, moving it around inside me. Oh my God, the pain I felt was shocking. When she had finished she pushed me to the floor as though she were brushing a crumb from her knee. Instead it was me, a child" (19). On the way to the hospital immediately after this incident, Fraser recounts being reminded by her foster mother that "I was a boong, and no one would believe me if I told them what really happened." Recalling her experience in the hospital, Fraser concludes: "The hospital doctors must have believed the story my foster mother told them: no one—no one at all—asked me what had happened to me" (20). After describing numerous other horrific experiences at the hands of her foster parents, she writes that as a child she had spoken to various people—school counsellors, psychiatrists, Welfare agents—about the abuse she and her sister were suffering but to no avail: "You know, I do not think the Welfare believed me. As far as I know, they took no action over any of the horrors I related" (20).

Throughout *Shadow Child*, Fraser repeatedly recalls incidents when she was not believed or not heard, which suggests that she uses her narrative as an attempt to finally be heard and believed, this time by a different audience. She employs graphic descriptions of her body being abused in order to claim authority and assert "certainty" in anticipation of her reader's doubts; as Scarry explains, in abuse narratives, "the sheer factualness of the human body will often be borrowed to lend that cultural construct the aura of 'realness' and 'certainty'"(14). Fraser also attempts to regain a sense of subjectivity by claiming the "I" of the autobiographical narrative. Fraser's comment that her foster mother brushed Fraser off her knee like a crumb, even though "it was me, a child" indicates the extent to which abuse affects self-identity. At this point in the narrative, Fraser recognizes the difference between herself as object (crumb) and herself as subject (child). Many Stolen Generations testimonies include comments about the effacement and erasure of subjectivity and identity at the hands of the abuser and in the midst of pain, for as Goodwin and Attias argue, "pain can destroy the notion of *me-ness*" (207).

In many cases, these witnessing narratives attempt to reclaim a "body-self" connection through the autobiographical "I." In Fraser's case, since she was silenced as a child by those who held administrative, parental, or physical control over her, her published account allows access to a speaking position through which she can rediscover her "*me-ness*." In other words, Fraser's acts of witnessing grant her access to a sense of self constructed through the autobiographical "I," since the self "is given content, is delineated and embodied, primarily in narrative constructions or stories" (Kerby 1).

Fraser's attempt to reclaim some sense of identity and agency derives, on some level, from her own experience with her racialized body that had

many times made her vulnerable. For Franz Fanon, the colonized, racialized body can never be silenced or denied meaning because such a body is
always already speaking and overdetermined by discourse: "The evidence
was there, unalterable. My blackness was there, dark and unarguable. And
it tormented me, pursued me, disturbed me, angered me" (117). Fraser's
own Aboriginal body torments her because it comes to be so intimately associated with the abuse she receives from her foster mother. Her body, as a
site of pain, also becomes a site of shame due to the racial slurs her foster
mother slings at her during these incidents. As Fraser recounts, "You know,
from the earliest time I can remember, she had the habit of grabbing me
by the back of the neck and pushing me at the mirror, and saying, 'Now
look! Look how ugly you are, you dirty boong—you're nothing but shit.' For
years afterwards, I could never look in a mirror without remembering her
words and thinking how ugly I was" (27). Peter Brooks argues that the
"relation to one's own body has its symbolic manifestation in a privileged
visual moment: self-reflection in the mirror" (14). Fraser's description of
her "self-reflection in the mirror" thus explains her struggle to overcome
feelings of insecurity throughout her life. In some sense, however, Fraser's
autobiography becomes an alternate self-reflection that counters the one
impressed upon her by her abusive foster mother. Her autobiography
restores a self-image that serves to counteract and resist the shame associated with her initial self-reflection. This process of self-reconstruction is
most evident in her description of why she started writing her autobiography: "It has been an experience writing this book. I would recommend
writing to anyone who has problems to come to terms with: it must be the
best therapy one can have....One night, I was so down, even alcohol could
not help, so with the kids in bed, I just sat down and started writing. The
pen took on a life of its own. I started feeling better about myself" (270).

As Fraser herself identifies, these acts which restore the voice and
reclaim self-identity hold little power if there is no audience to legitimate
such attempts. Such a response depends upon the recognition of the audience of the legitimacy and "truth" of the claims made by this voice through
the description of abuse and torture. The irony associated with the expression of either emotional or physical pain lies in the distance it creates
between certainty and doubt, because pain "comes unsharably into our
midst as at once that which cannot be denied and that which cannot be confirmed" (Scarry 4). Despite this seemingly unbridgeable distance between
the sufferer and the witness to that suffering, autobiography offers a means
by which to combat the "unconfirmability" of pain because of its generic
expectations associated with referentiality. Even so, Fraser attempts to

forestall any doubts that come with the distance between narrator and reader—victim of pain and witness to that pain—by claiming perfect memory in *Shadow Child*: "I do not know why, maybe it was because of Karen leaving, but from the time I was three years of age I can remember everything vividly....It just seems as though I woke up one morning with an absolutely clear head, and I can remember our life from that day onwards" (15). Fraser's constant references back to the reliability of her memory[7] not only highlight her ongoing insecurity about "being believed," but also gesture to the importance of memory as evidence for the authorization of her narrative.

After a lifetime of physical abuse and mental suffering, Fraser attempts once more to find someone in authority to "believe her." The final chapters of her narrative describe her attempts to gain an apology and compensation from the Western Australian government for the way she and her sisters were treated as children. She explains her reason for seeking compensation:

> During the course of 1989, after I had obtained some of the information about our past, Bev and I talked off and on about the problems of our childhood, wondering whether there was something we could do to bring such horrors out into the open. Late that year I sent a letter to then Premier of Western Australia, Dr. Carmen Lawrence, to ask for some help. I wrote the letter to her directly for a couple of reasons. To begin with, I was suffering so badly inside myself that I wanted some questions answered—I felt that because of the abuse that I and my sisters had suffered as State Wards, something should be done about it. And I needed to desperately know why! Why did we as children have to go through so much abuse? I thought that she might investigate this, as she seemed the compassionate type, and I believed in her....I never received a reply from Carmen Lawrence. In 1990, therefore, Bev and I decided to go and see a lawyer. When we first went to see the firm, we told them we wanted some answers as to why the State had handled our lives in that manner, and how they had had the right to do so. We wanted that type of response from the authorities—a full explanation, along with a well deserved apology. (234)

The government eventually dismisses her case and rejects her claim because, as a government official explains, "'There is no apology or explanation, because there is simply no money, okay?'" (254). Not only does this statement clearly identify the economic implications if governments were to assume responsibility for the Stolen Generations, but it also exemplifies, once again, the relationship between silence and oppression. Healing processes depend upon the sympathetic response of an audience to the proffered testimony. The fact that the government does not respond in any positive or sympathetic way to Fraser's claim only serves to exacerbate the pain of her memories, because she strongly feels that "the Department should be held accountable for what happened to me" (265). When she receives no answers from Carmen Lawrence, she once again feels betrayed by someone she "believed in." Nonetheless, Fraser's ongoing attempts to find justice and her efforts to relieve her own suffering through writing may become, according to bell hooks's own experience, the seeds of social and political change: "I say remember the pain because I believe true resistance begins with people confronting pain, whether it's theirs or somebody else's, and wanting to do something to change it. And it's this pain that so much makes its mark in daily life. Pain as a catalyst for change, for working to change.... I think that's why everywhere I am, my true comrades are...[those] who know that pain, who are willing to talk about that pain. That is what connects us—our awareness that we know it, have known it, or will know it again" (hooks 215).

In their autobiographical narratives, Aboriginal women use their abused bodies to assert a textual authority and a privileged speaking position from which to perform their acts of witnessing. Although the Australian government attempts to deny the full impact of these memories on the Australian national identity, the bodies of abuse victims represented in Stolen Generations autobiographical narratives refuse such denial by acting, to recall Fanon, as unalterable evidence, dark and unarguable, of the sordid history for which the government refuses to take responsibility.

UNDERSTANDING AND RESPONSE: THE DIALOGIC NATURE OF THE WITNESSING TEXT

> Understanding comes to fruition only in the response. Understanding and response are dialectically merged and mutually condition each other; one is impossible without the other.   — Mikhail Bakhtin (282)

> These voices and all the others of the Stolen Generations insist on a hearing, on understanding, and on response.   — Carmel Bird (116)

The wish to "be believed" and the desire to have certain horrific experiences validated through audience response gestures to a parallel wish that the story might continue to be told or remembered outside the literary space. Any act of witnessing invites the audience (the reader) to respond to the act of telling the story and to become responsible for carrying on the story after it has been told—a process Ross Chambers refers to as the "witnessing relay" (127).

Not surprisingly, this notion of a witnessing relay depends upon a perception of the narrative as legitimate, for unless readers understand the purpose for the narrative's existence, they will take no responsibility and accept no obligation. Fortunately, Aboriginal women's Stolen Generations autobiographical narratives have been authorized by the dominant non-Aboriginal audience partly due to the current political environment and the Australian government's investment in the Reconciliation movement. As a result, readers who witness abused and tortured bodies in the Stolen Generations narratives become implicated in the "witnessing relay"[8] and accept responsibility for carrying on the witnessing act. In other words, survivors of the Stolen Generations insist "that a kind of listening—a response, a taking on a responsibility—must take place" (Frow 355).[9]

Because recent Stolen Generations narratives construct discursive and moral sites around the tortured and abused bodies of Aboriginal people, they have initiated the recovery and reclamation of Aboriginal cultural memory in the service of political and social justice. De Certeau, who locates the body as a site of political struggle and organization, has identified this kind of process: "This *tortured* body and another body, the *altered earth*, represent a beginning, a rebirth of the will to *construct a political* association. A unity born of hardship and resistance to hardship is the historical locus, collective memory of the social body" (227). De Certeau's recognition of the connection between tortured bodies and tortured land resonates loudly in the Australian situation, for the struggle over Aboriginal land claims in Australia has much to do with the struggle over the bodies which were removed from that land. This struggle, in many ways, is the struggle over history and memory, for although the government stole both land and children from Aboriginal communities, the memories of the land and the memories carried in the bodies of those affected by the Stolen Generations remain intact. Although the Australian government believed that the best way to achieve assimilation was to physically remove Aboriginal children from their communities in order to effect a disconnection from cultural memory, it forgot that bodies carry within them the memories of generations past that are "sedimented in the body" (Connerton 72) and transmitted through bodily performance of ceremonies, dance, song, and oral storytelling. For Aboriginal people, the body acts as a recording device. As a result, Aboriginal bodies have recorded hundreds of years of colonization, and the stories that both the land and the bodies tell remain a challenge to a government whose attempts to deny history and erase the memories have failed.[10]

The use of representations of the abused body within the legitimated "truth-telling" genre of autobiography has facilitated this failure. The descriptions of exiled Aboriginal women's bodies serve to construct identification between the autobiographer and reader in order to first make transparent and then transcend the inherent differences between Aboriginal and non-Aboriginal histories. Aboriginal women attempt to transform the socio-political relationship with their audience in the space between the two processes of understanding and response, a space opened up by what American feminist Nancie Caraway calls "an oppositional pedagogy": "A discourse of horror is not a critical discourse. But it can be framed as an oppositional pedagogy. If our goal is affirmative, we can turn words of horror around to create a reading of empowerment, one which prefaces a longer political journey we need to take....The project of horror visited on the bodies and psyches of Black females is an interrogation which we must see as a projection of the collective mind...out of which emerges an alternate principle of personhood" (80). For Aboriginal women who write of abuse and torture, who use "words of horror" to educate their reading audience, autobiography allows the creation of "a reading of empowerment" that may also transform Aboriginal women's relationships to their own bodies. By filling their narratives with the horrors of history, Aboriginal autobiographers attempt to come out of the psychological exile imposed by abuse and affirm their own personhood; the moment of narrativization reaffirms the self for an audience who, the authors hope, will understand and respond accordingly.[11]

In order to resist or return from this state of exile, Aboriginal women have built bridges between text and context, between self and other, and between Aboriginal and non-Aboriginal histories. V.N. Voloshinov once wrote, "Word is a two-sided act. As word, it is precisely the product of the reciprocal relationship between speaker and listener, addresser and addressee....A word is a bridge thrown between myself and another" (86). This "bridging" effect is, of course, the basis on which the government's policy of Reconciliation has been developed, with the understanding that Aboriginal and non-Aboriginal Australians will attempt to meet halfway in their attempts to understand the implications of sharing the same continent and national history.[12] The metaphor serves as a positive representation of an act of invention, creation, and relation. Most of all, it reminds us that each word written or spoken and eventually published by an Aboriginal woman adds another step towards at least creating the public discursive and dialogic spaces necessary to continue the acts of witnessing and take advantage of the transformative possibilities that have been offered by Australian Aboriginal women's autobiographical narratives for over fifty years.

NOTES

1 For a recent discussion of Stolen Generations testimonies as dialogic forms, specifically in relation to post-secondary student responses to witnessing, see Rosanne Kennedy, "The Affective Work of Stolen Generations Testimony: From the Archives to the Classroom" (2004).

2 The life span of the Council for Reconciliation ended in December 2000. In its place, "Reconciliation Australia" was formed to continue the work that the Council had started. See <www.reconciliation.org.au> for more information on both Reconciliation organizations.

3 All testimonies from this report used in this chapter derive from Carmel Bird's edited collection, *The Stolen Children: Their Stories* (1998). As in Bird's text, only the first names of those who have testified will be used.

4 Ruth Hegarty also talks about the use of physical exile as a means of punishment in *Is That You, Ruthie?* Like Millicent, Hegarty recognizes that it is the isolation of exile, not the physical discomfort, that leaves the deepest scar: "I remember it so well. Even if we were locked up for only half the night to teach us a lesson, the very thought of being put away on your own in a locked cell, with high barred windows, no lights and very little ventilation, no bed and a drum in the corner—this was enough to terrorise any child. Just the isolation was enough without the fear and trepidation....Those experiences had the capacity to disempower any child. We who lived through them will bear the scars of this treatment for the rest of our lives" (43).

5 In her testimony for the Inquiry, Peggy recounts a similar punishment: "It was all about control, reform. The bald head was part of the dormitory system for punishment. If you had lice, you had your head shaved. But you could have your hair cut off for being naughty, doing anything naughty....Humiliation, because when you got your head shaved we were not allowed to put a beret or anything on our heads" (qtd. in Bird 82).

6 Although many people use metaphors with which to describe their pain ("it burns"; "it stabs"; "it is like a hammer pounding on my head"), Scarry explains that in some cases, "the sentences describing the accident may more successfully convey the sheer fact of the patient's agony than those sentences that attempt to describe the person's pain directly" (15).

7 At the beginning of her text, Fraser admits that her memory may be unreliable ("I was too young to understand the things that happened to us straight away, or to remember them in a clear way afterwards" [10]) but she counters that admission by calling on the collective memory of her sisters and on the memories that her traumatized body has carried: "It has taken me a long time to allow myself to recall those years, to take in what happened to me and my sisters, and to try to deal with the memories. What I will do here is to tell the story

as much as possible the way I lived it at the time. My sister, Karen, can recall a great deal, in fact she tells me she remembers events all too well" (10-11).

8   Amnesty International uses this notion of the "witnessing relay" as the moral ground on which its work stands. Scarry explains, "Amnesty International's ability to bring about the cessation of torture depends centrally on its ability to communicate the reality of physical pain to those who are not themselves in pain" (9).

9   Frow's comments reflect Dori Laub's discussion in relation to Holocaust narratives: "To a certain extent, the interviewer-listener takes on the responsibility for bearing witness that previously the narrator felt he bore alone, and therefore could not carry out. It is the encounter and the coming together between the survivor and the listener which makes possible something like a repossession of the act of witnessing. This joint responsibility is the source of the reemerging truth" (85).

10   According to Scarry, "The relative ease or difficulty with which any given phenomenon can be *verbally represented* also influences the ease or difficulty with which that phenomenon comes to be *politically represented*" (12).

11   The nature of that "second person" response and its implications has been discussed by Whitlock in her essay, "In the Second Person: Narrative Transactions in Stolen Generations Testimony."

12   This was also the metaphor taken literally in July 2000 when hundreds of thousands of Aboriginal and non-Aboriginal people walked across the Sydney Harbour Bridge in the name of reconciliation during Corroboree 2000 celebrations.

ADRIENNE KERTZER

CIRCULAR JOURNEYS AND GLASS BRIDGES
THE GEOGRAPHY OF POSTMEMORY

> I am conscious of having a relationship with the viewer, and I would like
> the viewer to have that experience of discovery, from their own experience.
> — Ydessa Hendeles (qtd. in Mays 96)

Shortly after Same Difference opened in spring 2002 at the Ydessa Hendeles Art Foundation in Toronto, Sarah Milroy reviewed the exhibit. In her article, Milroy linked Hendeles's background as the daughter of Holocaust survivors to her collection of close to 4,000 images of teddy bears, more than 1,800 of which were on display. Not having seen the exhibit, but driven both by my professional interest in Holocaust representation and children's literature and by a familial link to Holocaust survivors, I decided to visit Same Difference as soon as possible. Yet I was simultaneously suspicious of my own response, recognizing that in displaying any interest in this decidedly odd linking of teddy bears and the Holocaust, I was once again confirming my distance from my family's history.[1] On the two occasions that I subsequently visited the exhibit—once in April 2002 on my own, and a second time four months later with my husband and children—I did not take my mother.

Even imagining the possibility that photographs of teddy bears might be regarded as a more than a trivial response to the Holocaust separates me from my mother and my other relatives. The memories of that generation, as Marianne Hirsch proposes in *Family Frames: Photography, Narrative, and Postmemory*, differ from mine. My relatives' memories are "more directly connected to the past" (Hirsch 22). In contrast, what Hirsch calls postmemory is both more remote and more imaginary, a highly mediated form of memory separated by "generational distance" yet retaining a "deep personal connection" (22). Asserting that all memory is mediated, but postmemory is more so, Hirsch further defines postmemory as "the experience of those who grow up dominated by narratives that preceded their birth" (22). Regarding postmemory as familial, specific to the experience of children whose parents' narratives respond to "cultural or collective traumatic events" (22), Hirsch also sees it functioning in the memory work of later generations.

We might question how postmemory can be both specific to the experience of a second generation and descriptive of all succeeding generations. Is there not a difference, for example, between my postmemory, the ambiguous knowledge that governs how I respond to my mother's family photographs, and the inevitably more remote way that my children respond? Is there not an even greater difference when guests see a portrait of my mother's family in my living room but remain ignorant of the family history that explains the portrait's presence? It is precisely these differences that concern Hirsch as she assesses the ability of different "image-texts" to extend "the postmemorial circle" (251).[2] Arguing that "meta-photographic texts which place family photographs into narrative contexts" (8) offer the potential of moving from the artist's familial postmemory to an aesthetic response of affiliation, Hirsch is the first to admit that this pedagogical move does not always succeed. The move requires a moment of shock, a moment that startles us into adopting faces and stories that are not found in our family albums. If as hostess I hesitate to tell the guests in my living room that the elegantly dressed gentleman in the photograph was my grandfather, a few years before he died in Auschwitz, I am responsible for not providing the narrative that offers them the possibility of affiliation. I rarely tell my guests the incongruous narrative—the distance between my grandfather's proper appearance in the photograph and his improper ending in Auschwitz—that I tell myself whenever I look at the photograph. For even if I tell them the story, I cannot guarantee their response. The move to affiliative looking is "idiosyncratic, untheorizable" (Hirsch 93); we cannot predict with any certainty when and where it will take place.

The article that follows constructs a map of postmemory, one whose coordinates position it temporally within the second generation, and representationally within the discourse of adult texts. It asserts that postmemory's geography is a map that we rarely share with children, that the representation of memory in children's books is very different from the representation of postmemory in adult texts. Many of the paper's questions are locational. Are there representational markers by which we recognize postmemory? Are these markers always within the text—the novel that announces, for example, that its narrative perspective is that of the child of Holocaust survivors? Or is it equally likely that the markers of postmemory reside as they appear to in Same Difference in the relationship to the work—either the artist/curator's relationship to the installation or in the viewer's perception of the installation?

This article begins with Same Difference, an exhibit that I read about before I visited it. But characteristic of the circular journeys of postmemory—the adult returns to childhood memories—the paper ends by circling back to a place name that I heard repeatedly in my own childhood, but never saw represented in a public space until forty years later in the United States Holocaust Memorial Museum. In the space between these two journeys, the one to Toronto in 2002, the other to Washington, DC, in 2000, is a survey of the private landscape of postmemory: its features in adult fiction, its problematic status in children's literature, and the fragility of its work as pedagogy. That I circle here too, reconsidering a moment in a young adult book, Jane Yolen's *Briar Rose*, that I have discussed differently elsewhere, is not surprising. Postmemory journeys are by their nature endlessly repetitive.

THE GEOGRAPHY OF POSTMEMORY IN SAME DIFFERENCE

As might be expected from a second-generation writer, I begin with the personal—not the predictable memory of a miserable second-generation childhood, but the far more recent memories of visiting Same Difference. My repeated and failed encounters with Same Difference serve as a cautionary tale about our recognition of the art of postmemory, and how that recognition affects our response. These problems of response are puzzling, given that I am, like Hendeles, someone who grew up with parents directly affected by the Holocaust: "There are some people still around with real memories of Hitler. I only have the remembrances of growing up with these memories" (qtd. in Mays 96).

My postmemory knowledge does not necessarily privilege me. It does make me question the significance of biographical information provided by both Sarah Milroy and John Bentley Mays in their reviews of Same Difference. Both writers draw on interviews with Hendeles that inform us about her familial relationship with the Holocaust. Although Mays admits that his was a "failed interview" in which "her answers had nothing to do with the questions" (95), he still includes Hendeles's answers. Milroy quotes Hendeles saying that, as a child of survivors, she had no family albums, a comment that prompts Milroy to think of Same Difference as a strange kind of substitute. Like Milroy, Mays also commences his assessment by informing his readers that the best way to begin his account of the exhibit is to situate it within Hendeles's life. He quotes her: "I have very few pictures of myself, and there's little before the war" (93). Why is this information necessary? If both writers inform us that Hendeles is the daughter of survivors because they believe that it will help us respond to the exhibit, then why is this supposedly vital information not readily accessible to visitors of the exhibit? Once we have access to this information, what difference does it make?

One of the striking aspects of Same Difference is that it is an exhibit without a catalogue. In essence, Hendeles invites visitors into her semi-public space, not quite her living room, but not a conventional museum either. Not only is the foundation named after her but it is open for only a few hours a week; visitors enter by making a donation whose amount they are free to decide. Just as in my living room, the majority of photographs that make up the installation are not labelled. There are two ways in which we might read this: either Hendeles does not know the identity of the people photographed, or she regards that information as superfluous. In either case, we are left with photographs, objects that Hirsch identifies as particularly potent agents of postmemory because of their relation to the real, yet they lack an immediately obvious narrative frame that explains them. Certainly photographs may be all that remains after the real has vanished—Hirsch quotes Susan Sontag on photographs as memento mori—but as Hirsch rightly notes, we cannot read photographs outside a narrative frame. Hendeles refuses to provide such a frame. As tempting as it might be to conclude that the children (and the others) photographed holding the teddy bears in Same Difference no longer exist because they were Hitler's victims, this generalization clearly does not apply to all of the photographs. In a Holocaust museum, the museum setting functions as a narrative frame in that the images, we assume, must have some relationship to the subject of the Holocaust. In contrast, in the Ydessa Hendeles Art Foundation, the setting does not tell us that this exhibit in any way responds to the Holocaust. When the installation consists of so many untitled photographs, the visitor is left unsettled. She is driven less to an affiliative looking that allows her to adopt the images as her own postmemories than to a process of questioning that invites, then resists, any simple connection between the knowledge that drives the collector/curator and the exhibit that is all around her. It is as though Hendeles offers an installation that directly challenges the affiliative possibilities that Hirsch finds in the Tower of Faces in the United States Holocaust Memorial Museum in Washington, DC.[3]

Some of my questions about Same Difference are very personal. How do I separate the response generated by my particular postmemory from the influence of Milroy's article that instructs me about what the exhibit means? How do I silence the voice of the good daughter, the voice that inscribes me as a daughter of a Holocaust survivor, who whispers that when I am moved by Hendeles's exhibit, I am substituting postmodern play for the questions (and the images) I cannot deal with? Am I moved simply because I am relieved, just repeating in the space of Hendeles's gallery some of the relief I feel when reading about the Holocaust in the protected space of children's literature? Looking at photographs of bears relieves me from looking at photographs that document Holocaust atrocities. Same Difference is not a children's book, but like children's literature, it limits my exposure to the brutal facts of Holocaust history. In this protected space, I can indulge in the pleasures of aesthetic and intellectual response, pleasures I do not find in more recognizable Holocaust photographs.

Other questions are more general, directed at the significance of the details and overall design of the exhibit. Hendeles includes only two of her family photographs; they are the only photographs with labels that appear on the walls in the main exhibit room.[4] Just inside the door of the main exhibit space, to the left as the visitor enters the room, is one. The label reads, "Dorothy Hendeles, survivor of the Holocaust, with her daughter, Ydessa, born Dec. 27, 1948." Above it on the second level, is the other. It reads: "Jacob Hendeles, survivor of the Holocaust, with his daughter, Ydessa, born Dec. 27, 1948." Are the two photographs to the left because it is assumed that the visitor begins by turning to the left? Why should she?[5] Or are the photographs placed randomly to remind us that the Holocaust disrupted Hendeles's family story, that the family albums that stress "chronology, continuity, and repetition" (Hirsch 214) will not be found here? On my first visit, I did not even notice the two family photographs; entering the main gallery space and walking straight forward, I looked elsewhere, seeing instead a photograph of an unidentified child holding a teddy bear and sitting on a potty. In truth, I did not find the family photographs until my second visit, and I looked for them only after I overheard another visitor refer to them. Although I asked for directions, I still had trouble finding the photographs. Perhaps disoriented because I could reach the second level only by climbing a narrow winding metal staircase that led to a confined space, even when I found the labelled photograph, I was confused. Where was the father/survivor in the photograph? Then I realized that I had misunderstood the label: Jacob Hendeles, the "survivor of the Holocaust," was once simply another baby photographed with a teddy bear. Looking at the photograph, the visitor cannot know what would happen to the baby. Whatever meaning she wants to apply must engage with the categories that the organization of the gallery space both provides and repeatedly resists; the photograph of Jacob Hendeles is placed beside other photographs depicting children clutching teddy bears in bedrooms. Determined to find a narrative, the visitor is frustrated even though she may think that she knows the plot; certainly the absence of names for those photographed suggests the anonymity of the victims of genocide. Do the winding staircases that go nowhere represent chimney smoke? Do they suggest the vanity of searching for meaning in the Holocaust? The winding staircases lead to Jacob, but they are no Jacob's ladder. There is neither a divine resolution nor a coherent narrative here.

Many photographs are similar to those in my family albums—little girls with bows in their hair, family portraits that resemble many that I already know. Others do not resemble those in my mother's collection: pornographic photographs of naked women with teddy bears nestled between their legs, photographs of Hitler Youth with teddy bears, photographs apparently taken outside of Europe. But I kept returning to those that were familiar. Deprived of a catalogue, I fantasized a personal narrative in which my visit to Same Difference culminated in my discovering a photograph of my mother's family. This fantasy of heroic rescue was undercut by my knowledge that I often cannot recognize my mother in her childhood photographs, but it was hard to abandon. If being photographed holding teddy bears was so popular throughout the twentieth century, maybe my mother's family was also photographed. Surely if such photographs existed, they too might be circulating on eBay, the Internet auction house through which Hendeles accumulated her collection over two years of intensive trading. As a child, I used to imagine that my grandfather was not actually gassed at Auschwitz, that one day he would just show up. As an adult, I settle for a lesser fantasy.

In my determination to find a meaning, I circled back to the entrance room of the exhibit, and returned to a photograph of Sigmund Freud and his two dogs. Unlike most of the photographs in the main exhibit space, Freud's has a written entry beneath it, which characterizes him as an avid collector and mentions that his sisters died in the camps. A grammarian might characterize my previous sentence as a "cat-and-dog sentence"; what does the first clause have to do with the second? But this kind of dislocated cat-and-dog grammar is precisely what happens as the visitor attempts to link images and spaces. What does the entrance space have to do with the main gallery space, with the hallway, and the room that ends it all? Writing for the readers of *Canadian Art*, Mays is less interested than Milroy about interpreting Same Difference through the lens of Holocaust postmemory. He discusses how the exhibit demonstrates Hendeles's move from collector/curator to artist. Mays offers a series of tentative hypotheses: "If there must be a central theme to 'Same Difference,' then let it be collecting" (95), a statement that he immediately qualifies by adding, "But it is also a show about bears" (95). But does an exhibit about collecting and bears have anything to do with the Holocaust? If pictures could talk, what might Freud say? Mays does not discuss how the commentary beneath the photograph of Freud might serve as an ironic introduction to the exhibit; instead he reminds his reader that the Nazis used "mass media, especially photography" (97) to deceive.

Like Milroy, Mays infers the meaning of the exhibit through the impact of the concluding artwork: Maurizio Cattelan's *Him*, a statue of a half-size Hitler, dressed like a German schoolboy, kneeling with hands clasped. Milroy describes her shock at moving away from the main gallery space and discovering *Him*. The figure startled and clarified the exhibition for her. But forewarned, and always uncomfortable with the language of Holocaust transcendence that Milroy adopts, I was not so moved. Only someone for whom Hitler has become a mythical figure could be surprised that Hitler was once a child. Milroy also quotes Hendeles asserting that Hitler offered many in his society the false reassurance of the teddy bear. I take the point, but the human longing for the magic protection of teddy bears explains little, and, like Claude Lanzmann, I want to ask, "Well, is it because of all these conditions that the children have been gassed?" ("The Obscenity of Understanding" 207). Mays reads *Him* differently: "This is how Hitler wished to be seen when in power and after all was lost, how he wished to be remembered" (Mays 97). He interprets Cattelan's statue as ironically linking Christ, Hitler, and all the many people photographed with teddy bears. Teddy bears cannot protect anyone: "there is only one way out; the way we entered the world in the first place, and how we shall exit it; from nothingness, and back into it" (97). However clever this art history gesture to "extend hearts and hands to the victim of misunderstanding and hostility we see kneeling before us" (97), I think that Mays's conclusion misses the point of the exhibit design.

My son, Nicholas, had yet another response to *Him*. However, when he asked the attendant whether Hitler hated Jews because he didn't have a teddy bear as a child, she did not answer. Instead she directed us to the organization of the photographs in the hallway: the incremental move from photographs of one person with a teddy bear to photographs of many people with teddy bears. She drew our attention to the photograph of a team of soccer players in striped uniforms placed just outside the dead end that leads to *Him*. Unimpressed by the symbolism of striped uniforms, I was suddenly compelled by the gallery design; the visitor cannot get past *Him*. There is no exit. She can only turn around and retrace her steps through the exhibit space, forced by the design of the gallery to return to the photographs and see if she can possibly find a meaning that does not exclude *Him* yet allows a way out. But the only way out is through the entrance; journeys of Holocaust postmemory go nowhere. The journey is itself a dead end. Placing *Him* at the end of the exhibit space, Hendeles gestures towards the art of postmemory by pointing to its limitations. Postmemory goes only so far; around the corner is the historical amnesia that turns *Him* into nothing more than a grotesque schoolboy. There is no way to link the statue and the photographs. The statue is repellent precisely because I know who he is, and for that reason, I cannot participate in the gesture of forgiveness that his kneeling implies and that Mays finds so "wickedly ironic" (97). In contrast, the photographs of the people with teddy bears are distressing because I do not know who they are and cannot find any narrative to explain them other than the organizational patterns that led Hendeles to group them. The more I recognize structural patterns—teddy bears with phones, in the bath, on horses, with cameras, with hula hoops, with dolls, with celebrities (for example, Ringo Starr and Shirley Temple)—the less certain I am about what I am responding to. However appealing my longing to read Same Difference as the revenge of the collector, able to buy on eBay auction the detritus of people who could not buy their way to safety sixty years earlier, this reading simply does not explain all of the photographs.

According to Hirsch, "the agent of postmemory…gives narrative shape to the surviving fragments of an irretrievable past. But the stories do not add up" (248). What is "wickedly ironic" is surely the way the exhibit baffles the very categorizing impulse it subscribes to, the compulsion to categorize that produces racial hatred. Yet the exhibit traps me. Like the tourist who resents her dependence on a map but wants one anyway, if only to set it aside, what I really want as I retrace my steps through the gallery is a catalogue in which the collector explains the impetus for her collection. I want access to her private knowledge. I am aware of the contradiction: Milroy's description of *Him* may well have impeded my ability to be affected by it, yet here I yearn for a catalogue to help me understand the rest of the exhibit. Is the missing catalogue a deliberate artistic denial, a clever mockery by Hendeles of those who believe that the Holocaust can be represented and made sense of? If we cannot make sense of thousands of photographs of people clutching teddy bears, then how can we hope to make sense of the Holocaust in which so many more people were murdered, including possibly many once photographed with bears? If we cannot take in all of the photographs so carefully positioned in this one gallery in Canada, imagine trying to make sense of the collections of stolen goods found in the concentration camp warehouses, that other *Canada* that haunts my viewing.

Considering such questions, I noticed during my first visit that Hendeles was present, talking about the exhibit to someone else, pointing out organizational details that obviously I was not the only one to overlook. As I was leaving, I asked her when a catalogue would be available. She told me that she could not afford to publish one (a not-surprising comment given the prices that she paid for some of the images). So much for theoretical justifications behind the missing catalogue. Even in a postmodern gallery, sometimes an exhibit without a catalogue is just an exhibit without a catalogue.

THE ADULT LANDSCAPE OF POSTMEMORY

Undoubtedly the ambivalence that marks my response to Same Difference is exactly what characterizes me as a member of the second generation. Ambivalence is often attributed to the children of Holocaust survivors, both in their hesitancy about whether being members of this generation makes any difference in how they understand their lives, and in their resistance/attraction to knowing their parents' stories. How much do we really want to know? For Hirsch, ambivalence also characterizes the many artistic forms produced by postmemory. Because the children of survivors are often driven by ambivalent longings, desiring both to know what cannot be known—the destroyed past—and to "re-member, to re-build, to re-incarnate, to replace, and to repair" (243), Hirsch defines postmemory art as a "particular mixture of mourning and re-creation" (251).

Despite Hirsch's insistence that postmemory is not identical to memory, at times, the two are hard to distinguish. One such instance occurs when, immediately after suggesting that the children of Holocaust survivors are more than normally ambivalent in their curiosity about their parents' past, Hirsch makes an about-face and relocates ambivalence, suggesting that postmemory "may be less ambivalent and less conflicted" (243) than survivors' memories. A further blurring of boundaries occurs when Hirsch identifies herself as a child born in Romania hearing stories about Czernowitz, a place that no longer exists in the way that it did prior to World War II. But surely it is not her *postmemory* of Czernowitz—the place that she only hears about—but rather her own *memory* of being uprooted from Bucharest, the place where she was born, that leads her to assert, "This condition of exile from the space of identity…is a characteristic aspect of postmemory" (243). If for European-born Jews such as Hirsch home is "always elsewhere" (243), it may also be elsewhere for those who do not have second-generation memories of collective traumatic events. Just as certainly, a state of exile may have absolutely nothing to do with postmemory. It is my memory, not my postmemory, that explains why the home that no longer exists for me is a farm located in southern Ontario, not Nové Zámky, Komarno, and Dubnica, the places in Czechoslovakia where my parents grew up. Although Hirsch allows for various forms of postmemory, a further characteristic of its geography is the centrality of trauma in a narrative that overwhelms both the teller/participant and the second-generation listener. Central to Hirsch's understanding of postmemory is the premise that the second generation's "belated stories are evacuated by the stories of the previous generation shaped by traumatic events that can be neither understood nor recreated" (22). Hirsch's language mimics the parents' experience; not deported in reality, the children feel it is their own stories that are evacuated. This definition asserts more than just that the parents' memories are never the child's memories. It implies that the child remembers a childhood in which she was overwhelmed by the burden of postmemory. In keeping with this perspective, when writing of her own postmemories, Hirsch admits, "certain moments from my parents' history easily displace my own narrative" (226).

That such a response generates a feeling of inadequacy among the second-generation is commonplace. Think of the opening of volume 1 of Art Spiegelman's *Maus: A Survivor's Tale, My Father Bleeds History*. In it, Vladek, Artie's Holocaust-survivor father, dismisses his son's tears by a scathing comment about the trials of friendship under Holocaust conditions: "If you lock them together in a room with no food for a week…then you could see what it is, friends!" (6). Or consider Judith Kalman's "A Reason to Be," in which the narrator comments upon her parents' expectations that their daughters could do anything: "They made it sound easy.…if your standard was being gassed, tortured or stripped of everything you held dear, the rest would seem a breeze" (131). Even when postmemory writers proceed to challenge this second-generation convention of a childhood that cannot compete with the trauma of their parents' lives, they begin with the pattern in which the children, no matter how little they know about the details of their parents' past, know at least this much.

Although, in memoirs by the second generation, the expectation of secondary trauma produced by the Holocaust is often belittled (as it is ultimately in Spiegelman), it is taken far more seriously in fiction. The best example is the fiction of Thane Rosenbaum, where postmemory frequently exhibits the excess of hysteria; in the short story collection *Elijah Visible*, the narrator is so dominated by his postmemory that in "Cattle Car Complex" he convinces himself that a stalled elevator is a cattle car. Is it any wonder that this narrator believes Holocaust survivors were so damaged that they should never have had children? Rosenbaum makes the same point in *The Golems of Gotham*, a novel that presents an extreme example of a child, Oliver Levin, damaged by his survivor parents and the appalling postmemories that they give him. Considering suicide, Oliver is quick to distinguish his motives from those of his parents, who killed themselves in a Miami synagogue years after they survived the Holocaust. He seems traumatized by both postmemory and memory. Yet Oliver is also convinced that the children of survivors are different from other adults: "expose[d]...to second hand smoke, plagu[ed]...with cattle-car complexes" (334).[6]

All of these examples illustrate the hopelessness and despair implicit in Hirsch's definition. The second generation's stories are "belated" and "evacuated"; the traumatic events that shape the parents' stories cannot be understood. The second-generation writer, therefore, who seeks to understand the parental past as a narrative whose chapters include but do not focus solely on the Holocaust, writes against the darkness of much adult fiction about the second generation. When Elaine Kalman Naves writes a memoir of her family's past, *Journey to Vaja: Reconstructing the World of a Hungarian Jewish Family*, the childhood knowledge that she starts with is not the place where she ends. It is not simply that Naves now knows more than she did as a child; it is paradoxically that in knowing more about what happened to her father's family, she moves into the more affirmative space of the writer who writes for children. *Journey to Vaja*, published in the McGill-Queen's Studies in Ethnic History series, is not directed primarily at child readers, yet an interview with Naves and her daughter, Jessica, is featured in a special Holocaust Literature and Education issue of *Canadian Children's Literature*. In the interview, the daughter emphasizes how her mother's book taught her that "there was a life before the Holocaust" (Naves and Naves 36). This conclusion is supported by the mother's belief that *Journey to Vaja* will empower her children: "They can meet and love their ancestors through story form, and not just or only through the legacy of their loss" (47).

In contrast, adult fiction about the second generation often takes for granted readers' expectations of a despairing narrative in which the lesson, if there is one, is highly ambiguous: "My parents were Holocaust survivors. Need I say more, or should I just go ahead and ruin your day?" (Rosenbaum, *The Golems* 31). Clearly it is far easier to recognize postmemory in fiction than in exhibits that lack a catalogue simply because the narrative voice so carefully identifies the postmemory position for us. When Rosenbaum's protagonists name themselves as the children of survivors, we accept their identity because they fit our prior expectations. We know that they are children of survivors because they are miserable; they are miserable because they are children of survivors. Obviously there are children of survivors who write other stories, who do not dwell on the troubled dynamics of their familial relation to their parents' experience. But however complex the reality of the second generation as depicted in memoir, or as examined by psychologists and social workers in real life, in fiction, to dwell on the Holocaust for the second generation is to be defeated by it.[7] In *The Golems of Gotham*, Oliver's daughter, trying to save her father, asks the spirits of her grandparents if the Holocaust is responsible for everything. Her grandfather replies, "And you already know that the Holocaust is responsible for everything" (92).[8] Giving up on itself, the second generation turns to the third generation. Characters such as Oliver's daughter in *The Golems of Gotham* or Jesse, the grandson of survivors in Sonia Pilcer's *The Holocaust Kid*, are clearly meant to move the family beyond the paralysis of postmemory in which the Holocaust is responsible for everything.

POSTMEMORY AND CHILDREN'S LITERATURE

Hirsch interprets Spiegelman's dedication of volume 2 of *Maus: A Survivor's Tale, And Here My Troubles Began* to his daughter Nadja as evidence that the daughter will "carry on her father's postmemory" (36). If Nadja does so, she will inevitably deviate from the postmemory of her father's books, given that in her postmemory, her father's experience as the child of survivors will itself be a postmemory. Should Nadja turn to the writing of children's books about the Holocaust, she will have to transform the postmemory even more. The tension inherent in the dual meaning of Hirsch's definition of postmemory—a term that characterizes the experience of the second generation, but also applies to the memory work of later generations—is strikingly apparent in children's literature. In considering the future shape of postmemory, we might well consider its present and problematic status in children's books.

Postmemory's traumatic discourse is marginal to the memory evoked by children's historical fiction, the books that represent the Holocaust past in order to teach hopeful lessons about the future. Consider the difference between second-generation postmemory and the form of memory appropriate to children's books revealed by Elaine Kalman Naves in her interview with *Canadian Children's Literature*. Naves acknowledges that there is no right way of teaching children about the Holocaust: "there is no way of teaching it that is going to be okay, because it is not okay" (Naves and Naves 43). In contrast to this characteristically second-generation comment, her daughter Jessica appears far less conflicted, and declares her intention to teach children lessons about the Holocaust whenever possible. Naves admits that she cannot tolerate some of her own survivor/mother's stories; in contrast, Jessica says, "It doesn't bother me" (42). Despite the title of the article, what emerges is the sharp distance between Naves's response and that of her daughter. Jessica describes how she tells children about Auschwitz: "I explained that…there were many sad things done to Jewish people there.…that there were other times and places when bad things were done to other people" (39–40).

When the Holocaust is just another example of the sad and the bad, one that can be turned into a universal lesson about history, it is no wonder that the troubled discourse of second-generation postmemory is so rarely present. What is surprising is that trauma and postmemory do not necessarily disappear. Something strange happens to the traumatic memory found in adult texts when these texts are repackaged for child readers. The memory that drives the writer is both present and absent, often producing a traumatized narrative site whose traces and meaning are only apparent to the reader already familiar with other texts. That reader may well conclude that the traumatic memory is covered over simply because we protect child readers from the full horror of traumatic historical events in order to prevent an unintended secondary trauma (and also because publishers are reluctant to publish such works for children). And we do so for sound pedagogical reasons as well: children's literature is future-oriented. Whatever representation of historical trauma we give children, we frame it with the possibility of a future in which such trauma will not happen again.

Although there is plentiful evidence for the self-censorship of children's books, a version of non-familial traumatic postmemory may also account for some very odd narrative decisions. Such decisions do not apply to the simple suppression of traumatic memory that makes a Holocaust survivor such as Gerda Weissmann Klein publish decades after her memoir, *All but My Life*, a very hopeful, non-traumatic picture book, *Promise of a New Spring: The Holocaust and Renewal*. Protecting young readers by excising traumatic personal memories often occurs when female writers of Holocaust memoir later in their lives produce books for very young children. Isabella Leitner's *The Big Lie: A True Story* is another example where the survivor's traumatic memories of the Auschwitz gassing of her mother are simplified into a matter-of-fact statement, one death in a historical account of so many deaths. This is very different from the relentless return of traumatic memory in Leitner's three adult memoirs, but we might understand such narrative decisions as the survivor's conscious choice. The survivor chooses not to tell children because she knows what it is to be afraid as a child.

A different narrative situation is at issue when the children's writer is not herself a Holocaust survivor, but a writer who includes in her fiction traces of her own response to an autobiographical telling of trauma. These traces are illogical in narrative terms as though the writer does not fully control her writing. One example of this pattern appears in Jane Yolen's young adult novel, *Briar Rose*. Yolen's story about a granddaughter's quest to learn the truth about her grandmother's experiences during World War II was directly inspired by Claude Lanzmann's *Shoah*.[9] Although this inspiration is evident in multiple ways, for the most part, readers do not need to know Lanzmann's documentary to comprehend Yolen's text. However, there is one moment of narrative excess that is more than an obscure allusion to Lanzmann. In its dynamic of telling, but not telling, the passage exceeds the self-censorship of the children's author who does not want to frighten her readers; we might read its repetition as speaking to the traumatic impact upon Yolen of a particular testimony in *Shoah*. The reader unfamiliar with *Shoah* remains ignorant and is thus protected from trauma; Yolen, distressed by her viewing of *Shoah*, is unwilling to communicate her knowledge yet unable to repress it completely. The knowledge remains—a disturbing trace in the text of the afterlife of trauma—postmemory in this situation produced not through early childhood dynamics but through an aesthetic response.

Such a response offers one way of understanding a narrative reference that is incoherent otherwise. It is the moment in *Briar Rose* when the grandmother, who obsessively tells her granddaughter a traumatized, Nazi-inflected version of "Sleeping Beauty," insists that as the prince goes through the castle, no one is "stirring" (128). The granddaughter insistently asks the meaning of this word but the grandmother never answers her. The young adult reader, who will not likely have seen *Shoah*, may well wonder what the fuss is about. The reader familiar with the context of "stirring" in *Shoah* may suspect that the fictional grandmother's refusal relates to Yolen's traumatic postmemory, formed through her viewing of Lanzmann's film. Although she compulsively draws attention to "stirring," Yolen does not include the information derived from her viewing that would explain her reluctance. Most viewers of *Shoah* who recall Filip Müller's incredulity when he is first ordered as a *Sonderkommando* in

Auschwitz to "stir" the bodies in the crematorium will understand Yolen's reluctance. But what, other than traumatic postmemory produced through her watching of Filip Müller's testimony, explains her obsessive emphasis on the word?

THE SHOCK OF THE FAMILIAR: CIRCULAR JOURNEYS AND GLASS BRIDGES

Just as reading Sarah Milroy's review of Same Difference affects how I respond to Same Difference when I visit it, acts of narrative repetition affect our ability to recognize and respond to the personal narratives of postmemory. I've read this somewhere before, I think, and the sequence in which I read conditions my response. Reading Judith Kalman's collection of stories, *The County of Birches*, after I have read her sister's *Journey to Vaja: Reconstructing the World of a Hungarian-Jewish Family*, I constantly evaluate the truth of Kalman's fiction by its relationship to Naves's work. Despite Naves's admission that *Journey to Vaja* is "fictionalized but not fiction" (Naves and Naves 31), the details in Kalman that resemble the details in Naves resonate differently. Whenever Kalman's stories deviate from a detail that appears in Naves, I ignore the possibility that the two sisters may have heard different versions of the same incident, or that both accounts are fictional, and inevitably, if somewhat naively, assume that Naves's account gives me the historically accurate version.

For example, in Kalman's "Channel Crossing," the grandmother boarding the train for Auschwitz is stopped and asked about a white shawl that the grandmother always wore on Yom Kippur. Both Kalman and Naves say that the grandmother replied, "Clothes to die in" (Kalman 75; Naves, *Journey to Vaja* 256). In Kalman's story, Eichmann asks this question; in Naves, Eichmann's Hungarian assistant, László Endre, poses the question. My conviction that Naves's account is more accurate is not just an example of how my professional training in the fictionality inherent in all representation flies out the window when I respond to Holocaust texts. The response also foregrounds the problem of truth in postmemory narrative. Is postmemory narrative restricted to those who grow up in families affected by historical trauma, or is postmemory narrative a set of conventional features that can be imitated and appropriated? If it is the latter, a form produced by a predictable set of representational markers, we should be able to recognize Same Difference as mediated by postmemory without relying on the autobiographical information provided by Milroy and Mays. If it is the former, then my reading practice is not as naïve as it may appear. As absurd as it would be to claim that the features of postmemory representation cannot be imitated and appropriated, it would be equally problematic to insist that postmemory representation is always recognizable. The features of postmemory in Same Difference are not immediately recognizable; they are located in a web of relationships: Ydessa Hendeles's relationship to the exhibit that she curates, and the familial relationships that the viewer possibly brings to her perception of the installation.

It is also apparent that defining postmemory narrative by a set of conventional features can weaken the pedagogical possibilities that Hirsch imagines. If we recognize as postmemory narrative something that we have read before—whether it is Yolen's use of Lanzmann or Kalman's use of details that resemble those in Naves—repetition may also deaden us to the affiliative possibilities of postmemory. Hendeles uses repetition of teddy bear photographs to prevent any easy affiliation. In contrast, Hirsch praises the family photographs displayed in Yaffa Eliach's Tower of Faces in the United States Holocaust Memorial Museum. She imagines visitors to the museum entering the tower, and thinks of that moment as parallel to our taking up a family album, a moment in which visitors can look and know the past differently: "they can adopt these memories as their own postmemories" (Hirsch 255).

They can, but they may not. The pedagogical impact of postmemory is rarely predictable, and the devices by which it operates are equally surprising. Sixty-one years after my father barely escaped the fate of other Slovak Jews by entering Canada one month before the war, I stood in the United States Holocaust Memorial Museum staring at the names of Jewish communities destroyed in the Holocaust. At the museum doing research for a book that I had already decided could only be dedicated to my mother, I had relegated my father to a footnote. He had escaped Europe through the luck of being a farmer and qualifying to immigrate even under the restrictive policies in effect in Canada at the time. I knew that it was only luck that had saved him, but in my childhood postmemory of his story, Dubnica, the little Czechoslovakian village that he came from, was a kind of mythical place.

Forewarned by Hirsch's account of the Tower of Faces, I was prepared for the photographs I found there. As with Same Difference, knowing what I was supposed to feel when I saw the photographs, I felt nothing. But despite what I knew about my father's story, nothing had prepared me for what I saw on a glass bridge that Hirsch mentions but does not dwell on. It was not a photograph in the Tower of Faces that made me stop, but a series of three place names that I had never seen written together. I can recall wanting to stop other visitors and say, look at those names—do you see what they say? I didn't stop anyone. The moment was both intensely private and somewhat absurd. For what I saw were simply the names of the Czechoslovakian towns where my mother and father grew up: Nové Zámky, Komarno, and Dubnica. I understood the appearance of Nové Zámky and Komarno in this list; they were the towns that my mother lived in, but the name Dubnica made no sense. It was the first time in my life that I had seen the name written down. In my childhood memory, Dubnica was not a real place whose remaining Jews were vulnerable after my father left. Seeing its name publicly recorded in a list of communities destroyed in the Holocaust made me see my father's story differently. Recognizing what I had not seen before revised a postmemory that I already had, but the other tourists hurrying over the bridge did not stop. How could they see what the word meant to me?

NOTES

1 I discuss my relationship to the maternal side of my family's history in chapter 1 of *My Mother's Voice: Children, Literature, and the Holocaust.*

2 By "imagetext," Hirsch means any work that includes both image and a narrative context, including novels and memoirs that include fictional images, films, installations, and exhibits (Hirsch 8).

3 In *There Once Was a World: A Nine-Hundred-Year Chronicle of the Shtetl of Eishyshok*, Yaffa Eliach calls the installation in the United States Holocaust Memorial Museum The Tower of Life. Eliach, a child and one of twenty-nine survivors of the Nazi destruction of Eishyshok, collected the photographs of the shtetl's inhabitants. The exhibit in the museum contains 1,600 photographs in a tower-shaped room that extends over three floors. As Hirsch notes, we enter the space of the tower initially oblivious to its resemblance to a chimney.

4 There may be other family photographs; these are the only two that are labelled.

5 One possible answer is that Hebrew reads from left to right, but this answer is problematic given that the exhibit keeps rejecting any narrative that focuses only on the religious Jews who might recognize this pattern. Of greater significance, perhaps, is that the visitor, entering the main space, cannot turn right; there is no right way to make sense of this story.

6 Rosenbaum's metaphors reoccur throughout his work; *Second Hand Smoke* is the title of another Rosenbaum novel about the children of survivors.

7 See the variety of views expressed in Alan L. Berger and Naomi Berger, eds. *Second Generation Voices: Reflections by Children of Holocaust Survivors and Perpetrators.*

8 See Barbara Finkelstein on the "dubious option of turning the Holocaust in a TOE, a theory of everything" (159).

9 I give a different analysis of the relationship between *Briar Rose* and *Shoah* in *My Mother's Voice: Children, Literature, and the Holocaust* (66-75).

MARLENE KADAR [1]

....

THE DEVOURING

TRACES OF ROMA IN THE HOLOCAUST:
NO TATTOO, STERILIZED BODY, GYPSY GIRL

This article addresses the Holocaust as it was/is for Gypsies/Roma whose experience of the event is still largely unknown beyond their communities. One reason for our lack of knowledge has to do with Romany history. Gypsies comprise, according to Romany historian Ian Hancock, a largely non-literate culture, and so rely on oral traditions, such as song, for recording their histories ("Gypsies in Nazi Germany") and passing on their stories from generation to generation. The paucity of surviving or found records suggests that the vast majority of Roma, especially women and girls, could not document their lives. In this circumstance, scholars need to rely on other peoples' stories or witness stories and on examples of oral texts for auto/biographical inscriptions of Romany life in the Holocaust, or the *Porrajmos*, a Romany word meaning "Devouring."

In either case, I want to argue that another person's commentary on a life, however cursory, can stand in for a biographical text, whether it is an archival report authored by a witness at the time of loss or in remembered time, or a Nazi camp deportation list with unknown authors, unnamed scribes who are required to enumerate inmates for transit. Similarly, a personal lament can itself stand in for the autobiographical where no other finished, polished, printed, or published autobiographical or life-writing texts exist. Romany survivors have not recorded their experiences of the Holocaust in the usual fashion—that is to say, in the more conventional autobiographical genres: the memoir, the testimony, or the autobiography. Thus, we are lucky to find their stories in traces or fragments of autobiographical telling and, indeed, these traces and fragments must stand in for autobiographical genres if we are to recover the history of the Devouring. Thus, I want to propose the fragment and trace as member-genres in the taxonomy of auto/biographical practices.

In probing what she calls "difficult education," Deborah Britzman asks herself who and what are lost when history itself is lost? (*After Education* 1-32). Britzman's question is also my question. If the history of the individual Roma experience of the Holocaust is lost because we do not have whole, stable, authored, or published accounts that would fit into, for example, my own (flawed) 1992 definition of life-writing texts, what are we to do (Kadar, "Coming to Terms" 12)? Is that "who" us—and not only the Romany victims—and is that "what" a deeper, fuller account of both the different ways in which traumatic events are remembered, and a reconfiguring of the sub-genres of life writing so that we can reclaim lost stories, and thus, lost histories? Memory registers what it felt like, not exactly what it was like[2] and that slippage from "historical fact" to individual feeling and yearning is crucial to remember in our work in Autobiographical Studies, especially as it is used to understand traumatic events through fragment and trace. Can these kinds of texts tell us what it "felt like," even though they do not meet the literary standard of an autobiography? Can they also give us a sense of who is lost when the loss has rarely been documented in the first person narrative we describe as autobiographical?

My theoretical objective in this article is to question earlier assumptions about the nature of life writing as a genre-unity of texts about or in the form of the autobiographical and in which the fragment or the trace plays no part. Genres are policed, Leigh Gilmore writes, reproducing generic hierarchies that exclude impurities, both formal and asethetic ("The Mark" 5-6). Celeste Schenck pulls no punches: "beneath the Western will to taxonomize lies not only a defensive history of exclusions that constitute a political ideology but also a fetishizing of asethetic purity...which has distinctly gendered overtones" (283); I would add distinctly racialized, as well. Linda Hutcheon has said, "Some intellectual problems simply do not belong to a single discipline" (20) and this project is one of those. Julie Thompson Klein, Linda Hutcheon, and Giles Gunn all explain in their theorizations of interdisciplinary method that it is the subject itself that calls out for an interdisciplinary methodology. In this case, I have used historical and archival information to understand the *Porrajmos*, but in order to cover this subject fully I want to broaden the terms of life-writing texts to include traces and fragments as stand-ins for life stories and auto/biographical practices discussed elsewhere in this collection.

For my purposes, an interdisciplinary method deepens an appreciation of the mutability of knowledge, itself a fragment in Maurice Blanchot's sense: an unfinished separation that is always reaching out for further interpretation (58-59). In this article, I have tried to integrate historical knowledge about the Holocaust and the *Porrajmos* with autobiography theory and some theory about witnessing and its effects. Stories about the *Porrajmos* constitute what Britzman wisely calls "difficult knowledge," creating pain in the victims but also in the witnesses, both long ago and today, in the classroom (*Lost Subjects* 117-20). Dori Laub contends there are emotional and thus intellectual hazards to witnessing in the time of learning—the present—as well as in the time of loss and the original traumatic experience. Dori Laub and Shoshana Felman also argue that because there were no witnesses at the time of the trauma (they speak metaphorically to a degree), "the event could thus unimpededly proceed *as though* there were no witnessing whatsoever, *no witnessing that could decisively impact on it*" (Laub 84), so that witnessing must continue in the present. We perform this witnessing when we read Ida Fink's story or a haunting deportation list, when we listen to the Gypsy lament or look at the eyes in the portraits of children who have died in Hitler's camps, each of which I will discuss below. Practically speaking, however, since the fall of the Berlin Wall, archival collections in the former East Germany, such as those at the Ravensbrück (Fürstenberg/Havel, Germany) and Sachsenhausen (Oranienburg, Germany) Concentration Camps, have opened to western scholars and thus the repertoire of experiences narrated has increased. Thus, too, our opportunities to provide witness have also increased. Finally, for every time there is a season, and for a variety of complex cultural, psychoanalytic, and pedagogic reasons, only belatedly can certain stories be heard, even by the self/teller. There are many examples of Holocaust memoirs created late in the life of the survivor—both Ibolya Szalai Grossman's blended autobiographical text and Elizabeth Raab's memoir come to mind. We might also note what has become the ever-expanding "new" text known as the *Diary of Anne Frank*, and how much it has changed since the first English translation appeared in the US (see Ozick). Some of the changes have come about as new parts of the diary are "discovered" and members of Anne's family adjust to the life and loss of the diarist, young Anne Frank.

The three haunting images which are the subject of this paper—"no tattoo," sterilized body, Gypsy girl—are linked to the not-straightforward remembering of the *Porrajmos*, and each one bespeaks its own separate and remarkable dissonance. I have chosen to focus on these images because they poignantly speak to the little-known, often-contradictory information we have to date received about the experience of Roma in the *Porrajmos*. In order to address my questions about the images, I had to rely on fragments and traces of story and not on finished autobiographies. The power of the fragment or trace is undeniable. Maurice Blanchot provided the theoretical impetus to pursue the fragment and trace as genres that both contribute to our previous theorizations of the genre of autobiography, and also as necessarily unfinished genres that call out to us to *attempt* to finish them. I say attempt because the job can really never be accomplished. The time of loss has already been passed and yet the loss is still with us. How do we find auto/biographical texts that help us to realize this awkward state of affairs, especially when the autobiographer is essentially absent from the conversation we wish to have about the disappearance of possibly one-quarter of the Gypsy population of Europe? Thus, the auto/biographical fragment or trace can be used by life-writing scholars as a legitimate hermeneutical source, another auto/biographical practice, replete with stories about lives lost when finished stories do not exist.[3]

These images represent for me a certain dissonance in my own learning that cannot be resolved even with "new information" and even if we could fill in the absences in our knowledge about the Holocaust in general and the *Porrajmos* in particular. For me, the task at hand is to find a way to make the incoherence of our history meaningful, to make "the present able to live with itself" (Barnes 6). This is difficult to do in the face of both the horror of any state-sponsored systematic annihilation of a people, and in the face of mere traces and fragments of lives left behind, in the wake of genocide. In order to speak about specific texts, I must first speak about the status of traces or fragments—traces or fragments of memory, text, and story. I take my lead from a short story in which is embedded a theory of memory and trace. The traumatic nature of the event forces the memory to capture the remembrance as highly mediated, and yet this is all we have—highly mediated, partial, unfinished, or irregular narratives that at the very least infer an auto/biographical being, a being that bespeaks a self, however transitory. Traces of story and memory are interwoven, and yet as incomplete as they are, they achieve a status of permanence in our lives and in our cultural memory. At least, this is what Maurice Blanchot insinuates in *The Writing of the Disaster*.

"Traces" is the title of Ida Fink's dense three-page story, published in the 1987 collection, *A Scrap of Time*. In a highly neutral voice, the narrator describes what might seem like an everyday occurrence. She is sitting with an older woman whom we assume is Polish and Jewish. She witnesses the older woman's minimal reactions to a momentous photograph. The photograph reminds her of a horrifying day when the village's Jewish children are compromised by the ss officer's trickery and cruelty, and she explains in halting tones what transpired on that day. Fink's readers always remember the image of "traces of footprints" in the snow (135, 136). These footprints are the remains, the traces of a past traumatic event for the witness who is, we imagine, talking to the narrator/writer/Fink. They represent the impermanent and yet recorded remains, mediated by so many variables, including the weather (the snow records prints, but only as long as the cold temperatures remain), the passing of time (both the time of the story and the time of the remembering, and also the time of reading/learning), the quality of the photographic paper, the trauma of the interlocutor and, especially, the trauma of the witness(es). The witness in the story sees the footprints in the snow in a photograph, already just a copy of a copy—a "clumsy amateur snapshot" that is "blurred" (135)—but it jigs a shadowy, and yet precise, memory of an unnamed "butcher shop ghetto" somewhere in Poland, we assume, because it is on *Miesna* Street, or "Meat" Street (136).

The story is even further mediated by the witness's initial unwillingness to remember, but eventually the elderly woman narrates the memory of living in the animal stalls, like an animal. As shadowy as her memory is, it cannot be 'wasted.' She insists that "what she is going to say be written down and preserved forever, because she wants a trace to remain" (136). The trace she means is not represented in exact terms because it is unrepresentable; it is also not represented in the photo, except as absence. However, the photo expresses another image, a palimpsest, or a manuscript in which one text is written over another. This method allows a belated witnessing, a time that is rarely witnessed in its present. The palimpsest story is the one that truly haunts, and is more a trace than the story about the ghetto stalls. The ss discovered eight children (the eldest was seven years old) hidden in the attic of the *Judenrat*, or Jewish Council. These children, we are led to believe, refused to identify their parents—they remained silent—and were then all shot by the ss.[4] The narrator says that the witness to these traumatic events will "later...tell how they were shot" but later, understandably, never comes (137)—the survivor cannot bear any more memory. The story ends on that note, abruptly and without expression, and as readers we think we are all granted a reprieve. However, the temporary reprieve comes at a cost that will be borne by the culture in time to come. Readers rely on Ida Fink's story to teach us to tolerate times of losing and times of being lost, when the contentious history of a traumatic story "meets those other contentions, our selves" (Britzman, *Lost Subjects* 135). We can think of this moment of abandonment by the author as a repetition of crisis in witnessing that both Fink's narrator and reader feel. Psychoanalyst Dori Laub explains how this crisis is learned and repeated: "It was not only the reality of the situation and the lack of responsiveness of bystanders of the world that accounts for the fact that history was taking place with no witness: it was also the very circumstance of *being inside the event* that made unthinkable the very notion that a witness could exist, that is, someone who could step outside of the coercively totalitarian and dehumanizing frame of reference in which the event was taking place, and provide an independent frame of reference through which the event could be observed" (81). Fink's witness cannot provide that independent frame of reference for us, so memory becomes a method and "fiction," the medium, the contradictory dynamic of fits and starts, remembering and forgetting, finding and losing. Fink's story invokes the realization that "the lost ones are not coming back; the realization that what life is all about is precisely living with an unfulfilled hope" (Laub 91), while at the same time suggesting that the witness has an important role to play as a companion (92). Laub explains further that "the testimony is...the process by which the narrator (the survivor) reclaims his position as a witness: reconstitutes the internal 'thou,' and thus the possibility of a witness or a listener inside himself" (85). Readers of Fink's story take on the role of witnessing, too.

Dori Laub uses the example of National Socialism to explain what he means when he says that "no witness" was allowed to exist at the time of the horror (83-84). The Nazi system was foolproof: no witnesses on the outside and no witnesses on the inside. We can imagine Primo Levi's "grey zone" (see Levi 16; Agamben 24–26), where not even the children have the capability to bear witness and say, the emperor is naked; he has no clothes on (Laub 83). "The event could thus unimpededly proceed *as though* there were no witnessing whatsoever, *no witnessing that could decisively impact on* [*the trauma*]," Laub notes (84). Our need for what James Young calls "redemptory closure" cannot be fulfilled, and yet the traces must be followed at "memory's edge" (37–38).

For me, incorporating what Britzman calls "difficult knowledge" into interpretations of the history about the *Porrajmos* meant revising the genre of life writing. In other words, fragments of texts and traces of memories not only communicate the quality of difficult knowledge, but can also *stand in* for conventional finished forms of life writing, many of which are published as memoirs and autobiographies by Jewish survivors or their children.[5] However, to my knowledge, only one *Porrajmos*-memoir by a Romany woman exists, and so the history of the *Porrajmos* is again lost.[6] This loss is all the more complicated when we recall that some Roma lived in traveling caravans,[7] and their life stories may be more often recorded in song, or perhaps in less fixed texts, fragments, and traces of texts, spoken by a knowing "I" or by others, by witnesses.

In its crudest form, then, I imagine autobiographical traces being able to do the following work: the interpretation of a deportation list as if it were a biographical account, as a stand-in for more legitimate biography. For example—the authors of this biographical stand-in, a 1941 inter-camp deportation list (see fig. 1), are largely unknown Nazi officials or *kapos*[8] whose categorizations of inmates and the numbers used to replace names tell stories about their victims, some of whom are *Zigeuner* or asocial, marked as AZR (see, for example, prisoner names Gustave Fiehn, #14, and Joseph Papay, #43, in fig. 1). I will also interpret a collective and ever-changing lament, transmitted orally, as if it were an autobiographical account. I will begin by telling stories about the three images in my title, and I will end with a presentation of the lament. My primary objective is to use the three images as symbols of a modest correcting of received knowledge about the Holocaust and *Porrajmos* (the *Porrajmos* is itself a correcting of our notion of "Holocaust") and about the status of life-writing texts and autobiographical practices.

Liste der Häftlinge, welche am 10.12.41 nach Ahlmannsu/Hftl.Haß.überst.wurden;

Lfd.Nr.	Name	Vorname	Geb.Dat.	Hftl-Nr.	Hftl-Art	Transp.Liste
1	Bedzinski	Wenzel	18.9.11	4936	Pole	19
2	Blaszczak	Johann	14.1.09	3382	Pole	20
3	Bochenski	Stanislaus	20.3.04	5983	Pole	18
4	Boguslawski	Georg	9.10.11	5984	Pole	20
5	Bralczyk	Kasimir	4.3.17	70	Pole	19
6	Brenda	Ignaz	30.7.01	1191	Pole	18
7	Camons-Portillo	Eduardo	18.5.00	9082	Spanier	22
8	Criado	Jose	27.2.13	9154	Spanier	22
9	Czajkowski	Siegmund	21.1.02	142	Pole	18
10	Dobierzynski	Eduard	17.9.99	3515	Pole	20
11	Danielski	Ignaz	20.5.17	6097	Pole	18
12	Dojnikowski	Johann	10.7.10	1361	Pole	20
13	Dutkowski	Theofil	24.4.18	3449	Pole	20
14	Fiehn	Gustav	16.6.87	7496	AZR/Deutscher	18
15	Garcia	Francisco	4.10.17	9256	Spanier	22
16	Grabowski	Romuald	27.3.14	265	Pole	20
17	Heinrich	Hieronimus	25.3.02	3703	Pole	18
18	Herok	Johann	9.12.81	3705	Pole	21
19	Herwok	Heinrich	3.2.10	2136	Schutz/Deutscher	22
20	Jedrasiak	Stanislaus	7.4.21	3775	Pole	18
21	Jurkiewicz	Georg	10.9.12	7584	Pole	20
22	Kacsmarek	Josef	22.12.93	5203	Pole	20
23	Kaliszozuk	Johann	5.3.14	8052	Pole	20
24	Klimczewski	Johann	29.4.96	402	Pole	20
25	Koslowski	Thaddäus	14.2.94	459	Pole	20
26	Kryzinski	Josef	18.3.19	6543	Pole	20
27	Lebedaki	Stanislaus	21.5.01	7655	Pole	21
28	Lange	Siegmund	20.4.15	6598	Pole	18
29	Lossmann	Eduard	12.10.05	1951	Pole	18
30	Luczko	Georg	10.10.06	8586	Pole	22
31	Maczynski	Bronislaus	2.2.02	4112	Pole	21
32	Maniewski	Johann	9.7.17	8601	Pole	20
33	Marchewka	Josef	2.11.06	5429	Pole	17
34	Markowski	Stanislaus	11.10.14	8104	Pole	18
35	Max	Johann	13.12.03	2098	Pole	18
36	Mazanek	Alexander	15.3.21	4161	Pole	18
37	Migolski	Stanislaus	24.4.09	6728	Pole	21
38	Mirek	Josef	21.1.00	5469	Pole	17
39	Niemczyk	Franz	6.12.16	12690	Pole	17
40	Nowacki	Marian	2.2.09	8665	Pole	18
41	Nowacki	Stefan	31.8.22	5510	Pole	17
42	Odria-Ibarlucea	Jose	11.1.22	9511	Spanier	17
43	Papay	Josef	4.5.16	12631	AZR/Zigeuner	17
44	Pereda	Thaddäus	22.12.08	6555	Pole	22
45	Pastewnyczny	Ivan	23.5.13	12292	Pole	17
46	Pastor-Delgado	Antonio	25.12.20	11579	Spanier	17
47	Patajczak	Leo	2.6.16	6960	Pole	21
48	Rognas	Konrad	9.10.16	5637	Pole	18
49	Serwach	Johann	23.11.23	8815	Pole	17
50	Snaglewski	Roman	3.1.96	5700	Pole	21
51	Stefaniak	Johann	9.5.81	7176	Pole	21
52	Tomaszek	Josef	7.2.87	4693	Pole	20
53	Tomczyk	Felix	1.1.14	8890	Pole	19
54	Tost-Planet	Mariano	2.12.20	9746	Spanier	17
55	Turkowski	Siegmund	25.8.11	8896	Pole	21
56	Widynski	Marian	8.12.17	4763	Pole	20
57	Wieczorek	Wenzel	27.10.06	7287	Pole	21
58	Wisrucki	Johann	9.2.05	7289	Pole	18
59	Wojciechowski	Kasimir	26.2.93	4788	Pole	21
60	Wojcikowski	Johann	8.6.01	8929	Pole	17
61	Wisniewski	Johann	13.10.03	8924	Pole	22

Figure 1. Deportation List to Dachau Concentration Camp, 10 December 1941, found in Mauthausen Concentration Camp Archives, Vienna, Austria (July 1999).

No Tattoo

If I asked you if prisoners were tattooed when they entered Concentration or Extermination camps, what would you say?
"Yes."
If I asked you if all prisoners were tattooed, what would you say?
"Yes"; "probably"; or,"I don't know."
If I asked you where they were tattooed, what would you say?
"On the inner or outer forearm."[9]

Figure 2. *Arbeit Macht Frei* ["Work liberates," or "Work brings freedom"], Sachsenhausen Concentration Camp, Oranienburg, Germany, August 2002. Photograph: Marlene Kadar and Gary Penner

I was surprised when I learned that Romany girls who were sterilized in Ravensbrück Concentration Camp had been tattooed. Jack Morrison, an American historian who worked in the Ravensbrück archives soon after the fall of the Berlin Wall (2000), insists that no one was tattooed upon entering the camp. How could this be? I knew that memoirists who had been incarcerated in Ravensbrück bore tattoos on their bodies, most notably the Romany artist Ceija Stojka and the Romany singer Ruzena Danielova. As far as we know, no official documents from the period exist on the Nazi policies about tattoos. George Rosenthal and Josef Buszko explain that, for this reason, our knowledge about tattoos is anecdotal or remembered.

This is what I learned. Tattooing was an imperfect feature of the otherwise highly organized Nazi concentration camp system. We can understand it as one aspect of the larger system of categorizing prisoners as soon as they arrived at the gates of the camp. Ravensbrück Concentration Camp (which was really an extermination camp[10]) was designed expressly for women and girls and for the precise purpose of harnessing healthy bodies for long days of back-breaking labour in one of the many nearby colluding factories, such as Siemens Engineering. Even though it was primarily a factory/work camp, Ravensbrück ironically did not have the infamous National Socialist slogan above its gates: *Arbeit Macht Frei.* A nearby camp, Sachsenhausen, did have the slogan above the gates (fig. 2) emblazoned in iron in a style we remember from other camps, most notably Auschwitz.

In order to signal its benevolence, Siemens has recently set up a Holocaust Fund of twelve million dollars to pay compensation to inmates they used as slave labour at Ravensbrück. But this "sign" begs the question: how would a former slave labourer in the Siemens factory at Ravensbrück prove that she was there? The answer would have much to do with the successful numbering of inmates either entered at Ravensbrück or transported from other camps in order to work or die at Ravensbrück. Although the most vile form of numbering consists of burning a number onto the body, inmates were numbered in numerous other ways, thanks to the invention of the Dehomag (*Deutsche Hollerith Maschinen Gesellschaft*) Hollerith machine (Black 9) and punch card system during what Edwin Black has called "the I[nternational] B[usiness] M[achines]—Hitler intersection" (23–51). Victims and survivors of the Holocaust/*Porrajmos* are "numbered people," and as Black explains—referring to the "mental notes" of the Dutch prisoner, Rudolf Cheim, who was assigned to work in the Labor Service Office with the Hollerith punch cards and their coded numbers— prisoners were identified by descriptive and, yes, biographical cards (20–21). Each card had columns and punched holes detailing various aspects of one's identity: "Sixteen coded categories of prisoners were listed in columns 3 and 4, depending upon the hole position: hole 3 signified homosexual, hole 9 for anti-social, hole 12 for Gypsy. Hole 8 designated a Jew. Printouts based on the cards listed the prisoners by personal code number as well" (21). In our historical memory, tattooing is viewed as the most abject method of numbering human beings. But for the "numbered," it may have had positive connotations as well. We have learned from Jewish survivor remembrances that when prisoners entered Auschwitz Concentration Camp the question of tattooing had immediate dissonant life-death meaning for them. Anne Karpf, author of *The War After*, interviewed her own mother, Natalia Karpf. Natalia begins by saying, "We weren't in Auschwitz long, because in 1944 the front moved nearer and nearer, and they started talking about liquidating Auschwitz. One day there was an Appel again, and they said they are going to tattoo our numbers" (89). At the thought of having the painful and humiliating "operation," we are surprised to hear Karpf express relief. Karpf continues, "When they said that, we knew that we weren't going to the gas chamber, only they were going to transfer us somewhere else. So we were pleased about the tattoos, although it hurt…My number was A-27407, I think—I forgot already because I don't look at it [Checking] yes" (89).

Soon after, Karpf was transported to another camp for women, a small one of 3,000 women in Lichtewerden by Jagerndorf in Sudetendeutschland. Other inmates were transported to Ravensbrück, especially as the Russians advanced from the east. Another Jewish survivor, Carol Frenkel Lipson, A-24742[11] remembers that "We were worried when we weren't given numbers right away. We knew if we didn't get a number, we were destined for the crematorium. In Auschwitz a number meant life" (Adler 76-77). Lipson is grateful that her particular *Schreiber* [scribe] was "neat and gentle in her work." Josef Buszko claims that only 405,000 prisoners were registered at Birkenau or Auschwitz in this way, so not included in any form of registration were the "vast majority of the Auschwitz victims, those men and women who, upon arrival in Auschwitz II, were led to the gas chamber and killed there immediately. Also not included were those prisoners who were sent to work in other concentration camps not belonging to the Auschwitz system, such as Ravensbrück. Still another group of unregistered prisoners were those who were designated for execution after a short stay in the camp. That group consisted mainly of hostages, Soviet army officers, and partisans" (Buszko 110-11). Thus, the Gypsy girls and women who where sent to Ravensbrück from Auschwitz were likely tattooed, whereas those who were sent to the gas chambers immediately were not.

According to George Rosenthal, a survivor of Auschwitz and a historian, the Auschwitz Concentration Camp Complex (Auschwitz 1, Auschwitz-Birkenau, and Monowitz) was the only location in which inmates were tattooed in a systematic way—imperfect though the system was—during the Holocaust. Prior to tattooing, prisoners were issued serial numbers that were sewn on their garments. Different shapes, symbols, or letters were attached to the numbers in order to identify the status, nationality, religion, race, or sexual preferences of the prisoner. This practice continued during and alongside the period of tattooing, and this was also the practice at Ravensbrück.

In May 1944, numbers in the A Series—as with Natalia Karpf and Carol Frenkel Lipson—were first issued to Jewish prisoners, beginning with the men on 13 May and the women on 16 May. George Rosenthal explains that the A Series was to end with 20 000, and then the B Series was to begin, but an error "led to the women being numbered to 25 378 before the B Series was begun" (Rosenthal). This still doesn't make sense if we listen to Karpf, whose number was A-27 407, because A-27 407 comes after A-25 378, by which time the B Series *should* have begun. We cannot assume that the practice of tattooing was consistent or rational, nor can we know exactly how it was used to number Romany girls and women.

Tattooing began in Auschwitz in 1941 with Soviet Prisoners of War (Rosenthal). The soldiers who were not designated for immediate death were stamped with a metal plate (full of interchangeable needles) on the left side of the chest, and then dye was rubbed into the wound (Rosenthal). It wasn't until spring of 1943 that other prisoners were tattooed, even those who had been registered previously in another way. Notable exceptions included ethnic Germans, re-education prisoners, and inmates selected for immediate extermination (Rosenthal). Although in 1941 the tattoo was placed on the left breast, in later years, the inner or outer—as is the case with Ruzena Danielova—forearm was used (Black 352–53; Holý and Necas, 62–63). Black explains that "as the chest became obscured amidst growing mounds of dead bodies, the forearm was preferred as a more visible appendage" (353). For infants and little ones, the location was, however, the upper left thigh.

All *Zigeuner* (the German plural noun meaning "Gypsies") were tattooed with the Z for *Zigeuner*. Some of those tattooed late in the war were then transported from the Gypsy Camp at Auschwitz to work at Ravensbrück, which is why Ceija Stojka, for example, deported for work as a teenager, arrived at Ravensbrück already tattooed, Z-6399. On three occasions in 1944 during the time when tattoos were used more regularly, there were transports of Gypsies to Ravensbrück, totalling 1,107 women between the ages of 18 and 25 (Morrison 51). So although the Ravensbrück women should have no tattoo, the complex details of their transportation from one camp to another meant that they entered the "women's camp" *with* a tattoo.

Just because women were not tattooed on the body does not mean that inmates at Ravensbrück were not numbered. After undressing and showers, Stojka explains, *Zigeuner* received a small piece of canvas with three symbols on it: the black triangle, usually the symbol for asociality (the German word is *Asozial*, and the category was often used to indicate "Gypsy," but also others, such as prostitutes, unemployed people, and vagrants); the letter Z, the first initial in *Zigeuner*; and a prisoner number. Donald Kenrick and Gratton Puxon concur with Stojka's claim (129), although other sources say black was used for vagrants and lesbians, and brown for Gypsies (*Sinti and Roma* 7). This number was sewn on their civilian clothes because Roma were not always issued prisoner clothing.

The prisoner number, whether it was tattooed or sewn on or both, replaced the name of the inmate for the duration of her detention, and this is the most important point to be made. Although this action helped to dehumanize the inmates, it had other meanings for them as the genocide developed. It also served a practical purpose in a political system that legislated the extermination of Jews, Roma, and others. It enabled the ready identification of cadavers so that death lists could be kept and deaths registered and, I assume, in this way a new Series could be re-issued.

What can we say, then, about the meaning of the complicated and paradoxical phrase, "no tattoo"? I think there are a number of observations we can make here. Most importantly, we can speak about the tattoo or the Nazi camp number as a paradoxical auto/biographical symbol of both an erasure of identity and evidence of a life. The Ravensbrück women felt lucky that they did not have their numbers branded on their skin, but prisoners in other camps had reason to feel differently. With clarity and frankness, Carol Frenkel Lipson—A-24742—writes, "a number meant life" (Adler 76-77). Edwin Black describes a further wrinkle in the historical account: Dr. Mengele used his own private tattoo system on inmates he used for his barbaric experiments. When we add this to the mix, we must agree with Black that "Tattoo numbering ultimately took on a chaotic incongruity all its own as an internal, Auschwitz-specific identification system" (353). Although Ceija Stojka and other prisoners were inmates at Ravensbrück and had tattoos branded on their forearms, no tattoos were administered at that particular camp site. Instead, Gypsy women and girls who were healthy must have been deported from the Gypsy Camp at Auschwitz-Birkenau in order to provide slave labour for the conglomerate of factories on or near the Ravensbrück site, or at other camps, such as Bergen-Belsen.[12] We can therefore say that "no tattoo" embodies dissonance: it can be read as both a sign of "good luck" and as a further erasure of identity from history, and either way, it is an autobiographical trace, or a trace of the autobiographical. In some cases, the tattoo or its absence (no tattoo at all) is all that remains of the life, and thus in an eerie way the tattoos "persist on account of their incompletion" (Blanchot 58). While we want to preserve the autobiographical traces of "numbered people," we must remember that according to the 1948 Convention on the Prevention and Punishment of the Crime of Genocide, bodily mutilation, in addition to forcible detention and relocation, constitutes "deliberately inflicting conditions of life calculated to destroy a group." Here we have the ultimate irony: the trace of an autobiography lives within the tattoo, but the tattoo is also evidence of bodily mutilation, and therefore an act of genocide. At the same time as the group was being destroyed, the tattoo was a sign of the Nazi state's permission to live, at least for a short time.

Figure 3. Paintings by Ceija Stojka in the yard outside a central factory building, Ravensbrück, August 2002. Photograph: Marlene Kadar and Gary Penner

Sterlized Body

The second image, "sterilized body," is a blatant reminder that a sterilized body was a source of medical information for Nazi physicians and scientists inside the camps and for anthropologists on the outside. Anthropologists often worked for the Eugenic and Population Biological Research Station. Most famous among them is Dr. Robert Ritter, Hitler's race scientist in charge of the Nazi classification of Gypsies and an expert in "asocial youth." Ritter and his team of younger female race scientists invaded Romany caravans and homes, measured heads, and analyzed blood in order to feed their predetermined racist conclusions. Among these race scientists were two prominent women, Eva Justin and Sophie Ehrhardt. Ritter and Justin—a trained nurse who was often referred to as Ritter's "assistant"— concluded in 1936 that 90 percent of Roma were *Mischlinge* (mixed race) and therefore should be deported and exterminated (Morrison 50–51). Till Bastian explains the complex formulae that Justin and Ritter developed in order to determine various degrees of *"Zigeuner-Mischlinge"*: the more Gypsy blood, the more primitive, work-shy and, thus, asocial the person will be (Bastian 38–40; Lewy 140–43). The degrees of mixed-race blood were formulated "scientifically" using what was called a "scientific method," and a team of accredited anthropologists and behavioral scientists educated in Germany's most esteemed universities "gave form to the new ideology, or better religion, which at the time seemed to offer such promise for the salvation of the Fatherland and of capitalism" (Müller-Hill 93–96).

It may surprise us to learn that women were included in the carrying out of this "murderous science" (Müller-Hill). Women scientists observed and documented the Romany and Sinti communities of Germany and are often seen in photographs measuring head circumferences or examining other body parts (Lewy 46). Sophie Ehrhardt, for example, was a member of Ritter's team of anthropologists (Adolf Würth and Gerhard Stein were also members of the team). Although she was valued as a nurse, Eva Justin began to work with Ritter at the University of Tübingen. She went on to receive a doctorate in anthropology in 1943 after completing a dissertation about Gypsy children (Lewy 44). Gypsies, Slavic peoples, "social misfits" (including people with schizophrenia and epilepsy), and other individuals classified as asocial (AZR, *or asozial*) were reduced to "subservient depersonalized object(s)" by the bond that held "the psychiatrists, anthropologists, and Hitler together" (Müller-Hill 102). Most interesting for us is the fact that asociality was treated as a disease for which sterilization was one cure, and in the case of the Roma, asociality often stood in for *Zigeuner* or "Gypsy" and therefore can be read as a racialized category. This point has been made by others, most notably by Gisela Bock in 1983: "'Asociality' had been an important criterion in the sterilization courts…race hygiene theory had established the hereditary character of the disease, 'asociality' with such efficiency that it had become a central category of racism" (Bock 408, 412; see also Hancock, "'Uniqueness'" 57). Numerous non-Gypsy memoirs and oral testimonies report that groups of Gypsy women and girls suffered at the hands of Ravensbrück doctors, Karl Gebhardt, Rolf Rosenthal, and Gerta Oberhauser, among others (Morrison 241, 246–47). Oberhauser is remembered by memoirist Gemma Laguardia-Gluck, "Prisoner 44,139" (*My Story* 38) and other prisoners; and her various surgical operations are recorded in a variety of prison documents collected in the Ravensbrück Camp Archives. While conducting research in the archival collections at Ravensbrück (in Fürstenberg, the former East Germany) in the summer of 2002, I found a note writtten by Laguardia-Gluck, which attests to the sterilizations of Gypsy girls (Archive Mahn- und Gedenkstätte Ravensbrück, Box 32, 581-98). In a letter written to the Committee of Ravensbrück Prisoners (Report Number 590) soon after "liberation," Gluck writes, and I translate from the German "Dr. Oberhauser had forcibly sterilized completely healthy women in Ravensbrück Concentration Camp, including numerous children from the age of 8. The procedure used to sterilize was radiation, extremely painful—and in many cases led to death" (Box 91, 590). Others have commented that Oberhauser used "a high-powered X-ray machine" or a "High tension apparatus" in which one electrode was placed in the vagina and the other over the abdominal wall near the ovaries. This was "experimental medicine, to say the least," preferred to surgery by Dr. Clauberg because it was simple and effective (Lifton 269–302). Oberhauser, along with twenty-three other physicians and scientists (including Clauberg), was tried at the infamous doctors' trial in December 1946. She was sentenced to twenty years imprisonment for her crimes, but like many of her compatriots was released in 1952. She became a family physician in Stocksee, Germany, but her license was revoked in 1960.

Jack Morrison corroborates this archival fragment in the extensive Oberhauser files (*Band* 36: 40-375). He explains that Gypsy girls were subjected to a cruel ruse in Ravensbrück. Just before the New Year in 1945, the overseers—there were approximately 150 in Ravensbrück in 1944 (not including trainees) and all of them were women—came to the Gypsies with a deal. They said that the "authorities in Berlin" "had agreed to release any young Roma women or girls who would 'volunteer' to be sterilized" (52). Morrison reports that "almost all agreed to the procedure and signed the consent form" (52-53). In theory, the signatories were volunteers, but of course, none of them was released as promised. The young girls who were sterilized did not sign for themselves; tragically, the mothers of the victims signed for them, thinking they were doing the best thing for their children (53).

It is unlikely that the mothers understood what the procedure entailed: many would not have been literate, and, in any case, they might not be familiar with the word "sterilization." It has been reported by Morrison, Kenrick and Puxon, and others that the mothers of the young victims often signed documents they could not read or understand. Even if the mothers understood some of what they were told, like all prisoners, they were desperate for their children's freedom. Thus, we know that between 120 and 140 Romany women and girls were sterilized in Ravensbrück Camp, almost all in January 1945 (Kenrick and Puxon 148; Morrison 53). We know from Michael Berenbaum's study that "Dr. Clauberg sterilized all Gypsy women and their young daughters between the ages of five and eight" (qtd. in Feig 167)—"presque encore des enfants" writes a former prisoner (qtd. in *Avec les yeux des survivants* 24).

Involuntary sterilization was another way the Nazis tortured young Romany women and girls in order to ensure the erasure of Roma from history. If Romany women are sterilized, their history is lost, and a people are at risk of genocide. We are lucky to have at least biographical traces of stories about unnamed Gypsy girls and their sterilized bodies.

Gypsy Girl

The third image, "gypsy girl," invokes a variety of other images, but primarily the words connote absence, the absence of children from our cultural memory on a number of levels. There is a dearth of information about young Gypsy girls who survived the *Porrajmos*, but we know, for example, that by 1944 there were around 500 children at Ravensbrück, half of whom were Gypsies, not including infants. Rarely does the history we do have take race, gender, and age into account. A study could be made, for example, of the practice of "camp motherhood." Jewish survivors of Ravensbrück have commented that they would often become a child's "camp mother," a serious job of child protection, but one that gave the inmates pleasure (Hebermann 150–51). Odette Fabius and a group of French prisoners adopted an eight-year-old Gypsy girl: "Through her [the Gypsy girl] we felt ourselves to be mothers once again" (Morrison 263). Even the Tuberculosis Block at Ravensbrück had a "*Lagerkind* [camp child]," a four-year-old Spanish girl named Stella. As camp mothers disappeared or were exterminated, others stepped in to take their places. Because the few stories we do have about the Romany experience of the Holocaust are transmitted orally, our research methods need to be attuned to this kind of text and research methods adjusted accordingly.[13]

Before I begin the discussion of the performance/oral text, I would like to tell the story of Sidonie Adlersburg, a Romany child who has been memorialized in a "novel" by Erich Hackl (see fig. 4). The novel, *Abschied von Sidonie (Farewell Sidonia)* was published in 1989 for young readers and translated into English in 1991. It commits to public memory the genocidal crime of "Forcible transfer of children by direct force, fear of violence, duress, detention, and other methods of coercion," again, a pertinent clause in the 1948 "Convention on the Prevention and Punishment of the Crime of Genocide." Sidonie was taken by force, suffered enormous duress and fear of violence, until she was deported and exterminated. It is remarkable that a trace of her life story has been preserved and popularized in a fictionalized biographical genre by Hackl, and it is particularly compelling because Sidonie was indeed stolen by Aryans, when the usual (racist) legend insinuates that the Gypsies steal non-Romany children. This legend is enshrined in age-old anti-Gypsy verses and songs, such as "My Mother Said," written below.

Figure 4. Sidonie Adlersburg, a Romany girl born in 1933 and adopted as a young girl by an Austrian family in Steyr. She was removed from her family by town officials and deported to "the Gypsy Camp" at Auschwitz-Birkenau on 3 October 1943. Photograph from Dokumentationsarchiv des österreichischen Widerstandes, A-1010 Wien.

Sidonie was born to a Romany family in 1933, but grew up in the Austrian town of Steyr as a foster child of Josepha and Hans Breirather (Hackl 1–27). She was removed from her family as the institutions in the town colluded to sever her from their Aryan world. "Local welfare workers, the mayor, the school teacher and principal" all rushed to purge Sidonie, even though no command came from above ("The Case"). She was deported at the age of ten, in 1943, and died the same year in Auschwitz. I found this portrait of her in Vienna's *Dokumentationsarchiv des österreichischen Widerstandes* (Archive of the Resistance) in 1999. Sidonie would have been at greatest risk among camp children because she was under the age of fourteen and therefore possibly considered too young to be a productive labourer.

There is a great irony about the abduction and murder of Sidonie. One of the racist myths that supports what Ian Hancock calls "the Pariah syndrome" is that white children are always at risk of being "stolen" by Gypsies. The fear is deep-seated in Europe, even today, where this anonymously authored poem, "My Mother Said," was republished in 2000 in Eric Kincaid's popular *Children's Book of Rhyme and Verse*:

My mother said I never should
Play with the gypsies in the wood;
If I did, she would say,
Naughty girl to disobey.
Your hair shan't curl
And your shoes shan't shine

You gypsy girl,
You shan't be mine.

And my father said that if I did
He'd rap my head with the teapot lid.
The wood was dark; the grass was green;
In came Sally with a tambourine.
I went to the sea—no ship to get across;
I paid ten shillings for a blind white horse;
I was up on his back and was off in a crack,
Sally tell my mother I shall never come back.[14]

In Sidonie's story, the characters are reversed. The Gypsy Girl, and not Sally, is stolen from the white folk who love her, and she never does come back except in the current time as remembered. If we imagine what might have happened to Sidonie or another girl like her, our story might look like this: the girl is forcibly transferred from her home to a ghetto and then a concentration or extermination camp; she has no tattoo, she is sterilized, she is successfully purged from her community by her own neighbours and respected members of her community—physicians and teachers— and then murdered by the state and its leaders, lost to history.

Ian Hancock has determined that between one third and one half of the Gypsy population of Europe was lost in the "great devouring" ("The Roots of Antigypsyism" 38). There is, however, much debate about exact numbers for a variety of reasons, including the paucity of consistent records, and still unexamined records, the details of which are explained by Hancock ("Uniqueness" 48–49). As a consequence, the great misfortune is that Romany survivors often leave only traces of their experiences in other peoples' accounts, or in camp records newly released, and sometimes in song and poetry. Thus, their stories are often invoked by "traces" more than by complete texts that conform to the generic rules of autobiography. Fragments of historical information are then delivered to readers and other kinds of audiences in fragments or traces of auto/biographical genres. They are either taken down by a variety of amanuenses or transmitted orally by a community of singers, or in texts whose status may be read as auto/biographical in order to adjust the historical record accordingly. Indeed, such traces function as unfinished separations, but they are not always only "written," as Blanchot writes (58). In this sense, fragments that are sung are also, as Blanchot explains, prolongations which thankfully "persist on account of their incompletion" (58).

The following lament is one such "trace," but it tells us much about the Gypsy experience of the Holocaust. According to Susan Tebbutt, "Given that Romani is largely an oral language and that for many generations the nomadic lifestyle meant that the level of schooling was low, with a high incidence of illiteracy, it is hardly surprising that there are relatively few written works by Romanies" (133). The haunting tune is performed by an unnamed Slovak Gypsy in Tony Gatlif's film about the immigration of Gypsies from Northern India to Spain over 1,000 years ago, *Latcho Drom* (*Safe Journey*, France, 1993). It bespeaks both the autobiographical experience of the singer whose journey has not been safe at all, and who does bear the tattooed number on her forearm. The singer without a name wails her sorrow, but her song is not her own in the literal or generic sense familiar to contemporary theories of autobiography. The unnamed survivor has borrowed the song from another autobiography, that of the Romany singer Ruzena Danielova (1904–1988), Z-8259, who like Stojka was tattooed in Auschwitz and then sent to Ravensbrück. Danielova was born in Mutenice/Mutenic, Moravia. She performed the song often, and each time she did, it is reported, she began with a prologue and ended with an epilogue. The prologue goes like this, and I am translating from the French: "It is necessary that I say why I sing this song and I want the world to know about it. I was imprisoned for two years and I received the cruelest treatment" (Necas and Holý 22–23). And when she finished the song, she said, "my five children were killed at Auschwitz: Jenda, Majduska, Thomas, Misanek and Suzanka, and my husband also. He was a very good man. I am the only survivor in my entire family" (23).

The film version of the song, and the four-stanza "Oshwitsate," the first line of which is "Oh, at Auschwitz, there is a big house," has been translated by Canadian Romany historian and activist Ronald Lee, author of *Goddam' Gypsy*, and posted to the site of the Roma Community and Advocacy Centre. Another version of the song has been translated into French by Ctibor Necas and Dusan Holý and published in *Cahiers de Littérature Orale* in 1991: "*A Auschwitz il y a une grande prison.*" In both cases, the lyrics record an "unclaimed experience," to use Cathy Caruth's term for the nature of the belated experience of trauma. Yet the template for the song is pre-twentieth century (Stewart, "*Igaz beszéd*"; *The Time*). Recent research on Hungarian laments and ballads by Michael Stewart indicates that many versions of this song circulated, at least three of them before the war. In their book, *Zalujici Pisen* (Accusatory Song) (147–48), Dusan Holý and Ctibor Necas record eight versions of the song, including Slovak, Moravian, and Polish variants (94–96), and document its ancient roots. What do we make of this? Even more interesting is the fact that when Danielova began singing the song publicly, she did not claim to have composed it. By 1957, we are told, she changed her mind, and called herself the author. It is typical of oral traditions that communal songs circulate, but it is also true that by this time, Danielova wanted to put her imprint on the song and on the traditional communal material. We might say that she wanted to put her name to the song to recover the lost history of that sterilized gypsy girl with no tattoo. Danielova, however, was herself tattooed before arriving at Ravensbrück with the number Z-8259 (Holý and Necas 62). Dusan Holý and Ctibor Necas publish a photograph of Danielova with her left arm outstretched and her sleeve pulled up so that we can see the number on the top of her forearm (63).

The 1957 performance of "Oshwitsate" was also recorded by Radio Tchecoslovak of Brno. It was sung during a family birthday party and therefore not performed in a studio. Danielova's version, or so it is said, has been translated from the Romany by Ronald Lee:

> Oh, at Auschwitz, there is a big house
> Where the man I love is imprisoned
> He stays there, suffering his captivity
> And forgets about me.
>
> Oh, that blackbird
> He will deliver my letter for me,
> Take it to my husband,
> Who is confined at Auschwitz.
>
> Oh, there is starvation in Auschwitz,
> We have nothing at all to eat,
> Mother, not even a piece of bread,
> Those starving us are bad karma.
>
> Oh, if I only had a pitchfork
> I would kill the tormentors
> If I only had a pitchfork,
> I would kill the people starving us.[15]

Not only do I have to argue that the song be considered/stand in for a life-writing document in the absence of conventional forms of life writing such as autobiography or memoir, but I also have to underline the idea that autobiographical practices can only achieve the goal of representation and inclusion if the genre is expansive. Convention has it that "true" (Winslow 2) and "notable great" (Holman 49) autobiographies are stable, fixed, single-signature, written, and usually published personal accounts "of one's own history." Many life-writing theorists no longer think of autobiography in such limited terms and can therefore accommodate such

fragile and *un*fixed elements as song into our thinking about the autobiographical genres and practices. It is the gift of all autobiographical practices to illustrate where people have lived and how. "Oshwitsate," for example, illustrates in undeniably powerful terms where Gypsies have lived
during the *Porrajmos*, and what the experience has done to their families
and their people. The "I" of the first verse unites with the "us" of the
fourth, demonstrating the enduring strength of the community of Roma,
if not the individual singer. We understand that the singer's level of literacy is irrelevant in this case, another reason to make room for oral texts,
the primary aesthetic vehicle of non-literate communities. This idea is
underscored when we realize that the song has been used as a shared autobiographical text, and versions have been revised as needed. Helena
Malikova, Z-9953, sings a very different version of the song for Necas and
Holy than Danielova. The Czech scholars describe the performance as
trance-like—Malikova cares only about calling up a moment of profound
emotion from her soul, the emotion that is stirred by "an unclaimed experience," a trauma too great to be reproduced straightforwardly, a trauma
shared by an entire people—in this case, both traveling and sedentary
Roma of Western and Eastern Europe. Ian Hancock claims there was the
"Endlösung der Judenfrage" and the *"Endlösung der Zigeunerfrage"*—two final
solutions, not one (Hancock, *Pariah Syndrome*; "'Uniqueness'" 45-50). Preserving the song means preserving a dissonant trace of Romany history.

　　What is important to note is that autobiographical practices do reference verifiable historical information, but they also work with personal
experience and the rich character of personal responses to that experience. Thus, that which expresses more than what happened, that which
helps us to understand what the particular event *means* to the subject, can
be read as autobiographical. What is important is what it felt like, not
exactly what it was like. The song does not indicate exactly what transpired during the *Porrajmos*; but it registers the significance of what transpired for the singer—and it is for this reason that we can also have many
versions of the same event in the autobiographical genres. The song I mention here is based on improvised verses, free and crudely tailored. At the
same time, each version of the song is carefully structured and repeats
aspects of this structure with some regularity. The song delivers the experience of the singer, preserving the wailing, the sighs, and the knowing
dissonant cries. The song *stands in* for the memories of horrors of living in
the camps, and as such it functions like a stand-in for memoir. It is useless
to try to establish the "real" autobiographer or a fixed theme. All we have
are "traces" of the facts and the stories. The want of concord or harmony

is perpetual; the quality of being dissonant is consonant with the survivor's wish to live when, as Lawrence Langer puts it, living means enduring a death, enduring the haunting phrase "if only": if only the blackbird would deliver my letter/song; if only we weren't starving; "if only I had a pitchfork." If only, in the end, this pain of integrating mourning and sorrow taught us more about ourselves and our capacity to love, even as we love the numerous autobiographers who have stood in for that first historical witness in this song.

NOTES

1 An earlier version of this paper was presented as part of the Laurier Interdisciplinary Lecture Series on 24 March 2003. The author is grateful to the Canadian Centre for German and European Studies at York University for their generous assistance, and to Professor Christl Verduyn, Wilfrid Laurier University, for hers. I also want to thank the Centre for Jewish Studies at York University for their support. For assistance with research in Toronto, I am grateful to Shannon Gerard, Nancy Gobatto, Michelle Lowry, and Rai Reece; and to program assistants in the Graduate Programme in Interdisciplinary Studies at York University, Ouma Jaipaul-Gill and Jan Pearson; and in Germany, to the excellent staff at the Archiv der Gedenkstätte Konzentrationslager Mauthausen, Vienna and the Mahn- und Gedenkstätte Ravensbrück, Fürstenberg/Havel, especially Cordula Hoffmann and Mrs. Erler.

2 Deborah Britzman said this in a conversation about memoirs and the matter of veracity and memory, at York University, Toronto, 12 March 2003.

3 One might argue that all life stories are unfinished in the most cryptic sense of Blanchot's prose. But for the moment, I am taking Blanchot quite literally. The author's intentionality may be illusive, but the majority of readers know when a genre has enough shape to be assessed as "finished."

4 When I read this part of the story, I often think about the officers who were the parents of young children themselves, and the fact that orders to kill children were considered complicated by leaders in the SS. We know, for example, that many officers were indeed loving fathers even as they murdered other peoples' children. See, for example, "Report by the military chaplain, Dr Reuss, to Lieutenant-Colonel Groscurth, 1st *Generalstabsoffizier*, 295th Infantry Division" (Reuss 141–43), or *SS-Obersturmführer* August Häfner's heart-wrenching description on the killing of the children (Häfner 153–54).

5 Traces of Romany stories live in published memoirs such as Dr. Lucie Adelsberger's or Toby Sonneman's. Adelsberger was a Jewish prisoner doctor in the Gypsy camp at Birkenau; Sonneman is the daughter of a Jewish survivor who has traced the lives of members of the Mettbach-Höllenreiner family, "Sinti Gypsies in Germany and Austria" (5). Traces of the Romany experiences of the Holocaust also live in archival documents such as those found at YIVO Institute for Jewish Research in New York City (NYY). Protocol #3590, for example, records the story of Mrs. Aladár Berger, a survivor of the Csillaghegy ghetto (Csillaghegy is a suburb of Budapest, Hungary). Berger remembers two

"mass-graves at Pomáz" (a town four kilometres north of Budapest) where sixteen Jews were buried. It was reported to Berger by "the cemetery-guardsman" that the corpses "were stripped bare by Gipsies [*sic*]" (159). This Protocol #3590 was taken down by Franziska Pollák and translated by Jacques Sarlós for the Jewish Agency Palestine, pp. 153–59 (YIVO).

6   The memoir is written in German: *Wir leben im Verborgenen: Errinnerungen einer Rom-Zigeunerin* [We Live in Hiding: Memories of a Rom-Gypsy]. The book is the first part of Ceija Stojka's autobiography written with Karin Berger. It focuses on Stojka's youth in Austria and her time in Auschwitz, Bergen-Belsen, and Ravensbruck.

7   Although some Gypsies travel by caravan, it is well known now that only a fraction of the world's "nine million or so Gypsies are truly nomadic" (Hancock, "Uniqueness" 50, 54–57). Gypsies have been forced to keep moving in Western Europe, explains Hancock, but not in parts of Eastern Europe, where they were enslaved until 1864 (in Romania). Hancock explains, "By the 16th Century, a Romani child sold for the equivalent of 48 cents. By the 19th Century, slaves were sold by weight, at the rate of one gold piece per pound…Slaves were able to escape periodically and take refuge in maroon communities in the Carpathian mountains" ("Roma [Gypsy] Slavery" 3).

8   A *kapo* is a kind of "supervisory inmate," whose status in the camp is complex. Michael Marrus writes that *kapos* "directed the laborers and were themselves controlled by a small group of ss who remained in the background. The general impression is of a highly stratified system, in which the Nazis encouraged division and widespread corruption, broadly referred to in camp jargon as 'organization'" (129).

9   This text represents an amalgam of common responses to the questions posed here. The responses have been culled in the classroom and at other presentations over the last few years, 2000–2003.

10 Although Ravensbrück was designed primarily for girls and women, it also housed some 20,000 male prisoners at one point. The reason we question its status as a "concentration" camp, at least for the entire period of its operation, is that many inmates were expected to die there, and there is no question that gas chambers were operated on camp grounds until they were destroyed by the ss in the final days of the war (Morrison 289). In order to handle the dead bodies, crematoria were installed. In 1942, Ravensbrück implemented Himmler's Extermination Through Work program, which required the crematoria to complete the program (Morrison 243, 290–91; Black 19–22). Survivors estimate that 6,000 women were gassed during the two months in 1945 when the gas chambers operated (Morrison 291).

11 Because Lipson's number is lower than Karpf's, we might want to conclude she arrived before Karpf, but because of errors made by camp scribes, we have learned that we cannot necessarily make this assumption. This is another example of how difficult and complex the topic of numbering was.

12 Although many of the women whose stories are included in Joy Erlichman Miller's *Love Carried Me Home* were deported to Ravensbrück from Auschwitz, some were instead sent to Bergen-Belsen, including Alice C., Helen G. and Lily M. (27, 55, 64). Morrison explains that the reverse also happened: prison-

ers were sent from Ravensbrück to other camps. Morrison notes one incident in particular where a number of women and most of the children in Ravensbrück were sent to Bergen-Belsen (292).

13 Michaela Grobbel has explained how important oral performance is in our consideration of Gypsy autobiographies from Austria and Germany. She writes, for example, that a performance [of a song] is a "doing" and an "un-doing" at the same time. Very much like philosopher J.L. Austin's notion of the performative utterance (1962), which does not refer to some extra-linguistic reality but rather literally enacts and produces that to which it refers, this "it" of performance only exists in the precarious moment of the here and now. Thus, it is historically and culturally defined as part of a specific time and site, and— very importantly—bound to an individual body. Research in contemporary performance and ethnographic studies has taught us to see how culture is created and how it grows through various instances of local performance that contest assumptions and conventions. Performance, then, as a "doing and a thing done, drifts between past and present, presence and absence, conscience and memory," as Elin Diamond says (2).

14 Ian Hancock has reproduced another rhyme, "The Gypsies are Coming" ("Self-Identity" 52), where the story goes, "The gypsies are coming, the old people say./ To buy little children and take them away." There are many songs and rhymes that speak on this theme of kidnapping.

15 The original Romani version of this lament is printed at the website of the Roma Community Centre, Toronto, Canada.

"Oshwitsate"

Yai, Oshwitsate, hin baro ker
De odoy panglo mro pirano,
Beshel, beshel, gondolinel,
Yoi, opre mande po bishterel.
Yoi, oda kalo chirikloro,
Lidjel mange mro liloro,
Hedjoy, lidjoy, mro romiake,
Yoi, me, beshel, Oshwitsate.
Yoi, Oshwitsate bare bokha,
Na me amen, nane so xas,
Deya, ni oda kotor manro,
Yoi, o bokharis bi-baxtalo.
Yoi sar me yek furkeri djava,
Le bokharis murdarava,
Sar me yek furkeri djava,
Yoi, le bokharis murdarava.

THE AUTHORS AND THEIR ESSAYS

HELEN BUSS is Professor Emeritus in the Department of English at the University of Calgary and the author of numerous interdisciplinary studies of autobiography. Buss's *Mapping Our Selves* (McGill-Queen's 1993) won the Gabrielle Roy Prize in 1994. Buss also edited (with Kadar) *Working in Women's Archives* in 2001; as Margaret Clarke she has published novels, short stories, and poetry.

Buss's article, "*Katie.com: My Story*: Memoir Writing, the Internet, and Embodied Discursive Agency," analyzes the young adult "cyberself" of Katherine Tarbox as an autobiographical script that has consequences for her development as a young woman. Using a feminist autocritical method, Buss explores Katie's growing agency—from victim to scapegoat to survivor. The stages of Katie's growth are revealed in the form of the memoir and ultimately in her uses of the Internet.

CHRISTINE CROWE is Head of Credit Studies, Continuing Education, at the University of Regina. She teaches and researches in the area of Canadian and Australian Aboriginal autobiographical narratives and theories. She also works in the area of Aboriginal student retention and factors affecting first-year Aboriginal student success.

Crowe's paper, "Giving Pain a Place in the World: Australian Stolen Generations Autobiographical Narratives," considers the body as a tool for opening political and dialogic space, and explores how maimed and tortured bodies have been represented in Australian Aboriginal women's autobiographical narratives. Crowe also discusses Stolen Generation autobiographies as a way to achieve political change.

SUSANNA EGAN is Professor in the Department of English at the University of British Columbia. She has published extensively on autobiography, her most recent monograph being *Mirror Talk: Genres of Crisis in Con-*

temporary Autobiography (University of North Carolina Press, 1999). She is currently working on problems of imposture in autobiography.

Egan's paper, "The Shifting Grounds of Exile and Home in Daphne Marlatt's *Steveston*," focuses on Daphne Marlatt's long-poem cycle, *Steveston*, the fishing community at the mouth of the Fraser River just south of Vancouver. The poem gives rise to questions about Marlatt's autobiographical narration of exile and home. As an immigrant to Canada from Australia and Malaysia, Marlatt situates herself in this fishing community to which Japanese immigrants came from the end of the nineteenth century, expecting to return home, but from which they were removed for internment during WWII. Egan illustrates how Marlatt's attention to the constant movement of people and water and fish includes the movement of land and of horizons, so that the migrant situates herself in a shared impermanence that she defines in terms of particular place.

BINA TOLEDO FREIWALD is Associate Professor of English at Concordia University. Her areas of teaching and research include critical theory, women's writing, auto/biography and identity discourses, and Canadian literature. Recent publications include: "Nation and Self-Narration: A View from Québec/Quebec," *Canadian Literature* 172 (Spring 2002); "Translational and Trans/national Crossings: French-American Feminist Mis/Dis/ Re-Connections," *Works and Days* 20.1&2 (Spring/Fall 2002).

Approaching life-narratives as privileged sites for both the construction and interrogation of the nation, Freiwald's essay, "Gender, Nation, and Self-Narration: Three Generations of Dayan Women in Palestine/Israel," examines the auto/biographical writings of three women. These writings represent three generations of one of Israel's most public families, and offer insights into the making of the imagined community that is present-day Israel.

SHERRILL GRACE is Professor of English at the University of British Columbia, where she holds the Brenda and David McLean Chair in Canadian Studies, 2003-05, and is a Distinguished University Scholar. She has published widely on twentieth-century literature and Canadian culture, with books on Expressionism, Margaret Atwood, and Malcolm Lowry. Her most recent books are *Canada and the Idea of North* (2001) and *Performing National Identities: International Perspectives on Contemporary Canadian Theatre*, co-edited with A.R. Glaap.

Grace's paper, "Performing the Auto/Biographical Pact: Towards a Theory of Identity in Performance," explores some of the challenges faced by playwrights who create autobiographical plays. Drawing on recent theories of autobiography, Grace develops a theory of autobiography-in-performance and suggests how theatre practice differs from other autobiographical practices.

At the time of her death from cancer on December 31, 2004, in Vancouver, **GABRIELE HELMS** was Assistant Professor in the Department of English at the University of British Columbia, where she taught courses and conducted research in the fields of Canadian literature and culture and auto/biography studies. She is the author of *Challenging Canada: Dialogism and Narrative Techniques in Canadian Novels* (McGill-Queen's 2003), and co-editor (with Susanna Egan) of two special issues of the scholarly journals *Canadian Literature* (2002) and *biography* (2001). She has published several essays on life writing and Canadian literature and contributed to reference works such as the *Encyclopedia of Life Writing* and the *Cambridge Companion to Life Writing*.

In "Reality TV Has Spoken: Auto/biography Matters" Helms demonstrates what critics of autobiography can bring to debates about the proliferation and popularity of reality television shows such as *Survivor* and *Big Brother*. She examines how these shows draw on familiar strategies and discourses of auto/biography—such as the autobiographical pact, the confession, the diary, and the crisis-resolution plot—and she considers what these shows can reveal about contemporary modes of self-representation.

MARLENE KADAR is Associate Professor in Humanities and Women's Studies at York University, and the former director of the Graduate Programme in Interdisciplinary Studies. Her *Essays on Life Writing: From Genre to Critical Practice* (UTP 1992) won the Gabrielle Roy Prize in 1993. Kadar's research interests include the politics of life writing, including survivor narratives; the construction of privilege and knowledge in women's life writing; and Hungarian and Romani auto/biography in historical accounts, biographical traces, and fragments.

Kadar's essay, "The Devouring: Traces of Roma in the Holocaust: No Tattoo, Sterilized Body, Gypsy Girl," examines three troubling images in order to more fully appreciate the power of autobiographical traces and fragments in historical memory, especially in relation to the experience of Roma in the *Porrajmos*.

ADRIENNE KERTZER is Professor of English at the University of Calgary. Her book, *My Mother's Voice: Children, Literature, and the Holocaust* (Broadview Press, 2002), won the Canadian Jewish Book Award for scholarship on a Jewish subject. Her essay, *"Fugitive Pieces*: Listening as a Holocaust Survivor's Child," won the F.E.L. Priestley Prize. Forthcoming essays include

"The Problem of Childhood, Children's Literature, and Holocaust Representation," in *Teaching the Representation of the Holocaust*, ed. Marianne Hirsch and Irene Kacandes, MLA series Options for Teaching, and the entry on "Holocaust Literature for Children" in *the Oxford Encyclopedia of Children's Literature*, ed. Jack Zipes, Oxford UP. The author of numerous essays on Holocaust literature and children's literature, she is currently working on comedy and representations of trauma.

Kertzer's essay, "Circular Journeys and Glass Bridges: The Geography of Postmemory," constructs a map of postmemory, one whose coordinates position it temporally within the second generation, and representationally within the discourse of adult texts. Asking numerous locational questions, it asserts that postmemory's geography is a map that we rarely share with children, that the representation of memory in children's books is very different from the representation of postmemory in adult texts.

KATHY MEZEI is Professor in the Humanities and English Departments at Simon Fraser University. Her research interests are Canadian literature, Quebec literature and translation, modern British fiction, Virginia Woolf, and feminist literary criticism. Recently she has guest-edited a special issue of *BC Studies* (winter 2003/04) and a special forum of *Signs* (Spring 2002).

Mezei's essay, "Domestic Space and the Idea of Home in Auto/biographical Practices," examines how domestic spaces—houses and gardens—and the detritus of domestic life, along with everyday objects and rituals, function as structural and thematic devices in visual and literary representations, from photography to memoirs by Mary Gordon and Dionne Brand.

JEANNE PERREAULT is Professor in the Department of English at the University of Calgary. She has published widely in the fields of American women's writing, theories of subjectivity, race and gender, and Native Canadian and American literature.She is the author of *Writing Selves: Contemporary Feminist Autography*, and "Imagining Sisterhood, Again" for a special issue of *Prose Studies*, edited by Cynthia Huff (forthcoming).

Perreault's essay, "Muriel Rukeyser: Egodocuments and the Ethics of Propaganda," examines the unpublished materials Muriel Rukeyser produced during her period as a propagandist in the Office of War Information. Perreault argues that these papers can be read as "egodocuments" or life-writings, asserting Rukeyser's deeply held ethical and poetic sense of self.

CHERYL SUZACK is Assistant Professor of Native literatures in the Department of English at the University of Alberta. She has edited the critical edition of *In Search of April Raintree* and is at work on a teaching edition of Maria Campbell's *Halfbreed*. Her paper in this collection represents a longer project that explores the relationship between law and literature and the representation of Aboriginal/indigenous peoples as juridical subjects.

Suzack's essay, "Law Stories as Life Stories: Jeanette Lavell, Yvonne Bédard, and *Halfbreed*," begins by discussing the problematics of representation for Aboriginal women who have sought access to legal intervention through the courts. It explores how court cases assert a raced subjectivity for Aboriginal peoples that informs the logic of the court's decision-making process. Next, it analyzes how this legal context impinges on literary/critical debates about the politics of Aboriginal women's writing to illustrate how literature critiques state-imposed categories of race and gender subjectivity so as to assert cross-cultural community affiliations. The essay focuses on the reinstatement claims of Jeanette Lavell and Yvonne Bedard to offer an alternative social narrative of Aboriginal women's agency in relation to the politics of gender identity articulated through Maria Campbell's *Halfbreed*.

LINDA WARLEY is Associate Professor in the Department of English Language and Literature at the University of Waterloo. She has published widely on Canadian, Native, and postcolonial autobiographies and is currently writing a book about twentieth-century autobiographical works, in print and Internet genres, created by "ordinary" Canadians.

In "Reading the Autobiographical in Personal Home Pages" Linda Warley brings the methods of literary studies and new media studies together in order to conduct a close analysis of one academic's personal home page. She examines how particular design choices shape a "self" that at times conforms to familiar modes of self-representation and sometimes challenges them. The essay models one approach to analyzing multimodal autobiographical texts that are published online.

ACKNOWLEDGMENTS

We are happy to thank the Social Sciences and Humanities Research Council of Canada, the University of Calgary, the University of British Columbia, and the University of Waterloo for their wonderful support at key moments. The Centre for Feminist Research and the Office of Research and Innovation at York University provided Marlene Kadar and the editorial group generous assistance throughout the preparation of this manuscript. In particular, we would like to thank Vice-President of Research and Innovation, Stan Shapson, and Associate Vice-President Research, Suzanne MacDonald. Wilfrid Laurier University Press readers offered helpful suggestions; WLUP editors Jacqueline Larson and Carroll Klein, and copyeditor Lisa LaFramboise provided rigorous and kindly attention to the manuscript. Thanks also go to research assistants Nancy Gobatto, Shannon Gerard, and Philip Philip. Finally, we would like to thank our contributors for their enthusiasm and for allowing us to present these unpublished essays.

Acoose, Janice. "*Halfbreed*: A Revisiting of Maria Campbell's Text from an Indigenous Perspective." Armstrong, *Looking* 137-50.

Adams, Howard. *Prison of Grass: Canada from the Native Point of View*. Toronto: General, 1975.

Adams, Timothy Dow. *Light Writing and Life Writing: Photography in Autobiography*. Chapel Hill: U of North Carolina P, 2000.

Adamson, Jane, Richard Freadman, and David Parker, eds. *Renegotiating Ethics in Literature, Philosophy, Theory*. Cambridge: Cambridge UP, 1998.

Adelsberger, Lucie. *Auschwitz: A Doctor's Story*. Boston: Northeastern UP, 1995.

Adler, David A. *We Remember the Holocaust*. New York: Scholastic, 1989.

Agamben, Giorgio. *Remnants of Auschwitz: The Witness and the Archive*. Trans. Daniel Heller-Roazen. New York: Zone Books, 1999.

The Amazing Race 1-4. CBS. 5 Sep. 2001-27 Aug. 2003. <http://www.cbs.com/primetime/amazing_race>.

Anderson, Benedict. *Imagined Communities: Reflections on the Origin and Spread of Nationalism*. Rev. ed. London: Verso, 1991.

Andrejevic, Mark. "The Kinder, Gentler Gaze of Big Brother." *New Media and Society* 4.2 (2002): 251-70.

Andrews, William L. *To Tell a Free Story: The First Century of Afro-American Autobiography, 1760-1865*. Urbana: U of Illinois P, 1986.

Anthias, Floya, and Nira Yuval-Davis. "Introduction." Yuval-Davis and Anthias 1-15.

Archiv der Gedenkstätte Konzentrationslager Mauthausen, Vienna, Austria.

Archiv Mahn- und Gedenkstätte Ravensbrück, Fürstenberg/Havel, Germany.

Ardener, Shirley, ed. *Women and Space: Ground Rules and Social Maps*. London: Croom Helm, 1981.

Armstrong, Jeannette C., ed. *Looking at the Words of Our People: First Nations Analysis of Literature*. Penticton: Theytus, 1993.

———. "Unclean Tides: An Essay on Salmon and Relations." *First Fish, First People: Salmon Tales of the North Pacific Rim*. Ed. Judith Roche and Meg McHutchison. Vancouver: One Reel-U of British Columbia P, 1998. 181-93.

Ashley, Kathleen, Leigh Gilmore, and Gerald Peters, eds. *Autobiography and Postmodernism*. Amherst: U of Massachusetts P, 1994.

Attorney General of Canada v. Lavell—Isaac v. Bédard. [1974] S.C.R. 1349. Supreme Ct. of Can. 27 August 1973.

———. (Factum of the Anishnawbekwek of Ontario, Inc. at para. 8,9).

———. (Factum of the Appellants: Richard Isaac et al. at para. 5, 23iv).

———. (Factum of the Attorney General of Canada at para. 43).

———. (Factum of the Intervenants: The Alberta Committee on Indian Rights for Indian Women et al. at para. 5).

———. (Factum of the Intervenants: "Indian Organizations" at para. 20).

———. (Factum of the Interventants: The Treaty Voice of Alberta Association at para 2A, 2B).

———. (Factum of the Native Council of Canada [Intervenant] at para. 10).

Austin, J.L. *How to Do Things with Words*. Cambridge: Harvard UP, 1962.

Australasian Legal Information Institute. *Council for Aboriginal Reconciliation Archive*. 15 Jul. 2003 <http://www.austlii.edu.au/au/other/IndigLRes/ car/>.

Autopacte. 5 Oct. 2004 <http://www.autopacte.org/>.

Avec les yeux des survivants: Un parcours dans le mémorial de Ravensbrück. Ed. Lagergemeinschaft Ravensbrück/Freundesdreis, under the direction of Ursula Krause-Schmitt and Christine Krause. Stuttgart: Schmetterling Verlag, 2003.

Bachelard, Gaston. *The Poetics of Space*. Trans. Maria Jolas. Boston: Beacon, 1994.

The Bachelor. 1-4. ABC. 25 Mar. 2002-19. Nov. 2003. <http://abc.go.com/primetime/ bachelor/>.

The Bachelorette. ABC. Jan.-Feb. 2003 <http://abc.go.com/primetime/ bachelorette/>.

Backhouse, Constance. *Colour-Coded: A Legal History of Racism in Canada, 1900-1950*. Toronto: U of Toronto P, 1999.

Bakan, Joel. *Just Words: Constitutional Rights and Social Wrongs*. Toronto: U of Toronto P, 1997.

Bakhtin, Mikhail M. *The Dialogic Imagination: Four Essays*. Trans. Caryl Emerson and Michael Holquist. Austin: U of Texas P, 1981.

Bammer, Angelika. "Editorial." *The Question of "Home."* Spec. issue of *New Formations* 17 (1992): vii–xi.

Barnes, Julian. *England, England*. Toronto: Vintage, 1998.

Barson, Michael and Steven Heller. *Red Scared! The Commie Menace in Propaganda and Pop Culture*. San Francisco: Chronicle, 2001.

Bastian, Till. *Sinti und Roma im Dritten Reich: Geschichte einer Verfolgung*. Munich: C.H. Beck, 2001.

Bataille, Gretchen M., and Kathleen Mullen Sands. *American Indian Women: Telling Their Lives*. Lincoln: U of Nebraska P, 1984.

Bédard v. Isaac et al. [1972] *Ontario Reports* 2 391. High Crt. of Justice. 15 December 1971.

Ben-Gurion, David. *Israel: A Personal Story*. Trans. Nechemia Meyers and Uzi Nystar. New York: Funk and Wagnall, 1971.

Benjamin, David N., ed. *The Home: Words, Interpretations, Meanings, and Environments*. Aldershot, UK: Avebury, 1995; Brookfield, VT: Ashgate, 1995.

Benjamin, Jessica. "A Desire of One's Own: Psychoanalytic Feminism and Intersubjective Space." De Lauretis, *Feminist Studies/Critical Studies* 78-101.

Bennett, Susan. "Performing Lives: Linda Griffiths and other Famous Women." *Performing National Identities: International Perspectives on Contemporary Canadian Theatre*. Ed. Sherrill Grace and Albert-Reiner Glaap. Vancouver: Talonbooks, 2003. 25-37.

———. *Theatre Audiences: A Theory of Production and Reception*. London: Routledge, 1990.

Benveniste, Emile. *Problems in General Linguistics*. Trans. Mary Elizabeth Meek. Miami: U of Miami P, 1971.

Berenbaum, Michael, ed. *A Mosaic of Victims: Non-Jews Persecuted and Murdered by the Nazis*. New York: New York UP, 1990.

Berger, Alan L., and Naomi Berger, eds. *Second Generation Voices: Reflections by Children of Holocaust Survivors and Perpetrators*. Religion, Theology, and the Holocaust Ser. Syracuse: Syracuse UP, 2001.

Bergland, Betty. "Postmodernism and the Autobiographical Subject: Reconstructing the 'Other.'" Ashley, Gilmore, and Peters 130-66.

Bernstein, Deborah S. Introduction. *Pioneers and Homemakers: Jewish Women in Pre-State Israel*. Ed. Deborah S. Bernstein. Albany: State U of New York, 1992. 1-23.

Betsky, Aaron. *Queer Space: Architecture and Same-Sex Desire*. New York: William Morrow, 1999.

Beverley, John. "The Margin at the Center: On *Testimonio* (Testimonial Narrative)." Smith and Watson, *De/Colonizing* 91-114.

Bhabha, Homi K. "DissemiNation: Time, Narrative, and the Margins of the Modern Nation." *The Location of Culture*. 139-70.

———. "DissemiNation: Time, Narrative, and the Margins of the Modern Nation." *Nation and Narration*. Ed. Homi K. Bhabha. London: Routledge, 1990. 291-322.

———. *The Location of Culture*. London: Routledge, 1994.

Big Brother 1-4. CBS. 5 July 2001-24 Sep. 2003. <http://www.cbs.com/primetime/bigbrother/>.

Bird, Carmel, ed. *The Stolen Children: Their Stories*. Sydney: Random House, 1998.

Bird Rose, Deborah. "Dark Times and Excluded Bodies in the Colonisation of Australia." *The Resurgence of Racism: Howard, Hanson, and the Race Debate*. Ed. Geoffrey Gray and Christine Winter. Clayton, Austral.: Monash Publications in History, 1997. 97-116.

Black, Edwin. *IBM and the Holocaust: The Strategic Alliance between Nazi Germany and America's Most Powerful Corporation*. New York: Crown, 2001.

Blanchot, Maurice. *The Writing of the Disaster*. Trans. Ann Smock. Lincoln: U of Nebraska P, 1986.

Bock, Gisela. "Racism and Sexism in Nazi Germany." *Signs* 8.3 (1983): 400-21.

Bolter, Jay David. *Writing Space: Computers, Hypertext, and the Remediation of Print*. 2nd ed. Nahwah, NJ: Lawrence Erlbaum, 2001.

Bonner, Frances. *Ordinary Television: Analyzing Popular TV*. London: Sage, 2003.

Bontis, Nick. *Bontis.com*. 29 Aug. 2003. <http://www.bontis.com>.

Bornstein, Avram S. *Crossing the Green Line between the West Bank and Israel*. Philadelphia: U of Pennsylvania P, 2002.

Bourdieu, Pierre. *The Logic of Practice*. Trans. Richard Nice. Cambridge: Polity Press, 1990.

Bowden, Jean K. *Jane Austen's House*. Norfolk: Jane Austen Memorial Trust and Jerrold Publishing, 1990.

Braidotti, Rosi. *Nomadic Subjects: Embodiment and Sexual Difference in Contemporary Feminist Theory*. New York: Columbia UP, 1994.

Bramsted, Ernest K. *Goebbels and National Socialist Propaganda: 1925-1945*. East Lansing: Michigan State UP, 1965.

Brand, Dionne. *A Map to the Door of No Return: Notes to Belonging*. Toronto: Doubleday, 2001.

Bredhoff, Stacey. *Powers of Persuasion: Poster Art from World War II*. Washington: National Archives, 1994.

Brewster, Anne. *Literary Formations: Post-Colonialism, Nationalism, Globalism*. Melbourne: Melbourne UP, 1995.

Bridget Jones's Diary. Dir. Sharon Maguire. Perf. Renée Zellwegger, Hugh Grant, and Colin Firth. Miramax, 2001.

Briganti, Chiara, and Kathy Mezei. "House Haunting: The Domestic Novel of the Inter-War Years." *Homecultures* 1.2 (2004): 147-68.

———, eds. "Domestic Space Forum." *Signs* 27.3 (2002): 837-46.

Brilliant, Richard. *Portraiture*. Cambridge: Harvard UP, 1991.

Britzman, Deborah P. *After Education: Anna Freud, Melanie Klein, and Psychoanalytic Histories of Learning*. Albany: State U of New York P, 2003.

———. Conversation with Marlene Kadar. York University, Toronto. 12 Mar. 2003.

———. *Lost Subjects, Contested Objects: Toward a Psychoanalytic Inquiry of Learning*. Albany: State U of New York P, 1998.

Brooks, Peter. *Body Work: Objects of Desire in Modern Narrative*. Cambridge: Harvard UP, 1993.

Brown, Wendy. *States of Injury: Power and Freedom in Late Modernity*. Princeton: Princeton UP, 1995.

Buber, Martin. *I and Thou*. Trans. Walter Kaufman. New York: Scribner's, 1970.

Bunzl, Matti. "Theodor Herzl's Zionism as Gendered Discourse." *Theodor Herzl and the Origins of Zionism*. Ed. Ritchie Robertson and Edward Timms. Edinburgh: Edinburgh UP, 1997. 74-86.

Burgner, Robert L. "Life History of Sockeye Salmon (*Oncorhynchus nerka*)." Groot and Margolis 1-117.

Burlingame, Roger. *Don't Let Them Scare You: The Life and Times of Elmer Davis*. New York: J.B. Lippincott, 1961.

Burnett, Mark, with Martin Dugard. *Survivor: The Ultimate Game*; *The Official Companion Book to the CBS Television Series*. New York: TV Books, 2000.

Buss, Helen M. *Mapping Our Selves: Canadian Women's Autobiography in English*. Montreal: McGill-Queen's UP, 1993.

———. *Repossessing the World: Reading Memoirs by Contemporary Women*. Life Writing Ser. Waterloo: Wilfrid Laurier UP, 2002.

Buszko, Josef. "Auschwitz." *Encyclopedia of the Holocaust*. Vol. 1. Ed. Israel Gutman. 4 vols. New York: Macmillan, 1990. 107-19.

Butler, Judith. *Excitable Speech: A Politics of the Performative*. New York: Routledge, 1997.

———. *Gender Trouble: Feminism and the Subverison of Identity*. London: Routledge, 1989.

———. "Performative Acts and Gender Constitution: An Essay in Phenomenology and Feminist Theory." *Performing Feminisms: Feminist Critical Theory and Theatre*. Ed. Sue-Ellen Case. Baltimore: Johns Hopkins UP, 1990. 270–82.

Campbell, Maria. *Halfbreed*. 1973. Halifax: Goodread Biographies—Formac, 1983.

———. "You Have to Own Yourself." Interview by Doris Hillis. *Prairie Fire* 9.3 (1988): 44–58.

Campbell, Wanda. "The Hidden Rooms of Isabella Valancy Crawford and P.K. Page." *Literature and Architecture*. Spec. issue of *Mosaic* 35.4 (2002): 69–83.

Canada. Department of Indian Affairs and Northern Development. *Statement of the Government of Canada on Indian Policy*. Ottawa: Queen's Printer, 1969.

———. *House of Commons of Canada Bill C-297*. Ottawa: Canada Communication Group, 1996.

———. Indian and Northern Affairs. *Indian Status: What is the Present Law?* Ottawa: Queen's Printer, 1973.

Caraway, Nancie. *Segregated Sisterhood: Racism and the Politics of American Feminism*. Knoxville: U of Tennessee P, 1991.

Cardinal, Harold. *The Rebirth of Canada's Indians*. Edmonton: Hurtig, 1977.

Caruth, Cathy. *Unclaimed Experience: Trauma, Narrative, and History*. Baltimore: Johns Hopkins UP, 1996.

"The Case of Sidonie Adlersburg." *Learning from History*. 29 Sept. 2004 <http://www.holocaust-education.de/news/discuss/msgReader$107>.

Chambers, Ross. *Facing It: AIDS Diaries and the Death of the Author*. Ann Arbor, MI: U of Michigan P, 1998.

Chayot, Chuma. *Chuma Chayot*. Prepared for publication by Shlomo Even-Shoshan. Tel Aviv: Hakibbutz Hameuchad, 1963. [Hebrew].

Chew, Shirley. "One Cast of a Net: A Reading of Daphne Marlatt's *Steveston*." *Narrative Strategies in Canadian Literature: Feminism and Postcolonialism*. Ed. Coral Ann Howells and Lynette Hunter. Milton Keynes: Open UP, 1992. 61–70.

Chow, Rey. *Writing Diaspora: Tactics of Intervention in Contemporary Cultural Studies*. Bloomington: Indiana UP, 1993.

Clements, Theresa. *From Old Maloga: The Memoirs of an Aboriginal Woman*. Prahran, AU: Fraser and Morphet, 1954.

Coe, Richard, Lorelei Lingard, and Tatiana Teslenko, eds. *The Rhetoric and Ideology of Genre: Strategies for Stability and Change*. Cresskill, NJ: Hampton, 2002.

Coghill, Joy. *Song of This Place*. Toronto: Playwrights Canada, 2003.

Cohen, Mitchell. *Zion and State: Nation, Class and the Shaping of Modern Israel*. Oxford: Basil Blackwell, 1987.

Cole, Christina. "Daphne Marlatt as Penelope, Weaver of Words: A Feminist Reading of *Steveston*." *Open Letter* 6th ser. 1 (1985): 5–19.

Coleman, Debra, Elizabeth Danze, and Carol Henderson, eds. *Architecture and Feminism*. New York: Princeton Architectural Press, 1996.

Collignon, Béatrice, and Jean-François Staszak. "Espaces domestiques/Domestic Spaces Conference." Paris, 17–20 Sept. 2002.

Colomina, Beatriz, ed. *Sexuality and Space*. New York: Princeton Architectural Press, 1992.

Connerton, Paul. *How Societies Remember*. Cambridge: Cambridge UP, 1989.

Connor, Walker. *Ethno-Nationalism: The Quest for Understanding*. Princeton: Princeton UP, 1994.

"Convention on the Prevention and Punishment of the Crime of Genocide." 16 Aug., 1994. Office of the High Commissioner for Human Rights. 26 Apr. 2005 <http://www.unhchr.ch/html/menu3/b/p_genoci.htm>.

Conway, Jill Ker. *When Memory Speaks: Exploring the Art of Autobiography*. New York: Vintage, 1998.

Corner, John. "Documentary in a Post-Documentary Culture? A Note on Forms and Their Functions." Changing Media—Changing Europe, Programme Team One (Citizenship and Consumerism), Working Paper No. 1. 2000. European Science Foundation. Loughborough University, UK. 1 Aug. 2003 <http://www.lboro.ac.uk/ research/changing.media /publications.htm>.

Cottam, Rachel. "Diaries and Journals: General Survey." Jolly 1: 267-69.

Couser, G. Thomas. *Recovering Bodies: Illness, Disability, and Life Writing*. Madison: U of Wisconsin P, 1997.

———. *Vulnerable Subjects: Ethics and Life Writing*. Ithaca: Cornell UP, 2004.

Crenshaw, Kimberle. "Demarginalizing the Intersection of Race and Sex: A Black Feminist Critique of Antidiscrimination Doctrine, Feminist Theory and Antiracist Politics." *University of Chicago Legal Forum* (1989): 139-67.

Crewdson, Gregory. "Fox and Fence, 1991." *Architecture of the Everyday*. Ed. Steven Harris and Deborah Berke. New York: Princeton Architectural P, 1997. 66-67.

Curran, Beverly, and Mitoko Hirabayashi. "Conversations with Readers: An Interview with Daphne Marlatt." *Studies in Canadian Literature/Études en littérature canadienne* 24.1 (1999): 109-23.

Damm, Kateri. "Dispelling and Telling: Speaking Native Realities in Maria Campbell's *Halfbreed* and Beatrice Culleton's *In Search of April Raintree*." Armstrong, *Looking* 93-114.

Danylchuk, Jack. "Indian Women Once Banished, Court Told." *Edmonton Journal* 24 Sept. 1993: A7.

Davies, Philip R. "Introduction: Autobiography as Exegesis." *First Person: Essays in Biblical Autobiography*. Ed. Philip R. Davies. London: Sheffield Academic P, 2002. 11-24.

Davis, Cynthia J. "B(e)aring It All: Talking about Sex and Self on Television Talk Shows." Gammel 148-66.

Davis, Elmer. *By Elmer Davis*. Ed. Robert Lloyd Davis. Indianapolis: Bobbs-Merrill, 1964.

Davis, Elmer, and Byron Price. *War Information and Censorship*. Washington, DC: American Council on Public Affairs, 1943.

Dayan, Deborah. *Pioneer*. Trans. Michael Plashkes. Tel Aviv: Massada, 1968.

Dayan, Dvorah. *B'osher u'veyagon*. [*In Happiness and in Sorrow*]. Tel Aviv: Masada and Tenuat Hamoshavim, 1957.

Dayan, Moshe. *Moshe Dayan: Story of My Life*. London: Weidenfeld, 1976.

Dayan, Ruth, and Helga Dudman. *And Perhaps…The Story of Ruth Dayan*. New York: Harcourt Brace Jovanovich, 1973.

———. *Veuli…[…Or Did I Dream A Dream?: The Story of Ruth Dayan]*. Jerusalem: Weidenfeld and Nicolson, 1973.

Dayan, Yael. *Avi, Bito. [My Father, His Daughter]*. Jerusalem: Edanim, 1986. [Hebrew]

———. *My Father, His Daughter*. New York: Farrar, Straus and Giroux, 1985.

De Certeau, Michel. *Heterologies: Discourse on the Other*. Trans. Brian Massumi. Theory and History of Literature 17. Minneapolis: U of Minnesota P, 1986.

De Lauretis, Teresa. *Alice Doesn't: Feminism, Semiotics, Cinema*. Bloomington: Indiana UP, 1984.

———, ed. *Feminist Studies/Critical Studies*. Bloomington: Indiana UP,1986.

———. "Feminist Studies/Critical Studies: Issues, Terms, and Contexts." De Lauretis, *Feminist* 1-19.

Dekker, Rudolf, ed. *Egodocuments and History: Autobiographical Writing in its Social Context Since the Middle Ages*. Hilverum, Neth.: Verloren, 2002.

Derrida, Jacques. *Specters of Marx: The State of the Debt, the Work of Mourning, and the New International*. Trans. Peggy Kamuf. New York: Routledge, 1994.

Diamond, Elin, ed. *Performance and Cultural Politics*. London: Routledge, 1996.

Dokumentationsarchiv des österreichischen Widerstandes, Vienna, Austria.

Dolan, Jill. "Geographies of Learning: Theatre Studies, Performance, and the 'Performative.'" *Theatre Journal* 45.4 (1993): 417-41.

Donaldson, Scott. *Archibald MacLeish: An American Life*. Boston: Houghton Mifflin, 1992.

Döring, Nicola. "Personal Home Pages on the Web: A Review of Research." *Journal of Computer-Mediated Communication* 7.3 (2002). 22 Aug. 2003 <http://www.ascusc.org/jcmc/vol7/issue3/doering.html>.

Douglas, Kate. "'I cannot thank you enough for selecting me' (and rejecting me?): Survivor II and Its Elimination Confessionals." *M/C Reviews* 12 (4 May 2001). 24 Sept. 2002 <http://www.media-culture.org.au/reviews/sections.php?op=viewarticle&artid=106>.

Dovey, Jon. "Reality TV." *The Television Genre Book*. Ed. Glen Creeber. London: British Film Institute, 2001. 134-37.

———. *Freakshow: First Person Media and Factual Television*. London: Pluto, 2000.

Dowty, Alan. *The Jewish State: A Century Later*. Berkeley: U of California P, 1998.

Dudman, Helga. "Foreword." Dayan and Dudman, *And Perhaps* xi-xvi.

Dumont, Marilyn. *A Really Good Brown Girl*. London: Brick Books, 1996.

Duncan, Nancy, ed. *Bodyspace*. London: Routledge, 1996.

Dwork, Debórah, and Robert Jan van Pelt. *Auschwitz*. New York: Norton, 1996.

Eakin, Paul John, ed. *The Ethics of Life Writing*. Ithaca: Cornell UP, 2004.

———. *How Our Lives Become Stories: Making Selves*. Ithaca: Cornell UP, 1999.

"Editorial." *The New Republic* 26 Apr. 1943: 551-52.

Egan, Susanna. *Mirror Talk: Genres of Crisis in Contemporary Autobiography*. Chapel Hill: U of North Carolina P. 1999.

Egan, Susanna, and Gabriele Helms, eds. *Autobiography and Changing Identities*. Spec. issue of *Biography* 24.1 (2001).

Eliach, Yaffa. *There Once Was a World: A Nine-Hundred-Year Chronicle of the Shtetl of Eishyshok*. Boston: Little, Brown, 1998.

Ellerby, Janet Mason. *Intimate Reading: The Contemporary Women's Memoir*. Syracuse: Syracuse UP, 2001.

Ellis, John. *Seeing Things: Television in the Age of Uncertainty*. London: I.B. Tauris, 2000.

Emmett, Ayala. *Our Sisters' Promised Land: Women, Politics, and Israeli-Palestinian Co-Existence*. Ann Arbor: U of Michigan P, 1996.

Engel, Susan. *Context Is Everything: The Nature of Memory*. New York: W.H. Free-man, 1999.

Erlichman Miller, Joy. *Love Carried Me Home: Women Surviving Auschwitz*. Deer-field Beach, FL: Simcha, 2000.

Espanioly, Nabila. "Palestinian Women in Israel Respond to the *Intifada*." Swirski and Safir 147-51.

Fanon, Franz. *The Wretched of the Earth*. Trans. Constance Farrington. New York: Grove, 1963.

Fee, Margery. "Upsetting Fake Ideas: Jeannette Armstrong's 'Slash' and Beatrice Culleton's 'April Raintree.'" New 168-80.

Feig, Konnilyn. "Non-Jewish Victims in the Concentration Camps." Berenbaum 161-78.

Feldman, Yael S. *No Room of Their Own: Gender and Nation in Israeli Women's Fic-tion*. New York: Columbia UP, 1999.

Felman, Shoshana. "The Betrayal of the Witness: Camus' *The Fall*." Felman and Laub 165-203.

Felman, Shoshana, and Dori Laub, eds. *Testimony: Crises of Witnessing in Literature, Psychoanalysis, and History*. New York: Routledge, 1992.

Felski, Rita. "Feminism, Postmodernism, and the Critique of Modernity." *Cul-tural Critique* 13 (1989): 33-56.

Ferrier, Carole. "Aboriginal Women's Narratives." *Gender, Politics and Fiction: Twen-tieth Century Australian Women's Novels*. Ed. Carole Ferrier. 2nd ed. Brisbane: U of Queensland P, 1992. 200-18.

Fielding, Helen. *Bridget Jones's Diary*. London: Picador, 1996.

Fiffer, Sharon Sloan, and Steve Fiffer. *Home: American Writers Remember Rooms of Their Own*. New York: Vintage, 1996.

Fink, Ida. *A Scrap of Time and Other Stories*. Trans. Madeline Levine and Francine Prose. New York: Pantheon, 1987.

Finkelstein, Barbara. "Faith after the Holocaust: For One Person, It Doesn't Pay to Cook." Berger and Berger 156-71.

Frank, Anne. *The Diary of a Young Girl: The Definitive Edition*. Trans. Susan Mas-sotty. Ed. Otto H. Frank and Mirjam Pressler. New York: Doubleday, 1995.

Fraser, Nancy. *Unruly Practices: Power, Discourse, and Gender in Contemporary Social Theory*. Minneapolis: U of Minnesota P, 1989.

Fraser, Rosalie. *Shadow Child: A Memoir of the Stolen Generations*. Alexandria, AU: Hale and Iremonger, 1998.

Freedman, Marcia. *Exile in the Promised Land: A Memoir*. Ithaca: Firebrand, 1990.

Freire, Paulo. *Pedagogy of the Oppressed*. Trans. Myra Bergman Ramos. New York: Herder and Herder, 1972.

Freiwald, Bina Toledo. "Nation and Self-Narration: A View from Québec/Que-bec." *Canadian Literature* 172 (2002): 17-38.

———. "The Subject and the Nation: Canadian and Israeli Women's Autobio-graphical Writing." *Precarious Present/Promising Future?: Ethnicity and Identi-ties in Canadian Literature*. Ed. D. Schaub, J. Kulyk Keefer, and R. Sherwin. Jerusalem: Magnes, 1996. 10-31.

Freud, Sigmund. "The Uncanny." *The Standard Edition of the Complete Psychologi-cal Works of Sigmund Freud*. Vol. 17 (1917-1919). 24 vols. London: Hogarth, 1955. 217-52.

Friedman, James, ed. *Reality Squared: Televisual Discourse on the Real*. New Brunswick: Rutgers UP, 2002.

Friedman, Susan Stanford. "Women's Autobiographical Selves: Theory and Practice." *The Private Self: Theory and Practice of Women's Autobiographical Writings*. Ed. Shari Benstock. Chapel Hill: U of North Carolina P, 1988. 34–62.

Frow, John. "The Politics of Stolen Time." *Meanjin* 57.2 (1998): 351–67.

Fuchs, Miriam, ed. *Biography and Geography*. Spec. issue of *Biography* 25.1 (2002).

Gabe, Vida Zorah. "How Real Is Real?" *M/C Reviews* 12 (4 May 2001). 24 Sept. 2002 <http://www.media-culture.org.au/reviews/sections.php?op=viewarticle&artid=114>.

Gale, Lorena. *Je me souviens*. Vancouver: Talonbooks, 2001.

Gale, Maggie B., and Viv Gardner, eds. *Women, Theatre, and Performance: New Histories, New Historiographies*. Manchester: U of Manchester P, 2000.

Gammel, Irene, ed. *Confessional Politics: Women's Sexual Self-Representations in Life Writing and Popular Media*. Carbondale: Southern Illinois UP, 1999.

Garber, Marjorie. *Sex and Real Estate: Why We Love Houses*. New York: Pantheon, 2000.

Gefen, Johnathan. *Isha Yekara*. [*Lovely Lady*]. Tel Aviv: Dvir, 1999.

Gellner, Ernest. *Nations and Nationalism*. Oxford: Blackwell, 1983.

George, Rosemary Marangoly. *The Politics of Home: Postcolonial Relocations and Twentieth-Century Fiction*. Cambridge: Cambridge UP, 1996.

Gibson, Helen. "The Weak in Review." *Time Europe* 11 Jan. 2001. 2 Aug. 2003 <http://www.time.com/time/europe/webonly/europe/2001/01/weakestlink.html>.

Gill, Joanna. "Someone Else's Misfortunes: The Vicarious Pleasures of the Confessional Text." *Journal of Popular Culture* 35.1 (2001): 81–94.

Gilligan, Carol. *In a Different Voice: Psychological Theory and Women's Development*. Cambridge: Harvard UP, 1982.

Gilmore, Leigh. *Autobiographics: A Feminist Theory of Women's Self-Representation*. Ithaca: Cornell UP, 1994.

———. *The Limits of Autobiography: Trauma and Testimony*. Ithaca: Cornell UP, 2001.

———. "The Mark of Autobiography: Postmodernism, Autobiography, and Genre." Ashley, Gilmore, and Peters 3–18.

———. "Policing Truth: Confession, Gender, and Autobiographical Authority." Ashley, Gilmore, and Peters 54–78.

Godard, Barbara. "Between Performative and Performance: Translation and Theatre in the Canadian/Quebec Context." *Modern Drama* 43.3 (2000): 327–58.

Goldman, Anne E. *Take My Word: Autobiographical Innovations of Ethnic American Working Women*. Berkeley: U of California P, 1996.

Goodwin, Jean M., and Reina Attias, eds. *Splintered Reflections: Images of the Body in Trauma*. New York: Basic Books, 1999.

Gordon, Mary. *Seeing Through Places: Reflections on Geography and Identity*. New York: Simon and Schuster, 2000.

Grace, Sherrill. "Creating the Girl from God's Country: Sharon Pollock's Nell Shipman." *Canadian Literature* 172 (2002): 92–111.

———. "Writing the Self: From Joy Coghill to Emily Carr and Back…" *BC Studies* 137 (2003): 109–30.

Grant, Agnes. "Contemporary Native Women's Voices in Literature." New 124–32.

Gray, John, with Eric Peterson. *Billy Bishop Goes to War*. Vancouver: Talonbooks, 1981.

Greenfield, Liah. *Nationalism: Five Roads to Modernity*. Cambridge: Harvard UP, 1992.

Griffiths, Linda. *Alien Creature*. Toronto: Playwrights Canada, 2000.

Grindstaff, Laura. *The Money Shot: Trash, Class, and the Making of TV Talk Shows*. Chicago: U of Chicago P, 2002.

———. "Trashy or Transgressive? 'Reality TV' and the Politics of Social Control." *Thresholds: Viewing Culture* 9 (1995): 46–55. 26 Jul. 2003 <http://proxy.arts.uci.edu/~nideffer/ Tvc/section3/11.Tvc.v9.sect3.Grindstaff.html>.

Grobbel, Michaela M. "Performance in Gypsy Autobiographies from Austria and Germany." *Eine internationale zweisprachige publikation zuliteratur, film und kunst in den deutschsprachigen ländern nach 1945*, No. 7 (1999), 14 Sept. 2003 <httpp://www.dickinson.edu/departments/germn/glossen/heft7/romasinti.html>.

Groot, C., and L. Margolis, eds. *Pacific Salmon Life Histories*. Vancouver: U of British Columbia P–Govt. of Canada, Dept. of Fisheries and Oceans, 1991.

Grossman, Ibolya Szalai. *An Ordinary Woman in Extraordinary Times*. Toronto: Multicultural History Society of Ontario, 1990.

Grosz, Elizabeth. *Volatile Bodies: Toward a Corporeal Feminism*. Bloomington: U of Indiana P, 1994.

Grove, Valerie. "Introduction." *Mrs. Miniver*. 1939. By Jan Struther. London: Virago, 1989.

Guiney, Bob. *What a Difference a Year Makes*. New York: Penguin, 2003.

Gunn, Giles. "Interdisciplinary Studies." *Introduction to Scholarship in Modern Languages and Literatures*. Ed. Joseph Gibaldi. New York: MLA, 1992. 239-61.

Hackl, Erich. *Farewell Sidonia*. New York: Fromm International, 1991.

———. *Materialien zu Abscheid von Sidonie*. Zürich: Diogenese Verlag, 2000.

Häfner, August. "7. SS-Obersturmführer August Häfner on the killing of the children." Klee, Dressen, and Riess 153-54.

Hall, Chris. "Two Poems of Place: Williams' *Paterson* and Marlatt's *Steveston*." *Canadian Review of American Studies* 15.2 (1984): 141-57.

Hancock, Ian. "Gypsies in Nazi Germany." *Land of Pain: Five Centuries of Gypsy Slavery*. Buda, TX, 1985. Rpt. Centre for Holocaust and Genocide Studies. 6 Oct. 2004 <http://www.chgs.umn.edu/Histories_Narratives_Documen/Roma_ Sinti_Gypsies_/Gypsies_A_Persecuted_Race_3/gypsies_a_persecuted_race_.html>.

———. *Pariah Syndrome: An Account of Gypsy Slavery and Persecution*. Ann Arbor, MI: Karoma, 1989.

———. "Roma [Gypsy] Slavery." Typescript of article published in *The Encyclopedia of Slavery*. Ed. P. Finkelman and J. Miller. New York: Macmillan, 1997.

———. "The Roots of Antigypsyism: To the Holocaust and After." *Confronting the Holocaust: A Mandate for the 21st Century*. Ed. G. Jan Colijn and Marcia Sachs Littell. Studies in the Shoah 19. Lanham: UP of America, 1998. 19-49.

———. "Self-Identity Amid Stereotypes." *Transitions: Changes in Post-Communist Societies* 4.4 (1997): 38-51.

———. "'Uniqueness' of the Victims: Gypsies, Jews and the Holocaust." *Without Prejudice: International Review of Racial Discrimination* 1 (1998): 45-67.

Haraway, Donna. *Simians, Cyborgs and Women: The Reinvention of Nature.* New York: Routledge, 1991.

Harris, Geraldine. *Staging Femininities: Performance and Performativity.* Manchester: U of Manchester P, 1999.

Hawkins, Gay. "The Ethics of Television." *International Journal of Cultural Studies* 4.4 (2001): 412-26.

Hayden, Dolores. *The Grand Domestic Revolution: A History of Feminist Designs for American Homes, Neighbourhoods, and Cities.* Cambridge: MIT Press, 1981.

Hebermann, Nanda. *The Blessed Abyss: Inmate #6582 in Ravensbrück Concentration Camp for Women.* Trans. Hester Baer. Ed. Hester Baer and Elizabeth R. Baer. Detroit: Wayne State UP, 2000.

Hegarty, Ruth. *Is That You, Ruthie?* Brisbane: U of Queensland P, 1999.

Hendeles, Ydessa. *Same Difference.* Ydessa Hendeles Art Foundation, Toronto.

Henderson, Mae Gwendolyn. "Speaking in Tongues: Dialogics, Dialectics and the Black Woman Writer's Literary Tradition." *Changing Our Words: Essays on Criticism, Theory, and Writing by Black Women.* Ed. Cheryl A. Wall. New Brunswick, NJ: Rutgers UP, 1989. 116-42.

Heidegger, Martin. "Poetically Man Dwells…" Leach 109-19.

Hever, Hannan. *Producing the Modern Hebrew Canon: Nation Building and Minority Discourse.* New York: New York UP, 2002.

Hever, Hannan, Yehouda Shenhav, and Pnina Motzafi-Haller. "Epistemology of Orientalism [*Mizrahiut*] in Israel." *Mizrahim B'Israel: Iyun Bikorti Mehndash.* Hever, Shenhav, and Motzafi-Haller, eds. 15-27.

——, eds. *Mizrahim in Israel: A Critical Observation into Israel's Ethnicity* Tel Aviv: Van Leer Jerusalem Institute and Hakibbutz Hameuchad Publishing, 2002.

Hinz, Evelyn J. "The Dramatic Lineage of Auto/Biography." Kadar, *Essays* 195-212.

Hirsch, Marianne. *Family Frames: Photography, Narrative, and Postmemory.* Cambridge: Harvard UP, 1997.

——. *The Mother/Daughter Plot: Narrative, Psychoanalysis, Feminism.* Bloomington: Indiana UP, 1989.

Hitler, Adolf. *Mein Kampf.* Trans. Ludwig Lore. New York: Stackpole, 1939.

Hoffman, Eva. *Lost in Translation: A Life in a New Language.* New York: Penguin, 1989.

Holman, C. Hugh. *A Handbook to Literature.* Orig. by William Flint Thrall and Addison Hibbard. 3rd ed. Indianapolis: Bobbs-Merrill, 1972.

Holý, Dusan and Ctibor Necas. *Zalující Pisen: O Osudu Romu v Nacistickych Koncentracnich Taborech.* Brno: Vytiskla Polygra, 1993.

hooks, bell. *Yearning: Race, Gender and Cultural Politics.* Boston: South End, 1990.

Hubert, Renée Riese, with Judd D. Hubert. "Paging Self-Portraiture: The Artists' Books of Susan King and Joan Lyons." Smith and Watson, *Interfaces* 430-53.

Human Rights and Equal Opportunities Commission. *Bringing Them Home: Report of the National Inquiry into the Separation of Aboriginal and Torres Strait Islander Children from Their Families.* Canberra: Australian Government Publishing Service, 1997. 1 Oct. 2003 <http://www.austlii.edu.au/au/special/rsjproject/rsjlibrary/hreoc/stolen/prelim.html>.

Hutcheon, Linda. "Disciplinary Formation, Faculty Pleasures, and Student Risks." *ADE Bulletin* 117 (1997): 19-20.

Jameson, Fredric. "Is Space Political?" Leach 255-69.

Jamieson, Kathleen. *Indian Women and the Law in Canada: Citizens Minus*. Canada: Minister of Supply and Services, 1978.

Jay, Paul. "Posing: Autobiography and the Subject of Photography." Ashley, Gilmore, and Peters 191-211.

Jewish Virtual Library. "Tattoos." 28 Oct. 2003 <http://www.us-israel.org/jsource/Holocaust/Tattoos.html>.

Joe Millionaire 1-2. FOX. 6 Jan.-Nov. 2003. <http://www.fox.com/joem/>.

Jolly, Margaretta, ed. *Encyclopedia of Life Writing: Autobiographical and Biographical Forms*. London: Fitzroy Dearborn, 2001. 2 vols.

Jung, C.G. *Memories, Dreams, Reflections*. Rec. and ed. Aniela Jaffé. Trans. Richard and Clara Winston. New York: Pantheon, 1963.

Kadar, Marlene. "Coming to Terms: Life Writing—From Genre to Critical Practice." Kadar, *Essays* 3-16.

———, ed. *Essays on Life Writing: From Genre to Critical Practice*. Theory/Culture Ser. 11. Toronto: U of Toronto P, 1992.

———. "Life Writing." *Encyclopedia of Literature in Canada*. Ed. W.H. New. Toronto: U of Toronto P, 2001. 660-66.

Kalaidjian, Walter. "Muriel Rukeyser and the Poetics of Specific Critique: Re-reading 'The Book of the Dead.'" *Cultural Critique* 20 (1991-92): 65-88.

Kalman, Judith. *The County of Birches*. Vancouver: Douglas and McIntyre, 1998.

———. "Channel Crossing." Kalman, *County* 71-80.

———. "A Reason to Be." Kalman, *County* 122-44.

Kaplan, E. Anne. *Looking for the Other: Feminism, Film, and the Imperial Gaze*. London: Routledge, 1997.

Kapralski, Slawomir. "Battlefields of Memory: Landscape and Identity in Polish-Jewish Relations." *History and Memory* 13.2 (2001): 35-58.

Karpf, Anne. *The War After: Living with the Holocaust*. London: Minerva, 1996.

Kauffman, Linda S. *Discourses of Desire: Gender, Genre and Epistolary Fictions*. Ithaca: Cornell UP, 1986.

Kemp, Adriana. "State Control and Resistance in Immigrant Villages in Israel." Hever, Shenhav, and Motzafi-Haller 36-67. [Hebrew]

Kennedy, Rosanne. "The Affective Work of Stolen Generations Testimony: From the Archives to the Classroom." *Biography* 27.1 (2004): 48-77.

Kenrick, Donald, and Gratton Puxon. *Gypsies under the Swastika*. Hatfield, UK: U of Hertfordshire P and Gypsy Research Centre, 1995.

Kerby, Anthony Paul. *Narrative and the Self*. Bloomington: Indiana UP, 1991.

Kertzer, Adrienne. *My Mother's Voice: Children, Literature, and the Holocaust*. Peterborough, ON: Broadview, 2002.

Khalidi, Rashid. *Palestinian Identity: The Construction of Modern National Consciousness*. New York: Columbia UP, 1997.

Killoran, John B. "The Gnome in the Front Yard and Other Public Figurations: Genres of Self-Representation on Personal Home Pages." Zuern, *Online Lives* 66-83.

Kincaid, Eric. *The Children's Book of Rhyme and Verse*. London: Brimax, 2000.

King, Thomas. "Godzilla vs. Post-Colonial." *World Literature Written in English* 30.2 (1990): 10-16.

Klee, Ernst, Willi Dressen, and Volker Riess, eds. *Those Were the Days: The Holocaust through the Eyes of the Perpetrators and Bystanders.* Trans. Deborah Burnstone. London: H. Hamilton, 1991.

Klein, Gerda Weissmann. *All but My Life.* 1957. Rev. ed. New York: Hill and Wang-Farrar, Straus and Giroux, 1995.

———. *Promise of a New Spring: The Holocaust and Renewal.* Illus. Vincent Tartaro. Chappaqua, NY: Rossell, 1981.

Klein, Julie Thompson. *Interdisciplinarity: History, Theory, and Practice.* Detroit: Wayne State University, 1990.

Knapp, Bettina. *Archetype, Architecture, and the Writer.* Bloomington: Indiana UP, 1986.

Knelman, Martin. "Dearest Daddy." *Saturday Night* Oct. 1984: 73-74.

Knowles, Ric. "Dialogic Monologue: A Dialogue (with Jennifer Harvie)." *Theatre Research in Canada* 15.2 (1994): 136-63.

Kress, Gunther, and Theo Van Leeuwen. *Multimodal Discourse: The Modes and Media of Contemporary Communication.* London: Arnold, 2001.

———. *Reading Images: The Grammar of Visual Design.* London: Routledge, 1996.

Laguardia-Gluck, Gemma. *My Story.* Ed. S.L. Shneiderman. New York: David McKay, 1961.

Landow, George P. *Hypertext 2.0: The Convergence of Contemporary Critical Theory and Technology.* Baltimore: Johns Hopkins UP, 1992.

Langer, Lawrence L. *Preempting the Holocaust.* New Haven: Yale UP, 1998.

Lanzmann, Claude. "The Obscenity of Understanding: An Evening with Claude Lanzmann." *Trauma: Explorations in Memory.* Ed. Cathy Caruth. Baltimore: Johns Hopkins UP, 1995. 200-20.

———. *Shoah: An Oral History of the Holocaust: The Complete Text of the Acclaimed Film by Claude Lanzmann.* Rev. ed. New York: Da Capo, 1995.

LaRocque, Emma. "The Colonization of a Native Woman Scholar." *Women of the First Nations: Power, Wisdom, and Strength.* Ed. Christine Miller and Patricia Chuckryk. Winnipeg: U of Manitoba P, 1996. 11-18.

Latcho Drom [Safe Journey]. Dir. Tony Gatlif. New Yorker Films, 1993.

Laub, Dori. "An Event without a Witness: Truth, Testimony and Survival." Felman and Laub 75-92.

Laurie, Clayton D. *The Propaganda Warriors: America's Crusade Against Nazi Germany.* Lawrence: UP of Kansas, 1996.

Lavell, Jeanette Corbiere. "Award Address." *Justice for Natives: Searching for Common Ground.* Ed. Andrea P. Morrison. Montreal: McGill-Queen's UP. 19-25.

Lawrence, Roderick. "Deciphering Home: An Integrative Historical Perspective." D.N. Benjamin 53-68.

Leach, Neil, ed. *Rethinking Architecture: A Reader in Cultural Theory.* New York: Routledge, 1999.

Lee, Ronald. *Goddam' Gypsy: An Autobiographical Novel.* Montreal: Tundra Books, 1971.

Leitner, Isabella, with Irving A. Leitner. *The Big Lie: A True Story.* Illus. Judy Pedersen. New York: Scholastic, 1992.

Lejeune, Philippe. "The Autobiographical Pact." *On Autobiography* 3-30.

———. "The Autobiographical Pact (bis)." *On Autobiography* 119-37.

———. *"Cher écran": Journal personnel, ordinateur, Internet*. Paris: Éditions du Seuil, 2000.

———. "Looking at a Self-Portrait." *On Autobiography* 109–18.

———. *On Autobiography*. Ed. and fwd. Paul John Eakin. Trans. Katherine Leary. Theory and History of Literature 52. Minneapolis: U of Minnesota P, 1989.

———. *Le pacte autobiographique*. Paris: Éditions du Seuil, 1975.

———. "Reading Autobiographical Texts with APA." *Autopacte*. 27 Aug. 2003 <www.autopacte.org>.

Lepage, Robert. "Artist's Statement." Vancouver Playhouse Playbill. Sept. 2002. 4–6.

———. *The Far Side of the Moon*. Unpublished performance script. 2000.

Levi, Primo. *The Drowned and the Saved*. 1986. Trans. Raymond Rosenthal. New York: Vintage, 1988.

Lewis, Bernard. "First-Person Narrative in the Middle East." *Middle Eastern Lives: The Practice of Biography and Self-Narrative*. Ed. Martin Kramer. New York: Syracuse UP, 1991. 20–34.

Lewy, Guenter. *The Nazi Persecution of the Gypsies*. New York: Oxford UP, 2000.

Lifton, Robert Jay. *The Nazi Doctors: Medical Killing and the Psychology of Genocide*. New York: Basic Books, 1986.

Lionnet, Françoise. *Postcolonial Representations: Women, Literature, Identity*. Ithaca: Cornell UP, 1995.

Longley, Kateryna Olijnyk. "Storytelling by Aboriginal Women." Smith and Watson, *De/Colonizing* 370–86.

Lyons, Cicely. *Salmon: Our Heritage: The Story of a Province and an Industry*. Vancouver: British Columbia Packers, 1969.

Lyotard, Jean-François. "*Domus* and Megalopolis." Leach 271–79.

Man, Glenn, ed. *The Biopic*. Spec. issue of *Biography* 23.1 (2000).

Manganiello, Dominic. "Confessions." Jolly 1: 228–29.

Maracle, Lee. "Oratory: Coming to Theory." *Gallerie: Women Artists' Monographs* 1 (1990): 1–15.

Marcus, Clare Cooper. *House As a Mirror of Self: Exploring the Deeper Meaning of Home*. Berkeley: Conari, 1995.

Margalit, Avishai. *The Ethics of Memory*. Cambridge: Harvard UP, 2002.

Mar'i, Mariam. "The Emergence of a Palestinian Identity: Interview with Mariam Mar'i." Trans. Barbara Swirski. Swirski and Safir 41–44.

Marlatt, Daphne. *Ana Historic*. Toronto: Coach House, 1988.

———. "Between Continuity and Difference: An Interview with Daphne Marlatt." Interviewed by Brenda Carr. *West Coast Line* 25.1 (1991): 99–105.

———. "Entering In: The Immigrant Imagination." Marlatt, *Readings* 17–24.

———. *Ghost Works*. Edmonton: NeWest, 1994.

———. "Given This Body: An Interview with Daphne Marlatt." Interviewed by George Bowering. *Open Letter* 4th ser. 3 (1979): 32–88.

———. *How Hug a Stone*. Winnipeg: Turnstone, 1983.

———. "Long as in Time? Steveston." *The Long Poem Anthology*. Ed. Michael Ondaatje. Toronto: Coach House, 1979. 316–20.

———. "Perform[ing] on the Stage of Her Text." Marlatt, *Readings* 200–12.

———. "Preface." Marlatt, *Readings* i–iv.

———. *Readings from the Labyrinth*. Edmonton: NeWest, 1998.

———. *Salvage*. Red Deer: Red Deer College P, 1991.

———. "Self-Representation and Fictionalysis." Marlatt, *Readings* 122-27.

———, ed. *Steveston Recollected*. Victoria: Aural History, Provincial Archives of British Columbia, 1975.

———. *Taken*. Concord, ON: Anansi, 1996.

Marlatt, Daphne, and Robert Minden. *Steveston*. Edmonton: Longspoon, 1984.

———. *Steveston*. Vancouver: Ronsdale, 2001.

———. *Steveston*. Vancouver: Talonbooks, 1974.

Marrus, Michael. *The Holocaust in History*. 1987. Harmondsworth: Penguin, 1989.

Mason, Mary G. "The Other Voice: Autobiographies of Women Writers." Olney, *Autobiography* 207-35.

Mass-Observation Archive. 29 Aug. 2003 <http://www.sussex.ac.uk/library/mass-sobs/>.

Massey, Doreen. "Double Articulation: A Place in the World." *Displacement: Cultural Identities in Question*. Ed. Angelika Bammer. Bloomington: Indiana UP, 1994. 110-21.

———. *Space, Place and Gender*. Oxford: Polity, 1994.

Mays, John Bentley. "Bears." *Canadian Art* 19.3 (2002): 92-97.

McDowell, Linda. *Gender, Identity and Place: Understanding Feminist Geographies*. Minneapolis: U of Minnesota P, 1999.

McNeill, Laurie. "Teaching an Old Genre New Tricks: The Diary on the Internet." Zuern, *Online Lives* 24-47.

Mezei, Kathy, and Chiara Briganti. *Domestic Space: An Interdisciplinary Research Site on Houses, Homes and Gardens*. Dept. of Humanities, Simon Fraser University. 6 Oct. 2004 <http://www.sfu.ca/domestic-space/>.

———, eds. "Forum: Domestic Space." *Signs* 27.3 (2002): 813-900.

———. "Reading the House: A Literary Perspective." *Signs* 27.3 (2002): 837-46.

Michaels, Anne. *Fugitive Pieces*. Toronto: McClelland and Stewart, 1996.

Miller, Carolyn R. "Genre as Social Action." *Quarterly Journal of Speech* 70 (1984): 151-67.

Miller, Nancy K. "Representing Others: Gender and the Subjects of Autobiography." *Differences* 6 (1994): 1-27.

Milroy, Sarah. "Collective Memories: The Startling New Show Curated by Ydessa Hendeles Is No Mere Teddy Bears' Picnic—It's a Poignant Take on Coping with the Horrors of the Past." *Globe and Mail* [Toronto] 8 Apr. 2002: R1+.

Mohanty, Chandra Talpade. "Feminist Encounters: Locating the Politics of Experience." *Destabilizing Theory: Contemporary Feminist Debates*. Ed. Michèle Barrett and Anne Phillips. Paolo Alto: Stanford UP, 1992. 74-92.

———. "Under Western Eyes: Feminist Scholarship and Colonial Discourses." *Third World Women and the Politics of Feminism*. Ed. Chandra Talpade Mohanty, Ann Russo, and Lourdes Torres. Bloomington: Indiana UP, 1991. 51-80.

Mohanty, Satya P. "Us and Them: On the Philosophical Bases of Political Criticism." *Critical Conditons: Regarding the Historical Moment*. Ed. Michael Hayes. Minneapolis: U of Minnesota P, 1992. 115-45.

Morrison, Jack G. *Ravensbrück: Everyday Life in a Women's Concentration Camp, 1939-45*. Princeton: Markus Wiener, 2000.

Müller-Hill, Benno. *Murderous Science: Elimination by Scientific Selection of Jews, Gypsies, and Others, Germany 1933-1945*. Trans. George R. Fraser. New York: Oxford UP, 1988.

Munro, Alice. "What Is Real?" *Making It New: Contemporary Canadian Stories*. Ed. John Metcalf. Toronto: Methuen, 1982. 223-28.

Murray, Janet H. *Hamlet on the Holodeck: The Future of Narrative in Cyberspace*. New York: Free Press, 1999.

Naipaul, V.S. *A House for Mr. Biswas*. London: Deutsch, 1961.

Nannup, Alice, Lauren Marsh, and Stephen Kinnane. *When the Pelican Laughed*. Fremantle, AU: Fremantle Arts Centre, 1992.

National Indian Brotherhood. *Citizens Plus: A Presentation*. Edmonton: Indian Associations of Alberta, 1970.

Naves, Elaine Kalman. *Journey to Vaja: Reconstructing the World of a Hungarian-Jewish Family*. McGill-Queen's Studies in Ethnic History 25. Montreal: McGill-Queen's UP, 1996.

Naves, Elaine Kalman, and Jessica Naves. "'The Question Child' and Passing on Intergenerational Tales of Trauma: A Conversation with Elaine Kalman Naves." Interviewed by Judith P. Robertson and Nadene Keon. *Canadian Children's Literature* 25.3 (1999): 29-49.

Necas, Ctibor, and Dusan Holý. "A Auschwitz il y a une Grande Prison: Ausvicate Hi Kher Báro." *Cahiers de Littérature Orale* 30 (1991): 15-35.

Neuman, Shirley. "'Your Past…Your Future': Autobiography and Mothers' Bodies." *Genre Trope Gender: Essays by Northrop Frye, Linda Hutcheon, and Shirley Neuman*. Ottawa: Carleton UP, 1992. 51-86.

New, W.H., ed. *Native Writers and Canadian Writing*. Vancouver: U of British Columbia P, 1990.

Nichols, Bill. *Blurred Boundaries: Questions of Meaning in Contemporary Culture*. Bloomington: Indiana UP, 1994.

Nicolson, Nigel. *The World of Jane Austen*. London: Weidenfeld and Nicolson, 1991.

Nora, Pierre. *Les lieux de mémoire*. Paris: Gallimard, 1984.

Olney, James, ed. *Autobiography: Essays Theoretical and Criticial*. Princeton: Princeton UP, 1980.

———. *Memory and Narrative: The Weave of Life-Writing*. Chicago: U of Chicago P, 1998.

Ozick, Cynthia. "Who Owns Anne Frank?" *The New Yorker* 6 Oct. 1997: 76-87.

Paquet, Sébastien. "Personal Knowledge Publishing and Its Uses in Research." 1 Oct. 2002. Seb's Open Research. 5 Sept. 2003 <http://radio.weblogs.com/0110772/stories/2002/10/03/personalKnowledgePublishingAndItsUsesInResearch.html>.

Paradise Hotel. FOX. 18 June-1 Oct. 2003. <http://www.fox.com/home.htm>.

Paxton, Nancy L. "Disembodied Subjects: English Women's Autobiography under the Raj." Smith and Watson, *De/Colonizing* 387-409.

Peck, Janice. "The Medicated Talking Cure: Therapeutic Framing of Autobiography in TV Talk Shows." Smith and Watson, *Getting a Life* 134-55.

Personal Narratives Group. *Interpreting Women's Lives: Feminist Theory and Personal Narratives*. Bloomington: Indiana UP, 1989.

Peterson, Jacqueline, and Jennifer S.H. Brown. "Introduction." *The New Peoples: Being and Becoming Métis in North America*. Ed. Jacqueline Peterson and Jennifer S.H. Brown. Winnipeg: U of Manitoba P, 1985. 3–16.

Pilcer, Sonia. *The Holocaust Kid: Stories*. New York: Persea, 2001.

Poe, Edgar Allan. "The Fall of the House of Usher." *Collected Works of Edgar Allan Poe: Tales and Sketches 1831–1842*. Ed. Thomas Ollive Mabbott. Cambridge, MA: The Belknap Press of Harvard UP, 1978. 392–422.

"Poetess in OWI Here Probed by U.S. as Red." *New York Times* 7 May 1943: 4.

Pohl, Frances K. *Ben Shahn: New Deal Artist in a Cold War Climate, 1947-1954*. Austin: UP of Texas, 1989.

Pollock, Sharon. *Blood Relations and Other Plays*. Edmonton: NeWest, 1981.

———. *Doc*. Toronto: Playwrights Canada, 1984.

———. "Families." Interview by J. Hofsess. *Homemaker Magazine* 15 Mar. 1980: 41+.

———. *Getting It Straight*. In *Heroines: Three Plays*. Ed. Joyce Doolittle. Red Deer: Red Deer College P, 1992. 85–126.

———. *Sharon Pollock: Three New Plays* [*Moving Pictures, End Dream, Angel's Trumpet*]. Toronto: Playwrights Canada, 2003.

———. "Sharon Pollock: Writing for the Illegitimate Theatre." Interview by J. Hofsess. *Otherstages*. 10 Feb.1983: 3.

Popkin, Jeremy D. "*Ego-histoire* and Beyond: Contemporary French Historian-Autobiographers." *French Historical Studies* 19.4 (1996): 1139–67.

Poster, Mark. *What's the Matter With the Internet?* Electronic Mediations Ser. 3. Minneapolis: U of Minnesota P, 2001.

Pratt, Mary Louise. "Scratches on the Face of the Country; or, What Mr. Barrow Saw in the Land of the Bushmen." *'Race,' Writing and Difference*. Ed. Henry Louis Gates Jr. Chicago: U of Chicago P, 1985. 138–62.

Proust, Marcel. *A la recherche du temps perdu*. Paris: Gallimard, 1954.

Raab, Elisabeth M. *And Peace Never Came*. Life Writing Ser. Waterloo: Wilfrid Laurier UP, 1997.

Raday, Frances. "The Concept of Gender Equality in a Jewish State." Swirski and Safir 18–30.

Re Lavell and Attorney-General of Canada, [1971] *Criminal Law Quarterly* 236. Fed. Crt. of Can., Appeal Division. 8 October 1971.

Re Lavell and Attorney-General of Canada, [1971] *Ontario Reports* 1 390. York Judicial District County Crt. 21 June 1971.

Relke, Diana M. A. "'time is, the delta': *Steveston* in Historical and Ecological Context." *Canadian Poetry* 38 (1996): 29–48.

Rendell, Jane, Barbara Penner, and Iain Borden, eds. *Gender Space Architecture: An Interdisciplinary Introduction*. London: Routledge, 2000.

Reuss, Dr. "2. Report by the military chaplain, Dr. Reuss, to Lieutenant-Colonel Groscurth, 1st *Generalstabsoffizier*, 295th Infantry Division." Klee, Dressen, and Riess 141–43.

Rich, Adrienne. "Notes toward a Politics of Location (1984)." *Blood, Bread and Poetry*. New York: Norton, 1986. 210–31.

Ricou, Laurie. *The Arbutus/Madrone Files: Reading the Pacific Northwest*. Edmonton: NeWest, 2002.

————. "Phyllis Webb, Daphne Marlatt and Simultitude: Journal Entries from a Capitalist Bourgeois Patriarchal Anglo-Saxon Mainstream Critic." *A/Mazing Space: Writing Canadian Women Writing*. Ed. Shirley Neuman and Smaro Kamboureli. Edmonton: Longspoon/NeWest, 1986. 205-15.

Rideal, Liz, with essays by Whitney Chadwick and Francis Borzello. *Mirror Mirror: Self-Portraits by Women Artists*. London: National Portrait Gallery, 2001.

Rintel, Sean, and Sue McKay. "Interacting with Reality TV." *M/C Reviews* 12 (4 May 2001). 1 Oct. 2002 <http://reviews.media-culture.org.au/sections.php?op=viewarticle&artid=107>.

Robinson, Marilynne. *Housekeeping*. New York: Farrar, Straus, Giroux, 1980.

Roma Community Centre 26 Apr. 2005 <http://www.rcctoronto.org>.

Romines, Ann. *The Home Plot: Women, Writing and Domestic Ritual*. Amherst: U of Massachusetts P, 1992.

Roscoe, Jane. "*Big Brother* Australia: Performing the 'Real' Twenty-Four-Seven." *International Journal of Cultural Studies* 4.4 (2001): 473-78.

Rosenbaum, Thane. "Cattle Car Complex." *Elijah Visible*. New York: St. Martin's, 1996. 1-11.

————. *The Golems of Gotham*. New York: HarperCollins, 2002.

————. *Second Hand Smoke*. New York: St. Martin's, 1999.

Rosenthal, George. "The Evolution of Tattooing in the Auschwitz Concentration Camp Complex." *Center for Holocaust and Genocide Studies*. 5 June 2003 <http://www.chgs.umn.edu/Educational_Resources/Curriculum/Auschwitz_Tattooing/auschwitz_tattooing.html>.

Rouhana, Nadim N. *Palestinian Citizens in an Ethnic Jewish State: Identities in Conflict*. New Haven: Yale UP, 1997.

Rukeyser, Muriel. *The Collected Poems of Muriel Rukeyser*. New York: McGraw-Hill, 1978.

————. "Elegies Six to Nine. Sixth Elegy." Rukeyser, *Collected Poems* 247-50.

————. "The Book of the Dead." Rukeyser, *Collected Poems* 71-102.

————. *The Life of Poetry*. New York: Current, 1949.

————. Muriel Rukeyser Papers. Berg Special Collections. New York Public Library, New York.

————. Muriel Rukeyser Papers. Library of Congress, Washington, DC.

Ryan, Marie-Laure. "Introduction." *Cyberspace Textuality: Computer Technology and Literary Theory*. Ed. Marie-Laure Ryan. Bloomington: Indiana UP, 1999. 1-28.

Rybczynski, Witold. *Home: A Short History of an Idea*. New York: Viking-Penguin, 1986.

Sabbioni, Jennifer. "Aboriginal Women's Narratives: Reconstructing Identities." *Australian Historical Studies* 27.106 (1996): 72-78.

"Samuel Pepys' Diary." *National Post* 28 Sept. 2004: B2.

Sanders, Douglas E. "The Indian Act and the Bill of Rights." *Ottawa Law Review* 6 (1974): 397-415.

————. "Indian Women: A Brief History of Their Roles and Rights." *McGill Law Journal* 21 (1975): 656-672.

Scarry, Elaine. *The Body in Pain: The Making and Unmaking of the World*. New York: Oxford UP, 1985.

Schenck, Celeste. "All of a Piece: Women's Poetry and Autobiography." *Life/Lines: Theorizing Women's Autobiography*. Ed. Bella Brodzki and Celeste Schenck. Ithaca: Cornell UP, 1988. 281-305.

Scott, David. "The Aftermaths of Political Sovereignty." *Refashioning Futures: Criticism After Postcoloniality*. Princeton: Princeton UP, 1999. 131–57.

Scott, Joan. "The Sears Case." *Gender and the Politics of History*. New York: Columbia UP, 1988. 167–77.

Selzer, Jack. "Habeas Corpus." *Rhetorical Bodies*. Ed. Jack Selzer and Sharon Crowley. Madison: Wisconsin UP, 1990.

Sharoni, Simona. *Gender and the Israeli-Palestinian Conflict: The Politics of Women's Resistance*. Syracuse: Syracuse UP, 1995.

Silman, Janet. *Enough Is Enough: Aboriginal Women Speak Out*. Toronto: Women's Press, 1987.

Simmel, Georg. "Bridge and Door." Leach 66–69.

Sinti and Roma. Victims of the Nazi Era, 1933–1945. Washington, DC: United States Holocaust Memorial Museum, n.d.

Slaymaker, O., M. Bovis, M. North, T.R. Oke, and J. Ryder. "The Primordial Environment." *Vancouver and Its Region*. Ed. Graeme Wynn and Timothy Oke. Vancouver: U of British Columbia P, 1992. 17–37.

Smith, Sidonie. *Subjectivity, Identity and the Body: Women's Autobiographical Practices in the Twentieth Century*. Bloomington: Indiana UP, 1993.

Smith, Sidonie, and Julia Watson, eds. *De/Colonizing the Subject: The Politics of Gender in Women's Autobiography*. Minneapolis: U of Minnesota P, 1992.

———, eds. *Getting a Life: Everyday Uses of Autobiography*. Minneapolis: U of Minnesota P, 1996.

———, eds. *Interfaces: Women/Autobiography/Image/Performance*. Ann Arbor: U of Michigan P, 2002.

———. "Introduction: Mapping Women's Self-Representation as Visual/Textual Interfaces." Smith and Watson, *Interfaces* 1–46.

———. *Reading Autobiography: A Guide for Interpreting Life Narratives*. Minneapolis: U of Minnesota P, 2001.

———. "The Rumpled Bed of Autobiography." Egan and Helms 1–14.

Smith, Thomas R. "Agency." Jolly 1: 28–29.

Sonneman, Toby. *Shared Sorrows: A Gypsy Family Remembers the Holocaust*. Hatfield, UK: Hertfordshire P, 2002.

Spain, Daphne. *Gendered Spaces*. Chapel Hill: U of North Carolina P, 1992.

Spiegelman, Art. *Maus: A Survivor's Tale*. Vol. 1, *My Father Bleeds History*. New York: Pantheon, 1986.

———. *Maus: A Survivor's Tale*. Vol. 2, *And Here My Troubles Began*. New York: Pantheon, 1991.

Spivak, Gayatri. "Can the Subaltern Speak?" *Marxism and the Interpretation of Culture*. Ed. Cary Nelson and Lawrence Grossberg. Urbana: U of Illinois P, 1988. 271–313.

Stacey, Duncan. *Steveston's Cannery Channel: A Social History of the Fishing Community*. Document 4063K. Prepared for the Corporation of the Township of Richmond Planning Department, 1986.

Star, Susan Leigh. "From Hestia to Home Page: Feminism and the Concept of Home in Cyberspace." *The Cybercultures Reader*. Ed. David Bell and Barbara M. Kennedy. London: Routledge, 2000. 632–43.

Starobinski, Jean. "The Style of Autobiography." Olney, *Autobiography* 73–83.

Sternhell, Zeev. *The Founding Myths of Israel: Nationalism, Socialism, and the Making of the Jewish State*. Princeton: Princeton UP, 1998.

Stewart, Michael. "'Igaz beszéd'—avagy miért énekelnek a cigányok?" [True Words: Or Why Do the Gypsies Sing?] *Valóság* [Reality/Truth] 30 (1987): 49-64.

———. *The Time of the Gypsies*. Boulder, CO: Westview, 1997.

Stojka, Ceija, and Karin Berger. *Wir leben im Verborgenen: Erinnerungen einer Rom-Zigeunerin*. Vienna: Picus, 1989.

Struther, Jan. *Mrs. Miniver*. 1939. London: Virago, 1989.

Suleri, Sara. "Woman Skin Deep: Feminism and the Postcolonial Condition." *Women, Autobiography, Theory: A Reader*. Ed. Sidonie Smith and Julia Watson. Madison: U of Wisconsin P, 1998. 116-25.

The Surreal Life. 4 Oct 2004 <http://www.tvtome.com/tvtome/servlet/ShowMainServlet/showid-12331/>.

Survivor. 1-7 CBS. 31 May 2000-14 Dec. 2003. <http://www.cbs.com/primetime/survivor/>.

Swirski, Barbara, and Marilyn P. Safir, eds. *Calling the Equality Bluff: Women in Israel*. New York: Teachers College, 1993.

Tarbox, Katherine. *Katie.com: My Story*. New York: Dutton-Penguin, 2000.

———. Home page. 4 Oct. 2004 <http://www.KatieT.com>.

Tebbutt, Susan. "Challenging New Literary Images of Sinti and Roma." *Sinti and Roma: Gypsies in German-Speaking Society and Literature*. Ed. Susan Tebbutt. New York: Berghahn, 1998. 129-44.

Temptation Island. 1-3 FOX. 10 Jan. 2001-29 Sep. 2003. <http://www.fox.com/temptation/>.

Thomson, Kristen. *I, Claudia*. Toronto: PUC Play Service, 2001.

Thomson, R.H. *The Lost Boys*. Toronto: Playwrights Canada, 2001.

Tremblay, Michel. *For the Pleasure of Seeing Her Again*. Trans. Linda Gaboriau. Vancouver: Talonbooks, 1998.

Tremblay, Tony. "Reading the 'Real' in *Survivor*: Unearthing the Republican Roots in Reality Narrative." *Topia: A Canadian Journal of Cultural Studies* 9 (2003): 47-65.

Trudeau, Pierre. "The Values of a Just Society." *Towards a Just Society*. Ed. Thomas S. Axworthy and Pierre Elliot Trudeau. Markham: Viking, 1990. 357-85.

Tuan, Yi-Fu. *Topophilia: A Study of Environmental Perception, Attitudes, and Values*. Englewood Cliffs, N.J.: Prentice-Hall, 1974.

Turkle, Sherry. *Life on the Screen: Identity in the Age of the Internet*. New York: Simon and Schuster, 1995.

Turner, Edith. Notes on Steveston Museum, 3811 Moncton St., Richmond, BC.

Turner, Graeme. "Television and Cultural Studies." *International Journal of Cultural Studies* 4.4 (2001): 371-84.

Ty, Eleanor. "Writing as a Daughter: Autobiography in Wollstonecraft's Travelogue." Kadar, *Essays* 61-77.

van Kirk, Sylvia. *Many Tender Ties: Women in Fur-Trade Society, 1670-1870*. Winnipeg: Watson and Dwyer, 1999.

van Toorn, Penny. "Tactical History Business: The Ambivalent Politics of Commodifying the Stolen Generations Stories." *Southerly* 59 (1999): 252-66.

Venne, Sharon Helen. *Indian Acts and Amendments 1868-1975, An Indexed Collection*. Saskatoon: U of Saskatchewan Native Law Centre, 1981.

Verdecchia, Guillermo. *Fronteras Americanas*. 1997. Rpt. in *Modern Canadian Plays II*. Ed. Jerry Wasserman. Vancouver: Talonbooks, 2001. 313-31.

Vidler, Anthony. *The Architectural Uncanny: Essays in the Modern Unhomely*. Cambridge: MIT Press, 1996.

Voloshinov, V.N. *Marxism and the Philosophy of Language*. Trans. Ladislaw Matejka and I.R. Titunik. New York: Seminar, 1973.

Walker, Lynne. *Drawing on Diversity: Women, Architecture and Practice*. London: RIBA Heinz Gallery, 1997.

Warley, Linda. 7 Feb. 2005. <http://www.arts.uwaterloo.ca/~lwarley>.

Waskul, Dennis, and Mark Douglass. "Cyberself: The Emergence of Self in On-line Chat." *Information Society* 13 (1997): 375-97.

Wasserman, Jerry. "Daddy's Girls: Father-Daughter Incest and Canadian Plays by Women." *Essays in Theatre* 14 (1995): 25-36.

―――. ed. *Modern Canadian Plays II*. Vancouver: Talonbooks, 2001.

Wasson, Kirsten. "A Geography of Conversion: Dialogical Boundaries of Self in Antin's *Promised Land*." Ashley, Gilmore, and Peters 167-87.

Waugh, Evelyn. *Brideshead Revisited*. London: Chapel and Hall, 1945.

Weaver, Sally M. *Making Canadian Indian Policy: The Hidden Agenda*. 1968. Toronto: U of Toronto P, 1981.

Welsh, Christine. "Women in the Shadows: Reclaiming a Métis Heritage." *New Contexts of Canadian Criticism*. Ed. Ajay Heble, Donna Palmateer Pennee, and J.R. (Tim) Struthers. Peterborough, ON: Broadview, 1997. 56-66.

Whitlock, Gillian. "In the Second Person: Narrative Transactions in Stolen Generations Testimony." Egan and Helms 197-214.

―――. *The Intimate Empire: Reading Women's Autobiography*. New York: Cassell, 2000.

Whyte, John D. "The Lavell Case and Equality in Canada." *Queen's Quarterly* 81 (1974): 28-42.

Winkler, Allan M. *The Politics of Propaganda: The Office of War Information 1942-1945*. New Haven: Yale UP, 1978.

Winslow, Donald J. *Life Writing: A Glossary of Terms in Biography, Autobiography, and Related Forms*. Honolulu: University P of Hawaii, 1980.

Wollstonecraft, Mary. *A Vindication of the Rights of Woman*. 1792. New York: Norton, 1988.

Woolf, Virginia. *Three Guineas*. 1938. New York: Penguin, 1977.

Worthen, W.B. "Drama, Performativity, and Performance." *PMLA* 113.5 (1998): 1093-107.

Wynn, Eleanor, and James E. Katz. "Hyperbole over Cyberspace." *Information Society* 13 (1997): 297-327.

Yahoo! Directory. Personal Home Pages. <http://dir.yahoo.com/Society_and_Culture/People/Personal_Home_Pages/>.

Yanait [Ben-Zvi], Rahel. "Stages." *The Plough Woman: Records of the Pioneer Women of Palestine*. Ed. Mark A. Raider and Miriam B. Raider-Roth. Hanover: Brandeis UP, 2002. 109-15.

Yang, Mimi Y. "Articulate Image, Painted Diary: Frida Kahlo's Autobiographical Interface." Smith and Watson *Interfaces* 314-41.

Yeats, W.B. "The Circus Animals' Desertion." *Norton Anthology of Poetry*. Ed. Alexander W. Allison et al. New York: Norton, 1970.

Yesil, Bilge. "Reel Pleasures: Exploring the Historical Roots of Media Voyeurism and Exhibitionism." *Counterblast: The e-Journal of Culture and Communication* 1.1 (2001). 1 Aug. 2003 <http://www.nyu.edu/pubs/counterblast/issue1_nov01/media_art_review/yesil.html>.

YIVO Institute for Jewish Research Archives, New York, New York.

Yolen, Jane. *Briar Rose*. Fairy Tale Ser. New York: Tom Doherty, 1992.

Young, James Edward. *At Memory's Edge: After-Images of the Holocaust in Contemporary Art and Architecture*. New Haven: Yale UP, 2000.

Yuval-Davis, Nira. "National Reproduction and 'the Demographic Race' in Israel." Yuval-Davis and Anthias 92–109.

Yuval-Davis, Nira, and Floya Anthias, eds. *Woman-Nation-State*. Consulting ed. Jo Campling. London: Macmillan, 1989.

Zalis, Elayne. "At Home in Cyberspace: Staging Autobiographical Scenes." Zuern, *Online Lives* 84–119.

Žižek, Slavoj. *Looking Awry: An Introduction to Jacques Lacan through Popular Culture*. Cambridge: MIT Press, 1991.

Zuern, John, ed. *Online Lives*. Spec. issue of *Biography* 26.1 (2003).

———. "Online Lives: Introduction." Zuern v–xxv.

Books in the Life Writing Series Published by Wilfrid Laurier University Press

Haven't Any News: Ruby's Letters from the Fifties
edited by Edna Staebler with an Afterword by Marlene Kadar
1995 / x + 165 pp. / ISBN 0-88920-248-6

"I Want to Join Your Club": Letters from Rural Children, 1900-1920
edited by Norah L. Lewis with a Preface by Neil Sutherland
1996 / xii + 250 pp. (30 b&w photos) / ISBN 0-88920-260-5

And Peace Never Came by Elisabeth M. Raab with Historical Notes by Marlene
Kadar 1996 / x + 196 pp. (12 b&w photos, map) / ISBN 0-88920-281-8

Dear Editor and Friends: Letters from Rural Women of the North-West, 1900-
1920 edited by Norah L. Lewis
1998 / xvi + 166 pp. (20 b&w photos) / ISBN 0-88920-287-7

The Surprise of My Life: An Autobiography by Claire Drainie Taylor
with a Foreword by Marlene Kadar
1998 / xii + 268 pp. (+ 8 colour photos and 92 b&w photos) / ISBN 0-88920-302-4

Memoirs from Away: A New Found Land Girlhood by Helen M. Buss /
Margaret Clarke
1998 / xvi + 153 pp. / ISBN 0-88920-350-4

The Life and Letters of Annie Leake Tuttle: Working for the Best
by Marilyn Färdig Whiteley
1999 / xviii + 150 pp. / ISBN 0-88920-330-X

Marian Engel's Notebooks: "Ah, mon cahier, écoute" edited by Christl Verduyn
1999 / viii + 576 pp. / ISBN 0-88920-333-4 cloth / ISBN 0-88920-349-0 paper

Be Good Sweet Maid: The Trials of Dorothy Joudrie by Audrey Andrews
1999 / vi + 276 pp. / ISBN 0-88920-334-2

Working in Women's Archives: Researching Women's Private Literature
and Archival Documents edited by Helen M. Buss and Marlene Kadar
2001 / vi + 120 pp. / ISBN 0-88920-341-5

Repossessing the World: Reading Memoirs by Contemporary Women
by Helen M. Buss
2002 / xxvi + 206 pp. / ISBN 0-88920-410-1 paper

Chasing the Comet: A Scottish-Canadian Life by Patricia Koretchuk
2002 / xx + 244 pp. / ISBN 0-88920-407-1

The Queen of Peace Room by Magie Dominic
2002 / xii + 115 pp. / ISBN 0-88920-417-9

China Diary: The Life of Mary Austin Endicott by Shirley Jane Endicott
2002 / xvi + 251pp. / ISBN 0-88920-412-8

The Curtain: Witness and Memory in Wartime Holland by Henry G. Schogt
2003 / xii + 132pp. / ISBN 0-88920-396-2

Teaching Places by Audrey J. Whitson
2003 / xiii + 178pp. / ISBN 0-88920-425-X

Through the Hitler Line by Laurence F. Wilmot, M.C.
2003 / xvi + 152pp. / ISBN 0-88920-448-9

Where I Come From by Vijay Agnew
2003 / xiv + 298pp. / ISBN 0-88920-414-4

The Water Lily Pond by Han Z. Li
2004 / x +254pp. / ISBN 0-88920-431-4

The Life Writings of Mary Baker McQuesten: Victorian Matriarch by Mary J.
Anderson 2004 / xxii + 338 pp. / ISBN 0-88920-437-3

Incorrigible by Velma Demerson
2004 / vi + 178pp. / ISBN 0-88920-444-6

Auto/biography in Canada: Critical Directions edited by Julie Rak
2005 / viii + 272 pp. ISBN 0-88920-478-0

Tracing the Autobiographical edited by Marlene Kadar, Linda Warley,
Jeanne Perreault, and Susanna Egan
2005 / viii + 280 pp. / ISBN 0-88920-476-4